Finding Balance

Second Edition

Finding Balance

Balance

Second Edition

Fitness, Training, and Health
for a Lifetime in Dance

Gigi Berardi

ROUTLEDGE
NEW YORK AND LONDON

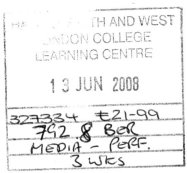
Published in 2005 by
Routledge
270 Madison Avenue
New York, NY 10016

Published in Great Britain by
Routledge
2 Park Square
Milton Park, Abingdon
Oxon OX14 4RN U.K.

Routledge is an imprint of the Taylor & Francis Group.
Printed in the United States of America on acid-free paper.

10 9 8 7 6 5 4 3 2 1

Library of Congress Cataloging-in-Publication Data

Berardi, Gigi.
  Finding balance : fitness, training, and health for a lifetime in
dance / Gigi Berardi.— 2nd ed.
    p. cm.
  Includes bibliographical references and index.
  ISBN 0-415-94338-8 (hb : alk. paper)—ISBN 0-415-94339-6 (pb : alk.
paper)
  1. Dance. 2. Dancers. 3. Physical fitness. 4. Dancing
injuries—Prevention. 5. Health. I. Title.
  GV1595.B47 2004
  792.8—dc22
                          2004017293

To my family, dancers extraordinaire

Contents

List of Figures

List of Tables

Acknowledgments

I acknowledge the support of my publisher, Richard Carlin, Executive Editor of Music and Dance at Routledge, without whose encouragement this book would not have been possible. Also at Routledge, I am grateful for the expertise and good work of editorial assistants Erin McElroy and Nina Sadd, who ushered the project through various stages, and also, in the Florida offices, my project editor Robert Sims and all those involved in the book's production—from copyediting to indexing.

The manuscript was read by copyeditor and advisor Barbara Palfy and master editor Jim Allaway, who waded through the early drafts to make the entire work more cohesive and consistent. Barbara Palfy was a constant source of encouragement for the revision of this project, as was K. C. Patrick, former editor-in-chief of *Dance Magazine*. The manuscript benefited enormously from Jim Allaway's editing of my long sentences with numerous meanderings (exactly the way I lecture); he also performed some major surgery on Chapter 2 (an initially long chapter on Injury and Injury Treatment), as well as on the hundreds of footnotes throughout, and lightened the technical terms, language, and discussion.

My original thought for a revised edition of *Finding Balance* was to simply update a few references and write new profiles. As explained in the preface, I had to do much more. The text is rewritten (in most parts) and I needed the expert counsel of colleagues in dance medicine and science (academics, writers, practitioners, teachers) to read individual chapters (many read the entire work) for tone and content. To all of them, I am exceptionally grateful for their careful read, (hardly shy) pointed remarks, notes on major omissions, and suggestions for deletions. These experts include: Matt Aversa, Glenna Batson, Rick Braver, Lorrie Brilla, Scott Brown, Steven Chatfield, Kitty Daniels, Jan Dunn, Linda Hamilton, Alec Kay, Elizabeth Kerwin, Yiannis Koutedakis, Donna Krasnow, Kenneth Laws, Marijeanne Liederbach, Stuart McGill, Sandra Minton, Marika Molnar, Craig Moore, Marsha Novak, Leslie Ochs, Boni Reitveld, Elizabeth Snell, Carol Teitz, David Weiss, and Ginny Wilmerding. Any errors or omissions in this final copy are mine and mine alone.

Angela Sterling deserves special acknowledgements for her beautiful photos that appear here, many of which were taken during a very long photo shoot in Bellingham and in Seattle. Her stunning and consistently high-quality work adds immeasurably to the book. Thanks also to other photographers whose work appears in this edition, mostly in the profiles as single photos: Nan Melville, Heather Eliot, Tom Caravaglia, John Deane, Paul Kolnik, Alanna Jankov, Bill Owen, Mila Petrillo, Terry Shapiro, Craig Schreiner, Adam L. Weintraub, Sandro DiSanto, and Liz Roth.

Pacific Northwest Ballet dancers and students (in Seattle), Nancy Whyte School of Ballet students (in Bellingham), and Sabine Chaland and Gael Lambiotte of the Dutch National

Ballet were willing models, for which I am grateful. Thanks also to the brilliantly intuitive physical therapist John McWilliams (who also edited parts of the manuscript and glossaries), master ballet teacher Cher Carnell, dancer and physical therapist Sydney Anderson, and dancer and movement therapist Kristen Torok. I also am grateful to dancers Alona and Matt Christman, who served as models. I thank Nancy Whyte, in particular, for her graciousness (and patience) in my work with students at her school.

Others who have helped in various ways and who I thank are (in alphabetical order): Tia Allaway, Jenny Blythe, Michael Blythe, Shawn Boeser, Karen Bradley, Mark Bussell, Maureen Callaghan, Judy Carney, Rose Cirelli, John Collins, Bob Dagger, Elaine Dalrymple, Nolan Dennett, Cindy DiBenedetti, Sarah Dillard, Susann Dillard, Jan Dunn, Hal Egbert, Jan Gal, Judy Gantz, Ed Gates, Michael Heiman, Paula Heiman, Jackie Heimbuch, Loretta Heimbuch, Adam Hewitt, Linda Kelly, Terri Kempton, Jennifer Lee, Carla Lillvik, George Liu, Claire Londress, Dianne Mannion, Kate McCarthy, Janet Martin, Craig Moore, Ann Neal-Levi, Amanda Ray, Kay Reddell, Teresa Rieland, Judy Roberts, Mitch Roberts, Dennis Scott, Dick Snyder, Liska Snyder, Allice Sullivan, Bruce Talbot, Jennifer Talbot, Nora Taylor, Thomas Welsh, and Arne Youngerman.

Sincere thanks and heartfelt gratitude are due the many dancers whose profiles appear in this revised version for the time and interest they showed in the project: Elizabeth Streb, Roxane d'Orléans Juste, Carrie Imler, David Parsons, David Zurak, Catherine Cabeen, Koichi Kubo, Li Chiao-Ping, Louise Nadeau, Bill Evans, Donald Byrd, Kelen Laine, Gus Solomons jr, Jan Dunn, Murray Louis, Gary Galbraith, Kent Stowell, Catherine Allaway, Jenifer Ringer, Melanie Skinner, Jamie Farquhar, James Fayette, Paul Bowler, Pat Graney, and Wendy Perron.

My most sincere gratitude to the dancers who train daily and perform nightly, who give me something to write about! I learn a lot from regularly watching the artists of the Pacific Northwest Ballet and writing for *Dance Magazine* and *Dance International*—as well as the daily, *The Olympian,* and public and community radio stations. Writing book reviews regularly for *Journal of Dance Medicine & Science* also adds enormously to my monitoring of the dance science scene. I am grateful for this position and for all writing assignments. The work allows me to observe—and question—constantly.

Lastly, I thank my family—my husband and my children—who are the most dazzling dance partners, creative musicians, and entertaining advice-givers an arts writer could hope for. They are a constant source of inspiration and unwavering support for all that I do. I hope that my little ones can hang onto their self-image so it is as positive and genuine in 10 years as it is now. To my family, I dedicate this book.

Gigi Berardi
March 2004

Foreword

Fitness, training and health for a lifetime in dance—what a huge topic! Or, rather, range of topics. And who better to pull a vast array of important material together in one resource volume than a woman who has not only danced herself but diligently studied the wide variety of tools and advice currently available to dancers? In this second, and extensively updated, edition of Gigi Berardi's comprehensive book, the glue that holds all the information together and compels our attention is her enthusiasm for dance and her love of dancers. Far too much has been written about the perils of a career in dance with little description of the rewards of being a dancer. We see over and over again that striving for goals that are just out of reach can shape remarkable characters and achieve astounding results. Perfectionists have many inspiring stories to tell, but for dancers to be truly successful, balance is, of course, the key.

The real sea-change in dance and dance education in the past couple of decades is the contribution made to dancers' health and well-being by dance medicine and science. Most professional dance institutions now incorporate therapy, injury prevention, nutrition, conditioning, Pilates, weight training, and the physics of dance as vitally necessary parts of the curriculum. At Pacific Northwest Ballet, these resources have been available to both professional dancers and students for more than 20 years. But so much information has become available so quickly that those of us responsible for training young dancers have trouble keeping up with advances in thinking and practice.

It is, therefore, difficult to overstate how valuable this volume is for us: artistic directors, ballet masters, teachers, and staff—all those making decisions regarding the future of the young people in our care. Just as importantly, the dancers themselves are becoming ever more knowledgeable and more concerned about developing and protecting the unique instrument each of them has been given.

Because dancers are a rare breed—unstinting in their devotion to their art form, they are deserving of every kind of help we can give them. Most importantly, Gigi Berardi's invaluable work will enable them to make wise decisions about caring for themselves.

Francia Russell
Co-Artistic Director
Pacific Northwest Ballet
April 2004

Preface
Warm-Up

Each year, tens of thousands of children in the United States take a dance class, step into a rehearsal studio, or watch a dance video. Dance is everywhere. Yup'ik children in Bethel, Alaska, grow up surrounded by their fathers and uncles (and a few mothers) beating out songs with drums and chants and representing them with dance steps. In the Canadian maritime province of Prince Edward Island, a teacher puts a young step dancer through his paces. For some children, it is the beginning of a lifetime in dance.

Wanting to be a dancer happens in so many ways. A small child sees a holiday performance of *Nutcracker*, or perhaps sees a big brother or sister dressed in a recital costume. Children want to be part of the magic—creating magic onstage, helping to create their own fairy tale world. And, depending on the teacher and learning environment, they may well develop the means and desire to last them a lifetime in dance.

I caught my first glimpse of such burning desire to dance—in the world of classical ballet at least—watching my neighborhood friend, Jarnie Olsen, who was a ballerina, coming home from class or preparing for a performance. She had point shoes and the feet to match, and she had received a scholarship one summer to go all the way to New York (we lived in North Hollywood, and New York seemed very, very far away)—she had earned a coveted place in a very competitive school. I didn't envy her that life—taken up by so many classes and so many rehearsals, but I did enjoy the thrill of seeing her perform. Sometimes I felt like the trip next door to her house was like entering another world, with all her costumes and shoes and the dance magazines adorning her room. As it turned out, rather than becoming a professional ballerina, she took on another challenging job: raising a family, including a pair of celebrity twins. She probably made the right choice, leaving the star status to her daughters. Yet the impression of what she went through, with all those hours of hard work, stuck with me for decades after.

As for me, my mother took me to ballet classes of various sorts when I was small. It wasn't until I was an adult at university that I took my first modern class. I was smitten, and eventually earned a degree in dance at UCLA. The dance program, now titled "World Arts and Culture," was a treasure trove of world dance. For technique, I took classes in dance of Bali, Indonesia, India, and Israel, as well as in Flamenco and Bugaku (Japanese Court Dance —my teacher was a royal prince, Mr. Togi). My first experience with cultural geography (which I now teach) was through dance. After earning my dance degree (which, I maintain, was more challenging than my previous graduate degrees combined—a M.S. and Ph.D.), I turned my heart, head, and hand to writing. I still dance, performing mostly as a Scottish Country dancer. And the thrill of taking a class (although I'm very picky as to whom I study with), seeing a dance performance (as the last one clapping in an audience), or interviewing a professional dancer has never waned. For me, dance makes the world go round. My experience with my own family now emphasizes that children need deep, positive experiences in dance and music early on, so that they can practice rejecting perfectionist tendencies and stay true to themselves and their dreams.

The first edition of *Finding Balance* took as a point of departure Suzanne Gordon's *Off Balance: The Real World of Ballet*, an exposé of ballet dancers struggling for control over their bodies and their working lives. Gordon argued that for many it was a losing battle. My objective in the first edition was to tell the story of those who stayed in dance, of those who had found some balance in their lives. Dance is more than an avocation—it is a calling. And a life in dance is a goal that is quite reachable, a theme evident in the profiles of dancers in the first edition. My idea for that edition was that it would be a glamorous coffee-table book, filled with beautiful images of older dancers still performing. Fortunately, my publisher (Charles Woodford) and editor (Richard Carlin) convinced me otherwise. They urged me to write a how-to book. I thought this might be a bit presumptuous for a nonprofessional dancer, so I decided I would base my fitness and training recommendations on interviews with professional dancers and on my graduate research and ongoing study in the science and art of dance.

Still, my academic sensibilities flared: How could I write such a book in nontechnical terms and still convey the foundational scholarship? My postmodern skepticism emerged. How to tell a story of fitness and training in dance? Which story? Which approach? Which truth? Whose truth? Clearly, I needed to depict multiple truths, urging dancers ultimately to find their own approach to training, health, and fitness.

Gordon's book emphasized the competitive nature of the classical ballet form: out of reach for those but the very thin and the very young. Yet my own experiences in dance were anything but, having started dance as a "late bloomer" (in college) and being surrounded by teachers in their 40s and 50s who continued to perform. Clearly, dancing could be considered a long-term career as well as an avocation.

Finding Balance was about breaking boundaries, challenging norms, and redefining self and audience expectations. This second edition of *Finding* Balance is directed also to the very young—to preprofessional dance students. Yet I still believe that dance is about more than age and DNA advantage—for brilliant dancers of all ages and shape continue to perform, having made wise choices about what and how to perform and about good, healthy, effective training. Examples of such individuals, ages 14 to 78, are profiled in this second edition.

I very early on abandoned my initial intention that the revisions for this second edition be minor—perhaps just changing the profiles and updating a few references. It became clear that the book needed to be rewritten. The dancers I had interviewed for the first edition of *Finding Balance* were mostly over 30. For this edition, about one third of those profiled are in their 20s (or close to it). Less than one quarter of the material in the first edition is included here. For Chapter 1, "Dance: A Challenging Profession," I wanted to soften the tone a bit (so it was not a diatribe on ballet) and broaden the audience to include dance students, those with fresh visions and dreams. Chapter 2, "Injury and Injury Treatment," needed a complete rewrite to bring it up to date. In contrast, half of the material is new in Chapter 3, "Technique and Training," and Chapter 4, "The Fit Dancer: Conditioning the Body for Strength, Endurance, and Flexibility," which contains guidelines for fitness regimens and is the result of reading, research, and interviews conducted with hundreds of dancers over the past 15 years. Likewise, half of the material in Chapter 5, "Nutrition,

Weight Management, and Diet for Dance," is new, discussing the issues surrounding the food pyramid with its carbohydrate base. Chapter 6, "Finding Balance," is completely rewritten. The profiles are new; in fact, only two of those profiled are featured in both editions—Murray Louis and Wendy Perron, both no longer performing but still making their mark in the world of dance. Interviews with dancers for the first edition were conducted between 1987 and 1989, and for the second, between 1992 and early 2004. Most of the references are new, with a few retained from the first edition; I wanted to keep some of the classic scholarly works that remain benchmarks against which later work is measured. The book also includes medical/dance glossaries, with some updates to the medical entries.

Since dance is very much about images, I needed to procure photos of consistently high quality. Former Pacific Northwest Ballet soloist and now Boston photographer Angela Sterling provides the stunning photography. Angela, herself, is a profound example of someone who has found balance by finding another outlet for her creative work—and thus another niche in the wide world of dance. "Models" in the photos are primarily dancers from Pacific Northwest Ballet and Dutch National Ballet. Also included are artists from the Nancy Whyte School of Ballet, students from the Whatcom Hills Waldorf School eurythmy program, and colleagues from Bellingham Physical Therapy.

In the time since I wrote the last edition, much has changed in the fields of dance training and dance medicine and science. I write about some of these changes in this edition, emphasizing two of the central themes of the book: that the dancer is a lifelong learner and that the science of dance informs the art. Especially useful, not surprisingly, is science that is based on studies with dance populations.

In the past 15 years, relevant publications include the newsletter, *Kinesiology for Dance*, which I co-edited for several years and which evolved into the refereed publication, *Kinesiology and Medicine for Dance*, joining other longstanding publications dedicated to arts medicine such as *Medical Problems of Performing Artists* and, more recently, *Journal of Dance Medicine & Science*. During that time, dancers of all kinds have come to be studied more. Pioneers of dance science and education in the United States such as Martha Myers, Ruth Solomon, Jan Dunn, Janice Plastino, Ernest L. Washington, Allan Ryan, Robert Stephens, Judy Gantz, and Larry Vincent grace the editorial boards of dance journals.[1] All of us were carrying the message that science, and in particular dance science, could enhance our understanding of dance teaching and performing.

Of course, in many ways dancers are their own best teachers. They have an intuitive understanding and feel for the dance science principles working in their own bodies. Dancers with no formal training in kinesiology speak from experience in the profiles here about what scientists and academics deduce from systematic investigation, for the dancers interviewed are *practicing* kinesiologists, and their stories and advice often have a firm footing in science. Their anecdotal information, the result of personal reflection, is often every bit as sound as the good science appearing in refereed literature.

In some ways I did not rewrite the book; the book rewrote me. In writing, I realized again how hard dancers push themselves. They are, at times, goal oriented and persistent to a fault. Such behavior helps in learning a demanding variation—or in succeeding in academic studies. This edition underscores the importance of developing a positive self-image, another theme of the book. Perhaps all dancers have a perfectionist tendency, but "perfection is the enemy of good enough." And it can lead to hyper-self-criticism that can destroy a promising career.

One other theme of the book is learning to work with limitations and setbacks (clearly this is related to the themes already mentioned). For example, Gus Solomons jr (profiled in

Chapter 3) notes, "age need not be a limitation. It is a resource of life experience and dance craft that enriches performance beyond technical virtuosity." Solomons says that, throughout his career, he never had enough money to realize all the production ideas he had, but it didn't matter: " . . . If you have 10 yards of fabric and your idea calls for a million, then what you need to do is find out how to make the 10 yards eloquent."

One last theme is how to find one's place in the world of dance. At least some dancers are working for what approaches a decent wage.[2] But, whether or not they decide to pursue a career in dance, I believe that the training young dancers receive can last them a lifetime. Their dance training will help in confidence building to get a job or to succeed in college. It will facilitate a life of motivation and achievement and encourage dancers to persevere, sometimes against high odds (see profiles of David Zurak, Li Chiao-Ping, Bill Evans, Catherine Allaway, and Jenifer Ringer for examples). Some dancers need to move on—to somewhere else in the world of dance, or beyond. Cirque du Soleil's Paul Bowler is taking up real estate (see Chapter 6 profile), Gus Solomons jr is considering a broader career in theater, including puppetry. Gone is the idea that professional dancers have one and only one career—especially in these times when even nondancers average three or four in their lives. The difference, of course, is that the dancer's identity is so completely wrapped up with being a dancer that the end of performing can be a real blow to the sense of self.

In the past 15 years I certainly have changed. In some ways I have become more positive —and knowledgeable—about dance, but I also have become more critical, for example, as I now look for good children's training. My feelings, however, are still much the same as with the first edition: that dance is inclusive, and that dance is a good fit for many talented and motivated individuals.

Yet if I am so concerned about inclusivity, then why is so much of the narrative in the book based on and directed towards one form of dance: ballet? The answer has to do with the high coverage ballet receives in the refereed literature—and thus the coverage it gets here as well. Also, ballet is one of the most unforgiving of dance forms in terms of body type; if people can let go of perfectionism in ballet, maybe there is hope for other dance forms. Further, some of the physical demands in ballet are not unique—hip turnout is needed for many forms: Scottish highland and country dance, certain forms of classical Indian dance, almost all of modern dance. Further, I cannot cover all forms for all students —the book would be too large! So world dance and social dance, jazz, and tap receive some mention, as do yoga and various somatic (body) disciplines (such as Feldenkrais work and Pilates), as practiced in the United States.

I write from what I know—from my years of involvement with dance writing, criticism, research, and performance; also, from working at a dozen different universities and colleges, the most affecting experience perhaps being my current work at a tribal college in Washington state, which has led to my study of how students learn. My Lummi Indian colleagues say, speak about only what you know. It may be embarrassingly little, but here it is.

The book is an overview of fitness, training, and health for a lifetime in dance. It is not an encyclopedia. Perhaps I have, in fact, tried to cover too much, said too little, raising more questions than answers. I have tried to use language that is appropriate, but not too technical; parenthetical expressions follow some terms, and definitions are also given in the glossaries. Photographs and anatomical drawings (by a young student, Emily Rhoades) illustrate some of these ideas. Additional technical or detailed information appears in the appendixes. In the text itself, I often give lengthy explanations, for the history of ideas is informative. Conventions I employ include an inclusive style for references to gender: I often alternate genders, or use both.

Although the first edition of the book was geared towards professional dancers and students, as well as teachers, the audience for this second edition has been widened to include preprofessional students and others with a keen interest in dance. Thus, this book is intended for all who have ever faced a physical, emotional, or psychological problem as they aspired to find a place in the world of dance—dancers, young and old (and their families), dance teachers, artistic directors, even dance audiences. It is based on the view that making decisions as to how dancers train, how they rehabilitate from injuries, how they condition themselves, and how they focus on goal setting and attainment all are parts of a lifelong learning process in dance.

Ultimately, dancers must find points of balance between body image and nutritional imperatives, what is aesthetically pleasing and what is anatomically possible, personal needs and professional achievements. Finding balance is an important part of growing up, feeling centered, taking charge. In dance it comes from practicing making good choices while recognizing the realities of the profession—physical demands, work schedules, a general obsession with youth and thinness. These attitudes need to be recognized not so much to deny as to refuse to be limited by them. Dancers stand on the shoulders of those who have gone before them and are themselves charged to advance an art form that has produced, embraced, and challenged some of the most remarkable people in the world.

1

Dance
A Challenging Profession

KEY CONCEPTS/THEMES

Each dancer needs to find her or his place in the world of dance
Developing a positive self-image is the key to achievement in dance
All dancers need to learn to work with limitations
The science of dance informs the art
The dancer is a lifelong learner

Dancers try to achieve the near-impossible. They aim for the ever-higher, bigger jump (Figure 1), with a picture-perfect landing. They strive for the full 180-degree hip turnout of classical ballet (Figure 2). They set their sights on precise, dizzying turns worthy of a figure skater.[1]

To achieve all this, dancers push themselves to the physical limit—in company class, in preprofessional schools, even in neighborhood studios. Few professional sports can compare with the demands that dance places on the body. As a prominent U.S. Soccer team physician, Bert Mandelbaum, puts it, "Dancers rank with elite athletes in terms of their need to compete and perform, regardless of injury and pain. . . . The psychological and physiological demands placed on dancers [elite and otherwise] are extreme."[2]

While a top cyclist may exert an effort equivalent to running a marathon every day for the 3 weeks of the Tour de France, and a major-league baseball pitcher may be at serious risk for overuse injuries such as chronic elbow and rotator cuff tendinitis—at least they ultimately are evaluated only on their skill in achieving a result, not on their body type. Dancers, however, must conform to a predetermined idealized look, particularly in classical ballet. As clinical psychologist Linda Hamilton notes, "In a just world, dancers would be judged on their musicality, talent, and physical grace [i.e., their skill]. Yet the first thing the audience spots is—the body."[3]

Figure 1 Gael Lambiotte of Dutch National Ballet rehearsing in the studio. (Photo by Angela Sterling)

Figure 2 Pacific Northwest Ballet's Louise Nadeau maintains full hip turnout, even in an extreme gesture — a deep penché arabesque from George Balanchine's *Rubies*. (Photo by Angela Sterling)

Of the millions of dance students and tens of thousands of semi-professional dancers in the United States, few have an ideal dancer's body. Even among professional dancers, the ideal physique is rare. Dancers face enormous cultural pressures to fit an ideal image. Dance students within just the normal range of weight, height, and anatomy can be at heightened risk for injuries as the body compensates for the physical demands placed on it.[4] This includes even highly limber dancers, who may have an easier time achieving the streamlined, hyperflexible look but may be at risk for injury due to strength deficits. Young dancers, in particular, are vulnerable to overuse injuries owing to their developing musculoskeletal system.[5] Ironically, a young dancer's greatest risk is at puberty, just as the intensity of dance training and performing increases and normal bodily changes undermine the ideal image of the thin, coordinated, flexible dancer.

Still, despite the risk of injury and the pressure to conform to some ideal image, the number of dancers is growing. By some accounts, more people are training in studios and participating in organized dancing than ever before.[6] Although the numbers are less than, say, the more than 40 million people who regularly participate in softball leagues in the United States, including all the informal social dancers makes the numbers impressive.

With so many dancers training, how many have an ideal body, or can expect to approach the technical brilliance of American Ballet Theatre's Ethan Stiefel or Pacific Northwest Ballet's Jonathan Porretta (Figure 3), the incisive performance quality of Roxanne d'Orléans Juste of the José Limón Dance Company or the buttery soft moves of Catherine

Figure 3 Pacific Northwest Ballet's Jonathan Porretta in Kent Stowell's *Silver Lining*. (Photo by Angela Sterling)

Cabeen of Bill T. Jones's group, the thrilling kicks of Ann Reinking or the enormous strength of Li Chiao-Ping and her Madison, Wisconsin–based dancers?

Author-physician Larry Vincent feels strongly that the ballet body is "born" as much as it is "created," and perceives an artistic "Darwinian selection" that operates as a relentless survival of the fittest (or thinnest) in professional ballet. Especially in ballet, many of the "wrong" bodies for dance, as well as the less skillful, seem to fall by the wayside early in training—during childhood—leaving those with bodies better suited for ballet to continue on the path to becoming professional dancers.[7] Social and world dance forms, as well as many schools of modern dance, may be more forgiving, but pressure on young people (especially at puberty) knows no boundaries.

Moreover, of the millions of dance students training in this country, few have been screened for anatomical vulnerability to injury.[8] Instead, an implacable process of deselection is at work (which, in this country at least, ultimately weeds out virtually all dancers by middle age). Researchers note that only 5 percent of the children beginning a complete course of instruction at the School of American Ballet complete the 9 years of training; this attrition occurs because of various physical and psychological factors.[9]

Vincent argues, "If you're intent upon performing (regardless of level), recognize and accept your physicality, and work within your abilities. Find a type of dance or company that your body is best suited for, rather than attempting to overhaul your body."[10] Finding a place in dance where you can thrive is a recurrent theme in this book.

However much having a nonideal body type may hinder a dancer in her or his career, there is no doubt that anatomical factors play an important role in causing injury. For virtually all dancers, even those who are perhaps "naturally" stronger, faster healing, and free from structural deformations or anomalies, there is a need to know one's body and work within its limits.

Because of one's physical limitations, dance practice must be smart as well as repetitive. Of course it is important for dancers to practice movement, but not if they have structural anomalies that prevent its correct execution or if they make harmful compensations for limited muscle flexibility—and, most importantly, not if they don't know the intent of the movement or have a good understanding of which muscles need to be strengthened before a movement can be executed. According to the late dancer-choreographer Erick Hawkins, "You don't practice practice; you practice *theory*, based on principles of kinesiology."[11] Insights from theory on proper conditioning and training, together with good technique, can help offset the risk of injury and, even for gifted dancers, enhance and lengthen their careers.

This book contains the knowledge needed to guide conditioning and training, so that those who are captivated by the art and exhilaration of dance can have a full life in the practice of it. An important part of the book are the dancer profiles and the excerpts of interviews with professional dancers, first conducted from 1987 to 1989 and then updated from 1991 to 2004 for this second edition. These materials expand on and support the ideas about injury and injury prevention, training and technique, conditioning and fitness, and working within one's limitations that are the main message of this book.[12]

Good technique is not solely a matter of good genes (which is basically good luck). Neither is dancing injury-free. Applying what has been learned over the years in dance medicine and science can enhance the art of dance—both in developing good technique and avoiding injury. With sound training and conditioning, and selection of the appropriate dance form and dance company, dancers can find ways to work within their innate structural limitations and functional restrictions.

This was certainly true for dancer-choreographer Bill Evans (profiled in Chapter 3), who overcame physical limitations to become a renowned modern dancer and teacher. Says the 64-year old Evans:

> For me, whether or not the dancer is born or made is really a balance between the two. I think the longer one continues to dance, the less it depends on the body you were born with. When I joined Repertory Dance Theatre, in 1971, everybody, including myself, considered me to have the least appropriate body for dance. But now, if you were to put me in a room with those same people, you'd say I had the best body for dance. Clearly, I've developed over the years. Sometimes those people with the [ideal] anatomy don't learn how to improve. When performance finally declines, they just give up. Never having the perfect body was a blessing. It allowed me to learn to dance.[13]

Access to information is critical to training and technique. In order to improve, dancers need information about *how* the movement is performed, including coaching for its intent. This must come from a teacher or other source (e.g., literature, videotapes) that the dancer respects and in a learning situation where the dancer feels safe. Some dancers are highly cognitive and analytical. They want to understand the physical mechanics of the movement they perform: how to find balance when turning, how to create the illusion of floating in the air, how to increase the height of a leg extension. For such learners, in particular, this book will be helpful. Dancers are voracious learners—the information in dance class is not enough; the learning process is lifelong.

In addition, recent information on dance kinesiology and physiology, although some of it is contentious, can help to debunk widespread negative images of dance. For example, although it is undeniably true that the female athlete triad (disordered eating, amenorrhea, and osteoporosis) is a concern in dance, studies show that dance actually may impart some benefits in terms of increased bone density.[14]

Thus, this book is intended for all those dancers and dance students who have ever faced challenging physical, emotional, or psychological problems—the vast majority of us—and are searching for information on recognizing, treating, and preventing injuries and managing their life in dance. The images and scholarly references in this book mostly refer to ballet and, to a lesser extent, modern dance, since these are the dance forms with which I am most familiar. However, the "lessons learned" from these forms apply directly to other social and world dance, tap, and jazz—wherever the show "must" go on and whenever technique such as above-average hip turnout (as in Scottish country dance) is desired.

Health professionals, teachers, coaches, and family members—the rest of the "team" who work and live with dancers—will also find this book useful. Finally, balletomanes as well as jazz and modern dance enthusiasts will find these insights illuminating in the world they watch so carefully.

Recognizing, treating, and preventing injuries is more fully discussed in Chapter 2. There the reader will find information about risk factors for injury, injury treatment, and rehabilitation including complementary and alternative medicine.[15] Technique and training are covered in Chapter 3, conditioning in Chapter 4, and diet and health in Chapter 5. Developing a healthy attitude toward dance, especially finding one's place in the field, is the focus of Chapter 6, a new chapter in this edition.

In reality, most dancers make at least several career transitions. The dance world is large, and should be seen more as a *sphere* than a ladder—from coryphée (or apprentice) to principal dancer. The dance world is populated with teachers and students, artistic directors, lighting and scenic designers, musicians, press and marketing staff, costume managers, ballet mistresses, touring staff, development, marketing, and communications experts, health therapists, dance medicine and science practitioners, dance psychologists and nutritionists, dance writers and critics, and—last but not least—the dance audience. Finding one's place in the world of dance, a theme of this book, is discussed more in Chapter 6, as is making relatively smooth career or role transitions—within and around the dance sphere.[16]

An important theme of this book is that dancers are not necessarily "natural born," but can be made—as long as a person has a strong enough desire to dance and has access to good training and information. The science of dance enhances the art and helps it develop. For many in dance, their work is a matter of learning to operate within limitations and finding a place in the dance world, wherever it may be.

THE DEMANDS OF DANCE

The image and presence of determined youth is prevalent in dance. In the popular media, driven young dancers are the heroes and heroines of movies such as *The Turning Point*, *Fame*, *Flashdance*, *Dancers*, *Billy Elliot*, *The Company*, and *Center Stage*—about young dancers pursuing their passion[17] for dance in a major dance school or company. These movies chronicle the trauma and drama of finding a place in a school or getting a break in the profession.

Certainly, dancers are driven to survive and to succeed. Some dancers virtually risk their lives for their art. They push themselves too much; they work too hard, truncating childhood, restricting eating, battling fatigue. The payoff is highly uncertain. Not only is professional dance emotionally and physically demanding, but employment may be short-lived. In addition, competition is fierce and opportunities for advancement are limited. In ballet, if dancers have not made it to soloist or principal status by the time they have reached age 25 or 30, it is unlikely they ever will.[18]

Pushing the Body Image

One of the greatest challenges for dancers is one they face every day. Their worst and most frequent critic is the mirror, which invites an obsession with body image that would put top fashion models to shame. For some dancers, especially adolescents, it is an obsession with thinness.

The romantic ballets of the nineteenth century promoted the sylph-like look, translated in the late twentieth century into willowy princes and fair maidens, with protruding clavicles and bone-thin arms, an image that dancers in many ballet companies still struggle with today. Fortunately, among some top-ranking professional companies, the desired body image is in the process of changing to that of a sinewy god or goddess (Figure 4), a muscular look that is much easier to attain than the ultra-thin sylph-like form.

Obsession with attaining a thin body does not even make physiological sense. Use of laxatives and diuretics or semistarvation is often counterproductive to maintaining low body fat and overall weight (see Chapter 5). Developing a positive body-image and healthy body is discussed throughout this book.

In his book *Competing with the Sylph*, Larry Vincent provides a concise and thorough discussion of body image in dance and eating disorders. He discusses the enormous pressures on the dancer to conform to an ideal weight, form, and age, and admits that

Figure 4 Pacific Northwest Ballet's Maria Chapman. (Photo by Angela Sterling)

> There are plenty of reasons why dancers have to be thin, should one bother to ask. But there are many reasons why the aesthetic considerations of dance should not be given carte blanche. . . . Not that . . . there will be much of a market in the foreseeable future for obese ballet dancers; still, let us cast aside our biases (as well as our knowledge of the exigencies of the dance world today) and assume a broader perspective.[19]

The point is that the dance world (at least parts of it) is big enough to accommodate many body types. This is not to say that the specter of the "Balanchine" look (an "anorexic Peter Pan on pointe," to quote Vincent) no longer permeates the field, but there are alternative images as evidenced by many of the photos of professional dancers and dance students throughout this book. Vincent is optimistic that more and more students will be able to find their place in dance. He notes that competitive ballet schools are becoming a bit more lenient about weight in preprofessional levels; "weighings-in" are used to identify the too-thin as well as too-heavy dancer; the health problems (gynecological and otherwise) associated with excessive thinness are receiving more attention in the literature.

Perhaps we are going through an aesthetic "swing," a return to seeing and appreciating difference—older and more full-bodied dancers on the stage. As Vincent observes,

> We are becoming older as a population, and the obsessive identification with youth may be waning. Feminist ideals have undoubtedly had a positive effect, not to mention the growing involvement of women in choreography. Role models are changing

as well . . . . We recognize that adolescent gymnasts, despite their technical virtuosity, are not always able to pull off the artistic aspects of a program that require a greater element of maturity.[20]

It is not just ballet dancers who need to pull back and ease off from an obsessive body image and/or work schedule. If the desire to dance is there and dancers truly want to continue to work, then men and women in many forms of dance must forge their own aesthetics, with confidence and perseverance.

Overuse and Overload: Practice Does Not Make Perfect

Clearly, trying to achieve the ideal in dance requires practice. Practice to make perfect is what the dancer's life is all about. Yet more than practice is needed. If dancers could achieve perfection merely through repetition, they would reach it—after all, there is an abundant opportunity for repetition in daily classes and rehearsals.

Instead, for the many with suboptimal technique or even subtle body limitations, frequent practice—or rather the lack of recovery from it—may produce overuse injuries that impede their quest. Even minor but very common anatomical, physical, and technical problems[21] can predispose the dancer to injury from the constant repetition of practice and performance.

Physical overload from training, rehearsing, and performing—and the overuse injuries that result—are problems common in professional dance work.[22] Overuse injuries are caused by dancers' repeated attempts to force their bodies beyond their innate limitations.

Figure 5 Sabine Chaland of the Dutch National Ballet. (Photo by Angela Sterling)

A movement such as extending the thigh at the hip in an arabesque intensifies the forces on the lower spine, especially when the leg is relatively long (Figure 5). Eventually, the chronic stress on the body results in premature deterioration of connective tissue in the pelvis and lower spine.

Certainly, the physical demands placed on the professional dancer are exceptional, and they are aggravated by at least one peculiarity of dance: the fact that dancers rarely wear shoes that are designed for shock absorption. Other athletes use protective footwear for shock absorption and skin protection; dancers (like gymnasts) do not, although some progress is being made in dance floor construction (see Appendix B). Eventually, chronic stress on the connective tissue in the foot, ankle, or leg may result in its premature deterioration. Repeated landings from aerial work can result in microtears to connective tissues and chronic inflammation (for more, see Chapter 2).

At the very least, proper technique is essential for injury prevention. For instance, dancers who land from jumps with their big toes lifted (to avoid rolling-in of the foot) are prone to stress fractures, commonly of the second metatarsal. Dancers who land heel-up, failing to make more complete contact with the floor, often suffer chronic injury. Poor technique or structural misalignment also are responsible for injuries such as plantar fasciitis, Achilles tendinitis, and shin splints.

The likelihood of injury is especially high when the dancers experience overload—an increase in the intensity of training or performance. As artistic director Oleg Briansky warns, "Dancers work too much—eight performances in a week. You don't allow horses to run eight times in a week."[23]

In professional ballet companies, corps dancers typically dance every night for most of the season. Often they dance in two or more ballets each night. One program in Pacific Northwest Ballet's 2002–2003 season presented four ballets per night, three of them with large corps contingents; two of the ballets were double-cast. In the eight performances of that program (which included Glen Tetley's *Voluntaries*, Paul Gibson's *Rush*, José Limón's *The Moor's Pavane*, and George Balanchine's *Concerto Barocco*, all demanding pieces) and allowing for the double casting, a typical corps dancer would have danced 12 ballets.

It is more difficult to generalize about injury rate among soloists and principal dancers, since many of the parts are suited to a particular type of dancer. In the same Pacific Northwest Ballet program, a principal dancer did not dance more than two ballets per performance. But owing to specific castings and to injuries, principal dancers have been known to dance in every ballet of the evening for most of the performances.[24]

Touring also takes its toll on dancers. Many companies, such as the prestigious Martha Graham Dance Company, tour extensively. This company announced[25] a 2003–2004 touring schedule with close to 2 dozen mainstage performances, lectures, and demonstration performances. These were presented over an 8-month period from the end of August through the following April, beginning and ending in New York state with travel to Seattle, Los Angeles, London, and several cities in Italy. This tour also followed a successful home season at the Joyce Theater in New York.

Not all dancers work in companies that tour extensively. Being a professional dancer does not necessarily mean performing every night, nor being on the road 6 months of each year. Dance opportunities come in all forms, shapes, and sizes (and with varying monetary incentives). Repeating a theme of this book: dancers have many options. Performing with a company of national repute that augments its home schedule with touring is but one.

In considering career and work options, younger dancers in training should understand just how demanding the rehearsal and performance regimens are in professional dance.

(They probably are starting to know this already—it is what they have been training for, for years.) They also should be aware of other career possibilities as in "academic" dance work —i.e., in dance programs and departments in high schools, colleges, and universities, or in conservatory teaching—where dancers can earn a salary for teaching or teaching combined with performing. Work as a somatics practitioner—either teaching in an academic institution or working in private practice—is also an option. Another alternative is dancing with a nonprofit dance company, which typically will have a varied performance schedule. A case in point is the nine-member Moving Arts Dance Company, based in Walnut Creek, California, whose 2003 season included a tour to Russia, Germany, and Hawaii and regional performances and residencies. Another is Li Chiao-Ping Dance in Madison, Wisconsin, which is associated with a university and performs an average of 10 times per year.

The strain of extended performing and touring schedules can be detrimental to the longevity of a dancer's career, since many companies and dancers do not follow good conditioning regimens. Yet, no matter how grueling the schedule, there are ways dancers can train and condition their bodies to avoid overload. Bill Evans and his company are a case in point. Every year, from 1976 through 1983, and again in 1985 and 1986, Evans toured for an average of 40 weeks and performed at least 100 times. How did he maintain balance and avoid overload? Evans explains that "Taking a real company class every day was our priority. Even when we did school residencies, we'd take the time for class and the children could come and watch. Many touring companies don't take the time to do it—for us, it was essential."[26]

The Show Must Go On: The Pressure to Perform

Given overuse and overload, less-than-ideal dance bodies, less-than-mindful repetition in classes, and demanding choreography, it is not surprising that injuries are common in dance. Moreover, dance injuries commonly occur in the lower body. When that happens, basic locomotion activities such as walking do not allow for a period of rest, unlike the situation with injuries to the upper body. Repeated "dancing through an injury" can eventually shorten a performing career.

For many dancers, it is not a question of whether or not they are injured, but how much and how often. Dancers do not stop dancing with most injuries—they feel they cannot. One of a dancer's biggest fears is being sidelined and replaced. According to Daniel Duell, a former principal dancer with New York City Ballet (NYCB) and director of Ballet Chicago, "The greatest debilitator in dance is the fear of pain and the setback of injury."[27]

Dancers simply cannot afford to miss an opportunity to perform, especially in a featured role. Missing performances may put their jobs and even their careers at risk. In addition, a scheduled performance may be in jeopardy since many modern dance and small ballet companies have few understudies.

Of course, it behooves artistic directors to be prepared—and they are. David Parsons notes that his troupe has no understudies. Instead, the dancers simply adapt during a performance, when injuries or other emergencies happen. Says Parsons, "My performers are adept at improvisation. This is not *Serenade* or *Swan Lake*. We know the audience doesn't know what the steps are, so we can dance with confidence that we can [improvise through the unexpected]—even in front of thousands of people. The show only stops when the lights go out."[28] Parsons should know. He has dealt with many unexpected crises, including audience members' heart attacks and even the death of a dancer, in his arms, in Lyons, France, after he had administered Cardiopulmonary Resuscitation (CPR).

Most of the time when an injury occurs or a performer is dancing with pain, the audience is oblivious to it, and the show does go on.[29] Dancers know that their company depends on them, and they do not want to acquire a reputation for being unreliable or for always being injured. And so the soloist landing from a grand allegro jump may actually be suffering from debilitating arthritis in his knees. A female corps dancer might suffer from abnormal tracking of the kneecap. A premier danseur may perform with multiple stress fractures in his lower leg. Mikhail Baryshnikov's inflamed foot was hardly noticeable in a performance of *Coppélia*.[30] Artistic director Danny Grossman, who describes himself as "in trouble from the waist down," danced in the Paul Taylor company for 10 years without missing a single performance.[31]

One week of rest may be all that is needed to recover from an ankle sprain, shin splints, or a mild muscle bruise, but one week to a dancer may seem like forever.[32] Even worse, sometimes complete bed rest is indicated. How is complete bed rest possible? The rent must be paid, classes must be taught.[33]

Allegra Kent, formerly of NYCB and currently an independent dance coach and writer, would agree that dancers are under pressure to return to work after they have been injured. Yet dancers must be as forgiving with themselves as they are gracious with their companies and listen to what their bodies are saying about taking time off to heal.

For dancers, as for everyone else, coping with pain is fatiguing. Yet there seems to be a stoic psychology about pain, as well as about injury and fatigue, that is peculiar to dancers. Researchers report that dancers of all ages and skills are trained to cope with pain and injuries, especially overuse injuries, in a particular way, exhibiting higher pain thresholds and tolerance than nondancers.[34]

This is perhaps to avoid the "disruption of self" emanating from the injury. It also is clear that factors such as the kind of injury (acute, chronic, overuse, recurrent; see Chapter 2), personality differences, knowledge and available information about prevention, treatment and rehabilitation, styles of coping, and social support networks influence how individual dancers approach pain and injury.

Many dancers dance with injury, pain, and discomfort, supported by a subculture in the dance community that reinforces tolerance of pain, perseverance, and ignoring injury. Unfortunately, this in turn encourages behavior that predisposes the dancer to risk of injury (primarily overuse injuries) and, therefore, chronic pain.[35]

Even Bill Evans, the exemplar of finding balance through injury-free dancing, recognizes that there is a pervasive subculture of pain in dance. He says:

> Teachers and co-directors are often irresponsible. They look at the short-term. But whenever a dancer comes into my environment, I try to instill in him or her patterns that will serve for a lifetime. Even though young dancers consider themselves invincible and mask pain by taking Ibuprofen, I really discourage that kind of behavior. A lot of it comes from teachers and directors, and the culture in general, glamorizing a performance with pain and injury, as in athletics. Someone dancing with an injury is a hero—that behavior gets applauded but should be discouraged.[36]

Francia Russell, in responding to an emergency on stage at the Seattle Opera House in 2002, adds: "There is the saying, the show must go on—but not at a dancer's expense. The dancer needs to take precedence. Of course, dancers are risk takers. It's difficult enough for them on stage, physically and emotionally. They deserve to feel that the management is taking care of them, in whatever way we need to."[37]

Any number of actions can be taken by artistic directors to reassure the injured dancer that she or he will not be replaced. These include providing help to modify dance activities and allowing the dancer to offer advice about who the understudy or replacement should be, assist in classes, coach other students outside class, and assist in rehearsals, all of which helps to assure the dancer that, although the show must go on, it is clear that future performances will include her or him.[38]

Older Dancers: Moving Out or Moving On?

Although many other kinds of athletes and performers would be considered in their prime in their 30s, for dancers, their 30s and 40s often portend retirement. Sometimes, even a retirement age in the mid-30s is generous. Besides demanding choreography, heavy work schedules that "wear down" the body, and poor conditioning that exacerbates physical deterioration, there is a standard of youth that permeates professional dance. Yet some choreographers, especially in modern dance, do not consider a dancer "mature" and in his or her "prime" until the age of 30. Despite some public expectations and physical constraints, dancers are increasingly dancing into their 30s, 40s, and far beyond.[39]

As former *Dance Magazine* editor-in-chief K.C. Patrick writes, in an editorial entitled "The Impolitic Body," " . . . it's not just that anybody can continue dancing all their lives; but [that] . . . anybody can begin to dance, even at a mature age, and perhaps perform professionally."[40] Elsewhere, Patrick adds, "The more mature dancer converts . . . openness to determination and staying power, and is less flash but no less flame—remember the blind Alonso, the arthritic Cunningham and Dunham, and hundreds more who continue to pour their passion for the art into our community."[41]

These days, more dancers who are mature are continuing to dance, often projecting a dramatic stage presence. Performing groups that include mature dancers are the 40Up Project, Dancers over 40, Netherlands Dance Theater III, Liz Lerman's Dance Exchange,

Figure 6 Carmen de Lavallade, Gus Solomons jr, and Dudley Williams performing as Paradigm. (Photo by Tom Caravaglia)

and Paradigm—a trio of dancers including Carmen de Lavallade, Gus Solomons jr, and longtime Alvin Ailey dancer Dudley Williams (Figure 6).[42]

Dancers do not have to be living legends with lots of audience good-will to perform on stage. Across the broad spectrum between Maya Plisetskaya and Ruth Page on one end of the fame and age continuum, and sylphlike teens on the other, it is clear that audiences pay to see a fairly wide range of body sizes and shapes and maturity, depth, and control. And, in recent years, more has been written about older dancers. *Dance Magazine* celebrated such a life in dance with its October 2003 story on Bill Evans.

As a younger dancer, Evans experienced considerable pain and injury. By age 30 he had severe pain in the lumbar spine, immobility in the cervical spine, and almost disabling knee pain, prompting him to look for a new technique, a new way of moving. Says Evans,

> I've always danced, beginning with my first dances at three. For me, it's the most reasonable way for a human to act. When I'm dancing . . . in rehearsal or performance . . . in that moment . . . of dancing . . . the physical, emotional, intellectual all come together. I can go through the rest of the day and never find anything like that. For me, dance is a spiritual activity—it's my spiritual practice. It regenerates my spirit.[43]

Overcoming an intimidating array of physical problems—including spinal immobility and pain and debilitating knee pain, Evans's technique today represents a heavy dose of dance medicine and science. It is a blend of anatomical awareness, kinesiological principles, body therapy, and movement repatterning, borrowing heavily from Irmgard Bartenieff's Fundamentals and Rudolf Laban's theories of effort, shape, and space harmony. Evans is not alone in his multidisciplinary study. It is dance medicine and science—sources of the scientific information to support dancers—that keep both young and mature dancers dancing.

FINDING BALANCE:
HOW DANCE MEDICINE AND SCIENCE CAN HELP

Another theme of this book is that dance medicine and science can augment the art of dance and help to enhance performance, reduce injuries, and prolong careers. As Karen Clippinger and Scott Brown wrote in their editorial for the 1997 inaugural issue of the *Journal of Dance Medicine & Science,* the field of dance medicine and science, although borrowing from work in sports medicine and fitness, is critical since dance places "unique demands on its practitioners."[44]

Dance medicine and science help one to understand the physical and psychological demands of dance, assess current methods of dance training and conditioning, and investigate ways to prevent and treat dance injures and related medical conditions. For dancers, dancing longer and dancing stronger is a matter of healthy dancing. For company directors, it also is a question of cutting expenses and maintaining a productive work force.[45]

Indeed, in the roughly one dozen years since the first edition of *Finding Balance* was published, the boom in scholarly research in the area of dance science has been astounding. With advances in such research and an increase in the number of specialists in dance medicine, dancers often do not have to stop dancing when injured. Instead, they can *selectively* rest body parts—especially when the injury is in the upper body—and limit certain movements. Following examination and diagnosis of the injury and the factors causing it, the specialist may recommend any of a number of actions: joint adjustments, manual physical therapy, selective exercise, possibly the use of a soft cast and stretching exercises, modifications in technique, various exercises in physical therapy, and proprioceptive retraining. All of these enable the dancer to continue activity during recovery from certain injuries (see Chapter 2).

Such rehabilitative work is also part—perhaps as much as half—of being a dancer. For many dancers, it is all of it—being lifelong learners, and feeling that the best technical years are yet to come.

FINDING BALANCE: THE DANCER AS LIFELONG LEARNER

The search for useful information in dance and dance science is a lifetime process; the information does not necessarily come easily. As artistic director Murray Louis said, "When kids come to dance, they're gorgeous, but [they're] dumb."[46] It seems that young dancers have to prove themselves—to themselves, to family, and to the dance world. Yet what they really have to do is use common sense. Gone is the "younger, thinner, stupider" archetype. Now, dancers are asking more questions and are learning to work within their limitations.

Louise Nadeau is a case in point. A principal dancer with Pacific Northwest Ballet who is known for her brilliant technique and injury-free dancing, Nadeau suffered from overuse, fatigue, and injury in spring 2003. "One needs to be aware of technique, especially in fast-paced ballets," says Nadeau. In attempting the relentless petit allegro of Balanchine's *Tschaikovsky Pas de Deux* (which she performed on the spring 2003 program), she repeatedly landed with her "heel up." She suffered from rehearsal overload, but has fully rehabilitated (see Chapter 2 profile). Within months after her injury, she performed a breathtaking Odette/Odile in Kent Stowell's *Swan Lake,* having taken the injury as an opportunity to condition her body and retrain.

During rehabilitation, dancers also can reevaluate their technique. Merrill Ashley discussed this in her book, *Dancing for Balanchine:*[47]

> When I am injured and have more free time than I am accustomed to, I find myself trying to form a clearer picture in my mind of what I want the overall effect of my dancing to be . . . . The improvement after long layoffs is due not only to the benefits I have derived from "starting from scratch" or observing others. During a period of recovery, all dancers are forced to be sensitive to the condition and the needs of their bodies in order to make important decisions about which therapies to try or which advice to listen to . . . After an injury, a dancer learns, at least for a short time, to heed his body if only because pain speaks a language almost anyone can understand. This heightened awareness should not disappear once a dancer returns to form; rather it should help him continue to learn about the way his body moves and reacts.

Dancer Keith Sabado, formerly with Mark Morris, felt that once you are injured, "there's a certain amount of knowledge that you gain from that . . . that allows you to perform." For Risa Steinberg, a former lead dancer with the José Limón company, the information was critical. After tearing the cartilage in her right shoulder, she was ready to embrace a new way of training. She began to identify the warning signs of pain and when she was being destructive to her body.[48]

Using "common sense" and "listening to your body," "knowing the signs of pain when destructive to the body . . . to be in control . . . and not a victim," are part of the healing process. For many dancers, this is a process of developing body intelligence and wisdom—a "thinking body."[49]

FINDING A PLACE IN THE WORLD OF DANCE

Dancers put up with the hard work of training and the pressures (counterpoints to the joy and excitement) of performing, no matter their age. Although the teenage dancer may not be able to imagine ever being as old as 30, in fact he and she someday will face the 30-, and maybe the 40- and even 50-year milestone, for the physical, emotional, and psychological demands of dance are enormous and continuing. That does not mean that they cannot be met. A career in performing dance is well worth the effort, but it takes work, commitment, and resolve.

As noted in a *Dance Magazine* editorial, "Twyla Tharp once told an interviewer that a life in dance is hard. Don't do this unless you can't not, she said. So why do we keep doing this if it's so hard? Because in some way we must. The very young are compelled to learn—it's a design feature for human survival. Adolescents' passion just bubbles out all over."[50]

Younger dancers must realize that only a very small percentage of dancers "make it" to prima ballerina, premier danseur, or favorite soloist in classical and modern dance companies. And some of those who do make it do not last long. Dancers must thus decide what is important for them in dance. If it is career longevity, they must be careful not to push themselves to the point where they no longer feel in control of their bodies, their training, and their health. They must recognize their limitations.

Professional dancers advise students to learn to face technical shortcomings and be willing to seek help in training and career choices. Wendy Perron offered, "You must keep the joy alive. To do this, recognize your limitations early on . . . I could have broken my body, but didn't. [At the Graham Studio] they wanted to discipline everyone and I was somewhat defiant."[51]

Perhaps the "survivors" always did have some limitations. In a sense, they were selected for longevity, because of their physical limitations. They could see that a "perfect" arabesque was not attainable. Patricia McBride, formerly with NYCB, reflected, "I didn't go for 200-degree extensions. I wasn't like Allegra Kent who could bend herself into a pretzel. I was unique, however, in my energy and love of dance." It is that love which is important, rather than the height of an extension, the perfect split leap en l'air. Jerel Hilding, formerly with the Joffrey Ballet, admitted, "I will not push, I will not force myself into some [position] which is unnatural. This may have inhibited my career since I would not push beyond a certain turnout, but it was never an obsession anyway. Dancers are injured because they put too much pressure on themselves."[52]

Audience expectations and preferences aside, how, what, and where can dancers perform when, for example, they have finished 10 rigorous and exhausting years in professional children's ballet school or have hit the "40-barrier" in modern dance, and want to go on. For all of these dancers, dance is their life—and they are going to do everything possible to ensure that they can continue with it.

Dancers *can* continue to dance in good health much longer, easily into their 40s, and often beyond. Essentially, they can dance as long as they want to. It is not just a matter of being lucky. We know that chronological age does not invariably render dancers physically dysfunctional, although not all of them have come to understand that.

Carmen de Lavallade, Dudley Williams, and Gus Solomons jr (of Paradigm) all know this, as do Murray Louis, Trisha Brown, and others whose names are less well known. The people who pay to see them perform also affirm that aging dancers have much to say in the practice of their art form. Modern dancers mentioned above who are over age 50 and are still performing may be the exceptions. But their stories (some of which are profiled in this book) tell us that dancers need not be fatalists about their career opportunities in professional dance, even as they age.

Probably one of the main requirements for continuing to dance is sustaining the desire to do so. That means putting up with the hard work of training and the pressures of performing no matter what one's age is. There is no doubt that the physical demands of dance are enormous. That does not mean that they cannot be met. This is especially true if dancers continue to look at themselves as lifelong learners. Those who continue to thrive in the profession look at life and dance differently, perhaps allowing the little things—anxieties, stresses, and disappointments—to fall through the cracks (see Chapter 6).

Dancers with staying power in dance are those who are impassioned with an art form and dance movement that respects the body's physical limitations. Such dancers see their work as a calling and are willing to explore mind-body connections that are critical for healthy dancing.[53] The pettiness and abusiveness that still exist in dance are also being recognized, and dancers are finding and redefining their own places in dance, including choice of dance form or style (Figures 7 and 8).

Ultimately, dancers must find a balance between training and performance, body image and nutritional imperatives, injury treatment and performance schedule, what is aesthetically

Figure 7 Dance is much bigger than ballet. Kristin Torok in a Wade Madsen solo. (Photo by Angela Sterling)

Figure 8 Eurythmist Ann Neal-Levi in Alia Hall, Whatcom Hills Waldorf School. (Photo by Angela Sterling)

pleasing and what is structurally possible, as well as personal needs and professional goals. Finding balance is an important part of growing up, feeling centered, and taking control.

Parents need to monitor the learning environment, mindful that when dancing stops being enjoyable for their children, then it is time to stop. For preadolescent and adolescent dancers, this can be difficult. They still need guidance, primarily in learning to make the right choices for themselves, especially when they are living and studying on their own. For the adult dancer, it is a question of making informed decisions, being willing to take control of one's life, and, if necessary, overcoming the obstacles one faces.

Jenifer Ringer, is, of course, an extreme case of this. A New York City Ballet corps member at 16 (in 1990), her still-maturing body meant a struggle with weight control and self-doubt, plummeting self-esteem, physical and emotional depletion, and injuries. She left NYCB in summer 1997 to find some balance, which meant taking time off to gain confidence in classes with a respected teacher, only to return to the stage the following year (she was promoted to principal in 2001), with a newfound love and sense of well-being for dance (see Chapter 5 profile).

The experiences of dancers who have found such balance in their training and professional lives are presented in profiles at the end of each chapter of this book. All are lifelong learners, using dance medicine and science to their advantage, finding their place in dance, acknowledging the challenges and following their calling. In reading these profiles, dancers everywhere and of all ages may be encouraged to acknowledge some of the tough realities of the profession—intense physical demands, relentless work schedules, obsession with youth (or age), with thinness or strength or height—not so much to deny as to refuse to be limited by them. In so doing, they will lead the way in helping others to find the balance in their lives that will allow them a life or two (Figures 9 and 10), perhaps even a lifetime, in dance.

Figure 9 Pacific Northwest Ballet's Paul Gibson performs in William Forsythe's *In the Middle, Somewhat Elevated*. (Photo by Angela Sterling)

Figure 10 Paul Gibson, as both choreographer and coach, rehearses dancers Melanie Skinner and Batkhurel Bold in his work, *Rush*. (Photo by Angela Sterling)

PROFILES

Elizabeth Streb

The work of Elizabeth Streb (Figure 11), who was the 1998 recipient of a MacArthur Genius Grant, has been seen in regular seasons in New York and on tour, in outdoor and indoor spaces all over the world, and on the *Late Show with David Letterman, ABC Nightly News, Larry King Live,* as well as other television engagements. Her work is a fascinating combination of the aristocratic (just how many people can master Elizabeth Streb's unique high-impact movement vocabulary and sense of daring?) and democratic (she invites the public to join her in her studio/laboratory/home, the Streb Laboratory For Action Mechanics (SLAM) located in Williamsburg, Brooklyn).

In a review in *Dance Magazine,* I wrote about her:

> . . . penchant for thrills . . . [in *Action Heroes,* whereby] the action occurs in a truss box, metallic scaffolding used for rock concerts, rising over 20 feet in the air. Other props are less visible but still critical—ropes, harnesses and padded gymnastics pads. These enable the dancers to . . . hurl themselves wildly and dive spread-eagled (a repeated motif in the piece), suspending in mid-air before landing on each other.

What is Streb's aesthetics that calls for her dancers to crawl, slither, leap, and levitate onto and over any prop they can—in addition to bunge jumping? Streb writes from her website, "Aesthetics of grace, the use or camouflage of gravity, the presence or absence of transitions, treatment of gender, the nature of spatial and temporal dimensions as well as the use of

Figure 11 Elizabeth Streb (Photo by Sandro DiSandro)

sound in theatrical presentations have been primary areas of exploration." [http://www .strebusa.org/pages/what.html]

For Streb, the rehearsal space and place is a laboratory for testing principles from different knowledge paths. Streb's creative process draws from the sciences and mathematics, uses specially designed and engineered equipment, and demands fearlessness and precision from her dancers. The result is work that is unique, compelling, and popular. She clearly loves the adventure of the choreography—the process as well as what's in the product at any point in time.

What characterizes Streb's work best is an almost insatiable curiosity for information—especially coming from different epistemologies or knowledge paths that converge. The study of different knowledge systems is almost recuperative for the hard-working Streb: "I take classes at New York University to study movement in different fields—mathematics, physics, architecture, philosophy. The study is a break for me, from flinging my body at walls. It's still rigorous, but similar—how to measure the area under a curve, how to choreograph specificity to an extreme action."

Streb calls herself a constant student, a lifelong learner:

> The classes for me are an escape from the intensity of performances and rehearsals. I go to class a few times a week and feel refreshed. Besides, you have to do it. Just as scholars have to know Greek, Latin, and German, say, movement practitioners probably should know about math and physics. It's not just enough to generalize about these points in space.
>
> For me, it's also about history—I want to study the accumulated knowledge base —fundamental motion ideas in physics, elemental shapes in geometry and trigonometry. There seems to be archetypal movements that can elicit a resounding reaction, a recognition form in dance. That's movement deserving as being part of a cannon.
>
> I guess my work is about the juncture of the body, space, and time—in a wandering way. It's still a humbling thing to put action on stage . . . how much can we actually know about it?

And artistic director Streb wears many hats in this demanding profession:

> Because the economy is so difficult in dance, a lot of time is spent fund raising to cover salaries in any one year. As an artistic director, I see this as part of my job—it's challenging and interesting for me. I see it as a responsibility of those who take on a new art form. You have to get established—this is how we build our vision in a stable way.
>
> I don't feel like I compete with others for money. Each artist goes to different foundations to ask for money . . . you certainly don't get everything you asked for. We always feel like we've won a gamble when something comes in—you have to make a game out of it. A serious game.
>
> Besides fund raising, the artistic director also is a human resources manager. You have to direct dancers. You have to have them get along. You have to collaborate. You feel like an individual artist, but have to wear a lot more hats—it's such a people discipline.

How important is technique to her work? Some observers might consider her work strenuous and potentially dangerous:

I'm not sure if our injury rate is higher. We've certainly done everything we can to avoid a worst-case scenario. Certain things can happen—the stakes are higher for us since the physical intensity is higher. In "punch the jump," people are supposed to land on the tramp[oline] at different times. Inevitably, there's a collision. In the past 25 years, I've had to memorize how you take care of people . . . part of it is, you just stop. It's like a small circus . . . things can happen that don't happen to other dancers. When these angels of the air crash, they can't work, everything is lost. This is why the technique is so important, and part of the technique is timing—you don't jump out of turn. It has to be precise—just like the conditioning for abdominal strength and trunk stability, the dancers have to work at it.

Fund raiser and people-manager extraordinaire notwithstanding, it's Streb's artistic and political vision that powers her choreography and career:

I'm 54 now, and am less able to pinpoint the next idea, the next piece out of the fear of repeating. You look at all the geniuses . . . and it's probably not a good idea to work on the same problem. . . . If you're a young mathematician, you're competing against the most brilliant people in the world—you don't want to work on something that others have been wrestling with for 300 years. I try to find the gaping holes, the unanswered questions.

Streb sees her work almost as a civic responsibility:

I ask, is there a civic duty we have as artists, or, do we just cast our ideas to the wind and see if they have any relevance in the real world? For me, I think our work should be public. When we're working in the Slam Lab, our doors are always open. It's a place where people meet to exchange ideas—from Ringling, Club Med, Noveau Circus, Cirque du Soleil; pedestrians, too.

There's a privacy in the dance world that's not the most fruitful way to promote growth. You have to let the outside in. Maybe it gets a little chaotic, but you might find something a little more wild as a result, a little more unpredictable.

Roxane d'Orléans Juste

For Roxane d'Orléans Juste, the works of José Limón are a masterful combination of movement, form, and ritual, with a subtext of hope, community, courage, and compassion. These dances sustain her, and she makes it her professional goal to keep the body of work alive. Besides serving as artistic associate and reconstructor of Limón's choreography, she is a principal dancer with the José Limón Dance Company. In 2003, Juste celebrated her twentieth anniversary with the company.

Times have changed, and dancers have changed, but what attracts the 21-year-old dancer to Limón is the same thing that attracted me back then. The work captivates your soul, not just with its physicality, but because it commands a singular state of alertness and awareness. Some works are especially vibrant. The challenge of the Limón repertory is that besides its great physical demands, it requires an insatiable curiosity—a love for movement, a love for the unknown, a willingness to give in to the force of gravity to truly find a renewal of energy. It is a metaphor for life! It requires one to be interested in the world's cultures and in the masterworks of great artists who deeply inspired José Limón. As an interpreter of his repertory and that of Doris Humphrey's, I have to investigate not only their point of view and the climate in which they lived but [reflect as well] on my own experience. I can only . . . be true to another artist's vision if I question and continue to discover, for myself, a creative mind and individual voice.

Juste was born and raised in Montréal, where she started ballet training at the age of four. Creative dance classes gave her free exploration of weighted movements, rhythms, swings, and speed in an imaginary world. She says it was a "great revelation," and [fit] with the mastering of precision, effortlessness, and lightness in ballet technique. She got her first big break in dance when traveling with her parents to Haiti, where she was exposed to Haitian folklore by Katherine Dunham and Lavinia Williams, with whom she continued her training in ballet. Williams, especially, took her under her wing when she was 11. In Haiti, she discovered the "earth and its sounds," learning that the torso was a living entity in dance, and achieving free-flowing movement of the body and the spine, or what she calls "release."

After her return to Canada, she studied in Sherbrooke and graduated from an Art and Science High School. Shen then pursued an interest in psychology in College. At the same time, she continued to dance with Pierre Lapointe, her ballet teacher and former "danseur" with Les Ballets Russes de Monte Carlo, and was encouraged to teach and inspired to choreograph. At the age of 20, she graduated from the National Ballet School in Toronto with the first official class of the School's Ballet Teacher's Program. She applied for and received a grant from The Canada Council for the Arts to travel to Europe to visit four major schools of dance: the Royal Danish Ballet School, The Paris Opéra, the John Cranko School (school of the Stuttgart Ballet), and the Hamburg Ballet School. For her studies, she observed the training of professional dancers and their differences in style. She then traveled to New York to continue her research at The School of American Ballet and studied contemporary dance, including Limón technique. She first saw the Limón company perform when she was a student in Toronto. Says Juste, "My memory was that there was such exuberance. The work was so powerful. I can remember the ensemble in a sweep of colors, as waves of movement."

Juste successfully auditioned for the company in 1983. She performed a solo choreographed by Eleo Pomare (with whom she had danced as a professional member of his company). She was then accepted into the Limón Company. Says Juste,

> One of the important things about the Limón technique is that you have to understand what weight really is, and how to use it following basic principles of opposition and resistance. The fall and recovery that looks so natural on stage, in the choreography, actually is more difficult to find in class. That's the physical part. In finding mental and emotional balance, I am very fortunate to have my husband's support and understanding—and to be able to share a mutual love for music, dance, and nature. We both seek transformation and growth.

Juste says that what injuries she has incurred have been from overuse, mostly in her lower body. But she has had good physical therapy, and any sprained ligaments have healed well. What also helps her is selectively resting injured body parts and keeping up with her Alexander Technique work.

> Early on in my career, my tendency was to overwork, to overstretch—just to overdo. Now, I try to have more balance in my life. The Alexander technique has

helped me in many ways. I am learning to ["listen" to my body in gaining] an over-all awareness of life and the inner self. The most important thing actually for me is not to stop dancing—if I stay away for more than one week, my muscles become tense. For my body, movement is oxygen.

In the Limón company, Juste is one of the more longstanding members. With that comes more responsibility and pressure:

I'm learning to manage overload. A few years ago, four of us had been members of the company for at least 9 years, now I am the only one. Longevity can be an asset but I sometimes suffer from overuse, repetitive motion, muscle fatigue, and dehydration. I still tend to take on too much, but I love what I do and look for ways to stay balanced in body and mind by working with somatic therapies including Feldenkrais and relaxation techniques.

[Work with the company] still attracts me, it is almost magnetic. Having guest artists create new works or having masterpieces reconstructed for us are wonderful opportunities. [Thus], we must stay current, versatile, and available to learning many dance "languages." Being part of the company is challenging; after many years we can enjoy some ease but we are still needing to reinvent ourselves. It's the best university in the world.

Carrie Imler

Carrie Imler is one of Pacific Northwest Ballet's (PNB) recently promoted principal dancers. She earned her unusual promotion—occurring mid-season, for only the second time in the company's history—following star performances in *Sleeping Beauty* and *Don Quixote*. She is known for her spot-on technique and elevation in jumps, and was included in a "25 to Watch" story on promising performers in *Dance Magazine* in January 2003. She got her rigorous training at Central Pennsylvania Youth Ballet in Carlisle, Pennsylvania, and the Pacific Northwest Ballet School in Seattle.

Imler is a cheerleader for PNB and a champion for dance in general:

Yesterday I was wearing my PNB jacket as I was shopping. Someone asked, "Are you with the ballet—oh, we love your work." I figure that as long as you're touching one person—it's worth it. I really love my work and I wouldn't trade it for anything. I think what really helps keep me going is being able to put everything in perspective, and then having performances to look forward to. Reaching one person in the audience makes all the training and injuries worthwhile.

This doesn't mean that Imler doesn't suffer from dance demons:

I've always struggled with the whole body image thing. I've always felt like I was a little bigger than most dancers. So, I work on my body image—physically and in my head. I'm 5'6", which really is a normal size for a ballerina. Still, I'm always aware of my size, especially when I'm looking in a mirror during class and rehearsal. Some days are better than others.

How does Imler control the obsession with the perfect dance look? "I focus on my work, my interpretation of a role—and I follow a good diet so I get the right balance of protein and carbohydrates. For toning up, I lift weights. If I need to, I go to the gym and work out a little harder."

Imler also focuses on her academic school work. She is part of a general effort by PNB, called "Second Stage" and headed by PNB trustee Rick Redman, to provide career counseling, mentoring, and grant money for dancers to take academic classes. A partnership with Seattle University provides for classes that fit into the dancers' demanding schedule. Introductory classes help dancers to move onto specially designed core classes and then into regular Seattle University courses. Taking one course every quarter for 4 years, the dancers can earn up to 2 years of education credits or the equivalent of an Associate of Arts degree:

> I'm taking classes now as part of a program that PNB created for dancers in the company or those who have recently left the company.[54] You can get a grant to go back to school, or open up your own dance school. Perhaps you need a Marley floor —some dancers have gotten a loan through the program.

Imler is part of the first cohort going through the university program:

> It was great when I heard about the partnership with Seattle University. I had tried taking random classes before and it was hard . . . there're only so many classes that fit into your schedule, like at 8:00–8:50. Now, I can take classes where the teacher comes to us [teaching close to PNB studios] on Monday nights after rehearsal. Class starts whenever we're done with rehearsals. If we get Monday off, he starts the class earlier in the day.
>
> I think that dancers are ideal students. Melanie Skinner [see Chapter 5 profile] also is in the cohort. At first it was a little strange . . . since we're always together and talk about ballet steps.
>
> And we were embarrassed when we had to do some peer review . . . letting someone else into a different part of our life. But most of us are getting used to it [close to 20 students were in the first cohort, ages 19–38]. I also enjoy using a different section of my brain rather than just using it for learning choreography. I depend on a different part, writing argumentative papers. So, it does not take away from the dancing. If I wasn't doing this I'd do something else—gardening or working on my house.
>
> Incorporating something else in my life, something new like university classes, is perfect for me to take my mind away from the pressures of training and rehearsal. I work well under pressure so it's easy for me to forget about school until the weekend. The classwork—writing poetry, doing assignments—develops another dimension of you as a person.

At least for now, Imler's college courses complement but won't displace her dance profession:

> Academics is about discipline and working hard to achieve a goal, as in dance. Just a bit of my interest in it all is that I am getting older, and it's natural to think about your career in dance, especially with the few injuries I've had—it gives you a new perspective But these are just basic courses. I'm not in a degree program, so I can still focus on my dance career.

Having other creative outlets is especially important when a dancer is rehabilitating. Imler had to take it easy after a minor injury during the PNB *Sleeping Beauty* production in

2003—she performed in the less demanding role of Lilac Fairy, rather than as Aurora. Imler says, "studying helps to keep your mind off not being at work." Back in full swing, Imler was rehearsing a new program at the time of writing: "We just started to learn the fourth move-ment of the *Brahms-Schoenberg Quartet* for the Balanchine Centenary. The individual solo parts in it are very difficult—big jumps and turns and fouettés. The whole program should be fun—this is what I've been training for."

David Parsons

David Parsons runs his own dance company of nine dancers and three administrative staff. His repertory of over 60 works, many with commissioned scores, is performed at City Center and the Joyce in New York, and in Spoleto, Italy, with the goal of making dance ac-cessible to the widest possible audience.

Parsons faces up to the demands of running a nonprofit dance company: at the time of the interview for this book, he was licking some of the 6,000 envelopes that needed to go out. "You have to be willing to do a lot of things to make it all work," he says, meaning what it takes to run a company.

> Basically, there are three types of dance—Broadway, major and regional ballet, and contemporary dance. Each has a completely different dance population—that's just the reality. Broadway jazz dancers will train in a completely different way to those in the contemporary dance scene.
>
> Dance has its own community, with new people coming and going, and you have to invest time in it. You can't just take class, be the hottest performer possible, and think that opportunity is going to knock at your door. It's intense and time-con-suming to learn about the whole concert dance world. But to really understand it, dancers have to take an interest in seeing what different choreographers are doing —you have to mix and network with others. The best performers are the ones who know what's going on. I know there're dancers in my company who graduated from Julliard yet never see dance. But then again, if you're performing all the time, who wants to go into a theatre?

Parsons danced with the Paul Taylor Company for almost 10 years (1978–1987). He also has had guest stints with the New York City Ballet, MOMIX, and the White Oak Dance Project.

> In a way, dancing with Paul Taylor was easy—I danced with him from the time I was 18 to 25 and I had a ton of energy. I did all the major works. Paul would use me because I was fearless—I wasn't afraid of injury . . . that was because of my age. I still think that the best injury prevention for dancers is to stay in shape and just dance.

To stay healthy, Parsons advises dancers to: "One, keep dancing—dance with a company with a lot of work where there's no long breaks. And, two, have a lifestyle that keeps you in shape, and performance is an important part of it. Not dancing and being fit is what leads to injuries." Parsons was 26 when he started his own company: "It was an absolute joy. We had a group of performers who were in love with what they were doing—in love with tour-ing and being together. The first years of a successful company when you have a repertory that presenters want is exciting."

Over the past 20 years, Parsons has produced and created dances for companies as diverse as American Ballet Theatre, Paris Opéra Ballet, Hubbard Street Dance Chicago, Batsheva Dance Company of Israel, Felds Ballet/NY, and New York City Ballet. He has had the chance to observe, choreograph, and rehearse many different types of dancers. He says he likes to begin setting a piece by using the vocabulary of the dancers. What does he look for in a performer? "Besides the prerequisite of making the [audience's] eyeballs pop out when you walk into a room, the dancer has to have that dancer passion—they also have to be willing to make a real team effort, especially with a company like ours."

Parsons says the dancers in his company, ranging in age from 22 to 36, are passionate, intelligent, and mature. They need to be fast and athletic, but also weighty and strong. They all receive health benefits and have enough work so that they don't need another job. Parsons likes to feature the choreography of his dancers,[56] much of which also has a sense of humor—like their artistic director.

> I had a pretty normal childhood, growing up in Kansas City, Missouri. I guess my sense of humor comes from growing up in a family of three boys. My family always loved good jokes. And working with and watching Paul Taylor, I could see that dance could have humor. Taylor believes that laughter is an emotion that should be dealt with. I saw what Taylor was doing and appreciated it.

Parsons is known for his inventive style and comic flair, "serving up laughter as the main course" because, according to some critics, "nothing is more serious than the business of amusing a New York audience." Some have referred to Parsons as the "wizard of modern dance." Parsons' sense of humor is evident in many of his dances: "To me, as a choreographer, it's the range of tone and emotion that is important to find. I'm the one in charge of the output. It's not that I make funny dances, but ones of different genres—that's what's exciting to [the audience]. Comedy breaks down the barriers of class and taste in an audience so everyone can enjoy the work."

David Zurak

Watching David Zurak (Figure 12) perform on stage with the Martha Graham Dance Company, it's hard to believe he took his first dance class when he was 23. Typically, "late-bloomer" professional modern dancers are involved in athletics earlier in their lives.

Zurak's story is unusual because he had not been an athlete. Far from it. He was a self-proclaimed computer geek from early on, when, in his final year of an electrical (biomedical) engineering degree program in Toronto, he saw a dance performance (Peggy Baker, formerly with Lar Lubovitch) that "gave him a new way of looking at the body; that first theatrical dance experience for me was—and I know this is a cliché—it was life-altering," says Zurak.

Zurak soon found that the movement he had seen was possible only with a lot of hard work. Zurak's progression into dance is a story of "finding teachers that work with and for you, and then having the courage to move on to develop as an artist." In fact, this is really the main message of Zurak's story: find what you need to be, to do, to study in order to develop as an artist; then, continue to reflect on and question your training and your work, in order to keep growing.

Zurak says he became the laughingstock of his electrical engineering graduating class when he let it be known he was planning to take dance classes. "I kept it bottled up for a

Figure 12 David Zurak of the Martha Graham Dance Company performs Graham's *Circe*. (Photo by John Deane)

year, and then I simply said, 'I need to do [dance].' I had to try it or I knew I'd be a very unhappy person. I took a few jazz classes."

His early approach to dance was purely scientific (in fact, his first job after graduation from university was a blend of his scientific training and interest in human movement—an engineering consulting job in neuromuscular rehabilitation); perhaps the intellectual approach got in his way, although it may have helped in dealing with the comments in his dance classes. At any rate, his ascent was not exactly meteoric. But, in the end, his hard work paid off with an audition for the summer intensive course at the National Ballet School of Canada; acceptance meant being in class with young children but also performing in showcases, including a piece that John Neumeier had created for the school.

Soon, he realized that catching up on the dance training he had missed would become a full-time job: He'd get up at 7 A.M. for a beginning Graham class at Toronto Dance Theatre, then go to the National Ballet School of Canada and take "tons of classes." Zurak says that he always was a closet Graham dancer. He says that the 10-year-olds in those ballet classes early on tortured him (as they would a big brother), his body was so tight, and that it took him years to open up. Says Zurak,

> So much of dance is about those who start very young; very little is mentioned about those who start as adults. I was so physically tight, Graham [movement] seemed impossible; I knew that ballet would help me to open up, even though taking class was touchy—there was a strong feeling that modern dancers don't take ballet, and vice versa. Yet that intensive study [1994–1996]—it was a kind of finishing school for ballet—was what I needed to learn about the fundamentals of coordination and line.

The study paid off—he appeared in *Les Grands Ballets Canadiens* as a contractual corps de ballet member for several years. Not one to rest on his laurels, Zurak kept moving on with his study of dance. "I'm a tall guy and was in danger of just being used as a partner in the corps," he says. "I knew that I wanted to be technically proficient and wasn't willing to compromise on that—even though I reminded myself constantly how inadequate my body was."

Zurak then studied with Dr. Arnold Spohr, Director Emeritus of the Royal Winnipeg Ballet, for 4 months in 1996, and found intensive workshops with Christine Wright (in ballet), Risa Steinberg (Limón), Irene Dowd (anatomy), and Diane Miller (Pilates). He currently is focused on supplemental training in GYROTONIC® practice (at Studio Riverside); along the way, he has earned certifications in osteopathic medicine through the Upledger Institute.

Reflecting on his training, he recalls particularly important influences: "Risa Steinberg[57] was so larger than life—her classes were beautiful and challenging. I was very inspired and moved by her. She had a great systematic approach to teaching. She's a master. It was important to me to be surrounded by that energy—and to always get good feedback."

Zurak credits Peggy Baker, artist-in-residence at the National Ballet School, who teaches the work of Irene Dowd, for his development of a good scientific understanding but also functional approach, and GYROTONIC® work at Studio Riverside to open up his tight body. His zeal for learning continued to motivate him:

> For me, it was not about getting work, somewhere, anywhere . . . but always developing as an artist. And that's also how I got to Montreal, and then New York, to take a few Cunningham classes. One Montreal-based artist I was working with at the time, Jose Navas, was very Cunningham influenced. So I checked the studio out and was offered a scholarship on the spot, and there was talk of me joining the understudy group. Should I drop everything? I finally let go of Canada, and relocated.

Zurak says he lost a lot of potential work in New York as a Canadian, but there were opportunities still. Soon after joining Cunningham on scholarship, he joined the newly reformed Lucinda Childs company and danced with her for a year.

At about that time, he incurred his first major injury—to his left hamstring and lower back. "When you have to deal with major injury . . . you either quit . . . or become a better dancer," says Zurak. He retrained again, with expert physical therapy, and functional ballet classes with Christine Wright: "Dance was still so much in my head—I had to work on that and still do. You can't think on stage—so much must be instinctive. I spent a lot of time finding out where my actual turnout was. And just because I had washboard abs didn't mean they were strong."

His progression to the Graham company followed.

> Soon after, a friend in the Graham company set me up to take a class with Christine Dakin. There was a talk about a scholarship. I was taken into the company as an apprentice but had never seen the company perform until [the night of the company's first performance after a 2-year hiatus due to legal struggles over dance copyright]. I remember the audience applauded for 10 minutes before any dance began.
>
> By September 2002, when I was invited to join the company as a new member, I really felt that I was on my way to becoming a solid contemporary dancer. I had taken Graham company classes for months. I had a lot of work to do, retraining again. I felt I was starting all over. But I also felt like I had come home. Even when

injured, I had to have faith in what I was doing. You need a commitment, a belief that it will work out, to never give up.

Zurak says he still struggles with understanding and transcending technique:

What is it? I am not drawn to high extensions or multiple pirouettes, but whether the technique enables the body to be used as a tool. Dance must be about more than technique but about communicating. So, in class, we do fundamental alignment and point and jump every day. But people who have learned to take this to develop their bodies as a vehicle of expression, who are fully connected—when I see them dance, I really feel something. If I'm bored, all I see then is turnout and legs. But in a great performance, I couldn't have told you what the steps were. That's what I hope to achieve in my dancing.

How to do it? For Zurak, the answer is Graham technique.

There is nothing like Graham . . . it connects to the human condition, to a humanity, to a timeless experience. The technique can be unbelievably challenging but it also is inspirational and audiences respond to that. The longer I'm there, the more I'm inspired. People are in the company, dancing, because nothing else speaks to them. It's wonderful to be part of it.

Zurak's hard work to get where he is helps him identify what a dancer needs to do: "Go after goals, get what you need, and retrain your body. I beat the odds, starting so late—and I'm thankful every day."

2
Injury and Injury Treatment

Given all the concerns raised in Chapter 1, the question naturally arises: Is dancing hazardous to your health? A reasonable response might be: "Not if you know what you're doing and you're physically capable." Indeed, many of the risk factors for injury can be managed. Dancers working within their limitations know that the joy and satisfaction from dancing is worth the effort and the challenge. Further, dancers can greatly extend their years of dancing by learning to minimize the risk of injury, much less enjoy a higher quality of life —i.e., good health in later years, after they stop dancing.

The risks are genuine. Dancers sprain ligaments in their back, herniate spinal discs, tear the cartilage in their knees. They strain their groin muscles and calves and are especially fearful of muscle spasms (related to stress and fatigue) but nonetheless try to dance through them. All parts of the body are at risk. While the majority of injuries occur to the lower torso and extremities, the highly mobile shoulder is also at risk.

Dancers subject their bodies to many of the same stresses that competitive athletes do, yet they also try to conform to a normative body image—an ideal look. Athletes protect themselves with shock-absorbing footwear and in many contact sports the equivalent of armor (helmets, shin guards, extra padding) to avoid injury. The physical challenges in dance are many (Figure 13),[1] especially when compounded by problems such as poor or restricted eating, hard and unresilient dance floors, and intense rehearsal schedules.

The pressure on young dancers is particularly strong. They face the challenge of training and dancing through growth spurts and physical, emotional, and psychological changes associated with puberty. At the other end of the age continuum, mature dancers face their own particular health risks owing to degenerative changes and loss of flexibility,[2] especially of the hip. For dancers of all ages, learning to work with restrictions and limitations is key to minimizing the risk of injury.

The definition of injury is subjective. To many dancers, anything short of being sidelined for a week or requiring surgery is hardly an injury.[3] Thus, many dancers interpret "injury" in the most practical way: something that prevents them from dancing. Chronic injury eventually can destroy a career. An off-balance landing, a poorly timed lift, a slippery floor, or unforeseen obstacles in the wings can cause a rapid-onset acute injury—a sprain, strain, fracture, or dislocation—also jeopardizing one's career in dance. With perhaps one third of

Figure 13 Many moves in dance require considerable strength and flexibility, as in a position of full hip extension (an arabesque) with the torso upright, as danced by Alona Christman. (Photo by Angela Sterling)

injuries in dance considered unforeseen or acute,[4] there is plenty of room for chronic injuries. These are recurrent or long-lasting injuries resulting from low-level stress. Chronic injuries have a more insidious onset and, for the purposes of this discussion, can be grouped under the term "overuse."[5] These are injuries that can be prevented from worsening if intervention such as activity modification and rehabilitation occurs early.

What exactly is an "injury?" Marijeanne Liederbach, of the Harkness Center for Dance Injuries, Hospital for Joint Diseases Orthopaedic Institute in New York,[6] defines an injury as pain or physical dysfunction resulting in impaired performance or missed participation in class, rehearsal, or performance.[7] Others might consider "injury" in terms of what it costs the dancer's company[8] or, more broadly, "any complaint about which dancers have questions."[9] Dance students raising questions about problems early, when intervention is most likely to be effective, are likely to benefit from health or medical treatment.[10]

The relationship between the way injuries are dealt with and the longevity of a dancer's career is clear. Robert Stephens, co-editor of *Dance Medicine: A Comprehensive Guide*, points out that "very few dancers escape the tragedy of careers cut short by injury . . . The dancer's 'Achilles heel' is a reluctance to face the need for effective injury prevention programs . . . [especially important] when one is preoccupied with the ferocious demands of acquiring and maintaining . . . technique."[11]

There is little doubt that technique class of various sorts is essential for optimal training and performance. It also is necessary for the physical and mental conditioning that prepares the dancer for that day's rehearsal[12] and provides the feedback needed to refine technique.

When dancers are injured, however, there still are ways for them to experience many of the benefits of class while allowing for selective rest of injured areas.

This chapter discusses the many things dancers can do to recognize, treat, and, most importantly, prevent injuries. Throughout this book I emphasize that, for the sake of dancers' health and longevity, changes need to be made in the dance subculture so that injuries are addressed early on. Particularly common are overuse injuries, including stress fractures, Achilles tendinitis, shin splints, and knee disorders[13] (Table 1).

To protect themselves, dancers must be cautious and deliberate, with good technique as a foundation, and make the right choices about conditioning, eating habits, and safe and effective training. Maintaining this cautious approach and still enjoying and even excelling at dance is not impossible. For younger dancers, practice at making good choices early on will be critical to maintaining the levelheadedness they will need as teens and young adults.

Table 1 Overuse Injuries of the Lower Extremity and Causes/Risk Factors

Type of Injury (partial list)

Stress fractures of the metatarsal bones of the foot and tibia

Plantar fasciitis and strain of the plantar fascia

Achilles tendinitis

"Shin splints" (referring to a group of injuries characterized by lower anterior leg pain)

Patellar (kneecap) injuries/disorders (tendinitis, patellofemoral syndrome)

"Snapping hip"

Possible Causes/Risk Factors*
Anatomical or Biomechanical

Structural anomalies (e.g., related to differences in leg length, femoral anteversion or rotation of the femur in the hip socket, tibial torsion or outward twisting of the tibia)

Alignment deficits

Abducted gait (a ballet dancer's "duck walk")

Hypermobility

Muscular imbalance (typically muscles of the ankle, lower leg, or upper thigh)

Forced or asymmetrical turnout (and excessive movement at the knee, ankle)

Inadequate warm-up (a contributing factor to most injuries)

Excessive pronation (lifting the outside edge of the foot)

Excessive inversion (ankle rolling out, sickling)

Training and Environmental

Overload in training (a sharp increase in the intensity of training, rehearsal, performance, and/or touring)

Physiological: poor nutrition, disordered eating, smoking, menstrual dysfunction or irregularity

Suboptimal equipment, especially floors and room temperature

Choreography (e.g., ball-to-heel "stage running," allowing little contact with the floor)

Repeated jumps and leaps on unresilient floor surfaces

Insufficient stamina (and other fitness components) leading to fatigue

Psychological and Psychosocial

Response to stress and competition (depression, overanxiety)

*Sources include: Delmas J. Bolin, "Evaluation and management of stress fractures in dancers," *Journal of Dance Medicine & Science* 5/2 (2001): 37–42; Stephen F. Conti and Yue Shuen Wong, "Foot and ankle injuries in the dancer," *Journal of Dance Medicine & Science* 5/2 (2001): 43–50; Gretchen Kerr, Donna Krasnow, and Lynda Mainwaring, "The nature of dance injuries," *Medical Problems of Performing Artists*, 7/1 (1992): 25–29; Lyle J. Micheli, "Dance injuries: An overview," paper presented at the Boston Dance Medicine Conference: Update 1998, Boston, October 10, 1998, In Proceedings, *Journal of Dance Medicine & Science* 3/1 (1999): 28–32; J. Christopher Potts and James J. Irrgang, "Principles of rehabilitation of lower extremity injuries in dancers," *Journal of Dance Medicine & Science* 5/2 (2001): 51–61; and, Stuart Wright, *Dancer's Guide to Injuries of the Lower Extremity: Diagnosis, Treatment, and Care.* (New York: Cornwall Books, 1985).

TYPES OF INJURIES IN DANCE AND RISK FACTORS

Most of the injuries sustained by dancers involve the lower extremities, with up to 80 percent of injuries in dance involving the foot, ankle, and knee.[14] The lower extremities are particularly at risk due to the large amount of jumping (made worse in ballet by hip turnout requirements and point work). But injuries to the upper torso also are not uncommon, many resulting from lifting other dancers. Upper-extremity injuries include shoulder dislocations, elbow tendinitis, wrist sprains, and fractures of the lower finger bones, the metacarpals[15] (see Appendix A: Anatomy Basics).

Although much attention has been focused in dance medicine literature on injuries in ballet, researchers David Jenkinson and Delmar Bolin document injuries in other "disciplines in dance" as well.[16] These dance forms include Irish, Scottish,[17] Yup'ik Eskimo, and circus dance as well as professional flamenco, modern,[18] hip-hop, ballroom, and even some martial arts. With Yup'ik Eskimo dancing, injuries are reportedly few, in part owing to the strong pelvic stability of dancers, and are mainly limited to some overuse injures among males in drumming.[19] With Cirque du Soleil performers in "Mystère" in Las Vegas, Nevada, injuries were sporadic and tended to be acute rather than chronic, as with Paul Bowler's recent shoulder dislocation, and related muscular tears (including rotator cuff).[20]

For Flamenco dancers, knee problems are one of several typical injuries reported.[21] Injuries are related to the percussive dance steps and use of high-heeled shoes,[22] with constant demands placed on the calf muscle since much of the weight is on the forefoot (on half-toe).[23] Technique can correct this to some extent, as with the encouragement of a "whole body arch," to avoid excessive hyperextension of the spine. Poor alignment and stability of the spine leads to ways of compensating that act to diminish the body's capacity to adjust to high compressive forces. Muscular imbalance, weak abdominals, and tight lumbodorsal fascia, resulting in poor stabilization of the lower torso, also put the dancer at risk for injury.

A survey of dancers trained at the Nishikawa School of Japanese traditional dance also showed that knee injuries are common.[24] For a Broadway show using ballet technique, researchers reported an overall injury rate of 40 percent among the performers.[25] In Scottish Highland forms, dancers sustain lower body injuries similar to those in ballet. The Achilles tendon especially is at risk with Highland dance, since the dancers are continuously dancing on half-toe; weak front lower leg muscles put the dancers at risk for injury. For competitive Highland dancers, muscle imbalances of the lower limb are common—with the plantar flexors more developed than the dorsiflexors.[26]

Overuse injuries are common with all these dance forms, especially where exaggerated turnout is expected and dancing on toe or half-toe is typical. Faulty technique, anatomical limitations, poor muscular strength, and muscle imbalances are just some of the many risk factors.

Risk Factors

Many of these factors for injury are the same, irrespective of style of dance.[27] These include: dancing on unresilient dance surfaces (see Appendix B: Dance Flooring); lack of protective footwear or poorly fitting shoes with poor shock absorption (see Appendix C: Feet First: Dance Footwear and Footcare, and Appendix D: On Point); anatomical limitations (such as unequal leg length, asymmetrical hip turnout, or limited dorsiflexion of the big toe)[28]; inadequate technique or inefficient movement mechanics; insufficient muscular strength and endurance; muscle imbalance involving tight and/or weak muscles (e.g., tight calf muscles owing to extensive work on half-toe in ballet, Scottish country dancing, and Flamenco); poor caloric intake (perhaps related to the female athletic triad syndrome: disordered eating, amenorrhea, and osteoporosis); returning to dance before adequate recovery from an injury; and psychological factors related to dance subcultures of tolerance for pain and injury as well as the stressful and competitive nature of professional dance. These risk factors can be considered to have three general categories of origins[29]: occupational demands, movement demands, and training oversights.[30]

Occupational demands have to do with a variety of pressures: the aesthetic appeal of a particular "ideal"—a waiflike body, or an overarched or rigid "cavus" foot (absorbing shock poorly); demands and expectations regarding above-average strength and flexibility; and stresses related to the "business of dance," such as having little professional or financial security.

An example of a risk factor related to occupational demands is dancing in point shoes, which typically are made of cardboard, satin, and leather and are poor shock absorbers. When performing relevé on point, for instance, the bone-on-bone forces at the ankle are many times the body weight of the dancer. Further, tight, poorly fitting point shoes prevent the foot muscles and proprioceptive receptors from being fully utilized. Another example of an occupational demand is the general physical tendency among some dancers toward joint looseness, or hypermobility. Accomplishing such extreme ranges of motion may predispose the dancer to injury.

Movement demands and the *dancer's technique* can reveal insufficiencies in strength, endurance, and range of movement. For example, in order to meet the "classic" aesthetic norm

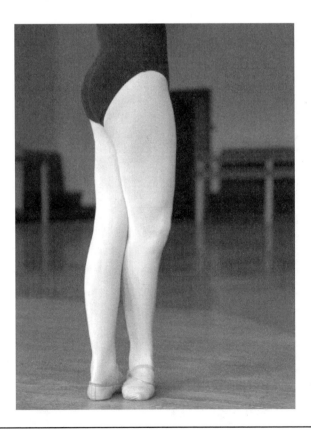

Figure 14 Dancers with insufficient external hip rotation compensate with added movement at the pelvis, knees, and ankles to achieve an anatomically impossible fifth ("heel-to-toe") position. (Photo by Angela Sterling)

of 180-degree hip turnout that is still prevalent in some preprofessional ballet schools, dancers with insufficient hip rotation compensate with added movement at the pelvis, knees, and ankles to achieve the look (Figure 14). As mentioned earlier, hip external rotation also can result in overdeveloped lateral leg muscles, creating muscular imbalance. Further, the hip piriformis muscle can become short and tight with chronic turnout stance, limiting pelvic and lumbar movement owing to persistent piriformis spasm. In short, torso and lower body alignment is compromised.[31] For these and other reasons, dance educators and medical/health professionals eschew this unattainable and damaging norm (Figure 15).

Another example of injury risk from movement demands is a dancer's repeated efforts to deepen her demi-plié beyond the bony limits of her anatomy or the flexibility of her Achilles tendon.[32] It is true that during growth the skeleton still may be molded to some extent. The "late starters" (preprofessional dance students starting after puberty/adolescence), however, are a particularly injury-prone group. They lag behind in technique and physical skills, wanting to improve faster but with bodies (after their growth period) that may adapt slower.

Dancers also are asked to use odd bases of support, such as knees, buttocks, spine, neck, upper extremities, or head, often without any specific instructions, safety measures, pre-conditioning work, or warmup, with resultant injury. Other movement demands include those required to maintain a square torso, even against the large movements of the lower limbs; this creates a need for extreme hip and lower spine hyperextension and substantial

Figure 15 External hip rotation: A slight adjustment improves alignment. (Photo by Angela Sterling)

spinal rotation (see the discussion in Chapter 1 of the dancer's long-limbed arabesque being a challenge).

Training oversights readily result in overuse. Given that professional ballet dancers average close to 45 hours per week of practice and performance, together with extreme occupational demands and less-than-ideal technique, it is not surprising that overuse injuries result. With dancers performing as many as 200 jumps per class, there is little leeway for improper mechanics on jump landings, such as no heel contact, due to a lack of control when rolling down through the foot. Young dancers especially are at risk during summer courses, when a student who took three to five classes per week during the school year suddenly takes three to five classes per day. Research indicates that increased muscle damage, muscle soreness, and musculoskeletal complaints related to fatigue occur with an increase in training.[33] Many of the overuse injuries can be managed by strengthening programs for the abdominal muscles (core stabilization), quadriceps/vastus medialis (for knee complaints), and tibial and peroneal (lower leg) muscles (for ankle complaints).[34] This supports the view that summer programs should include conditioning sessions. Further, young dancers should notify the healthcare team when problems persist more than 3 or 4 days. Teachers need to use such feedback perhaps as an indication that supplementary conditioning is needed or that overtraining is a problem.

Fatigue is an important factor in injury.[35] The majority of ballet injuries occur between 4:00 and 6:00 P.M., when physical and mental fatigue build up after a long day of class and rehearsal[36] (or academic classes for school-aged children). Overload—an increase in the intensity and frequency of performance—is another risk factor.

Overload brings fatigue and exhaustion, which predispose the dancer to injury. Complaints of fatigue and increased exertion are verbal cues that should serve as a red flag.[37] Technique may lag; the experience of Pacific Northwest Ballet principal dancer Louise Nadeau gives an instructive example (see Nadeau Profile, later in this chapter).[38]

Occupational demands—especially the pressure of conforming to an ideal look—were discussed in Chapter 1. Here I focus on the risk factors arising from movement demands and the dancer's technique and from training errors, leading to overuse injury.

Specific training issues for young dancers include point work and turnout. For point, children need a history of 3 to 4 years of technical ballet training to build alignment of the foot with the tibia and the spine, good range of motion in the ankle, solid footing, lower leg and core (trunk) strength, and good balance. This training also should include proprioception work so that the child is as stable on one foot as she is on two. One way to test for proprioception is to have the dancer hold a passé on demi-point while maintaining good, stable alignment of the pelvis, hip, and ankle and minimal shaking (Figure 16). Further, the weight should be centered on the ball of the foot as well as directed to the bottom of the toes. The child should be able to hold this position for 15 to 30 seconds in addition to having adequate ankle flexibility (for adequate point). Otherwise, the child risks straining muscles and causing abnormal stress to joints of the ankle, knee, hip, and spine.[39]

Turnout is especially challenging for the child dancer, who often has relatively weak abdominal muscles and has difficulty stabilizing the torso and pelvis. Injury may result, especially with repetitive extension, as in arabesque or attitude, in turnout position.[40]

In a study conducted by psychologist Linda Hamilton and her colleagues, turnout seemed to be one of the "up-or-out" decisive factors in the attrition of ballet students in the New York City Ballet's School of American Ballet.[41] Reduced turnout was present in 25 percent of the second-year dropouts and 40 percent of the third- and fourth-year dropouts, but not in the students who made it through training. Dropouts reported an earlier age of menarche,

Figure 16 For point work, children need good range of motion in the ankle, foot and lower leg, as well as technical ballet skills, and stability on one foot. One test is to have the dancer hold a passé in demi-point while maintaining good and stable alignment of the pelvis, hip, and ankle. (Photo by Angela Sterling)

had more major injuries, and displayed a certain lack of strength and flexibility, a poorer point, and more restricted eating behaviors. Dropouts also tended to be thinner and have a poorer body image. The authors note that more than half of the sample dropped out of training during adolescence. Only 15 percent of students were accepted into a national ballet company. These findings suggest a "survival-of-the-fittest" phenomenon in some pre-professional ballet schools.

However, a more conservative but still visually acceptable turnout of 140 degrees allows for more control of the pelvis, spine, hip joint, and knee (Figure 17); this reduced angle of turnout should be recommended in teaching and performing. The Royal Ballet in London, for example, is well known for valuing purity of line over arbitrary and damaging norms of turnout and extension.

Trying to achieve more turnout is fraught with risks. Dancers compensate for their less-than-ideal turnout by externally rotating the lower leg at the knee (referred to as "screwing out the knee," especially in plié) and pronating the foot (producing stress on the outside of the kneecap) or by swaying the lower back (hyperextending the lower spine), possibly resulting in stress injuries to the spine. Physician Lyle Micheli, in describing the normal biomechanical development of the lower extremities in order to recognize abnormalities, warns of "forcing turnout."[42]

Figure 17 A more conservative but still visually acceptable turnout of 140 degrees. (Photo by Angela Sterling)

For dancers in general, many injuries are due to excessive pronation, supination (especially in relevé or point work), and abnormal pelvic movement. These positions and movements represent harmful compensations in achieving a "perfect" hip turnout (90 degrees of external rotation in each hip).[43]

A brief look at several types of injuries illustrates the effect of such risk factors:

- *Stress fractures*: Studies conducted at the National Ballet School, Toronto, Canada, over the past 25 years found that stress fractures of the second metatarsal, fibula, and tibia (bones of the foot and lower leg) and of the lumbar spine (see Appendix A: Anatomy Basics, Figure 93) were common among dancers (mostly female) 15 to 19 years old. The studies showed that at least half of the injuries were associated with anatomical variations, such as a longer second metatarsal as well as common biomechanical abnormalities, such as pronated ankles and genu valgum ("knock-knees").[44] Researchers comment that "young, skeletally immature females involved in intensive ballet training are especially susceptible to stress fracture development."[45] Repetitive loading with demanding movements, predisposition to amenorrhea, and restricted caloric intake also contribute to this condition.[46]

- *Inflammation of the plantar fascia of the foot, Achilles tendinitis*, and *shin splints*: These conditions can be attributed to poor technique or inherited structural misalignment, as well as problem floors. Dancers who land with their "heel up" (i.e., with the heel of the foot not making contact with the floor) risk chronic injury. Dancers with shallow plié or weak quadriceps or tight calf muscles also will have problems rolling through the entire foot in fast-tempo ballets. In contrast, strong quadriceps help to stabilize the knee joint and control the plié movement.
- *Snapping hip*: This condition occurs with a tight iliotibial band snapping over the greater trochanter of the femur, or more commonly—for dancers—a tight iliopsoas tendon (hip flexor) snapping as the leg is raised or lowered, especially in développé à la seconde. Both can be addressed by correcting the dancers' alignment, stretching and manual therapy, and increasing lumbo-pelvic stabilization and strength.[47]
- *Patellofemoral syndrome*: In many dance forms, excessive loading of the patella results in patellofemoral pain or syndrome. When jumping, practicing lunges, or using the step or bench, many students in aerobic conditioning classes unnecessarily contract their quadriceps tightly during an entire plié producing constantly high patellofemoral compression forces.[48] (See Appendix A: Anatomy Basics, for a discussion of eccentric contractions.) The situation is aggravated by a pronated ankle, anterior (forward) pelvic tilt, varus alignment (bowlegs), or externally rotated gait.

Rehabilitation of this patellofemoral syndrome involves conditioning for strength of the quadriceps, inner thigh muscles, hamstrings, gastrocnemius, and soleus as well as stretching of the iliotibial band.[49] Treatment involves strengthening the inside quadriceps muscle and stretching the iliotibial band, hamstrings, and quadriceps. Giving feedback in technique class—for example, to avoid overuse of the quadriceps—also helps. To help in ensuring proper alignment, the teacher can emphasize that the dancer's knees should be well aligned with her feet in lunges[50] and that external hip rotation should be used to initiate plié and adduction to return to the starting position.[51]

The Preadolescent and Adolescent Dancer: Special Considerations

The preadolescent and adolescent years are crucial for dancers. This is the time when health and work habits are set that carry through years of practice and training. This also is a time when the physical development of a young dancer makes him or her particularly vulnerable to physical injury that may persist for a long time. Moreover, the young dancer is fully reliant on the guidance and judgment of adult instructors and mentors. With classical ballet, one might think that the exposure young dancers receive to the expectations and demands of the profession from the early age of, say, 8 or 10 years old would prepare them for the training pressures throughout adolescence.[52] But it manifestly does not.

Adolescence, with its accompanying growth spurt that can last 2 years, comes at about the age of 11 to 13 in girls and 12 to 14 in boys.[53] It begins with the onset of puberty and continues through the teenage years. Although the onset of puberty can occur anywhere from ages 9 to 16, it more typically occurs at 11 to 14 years.[54] This is a time of enormous physical, psychological, and social changes, accompanied by a host of self-esteem and identity issues. This is a vulnerable time for the young dancer.

The physical changes alone are daunting. As mentioned in Chapter 1, the teen and preteen dancer experiences sudden increases in height and decreases in muscle strength, flexibility, and coordination; hormonal changes; and brain tissue changes—all of which can be overwhelming.[55] The nervous system struggles to keep up with such changes, and coordination and balance may be compromised. Muscle imbalance and tendon inflexibility may result. Growth plates are particularly vulnerable, especially in areas such as the knees, where much of the growth takes place. Trauma to the growth plate cartilage is likely.

The physical changes associated with puberty occur at the same time that young girls and boys are entering a period of intensive training in dance. The pressure to achieve strong technique increases for preteens and teens as the competition intensifies. Risk factors such as poor diet, muscle imbalance, and poor technique become more critical for the prepubescent dancer. The young female dancer suddenly finds her body assuming a more curvy shape and having less strength, coordination, and control. Young dancers thus are especially vulnerable to injury and need special consideration.

Self-esteem is at risk. As the adolescent dancer extends his leg, he may sense a loss in strength and flexibility. Holding an attitude or turning in pirouette position may be harder because of decreased coordination and balance. It may be more difficult to maintain proper alignment of the pelvis owing to the increased leg length relative to the torso. This all adds up to the dancer perceiving him- or herself as less capable. Moreover, changes in body shape and size may cause plummeting self-esteem as the goals of svelte, thin, and perfect (for both genders) are ever more elusive.

Dance students need support during such transitional times. The students need to know that the changes are temporary. Once this time period is complete, balance and coordination should return.

It is important that health practitioners and professional schools recognize the dancer's vulnerability during the adolescent growth spurt. Physician Lyle Micheli recalls being impressed during his visit to the North Carolina School of the Arts, when a dance teacher pointed to a young male student who was sitting out the class, and said, "That boy over there is going to be a wonderful dancer, but he is in his growth spurt now, so we are backing off his training."[56]

Indeed, it is important for educators to remember that adolescents are not little adults. One of the biggest challenges in training young dancers is dealing with the growth spurt. This period is made more problematic because it occurs just as dancers are focusing on career goals and increasing their training intensity. Key points, then, to consider for adolescent training are:

1. Sites of injury are often the sites of rapid growth.
2. "Growth plates," located at the ends of long bones near the joints of the adolescent dancer (as with all children) are prone to injury.[57]
3. Bones grow faster than soft tissues, resulting in muscle tightness as well as possible bilateral asymmetry.
4. Temporary loss of joint flexibility may result from increased muscle-tendon tightness.
5. Temporary decreased strength and coordination are to be expected.[58]

Family members and teachers as well as healthcare providers need to understand the normal development of the young dancer, encouraging adolescents who are temporarily "too tight" or "too loose" to avoid making harmful compensations to achieve a certain look in dance.[59]

The implications for training are clear. Teachers must go slowly, avoid increasing abruptly the frequency, intensity, and duration of training sessions, and be patient with young dancers as they slowly regain balance and coordination. It may well be that ballet class is not enough to achieve both a strong technique and a well-conditioned body. Perhaps different conditioning or less training is needed.

This doesn't mean that the dance teacher needs to become a mental health professional for the adolescent or aging dancer, a strength trainer for the soloist, or a nutrition counselor for the prepubescent dancer. But good teaching means good listening and observing. Dealing with young and stressed dancers is one of the greatest challenges dance educators face. Perhaps dance professionals should not underestimate their roles as educators and mentors in supporting this transition and important life passage. In devising practical strategies for assisting injured dancers, teachers can advise on modification of dance activities, alternative movements during dance practice, exercises outside the studio, and psychosocial strategies for recovery.[60] In everyday class work, teachers also need to provide a safe and positive learning environment, one in which the students have opportunities to creatively and deliberately, through trial and error, apply what they are learning.

Teaching is, fundamentally, helping students to grow new dendrites, synapses, and neural networks.[61] Learning can be considered the growing of such new structures in the brain. This growth results from practice—making and correcting mistakes and then trying again. Mistakes are thus an important part of learning. This is not a good time for adolescents to be inundated by pervasive messages of perfectionism, particularly having to do with an ideal look; depression, a sense of hopelessness, and loss of self-esteem may result. Bad habits such as restrictive eating or overworking also may result.

Emotions affect learning in significant ways. Positive emotions promote the growth and functioning of brain structures. By contrast, dancers react to fearful learning situations by putting on the brakes in terms of dendrite growth.[62] Thus, the dance class environment needs to be supportive and encouraging, exhibiting the teacher's unconditional belief in the students' desires and innate abilities to learn.

Adolescent dancers want to exercise their ability to make choices in a more democratic, less autocratic way. They think they know what they want but may not have the influence or resources to make it happen. This is especially a problem for girls; studies abound documenting how preadolescent girls give up their individuality, especially in professional dance. For girls to imagine something else, their healthcare team needs to support training that encourages establishing high but healthy expectations, and goal setting and attainment.[63] The young dancer needs to develop coping skills, cultivate imagination and curiosity, and value challenge and creativity.

Boys, too, do not pass through this period unscathed. Like girls, they need role models for what researcher Susan Lee calls "emotional literacy," and for building self-esteem and their own unique identities.[64] Healthy role models are teachers and peers who practice normal eating habits, do not smoke, and take time to recuperate from intensive training sessions.

In the throes of conflict over identity and independence, patience is needed in attaining goals. Young dancers should consider their work as a form of self-expression and confidence building, rather than as a ticket to placement in a company.

Such self-confidence also helps in countering the incidence of disordered eating among dancers. With some studies reporting up to 22 percent incidence of disorders compared to 1 percent in the general population,[65] the young female dancer's healthcare team needs to be aware of both menstrual problems and unusual eating habits. Some indications are a child who avoids eating with others or exercises excessively. Management of eating disorders must be multidisciplinary and should include physicians and other healthcare providers, a psychiatrist or psychologist, nutritionist, and family and friends.[66]

A physical dimension to training young dancers is their vulnerability to stress fractures. Disordered eating and overwork increase the risk. A certain amount of physical stress, such as jumping and point work, but with sufficient rest, seems to promote increase in bone density and thus bone strength.[67] On the other hand, when repetitive stress is excessive and compromises new bone formation, microscopic cracks that can develop into overt fractures may result. Those dancers with restricted eating, menstrual abnormalities, or muscle imbalance are at particular risk. Poor ballet technique and hazardous environmental conditions such as hard floors or poorly fitting point shoes also add to the risk.[68]

The risk of stress fractures is further complicated if a young dancer exhibits the female athlete triad: eating disorders, amenorrhea, and osteoporosis. Dancers suffering from eating disorders may be preoccupied and stressed with thoughts of eating and body weight,[69] even when they are told they should increase their body weight.[70]

Recommendations for Training

Clearly there should be guidelines for training. Attention should be given to understanding each dancer's unique anatomy, to building good technique, to avoiding overload (incorporating rest and recuperation—and conditioning—into a training program), and to monitoring the volume and intensity of dance training. For example, it may be inappropriate to try to increase muscle power by maximal loading during adolescence. Training in healthy adolescents does not necessarily result in maximal physiological extension of the lumbar spine, and attempts to exceed the limit may only cause strain on specific anatomic structures of the lumbar spine. Researchers warn that this must be taken into consideration when choreographing pieces on adolescents.[71]

Combining "controlled strength" training with a focus on the spine and pelvic musculature is the key to working with the adolescent's reduced or compromised flexibility, balance, and coordination during the growth spurt.[72] As the adolescent dancer increasingly becomes aware of his or her ever-changing body, it is a good time for practicing positive attitudes (see Chapter 6).

Furthermore, the dancer's healthcare team needs to pay careful attention to problems that may develop from muscle imbalance. For example, it is very easy for the hip external rotators to become stronger than the internal rotators, causing a lateral snapping hip syndrome or a trochanteric bursitis; a weakness of the quadriceps muscles to lead to "jumper's knee" (pain at the lower tip of the kneecap); constantly used calf muscles to favor the onset of tendinitis; tight hip flexors to cause an increase in lordosis or swayback; and temporary abdominal and spine muscle imbalances, especially during growth spurts, to produce what is referred to as mechanical low back pain.[73] Low back pain is a condition commonly seen in younger dancers. Through technique analysis, imaging exercises, and observation of biomechanics, appropriate femur placement in développé en avant and à la seconde, for example, can be addressed. Or, in considering a "snapping hip" syndrome, researcher and educator Ruth Solomon recommends several approaches.[74]

Muscular (strength) imbalance is a particular concern during periods of growth and relative muscle tightness. The healthcare team should note if pain increases with dancing or daily activity. If so, a medical diagnosis should be made; selective rest and modification of activity may be necessary. The dancer may need to avoid deep or grand plié, jumping, and direct pressure on the knees.

If a student dancer is injured, the period of rehabilitation should be seen as a time of growth and understanding for both the dancer and teacher. It should be viewed as a opportunity to increase technical understanding, to work on artistry, and to learn more about how the body functions. During rehabilitation, center-floor point work, difficult lifts, jumps, kneeling sequences, and other stressful movements should be avoided. Rather, the

Figure 18 Body conditioning exercises can be used to good effect during the technique class time — in this case, conditioning for muscular endurance of the lower anterior leg muscles (an aid in preventing shin splints). Laura Tucker, Janelle Keiper, and Jessica Dill demonstrate. (Photo by Angela Sterling)

emphasis in class should be on spine and pelvis stabilization (see Chapter 4) and the development of proprioceptive skills. Also, body conditioning exercises can be used during the rehabilitation period (Figure 18).

The challenge for dance instructor and student is to find ways to accommodate the needs of the student who is in the midst of a growth spurt. One way to do this would be to take a floor barre and do supplemental conditioning that emphasizes core stabilization. It is prudent for teachers to postpone high-profile competitions or exams until after this period in order to lessen the pressure on the dancer.[75]

Screening or monitoring by the healthcare team is essential at this time.[76] Attention by the team provides critical support for the young dancers and can help them realize that the changes they are experiencing in technical skills and loss of flexibility are likely temporary. The team can help to counter an expectable slide in self-confidence and self-esteem that results from a perceived loss of technique together with normal adolescent emotional challenges. Young dancers need help. The team can provide it, and should. In university settings, heads of dance departments can join with psychologists from the university counseling centers to create courses or seminars designed to deal with the psychological and physical health needs of their student dancers.[77]

Dance screening is a critical part of overall healthcare support. It was the topic of the first special issue of the *Journal of Dance Medicine & Science* in 1997, its inaugural year.[78] The issue includes screening protocols used by the Israel Dance Medicine Center, Harkness Center for Dance Injuries, Boston Ballet, and School of American Ballet. These include relatively quick, easy tests for a large number for dancers, as well as more detailed screening. Standardized screening procedures are, of course, a necessity.

TREATMENT AND REHABILITATION

Although some dancers may have difficulty recognizing injury,[79] in medical circles an injury can be considered to be pain or physical dysfunction resulting in impaired performance or missed work in class, rehearsal, or performance.[80] (I am using "medical" in the broadest sense: the science and art of dealing with the prevention and alleviation of injury and disease as well as the maintenance of health.) Injuries produce varying physical effects such as contracture of the skin, fascia, muscle, or joint capsule that prevents normal mobility or flexibility, an increase in adhesions (abnormal adherence of collagen fibers to surrounding structures during immobilization or following trauma and/or surgery, which reduces normal elasticity of new tissue), reflex muscle guarding (the prolonged contraction of a muscle in response to a painful stimulus that functionally splints the injured tissue against movement), muscle spasm, and muscle weakness.[81]

How an injury affects a dancer's performing ability depends on several factors, including the severity and frequency of the injury, the repertory and roles that are being performed,[82] and the treatment that is prescribed and followed. For all injuries, a medical diagnosis should be established, the causal factors identified (as discussed earlier), and any technical errors corrected. Indeed, a diagnostic process proposed by P. E. Greenman highlights the importance of considering anatomical limitations with the mnemonic "ART": A, assessment of the asymmetry of bony parts (e.g., differences in shoulder height, degree of turnout between hip joints); R, range of motion deficiencies or excesses, representing either hypermobility or hypomobility; and T, abnormal soft and connective tissue texture (in the skin, fascia, muscle, ligament, etc.).[83]

Rehabilitation begins with evaluation by the healthcare team, especially to determine if the injury was caused by faulty technique. It typically includes a thorough medical evaluation. For complete rehabilitation, proprioceptive (balance and coordination) rehabilitation, neuromuscular repatterning, and technique assessment are all recommended in addition to conventional therapeutic practices.

The *acute stage* of an injury, lasting through the first 4 to 6 days, or longer, involves various physiologic processes, such as increased blood flow and swelling, as part of the inflammatory reaction. During the acute state, irritating chemicals are released, and edema, muscle guarding, and spasm contribute to restrict movement.[84]

Rest, ice, compression, and elevation (RICE) are especially important for the dancer immediately following injury and for the first 48 hours. As the dancer experiences pain and impaired movement during the initial inflammatory stage of healing, rest and protection of the injured area are important to control pain, edema, and muscle spasm. As soon as possible, the damage should be evaluated and a medical diagnosis and treatment plan established.

The first line of attack for short-term minor injury treatment should be the application of ice. Cold minimizes hemorrhaging, although compression is usually needed to reduce swelling in surrounding tissues. Both blood flow to the injured site and muscle spasms are reduced. Further, the analgesic effect of the ice may allow the joint to remain relatively mobile, thus helping to prevent the formation of scar tissue and adhesions. If the joint is not allowed to be mobile, collagen that is weaker and less elastic than the original structure will grow into scar tissue. Eventually, adhesions are produced. These are strands of collagen located at the site of swelling. They restrict the mobility of the joint, making the area more susceptible to reinjury upon the resumption of activity.

In cryotherapy, the systematic use of ice for injured tissues can be achieved by using ice packs (applied indirectly) for no more than 20 to 30 minutes at a time, ice baths for even less time, or ice massage. For ice massage, water can be frozen in a disposable cup or even frozen-juice container, with the top peeled or cut away, allowing the ice (for a limited time) to come into contact with the skin.

The next stage of an injury, the *subacute* or *healing stage*, begins 14 to 21 days after injury. This stage usually lasts 10 to 17 days but may last up to 6 weeks. Early movement, as tolerated and under advisement of the healthcare team, is very important to avoid the adherence of tissues and weakening of connective tissue. If the inflammatory process is prolonged, healing is compromised and, without appropriate stress, the orientation of the developing fiber will be random, with excessive cross-linking of fibers. This leads to the formation of dense, inflexible tissue, which is difficult to rehabilitate.[85] Thus, early movement is required to achieve a strong, mobile scar at the site of the injury in order to achieve complete and painless function. Any movement tolerated at this stage is beneficial as long as it does not increase inflammation and pain. The dancer most likely will feel resistance at the end of his or her range of motion (ROM). As discussed later, manual therapy at this point, involving gentle movement of the injured site to minimize adhesions, helps to maintain the mobility of the joint.[86] Such mobility, in turn, is essential to maintaining proprioception.

In late-stage tissue repair, the *"chronic" stage* of uncomplicated tissue healing, tissues mature as collagen fibers become thicker and reorient along the lines of tensile loading.[87] The fibers are readily remodeled with persistent, gentle stress (range of motion exercises, etc.), but the thicker the tissue, the longer the process of remodeling. This remodeling remains possible for up to 10 weeks, but if the tissue is not properly stressed before then, the fibers adhere to surrounding tissue to form a restrictive scar. As collagen matures and thickens, it becomes more resistant to remodeling.[88] Old scars with thick, inflexible tissue may even require surgical release, as was the case with an injury to Paul Bowler of Cirque du Soleil (see Paul Bowler profile, Chapter 6).

Psychological factors are perhaps equal in importance to physical processes in injury rehabilitation. The image many dancers form of themselves (i.e., their personal and cultural identity), is often defined by their work, so that anything that stops them from dancing is a threat to their identities. Thus, healing should also include time for self-reflection, perhaps with outside psychosocial services and intervention.

Multidisciplinary Approaches and Complementary Therapies

Much attention has been given to the team approach in rehabilitation. The approach is particularly important since correcting faulty technique requires an understanding of the many dimensions of injury. It involves dance instructors and coaches, company artistic staff (anyone who trains dancers on a daily basis), and the dancer.[89] A multidisciplinary approach practiced by a healthcare team would seem to be most effective in healing and identifying the causal factors of injuries and facilitating the return to dance with full function.

Dancers should choose wisely in selecting a healthcare team. Health professionals who may work with dancers include general practitioners, internists, neurologists, physiatrists, psychiatrists, orthopedists, podiatrists, osteopaths, chiropractors, physiotherapists, psychotherapists, dietitians, nutritionists, and kinesiologists (Table 2).[90] Many of these practices and specialties are covered by insurance policies.

For many in dance, an important part of the team may be what physician and journal editor Scott E. Brown calls Complementary and Alternative Medical (CAM) therapists.

Table 2 Health Practitioners for Treatment of Dance Injuries[a]

Acupressure therapist (certified, licensed)

Acupuncturist (M.S.A.; certified, licensed)

Athletic trainer (A.T.C., M.S., M.S.P.E)

Body/Movement therapists[b] (D.T.R., C.M.A.; certified, licensed)

Chinese and other oriental medicine practicioners[c]

Chiropractor (D.C.)

Dietician (R.D.)

Healer (spiritual, e.g., laying on of hands)

Homeopath (certified, licensed)

Integrative medicine practitioners[d]

Kinesiologist (M.S. and/or Ph.D.)

Manual therapist[d]

Massage therapist (certified, licensed)

Naturopathic medicine (N.D.)

Nutritionist (M.S. and/or Ph.D.)

Osteopathic physician (D.O.)

Physical therapist (P.T., M.S., M.P.T.)

Physicians and surgeons (M.D.)

   General practitioner (M.D.)

   Internist (M.D.)

   Neurologist (M.D.)

   Orthopedist (orthopedic surgeon) (M.D.)

   Physiatrist (M.D.)

   Psychiatrist (M.D.)

Pilates practitioner (certified)

Podiatrist (D.P.M.)

Psychotherapist (L.C.S.W., M.F.C.T., Ph.D.)

Rolfing practitioner (certified, licensed)

Shiatsu practitioner (certified, licensed)

[a]This list is exemplary, rather than all-inclusive, and can be used for those seeking general conditioning and holistic wellness as well as injury treatment and rehabilitation. The list is organized alphabetically to avoid any implications about the extent or purview of the work of each category of healer. The more common physicians and surgeons are in an easily recognizable and separate group—certainly the largest group with a common degree (M.D.).

[b]Body/movement therapists practice any one of a number of body therapies or somatic reeducation (Alexander Technique, Laban/Bartenieff Fundamentals, Feldenkrais, Ideokinesis, Skinner Releasing Technique, among others). Practitioners of Body-Mind Centering who have worked with Bonnie Bainbridge-Cohen also are included. Certified Movement Analysts (C.M.A.s) are well versed in Bartenieff Fundamentals, and possibly other somatic practices.

[c]A variety of certifications and degrees are possible, including extensive apprenticeships rather than degree programs. Many are listed on the Worldwide Web, e.g., http://schools.naturalhealers.com/bastyr/.

[d]Represents an integration of many of the specialties given in this table; for an example, see William Weintraub, *Tendon and Ligament Healing: A New Approach Through Manual Therapy* (Berkeley, CA: North Atlantic Books, 1999), pp. 70–75.

Brown reports on the work of the Office of Complementary and Alternative Medicine (OCAM) of the National Institutes of Health in guideline development for CAM.[91] CAM is defined, according to the NIH, as "those practices that do not form part of the dominant system for managing health and disease"[92] or medical interventions not taught widely at American medical schools or generally available at American hospitals.[93]

CAM practitioners include those in the well-established disciplines of chiropractic and osteopathy as well as the practices less well understood by standard western clinical medicine, such as acupuncture, homeopathy, herbal medicine, cognitive biomechanics, and others. The amount of published data attesting to the efficacy of each of these varies.

Daniel Nagrin provides a thoughtful discussion in *How to Dance Forever* on healing and self-healing, and on the restorative nature of touch therapies in general, which include realigning scar tissue in physical therapy, massage and self-administered massage, but also shiatsu and pressure point therapy. Sometimes application of ice is needed to reduce swelling after the tissues have been manipulated "deeply" (at bony attachments). Nagrin calls his own work in this area "pressure therapy." It consists of applying direct pressure to an injured area.[94]

CAM also includes self-care disciplines such as yoga, Ayurvedic, diet, and various spiritual healing practices. It also encompasses what has been referred to as "body therapies" or somatic reeducation and includes the somatic disciplines of Alexander, Feldenkrais, Body-Mind Centering, autogenic training and functional relaxation, and Skinner Releasing Technique. Some of these approaches can be grouped under the term "somatic training," which is characterized by attention to "sensory reeducation, anatomical knowledge, release of tension, and proper biomechanical use of the body during execution of dance movements."[95]

Perhaps one of the main reasons that complementary therapies are so critical in dance is that they are particularly effective in dealing with the multiple and multifaceted risk factors involved in dance injuries. Furthermore, for those dancers who are not covered by insurance, therapies involving nonmedical healers (that are affordable) are popular because of the high and fast-increasing costs of conventional medical care. This is not to downplay the comprehensive services offered by some medical clinics with a long-standing history of offering services on a sliding scale.[96]

At the same time, there is no doubt that partnerships between CAM and mainstream medicine are becoming more common—practices "that mutually reinforce a belief system to cause a positive impact on health status."[97] Although the wealth of proven medical science is available to dancers, conventional medicine delivery itself is becoming more responsive to dancers' requirements.[98]

A comprehensive approach to rehabilitation should be inclusive of both conventional medicine and CAM, espousing convergent philosophies. *Journal of Dance Medicine & Science* co-editor and physician Scott Brown notes that, " . . . traditional medicine and CAM are not philosophies that propose mutually exclusive and irreconcilable theories. A truly holistic view would allow for both complementary and alternative medicine and traditional medical practices to become part of a comprehensive treatment plan."[99] Indeed, it is a falsehood to paint the "established" disciplines of mainstream and conventional medicine as pitted against CAM; even in mainstream medicine, there are healthy and real debates that have implications for treatment options. A case in point is the differing emphases in physical therapies placed on fascial networks (anatomy trains) and manual therapy.

Clearly, a variety of approaches can be used to achieve the principles of rehabilitation. For the purposes of brevity and accuracy, I refer to complementary and alternative medical practices as simply "complementary therapies" (dropping alternative) in the following discussion (and referring also to the therapies as "complementary adjuncts," "somatic disciplines," or "somatic reeducation"). Such therapies refer to those that emphasize holistic, mind-body changes in posture and movement and that are not yet part of the dominant system (in North America, at least) for managing health and disease.

Rehabilitation

The underlying principles and assumptions that are followed in injury rehabilitation are as important as the technical approaches used. Many approaches are possible. Indeed, quite often in rehabilitation a plateau response is reached and a new approach must be tried. Also, individual patients respond to different therapies in different ways, so it behooves the therapist to try a number of approaches. This affirms the notion that dance rehabilitation is as much an art as it is a science. In the words of Marijeanne Liederbach of the Harkness Center for Dance Injuries, it "is a dynamic process that ultimately depends on careful communication between the dancer and therapist."[100]

A total rehabilitation program conventionally consists of several parts: a thorough evaluation by a medical/health professional, looking at the dancer's health and working environment; sessions of therapeutic and rehabilitative work; self-help exercises, which may include strengthening and flexibility programs, balance or proprioception work, general physical and psychological conditioning, and fitness training; and counseling for injury prevention (such as changes in dance technique, diet, training schedules, and warm-up routines).

Rehabilitation is not a passive process for the dancer; neither is it a "quick fix." It requires more than just showing up for a session. Rather, it represents a process of education, an attitude, an act of taking control of one's life in order to take time to heal and condition the body. The saying, "It is your body, not just any body," suggests a commitment to processes and practices of healing that are individualistic.

In the words of Allan Ryan and Robert Stephens, co-authors of *The Dancer's Complete Guide to Healthcare and a Long Career*, "every step in the [rehabilitation] process is part of a coordinated chain which is connected with the succeeding steps to reach the desired goal. As far as the dancer is concerned it is an active rather than a passive process."[101] The rehabilitation process will vary, depending on the injury. It may take 7 days (for a mild ankle sprain, shin splints), 7 weeks, 7 months (for some fractures), or longer before complete healing and rehabilitation occurs.

Marijeanne Liederbach's perspective on rehabilitation as an active process is generally the same.[102] In her view, the essential elements of rehabilitation include a skilled, sensitive therapist who is familiar with the world of professional dance, understands the many risk factors involved and the importance of good technique, and is able to create a style-specific, progressive rehabilitation plan. Rehabilitation also requires a highly motivated dancer, committed to self-management, and one who understands the underlying causes of the injury itself. The clinician-in-charge must understand the dancer's work setting and the demands placed on him or her, combined with the dancer's functional ability.[103] In short, communication is essential.

Physical Therapy

In a conventional rehabilitation program, the physician, podiatrist, or osteopathic physician may prescribe the general course of treatment, with a physical therapist developing and administering it. A physiatrist (a physician specializing in medical aspects of rehabilitation) also may be involved. The ideal rehabilitation situation features therapists with considerable clinical experience working with dancers, so they also can address the faulty technique that is causing the injury to occur and recur (Figures 19 and 20).

For all physical therapy approaches, the first task is to observe movement patterns and formulate a list of musculoskeletal restrictions that interfere with normal movement. The therapist, together with the dancer, establishes goals and a concrete plan for full return to

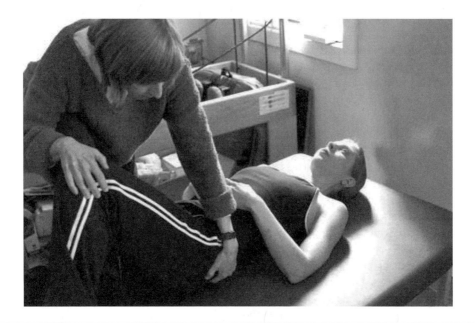

Figure 19 The physical therapist typically makes a functional diagnosis after a medical diagnosis delivered by a physician. For all physical therapy approaches, the main objective is to look at movement patterns, see where restrictions are, and address them, drawing on sports and applied physical therapy as well as CAM (complementary and alternative medicine) approaches, to assist in restoring functional movement. Seattle physical therapist Marsha Novak, who has a master's degree in kinesiology and is a guild-certified Feldenkrais practitioner, is seen here giving a Feldenkrais functional integration (FI) lesson. Unlike in traditional physical therapy, where the clinician looks for a "problem to fix," Feldenkrais uses a sensory-motor learning model. The gentle hands-on work profiled here can facilitate learning. In this part of the lesson Novak is helping former Pacific Northwest Ballet principal Julie Tobiason to "differentiate" movement of the pelvis from movement of the femur. The ability to do this is a prerequisite for appropriate hip turnout mechanics. (Photo by Angela Sterling)

performance. Physical therapists also can offer general conditioning as well as therapeutic programs. Above all, particularly if they have clinical experience working with dancers, they should address technical deficits.

Physical therapy makes use of different modalities such as hot packs, cold packs, ultrasound, joint mobilization, "spray and stretch," electrical stimulation, and deep-tissue or cross-fiber massage and other tissue mobilization techniques, as well as "Functional Footprints" and other educational tools (Figures 21 and 22). These techniques can include various friction massages to keep the ligaments and other tissue moving freely across the joint, and muscle lengthening using gentle contract-release techniques. Potts and Irrgang give a variety of stretching techniques for soft tissue: Massage Myofascial Release, joint capsule release, and joint mobilization as well as mobilizing soft-tissue adhesions and stretching muscles through techniques such as proprioceptive neuromuscular facilitation.[104] The goal is to rehabilitate to the point where the dancer can embark on a self-healing regimen, with new tools and new knowledge.

Proprioception, defined as "the physical awareness of the movements and position of your body,"[105] is particularly important in rehabilitation. Proprioceptors include muscle spindles that detect change in the length of muscle fibers, Golgi tendon organs that detect tension applied to the tendon during various muscle contractions, and unencapsulated endings in joint capsules and ligaments.[106]

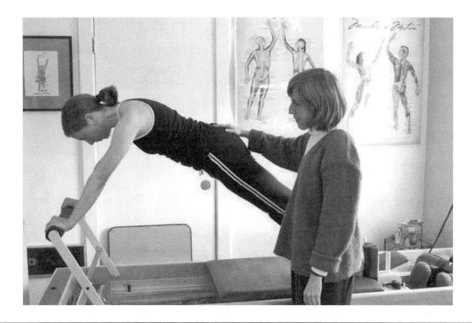

Figure 20 Physical therapy practices that take a holistic view: Physical therapist Marsha Novak uses both Feldenkrais and Pilates work in her practice. Here, she works with Julie Tobiason on core strength exercises using the Pilates reformer. This exercise is useful for general conditioning and spinal rehabilitation. (Photo by Angela Sterling)

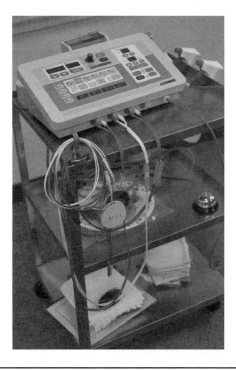

Figure 21 Electrical stimulation and ultrasound are combined in this machine. (Photo by Angela Sterling)

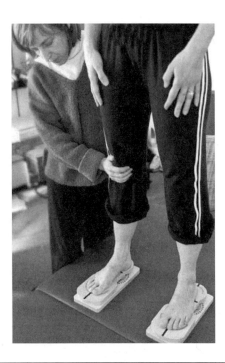

Figure 22 Also useful in physical therapy practice is "Functional Footprints," used to teach and improve appropriate turnout mechanics. The forward and backward play allows dancers to sense if their weight is too far forward or back. Functional Footprints can also be used for other balance and proprioceptive training. (Photo by Angela Sterling)

An acute injury leads to rapid loss of proprioception, even with just a few days of immobilization. Proprioceptors should, in fact, be considered signal sources that are themselves capable of being injured.[107] Proprioception is thus an important part of dance for the coordination, timing, and balance it develops.[108] Proprioceptive and balance retraining play a key role in rehabilitation. As the dancer can tolerate weight bearing, the physical therapist can assist with exercises in a normal progression from eyes-open to eyes-closed, and with distraction (i.e., standing on an unstable surface like a balance board) (Figure 23)[109] or using an exercise ball (Figure 24).

Once normal joint mechanics are restored, strength needs to be increased by progressive exercises. Power gains (exerting force with speed) can be addressed with plyometrics exercises, emphasizing quick, powerful movements. Integrating all of these aspects takes time, but it seems to be a very effective approach in rehabilitation, as is any self-administered strengthening program, for example, involving the use of Therabands (Figure 25).

Manual Therapy

Although there are many schools of physical therapy, a popular one emphasizes the mobilization of tissues, working with what is believed to be highly responsive, functionally active connective tissue to restore it to proper tone, length, and thickness. The focus is on optimal structural alignment in relation to movement repatterning via manual therapy.

Much has been written on such manual therapy of myofascia practiced by massage therapists, osteopaths, and physiotherapists. Myofascia refers to the muscle tissue and the accompanying web of connective tissue (fascia). In his classic work, *Anatomy Trains,* Thomas

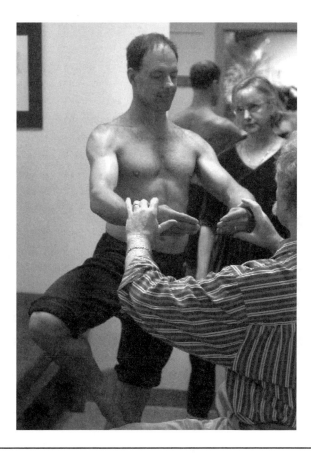

Figure 23 Exercises for proprioception involve closing selective sensory areas, eventually balancing on an unstable surface with eyes opened and closed. (Photo by Angela Sterling)

Myers writes on the history of such movement reeducation therapy.[110] Myers credits the Myofascial Release work of Ida Rolf as one of his main influences, as well as Moshe Feldenkrais and F. M. Alexander. Myers' hypothesis is straightforward: muscles operate across functionally integrated bodywide continuities within the fascial webbing. These form the warp and weft of the body's connective tissue fabric, forming traceable "meridians" or lines of pull of myofascia.[111] Strain, tension, fixation, and compensations are distributed along these lines.

Myers considers how these lines of pull affect the structure and function of the body. He identifies 11 such meridians, of consistent direction and depth. For example, the superficial back line connects the entire posterior surface of the body from the bottom of the foot (plantar fascia) to the top of the head. This line is restricted by tight hamstrings, lumbar lordosis (swayback), or chronic hyperextension in the upper cervical spine. Any method to release the tightness communicates to the tissues throughout (physical therapist John McWilliams illustrates this holistic approach to healing; see Figures 26 through 29).

Efforts at loosening sections along different parts of the myofascial meridians is needed for good alignment (e.g., knee tracking) to retrain movement patterns in the body. Practitioner William Weintraub makes a convincing argument that the use of manual

Figure 24 Certified Pilates instructor Jane Erskine works with dancer Jessika Anspach. These exercises use body weight for resistance and an unstable surface for additional training for balance and proprioception. The sequence begins with drawing the ball in while maintaining a neutral (i.e., stable) spine and extending the legs, then increasing the difficulty of the exercise by raising one leg. (Photo by Angela Sterling)

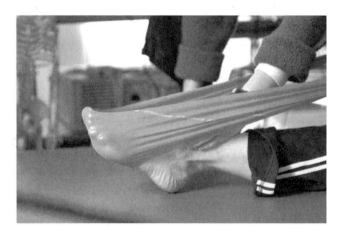

Figure 25 There is much the dancer can do at home with foot and ankle strengthening using rubber tubing or bands for strengthening, for example, the plantar flexors. (Photo by Angela Sterling)

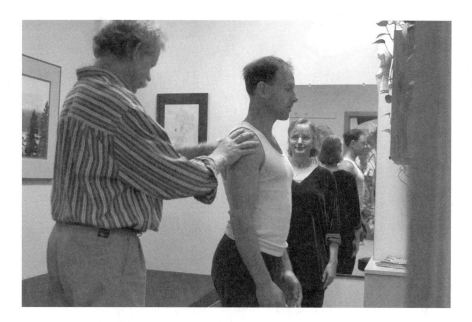

Figure 26 The healthcare team, consisting of dancer (Matt Christman), yogi and dance teacher (Cher Carnell), and physical therapist (John McWilliams), needs to first identify areas of tightness and restriction at the site of injury and throughout the anatomy train. (Photo by Angela Sterling)

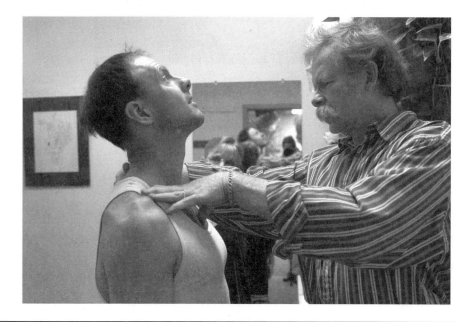

Figure 27 Restrictions in the body along the front of the torso mean fewer movement cues, for example, in aiding the dancer to control pirouettes. Manual therapy aims to mobilize fascia; here, in the anterior upper torso. (Photo by Angela Sterling)

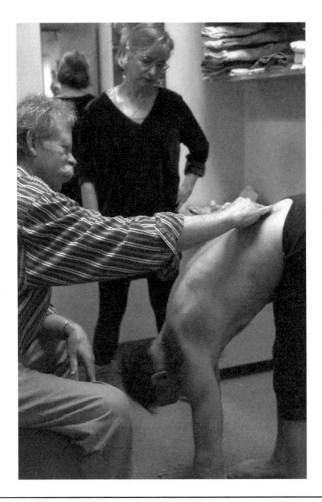

Figure 28 Areas of tightness in fascial webs involving the lumbar and pelvic region through the limbs to the feet affect mobility and stability in the entire body. (Photo by Angela Sterling)

therapy in conventional healthcare needs to be reevaluated, especially given ideas concerning an expanded neural role for ligaments and tendons.[112] He argues that manual therapy can play a pivotal role in rehabilitation for dancers recovering from serious, chronic tendon and ligament injury.[113]

Physical therapy, like many healing approaches, requires a commitment to rehabilitation that entails perhaps two to three visits each week for several months, with visits becoming less frequent as healing progresses. How does one find a good physical therapist? There are many top-notch dance physical therapists around the country. Directories of healthcare professionals are available, such as the *Dance Medicine Resource Guide* (published by J. Michael Ryan Publishing, Inc., and originated by healthcare professional Jan Dunn) allowing dancers and dance company management to easily locate physical therapists and other health professionals around the world. Physical therapy could be a financial strain if the dancer's individual or group insurance does not cover it. Some clinics and practices offer services for dance students and professionals on a sliding scale. For more, see the *Dance Medicine Resource Guide*, or contact organizations such as the International Association for

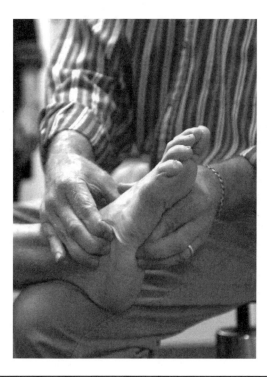

Figure 29 Cross-friction massage eases the restrictions surrounding the cubic bone of the foot; any method to release the tightness communicates to the tissues above. (Photo by Angela Sterling)

Dance Medicine & Science (http://www.iadms.org/) or Dance/USA (http://www.danceusa.org/). Note, too, that health insurance coverage varies according to company and also by country, with a larger proportion of dancers in the Netherlands, for example, enjoying more extensive benefits than dancers in the United States.

Dancers and others in the dance world should realize that many, if not most, dance injuries can be treated conservatively with rehabilitation and modification of the dancer's movements as well as by giving careful attention to modifying technique. For example, technique may need to be changed so that a dancer does not lift his partner from a flexed, poorly stabilized position of the spine (which amplifies disk pressure) and poor hand placement in an overhead lift (see Chapter 3). However, for other injuries (e.g., a torn anterior cruciate ligament) or for overuse injuries (such as ankle tendinitis) that do not respond to conservative treatment (over the period of, say, a year), surgery may be indicated.[114] In such cases, a second (or third) opinion may be warranted.[115] It is important that the dancer relies on a healthcare team that understands both the demands of dance and the dancer's passion for his or her work.

Complementary Adjuncts

Complementary adjuncts in rehabilitation include GYROTONIC® work, Physioball Conditioning, and Conditioning with Imagining (C-I) training, as developed by Donna Krasnow at York University,[116] and other somatic practice developed by leaders in the field such as Glenna Batson,[117] Eric Franklin,[118] Sandra Minton,[119] and Ruth Solomon.[120]

Krasnow's C-I training uses imagery work from Bartenieff Fundamentals, as well as the work of Irene Dowd and Lulu Sweigard (discussed later in this chapter). Krasnow also includes Pilates-based floor exercises, floor barre work developed by Zena Rommett, and class work with Ruth Solomon of the University of California, Santa Cruz. The training is based on several principles, including mind/body integration, progression of tasks from simple to complex, alternating work in strength with endurance or flexibility, and specificity— whereby much of the conditioning work can approximate dance movements, for example, wall slides simulating a plié series (with feet moving from parallel to turned-out first position to second position and back). Another example is a weight-bearing full knee extension becoming a tendu or dégagé series, with resistive bands (Figures 30 and 31).[121]

Pilates

Rehabilitative work such as Pilates may be especially helpful in promoting core strength and stability, initially in a partial or non-weight-bearing state (for example, with supine, prone, seated, and exercises).[122] Besides its rehabilitative importance, Pilates work also has an important role in conditioning (see Chapter 4).

Just like many of the somatic therapies, Pilates body work was built from personal experience, in this case the personal experience of Joseph Hubertus Pilates.[123] Pilates, drawing on a background of gymnastics, boxing, circus performing, and nursing, developed his work

Figure 30 Dancer Alona Christman demonstrates rehabilitative work that approximates dance movements, for example, in the form of a tendu or dégagé series, with resistive bands. (Photo by Angela Sterling)

using a simple spring resistance–based apparatus and began devising ways for patients to begin exercise programs while still bedridden. What Pilates eventually developed was a system of mental and physical conditioning, which made important contributions to an understanding of focus, mental concentration, core strength, use of the breath to facilitate movement, control of complex movement patterns, and combining strength and flexibility into one program. Many contemporary Pilates instructors have incorporated recent concepts of functional movement, clinical protocols, and correct biomechanics into the work. Contemporary Pilates environments often emphasize less posterior pelvic tilt and more neutral pelvis and spine than in the original Pilates work.

Changes also have been made in Pilates' original machines, particularly the Reformer, so now it may have a foot board as well as a smaller toe-heel bar.[124] In addition, contemporary versions of the Reformer frequently use a riser and ropes instead of the traditional leather straps attached to the wood frame. The riser and ropes allow for decreased lumbar spine compression and for a more biomechanically correct position in various exercises.

Especially important with Pilates' work is its emphasis on muscle imbalance and alignment problems, particularly pelvic and spinal stabilization. The foot board on the Reformer also can be used for jumps, allowing them to be incorporated into the program early in rehabilitation. The dancer can lie on a sliding platform (carriage) and "jump" against a spring resistance rather than gravity. Dancers working on strengthening their ankles for point work can use the machine by rolling up to point, against resistance, and progressing to more resistance and complex movements.

Figure 31 Strengthening with Therabands. (Photo by Angela Sterling)

Researchers from Queensland University in Australia have worked on the relevant musculature for stabilization and control of the abdominals and torso, focusing on the power musculature, rather than endurance musculature; contemporary Pilates practitioners incorporate much of the Australian work into their programs (a brief discussion is given in Chapter 4, in the sections titled, "Pilates").

Because initial exercises on the Reformer can be done in a supine position, there is little weight bearing for the injured limb. Gentle ROM activities can be accomplished with small amounts of gradually increasing resistance. The movements can be dance-specific, such as plié and relevé, paying careful attention to torso stability. (See Fgures 74–78 in Chapter 4 for a sample combination rehab/conditioning program demonstrated by former Pacific Northwest Ballet principal, Lisa Apple.)

What makes the Pilates system especially good for rehabilitation is its flexibility and the adaptability of the apparatus, allowing injured dancers to develop strength while not affecting the injured area. It is well suited for dance, with its emphasis on core strength, pelvic and scapular stabilization, coordination and balance, full-bodied movements (with resistance in the full range of movement—essential for the usually very flexible, hypermobile dancer), breath, and concentration. Pilates is good for overall fitness as well, using increases in spring tension or the challenge of gravity for progression. It is not surprising that Pilates is practiced worldwide and flourishes today as a treatment and conditioning option for dancers everywhere.

Sample Rehabilitation Program

Rehabilitation programs thus have three general steps:

1. Evaluation by a healthcare "team," the composition of which will vary depending on the type and extent of injury. The team typically should include the dancer, the dance teacher, and appropriate health (including complementary therapy) specialists and medical providers, the latter of which establish a medical diagnosis and possible prognosis.
2. Therapeutic and rehabilitative work, which may include physical therapy, massage, somatic disciplines, acupuncture, Rolfing, Shiatsu, and so on. It also may include counseling on injury prevention, such as changes in technique, diet, and training.
3. Self-help strengthening and flexibility exercises, proprioception work, general fitness, use of somatic practices, and such.

Examples of rehabilitation for ankle tendinitis and for low-back disorders using these three steps are given below.

Ankle Tendinitis[125]

1. DESCRIPTION/EVALUATION: Tendinitis around the ankle joint can be either acute —resulting from accidental injury to the ankle—or chronic. In chronic tendinitis, the injury is recurring, i.e., not healing within an acceptable time (say, 3 to 6 months). Improper dance technique or anatomical variations can be contributing factors to the injury. Problems with technique include excessive rolling in (eversion, "winging") or rolling out (inversion, "sickling") of the ankle.

    In addition to improper dance technique, anatomical limitations, such as a high instep (cavus foot), and poor strength or flexibility of affected muscles and tendons also cause injury. In addition to recommending a course of physical therapy and conditioning, the evaluation may indicate the need for corrective devices or "orthotics." An orthotic shoe insert limits excessive rolling in of the ankle and repositions joints to alleviate pressure put on muscles and tendons.[126] Also, the patient may follow a course of extensive manual therapy practices or neuromuscular reeducation to establish more optimal musculoskeletal support throughout the whole body.[127]

2. THERAPEUTIC AND REHABILITATIVE WORK: This can be practiced with any number of healthcare specialists, including physical therapists and somatic practitioners certified in, for example, Acupressure Therapy, Body-Mind Centering (BMC), and other therapies as well as those with graduate work in biomechanics.[128] Rehabilitation could include (initially) weekly manual therapy to free restrictions of the lower spine and foot (especially the tarsal bones), as well as fascial release for the foot joints.[129]

   To learn more efficient movement patterns, an "epiphany of kinesthetic learning" is needed to retrain the body.[130] For example, therapies involving visualization help to develop good alignment and efficient movement patterns,[131] emphasizing the initiation and completion of simple and complex movements, which are components of the dancer's pedestrian and dance vocabulary. In the case of an Achilles tendon repair patient, rehabilitative work could include establishing new patterns of efficient movement by visualizing lines of movement traveling through the body,[132] or, for example, building on Lulu Sweigard's work, Eric Franklin gives vivid images for sensing the extensor muscles of the spine. Franklin makes a convincing argument to develop "the use of imagery beyond the original scope of ideokinesis and the nine lines of action [so as] to work with skeletal musculature or organ musculature . . . "[133] The goal is to change the habitual patterns of neuromuscular activity by imaging or imagining the efficient movement once the muscles and connective tissue are strong enough to support it.

3. SELF-HELP—STRENGTHENING AND FLEXIBILITY EXERCISES, GENERAL FITNESS: Exercises needed to correct poor alignment and muscle imbalances include strengthening the inside thighs and stretching the stronger outer hip and thigh muscles. Also, the muscles in the front of the leg must be strengthened (an exercise that also increases muscular endurance along the front of the leg can be done standing or in a deep lunge position, without using a band: tap the foot, heel planted firmly on the ground and the foot flexing maximally to the point of reasonable discomfort; see Figure 18). The patient also will benefit from a general fitness program.[134]

   Training also includes exercises advancing from stable surfaces (toe presses) to unstable, in addition to varying texture—sand pits, beams, trampolines. Difficulty is added by balancing on one leg, with eyes closed—perhaps adding arm and leg gestures, which is a form of proprioceptive training.[135] There are any number of systems that promote proprioceptive abilities and balance,[136] including hygienic eurythmy, which dates from the beginning of the twentieth century. These systems use varying approaches to achieve the same optimal performance (Figure 32).[137] The true test is the dancer's eventual athletic and expressive performance.

Low-Back Disorders

1. DESCRIPTION/EVALUATION: Repetitive lumbar compression is the result of lifting and jumping with insufficient regard to proper biomechanics and overuse; this strains the lumbar musculature. Musculoskeletal imbalance and hyperlodosis (swayback) to compensate for inefficient hip turnout are the most significant factors that predispose dancers to develop compressive or excessive strain syndrome. The imbalance may involve a tight psoas muscle,[138] weak abdominal and paravertebral musculature, or a hamstring/quadriceps imbalance.[139] Overload in training, environmental factors such as unresilient floors, tight costumes, or lifting a partner mismatched in

Figure 32 Eurythmy is but one approach to movement that develops proprioceptive abilities and balance as demonstrated by Adam Hewitt and children of the Whatcom Hills Waldorf School. (Photo by Angela Sterling)

height or weight or with improper timing also may be to blame. A comprehensive medical evaluation should rule out pathology such as spondylosis (a degenerative disease), stress fractures, and slipped lumbar disk (herniation).

2. THERAPEUTIC AND REHABILITATIVE WORK: Recommended techniques are manual mobilization of the lower-thoracic/upper-lumbar spine, shoulder-girdle stretching, proprioceptive exercise, and hip stretching assisted by a physical therapist. Any of a number of soft tissue treatments will reduce muscular spasms and relax the tissues. Physical therapy adjuncts may include massage, ultrasound, electrical stimulation, heat, and ice. Conditioning programs that focus on abdominal and back extensor strengthening, hip flexor stretching, and exercise to release tension in the low back area can help to relieve lowback pain. Rehabilitation also could easily include Pilates work.

3. SELF-HELP—STRENGTHENING AND FLEXIBILITY EXERCISES (with an emphasis on core stability): Stretching exercises include those for tight hip flexors. Hip flexors must be stretched to allow production of normal range of motion at the hip joint. Most of the work here involves dynamic core stabilization. Examples abound, although one of the simplest yet most effective programs is that presented by researcher Stuart McGill.

McGill's core health and stabilization program includes a hip flexor stretch (Figure 33), a psoas stretch requiring the torso to be laterally bent away from the extended hip, and three stabilization exercises that sufficiently challenge muscles, spare the spine of high load, and ensure sufficient stability. The program includes curl-ups for

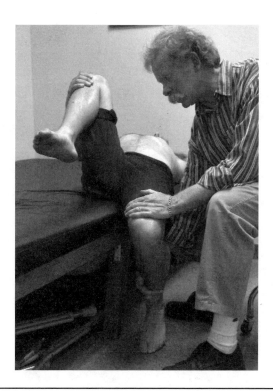

Figure 33 Stretching exercises for the hip flexors aid in easing low-back pain; here, the dancer is reaching his heel to the ground, aided by physical therapist John McWilliams, eventually progressing to raising the other leg. (Photo by Angela Sterling)

the rectus abdominus; variations of the side bridge for the obliques, transversus abdominis, and quadratus (see an advanced form of this exercise in Figure 34); and leg and arm extensions leading to progressions of the "birddog" for the back extensors (see Figure 68 in Chapter 4)—all held for no longer than 7 to 8 seconds. McGill notes that endurance seems to be more important than strength (heavy loads), so programs should emphasize more repetitions of the exercise rather than increasing the duration. See Chapter 4 for more discussion and illustrations.[140]

In core stabilization exercises, a neutral spine position is assumed, then the muscles of the side, stomach, and back are activated. In the neutral spine position, a vertical compression force applied through the shoulders should not reveal any evidence of strain of the lumbar structures. Rather, the feeling should be of "support," with the navel drawn in toward the spine, not to flatten the lumbar curve, but to fully stabilize the deep abdominal muscles. It is these muscles that will assist in supporting the lower spine during lifting and jumping movements. However, the spine cannot obtain the necessary motion of dance while remaining in neutral. Exercise and physical therapy need to progress to allow the dancer to learn motor patterns that are safe for the spine yet accomplish the demands of the greater ranges of motion.

Many rehabilitation protocols include self-managed conditioning work (flexibility, strength, and endurance exercise) as well as physical therapy modalities, both of which are important to achieve preinjury conditioning levels. Lasting gains in rehabilitation means muscles are functioning at full capacity (i.e., performing tasks that approximate certain dance movements, rather than being satisfied with dependence on clinical measurements).

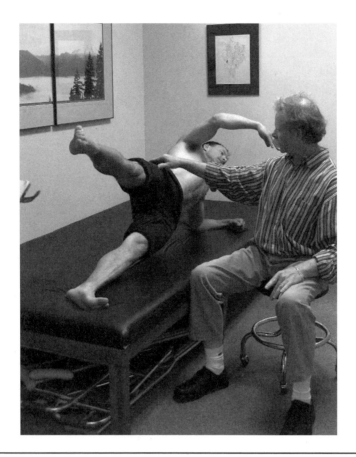

Figure 34 Abdominal stabilization work, including an advanced version of side bridge. (Photo by Angela Sterling)

The program thus must progress the athlete beyond normal clinical measurements, but challenge the dancer to accomplish desired movements with appropriate coordination and timing of deep and superficial stabilizing muscles, and protecting the spine from moving into a painful, nonphysiological range of motion.

Transitional Class

Understandably, the rehabilitating dancer is eager to return to technique class, which is an essential part of dance training, conditioning, as well as performance and artistic enhancement. But returning to class or rehearsal too soon may put excessive stress on connective tissues. Thus, having an alternative to regular company class, which incorporates many of the above approaches, is attractive. Such a transition class has been offered at the Boston Ballet for a number of years. The class combines therapeutic exercises with technical work to meet both artistic and rehabilitative goals.

At the Boston Ballet, the class usually includes 2 to 15 dancers, a physical therapist, dance instructor, and accompanist.[141] Held three times a week for an hour and a half, at the same time as company class, it allows the dancers to be carefully and regularly observed. The physical therapist and instructor meet previously to discuss each dancer, so that any harmful compensations or preexisting technique problems can be considered. The physical therapist also helps to monitor the dancer's progress and adjust conditioning and therapeutic programs.

Dancers are allowed to take the entire class when they can bear equal weight on both feet (including in demi-plié) and balance on either leg with a flat foot. The class begins with several warm-ups (therapeutic and general) and injury-specific exercises for each dancer. Barre exercises are followed by center work, depending on each dancer's injuries, continuing instruction on alignment and technique, and a "cool-down." Approximately half the class is spent as a floor barre or modified barre.

This hands-on "team" approach is generally welcomed by the dancers. Participating dancers view it as an opportunity for individual improvement of technique and performance, and not as a setback. As one dancer commented, "It is very helpful to have an alternative class to company class not only when you are injured but if you're just not feeling well and may not be able to take the pace of company class. Having this as an option helps to prevent injuries."[142]

Thus, one sequence for the rehabilitating dancer is to take a floor or pool barre (aquatic physical therapy may be useful, especially with moves that approximate dance and even use a modified barre), progressively adding more of the basic skills.[143] This could be followed by a flat-foot barre, and then a beginner's barre or, alternatively, a special transition class (as discussed above) to allow the dancer to concentrate on alignment, stability, and improved technique. Activities in the studio should involve limited movement with focus on alignment and stability; restricted tissue loading (padding, taping, etc.) may be necessary.[144] Injured dancers who are beginning a process of reeducation and training to prevent further trauma to connective tissue will find the somatic disciplines of movement reeducation especially useful for rehabilitation. Some somatic work integrates a number of different approaches. A discussion of relevant somatic disciplines used for training healthy dancers, as well as those who are injured, is given in Chapter 3.

PARTING WORDS: FOR THE DANCER, THE COMPANY, THE HEALTHCARE TEAM

The ultimate goal of rehabilitation should be to return the dancer to full, pain-free function and to give the dancer new insights into injury prevention and changes in technique. During rehabilitation, the dancer may learn poor alignment and poor movement patterns even while undertaking and completing a rigorous conditioning program. Harmful compensations may result, which are obvious in pedestrian activities, if not in technique class. For example, the dancer can perform a double pirouette in class but walks with a limp, or can perform that pirouette barely on half-toe, thus putting great stress on the Achilles tendon. It is thus critical for the dancer to include training and conditioning work that emphasizes correct movement patterns from the beginning of the rehabilitative program. Complementary adjuncts can help.[145]

Certainly, even in conventional treatment, different approaches are needed for different tissues (muscles, ligaments and tendons, cartilage, and bone). Many health professionals agree on the principles of tissue healing, but differ in the approaches they recommend. As with many dancers, who are drawn to a healthcare model based on the self-corrective powers of the human body, choices must be made in terms of systems of therapy and therapist. In many cases, systems are compatible. A good example of convergence can be seen with the Alexander Technique, a method of movement reeducation prescient in respect to what is known about neuroscience today. Conscious, directed awareness while moving is key to completing the process of recovery to full health (dancing), i.e., a balance between appropriate therapies and active self-direction.[146]

Once back in the studio, the dancer can eventually enjoy unrestricted dance movement using good technique and alignment, but this should happen only with a prescribed warm-up and when the dancer has developed a heightened awareness of dance-injury prevention, including nutritional and psychological needs. Consideration of dance psychology (which, following the lead of sport psychology, has emerged as a field of study in the last few years)[147] also plays an important part in rehabilitation.[148]

Certainly, dancers must be motivated and patient for rehabilitation to be effective, especially with rehabilitation protocols that depend heavily on self-work.[149] When dancers describe their own self-education during rehabilitation from an injury, they use terms like "listening to your body," "using common sense," and knowing the signs of "good" pain versus sharp and acute "bad" pain. In sum, successful rehabilitation requires the cooperation of an extended team: the dancer, the various healthcare professionals and therapists, dance teachers, coaches, administrators, and family. It involves not only pain relief and restoration of full range of motion, but also restoration of confidence in the dancer's dancing ability. In fact, dancers usually are highly motivated to self-rehabilitate. However, for professional dancers, company support also is important.

From a company perspective, injuries are expensive in monetary terms as well as in their effects on individual dancers' careers. A long-term study of the Boston Ballet found that by monitoring injuries closely, contracting with a variety of healthcare providers to treat the dancers upon referral by the company physician, and paying these providers directly while only claiming "major" expenses against worker's compensation insurance, the company has saved in excess of $1.2 million dollars on insurance premiums.[150]

In sum, in treatment and rehabilitation, dancers should:

- Expect to be understood by practitioners and keep open the lines of communication with teachers and practitioners.
- Continue to report injuries and communicate about their progress with rehabilitation.
- Seek information from those with sound teaching and support practices, which means asking good questions to get the assistance they need.
- Expect their dance companies and teachers also to become educated about rehabilitation and injury prevention.

Much has been said in this chapter about risks in dance: the occupational and movement demands of dance, one-size-fits-all training, and overload in training and rehearsal. The situation is made more stressful when dancers feel governed by others in their training, as they often do.[151] Dance injuries are correlated with dancers having less influence on their training and work. It is the dancer herself or himself who should decide on how much training her or his body and mind needs.

For injury prevention and improved rehabilitation, dancers and their team should pay more attention to the extent of self-control, or influence in the work situation, that they have. Better dancer education and health programs are seen by researchers Eva Ramel and Ulrich Moritz (based on their work in three theaters with resident ballet companies in Sweden[152]) as ways to enhance dancer's body awareness and self-esteem. These programs also allow the dancers to feel they have a greater stake in the company,[153] as well as take more self-responsibility. Ramel and Moritz's recommendations include:

- Offering of an orientation class covering details about company practices as well as health and diet resources and interventions. These classes are similar to the training sessions that Cirque du Soleil requires for artists appearing in its productions world-wide.[154]

- Offering of a greater training variety with warm-up before class, aerobic and mental training, and emphasis on long-range goals.
- Encouragement of sabbaticals and leaves.
- Encouragement of supplemental conditioning.
- Better organization of class schedules and rehearsals.
- Establishment of protocols for rehabilitation, with goals that need to be "SMARTER" (borrowing from sports psychology): Specific, Measurable, Attainable/Acceptable, Realistic, Time-based, Evaluated, and Recorded.[155]
- Offering of a transition class for dancers recovering from an injury.
- Individual assessment of each dancer every year, and follow through on the findings.
- Establishment of a mentoring program for new and junior dancers.
- Establishment of a plan for voluntary assistance before retirement or at other times when a dancer changes careers.

Company-sponsored dancer education programs can be very effective.[156] Dancers need education about healthy ways to maintain weight and psychological support for those who are feeling tremendous pressure to conform to ballet's technical standards and ideal look (Figure 35). These dancers tie their identity and self-worth to performance and physique; but to be healthy, dancers need to learn how to work within their own limitations.

Figure 35 Laura Tucker (foreground) and Allison Constantin of the Nancy Whyte School of Ballet. Young dancers need to find schools that promote healthy ways to maintain weight, provide the necessary psychological support for those who are feeling various pressures to conform, and are attentive to the goals of all students. (Photo by Angela Sterling)

PROFILES

Catherine Cabeen

Catherine Cabeen (Figure 36) makes even often-performed moves seem completely fresh. With balances that seem like forever, this 26-year-old has been referred to in the press as "the perfect dancer."[157] As a member of the Bill T. Jones/Arnie Zane Dance Company, she enjoys wide exposure, from performances at the Lincoln Center to an open-air stage in Lyons, France. A recipient of numerous merit awards, including a demonstrator scholarship with the Martha Graham School of Contemporary Dance, Cabeen can also be spotted in the "Free to Dance" documentary, part of the PBS Great Performances series, and even in the occasional art gallery or dance studio, freelancing as a choreographer.

Dancing is the only profession Cabeen has ever had. Her early preparation included training at Cornish College of the Arts in Seattle. She moved to New York City when she was 17, danced in the Martha Graham Dance Ensemble and with the Pearl Lang Dance Theater when she was 19, and then joined the Bill T. Jones/Arnie Zane Dance Company when she was 20.

Although in many ways this young dancer has "made it," dancing with a big-name contemporary company, she recognizes that you can never be too smug:

> Dance is demanding. You can't lean on what you've done in the past. In an ephemeral medium, you have to stay on top of things constantly. Even if you have a great resumé (as Dudley Williams once told me), you're only as good as your last performance. In the visual arts, you can accumulate a body of work that supports your identity and is evidence of your skills. In dance, you can't. You're constantly relying on faith that the dance is within you. Of course, another pressure is that you're not going to make a lot of cash that you can rely on in retirement. So you want to be sure you are enjoying your life as you live it. To dance with a company is a great opportunity to connect to something larger than oneself.

She also has had to deal with the injuries that so many dancers face:

> My most major injury was a fall onto my lower back my first year in the company. I threw myself into a dive roll and strained the insertion of my psoas into my spine. That injury was a great lesson. It was very painful and I had to really look at my dancing in terms of technique and artistry rather than my tricks—I always had a flexible back and could show off. Even the minor injuries are a wake-up call to the ego.

Cabeen recognizes that many of the injuries can be attributed to overload and has developed her own contemplative way of visualizing and coping with injuries (Figure 37):

> When I'm injured, I'm usually trying to do too much, like when I hurt my knee after I stayed up all night to get in a proposal for my choreography. I say, "hey Catherine, you aren't immortal, calm down; don't act like more than you are."
>
> To help deal with back injuries I draw pictures. I draw a human being, and with brightly colored markers. As I feel the injury, I color it in. Since most injuries come from imbalance, it also helps me to meditate, to think about whatever else could have caused this, what has brought this into my life. I believe that everything's connected. This is a calm, seated activity, which I need so that I don't go crazy while incapacitated. It helps to think about it and track it.

Figures 36 and 37 Catherine Cabeen of Bill T. Jones/Arnie Zane in Jones' *Some Songs*. (Photo by Mila Petrillo) Catherine Cabeen sketches as part of rehabilitation. This sketch refers to an injury of the lower back and right shoulder and various release techniques. "Tower-XVI" refers to the Tarot. The injury occurred while partnering. As it healed, Cabeen developed a new understanding of her limbs relative to her core.

Cabeen is not shy about using both mainstream and complementary medicine for tuning up her alignment and technique as well as rehabilitating from an injury. For Cabeen, technique is the dancer's health insurance:

> Every injury makes me a better dancer because it gives me an opportunity to work on my technique, which has to be spot on. I become more conscious of alignment and it puts my ego in check. I study a lot of yoga. It definitely helps, especially with alignment. Yoga is a great middle step in transition between physical therapy and the dance studio. It also helps with the mind and spiritual dimensions of the work. I also see a great acupuncturist in New York City for a tight iliotibial band problem, which affects my knees. I've seen a lot of chiropractors, which is a first step to doing the necessary physical work for, say, a healthy spine.

Cabeen knows what she needs to do to keep herself healthy, whether it's poetry (she was nominated as poet of the year 2002 by the International Society of Poets) or drawing (art therapy) or restorative classes such as ballet with New York City's Christine Wright. As a result of her study and introspection, she has developed her own perspective on dance:

When I was performing, early on in New York, I was told by an artistic director, "you will never be a dancer because you are not angry enough." She was a great teacher in my life and had a lot to teach me—it's so important that you realize that your teachers exist in a different generation. Anger is, in fact, a big part of modern dance as a form of protest and commentary on the human condition. I understand what she was asking for. But contemporary art is complex and there is space now for other kinds of expression. My time with Graham helped me appreciate the roots of modern dance, and the anger that Pearl Lang was talking about.

Working with Bill is being part of something larger than me. We're in a twentieth anniversary tour with Bill's company now, and the touring is intense. I'm an interesting juxtaposition in his work and I feel really blessed to be a part of it. I wouldn't have been a modern dancer if I wanted to be a star! But dancing in a company of this caliber I am able to share important things with my family. Some of them are racist and homophobic, yet I can say, "Hey, come look at this dance I'm in with a black woman . . . ." I really believe that dance can change the world, and help us all to work together and feel connected. Dance can make a difference.

========

Koichi Kubo

Japanese-born Koichi Kubo is celebrated for his technical brilliance, winning the silver medal at the 1989 Moscow Ballet Competition—the highest medal awarded that year. He has dazzled audiences internationally with his dead-on pirouettes and turns à la seconde, and his floating grand jeté. A member of the Colorado Ballet since 1991, in the last several years he has made the transformation from competition dancer to danseur noble, with attendant fortitude, charm, wit, and musicality (Figure 38).

Yet at age 30, in 2003, he faced one of a dancer's greatest challenges: a torn anterior cruciate ligament (ACL) and meniscus injury, a tissue group known in dance and sports medicine as "the unhappy triangle." Although his rehabilitation has gone well, Kubo says, he doesn't yet have his strength back yet. "It's really frustrating because my muscles still remember how to jump but the strength doesn't necessarily follow."

Kubo was injured during a guest performance of *Le Corsaire:* "When I did *Corsaire* in Japan, I landed from a jump and my knee just didn't hold. I had never had any problems with that knee before. I had no major injuries before this—I thought I'd never have a big injury in my life. I was wrong."

While in Japan, he tried to start his rehabilitation with physical therapy. "Originally it was thought that the ligament wasn't torn at all, even though my knee was very swollen. A few days later in a Japanese hospital, I had an MRI, which showed that the ACL was torn. I had a consult in San Francisco, and decided not to have surgery for 5 weeks. There was some discussion about the need to wait in order to get back my full extension."

Kubo had the ACL repair surgery in Colorado in August 2003 (his medical team included physicians for the Denver Broncos and other professional sports teams). Rehabilitation has included physical therapy, exercises using Therabands, resistance machines, free weights, and Pilates. His return to a modified dance class (in mid-November) meant barre exercises only at first, then (in mid-December) small jumps. He had to take particular care as to when and how to work his external hip rotation, which would also affect the knee:

I don't see this as a really negative experience. I had been dancing 13, 14 years without a break—maybe this was a sign that my body needed a break. I'd like to come back for the next Balanchine program to do *Rubies* and then *Rodeo*; we'll see. I'm

Figure 38 Koichi Kubo partnering Sharon Wehner in Colorado Ballet's *Coppélia*. (Photo by Terry Shapiro)

still working with the physical therapist and doing exercises on my own—very carefully. Ballet is my life. I'm determined to come back even better than before. This gives me a chance to focus on my artistry. I'm taking one day at a time.

Li Chiao-Ping

Dancer, choreographer, and artistic director Li Chiao-Ping's (Figure 39) style of dance is a unique blend of acrobatics, modern dance, and Chinese martial arts—much of which she studied as a little girl, née Nancy Lee, growing up in San Francisco. Li now teaches at the University of Wisconsin, where she also choreographs and performs with her company, sometimes in collaboration with her partner, videographer/artist Doug Rosenberg.

Li has earned a reputation for a fierce presence on stage and consummate execution of theme and movement. As a child, she fought racial and gender stereotypes. Li's oeuvre of over 60 dances explores themes of culture and identity through abstract, composite characters that inhabit emotionally oddball worlds. *Chi*, her signature piece, is based on a concept of life force or inner energy. More recently, she has been challenging expectations of what an injured dancer can and cannot do in what may be her bravest role yet—in her own recovery from a near-catastrophic automobile accident in 1999 that resulted in nine surgeries and a near-amputation. Li says, "Most of my injuries had been of the run-of-the-mill, sprained-ankle type—nothing that would prepare me for my January 11, 1999, accident when the car I was riding in slid on black ice and was broadsided by a tanker truck. I was faced with losing my foot and my life."

Li experienced a "degloving" of the foot where all of the skin and much of the fascia ripped away—which complicated her recovery since the chances of infection were so great —in addition to avulsion of the tendon. She also broke her heel. Many of the surgeries involved skin and vein grafts, only some of which were successful. Early on, she was told by her orthopedic surgeon to get used to the idea of a prosthetic limb and to be prepared for eventual amputation: "When I learned it was that serious, I did everything possible to keep the foot. We were at a [University of Wisconsin] research hospital, and the team pulled some miracles. I really consider the surgeons as artists."

Today, her range of movement is limited: "I can't fully balance on the foot. However, I am dancing and performing and teaching technique and doing everything else. I can't yet run a marathon, but I can jog on a treadmill, which is all I wanted to do anyway."

A watershed accomplishment is that she has started to perform with her company: "After I got out of the hospital, I had a long recovery period ahead of me. The recovery is still going on. It's a big change for someone whose identify is enmeshed in being a dancer." Li recalls that she had to work to allow her foot to hang down, to retrain her vascular system to handle "all the gravity."

Staying mobile and rebuilding strength was important says Li:

> Overall, my entire body had weakened. Lying down for so long (6 weeks in the hospital), I had little general strength. I was compensating by favoring my right leg and hip. One of the smart things I did right away was to work with a massage therapist to release restrictions. I worked with an acupuncturist as well, and with various somatic therapies to help develop my body awareness in space [proprioception]. When I could bear weight, I exercised with a balance board and certain machines.

Figure 39 Li Chiao-Ping in 2002 in *Grafting*. (Photo by Craig Schreiner)

For rehabilitation, Li tried a variety of approaches:

It was very frustrating. It was certainly beneficial to feel that I was doing something. But it also was frustrating because I felt like I wasn't doing enough of the right thing. The physical therapy wasn't necessarily wrong, it's just that it would have been great if acupuncture and massage had been covered by insurance. Eventually, I was able to get my health insurance to cover the Pilates work. The Pilates was essential in my recovery because so much of the conditioning could be done in a reclining position. I love Pilates and am almost certified in it. I work with the machines—the Reformer, the Cadillac, pointing and flexing exercises in the [Wunda] chair. With the Reformer, I didn't have to stand up and could work with one leg or both, or my arms—there was a lot I could do. It was kind of fun. The rehabilitation wasn't monotonous.

Li eventually got a second medical opinion. A surgeon recommended a regraft due to the excessive scar tissue buildup. For the first 12 weeks after the accident, Li's foot had been immobilized to maximize the success of the skin graft. A metal rod screwed to her tibia and the top of the foot helped ensure that the graft would not break. The scar tissue buildup was due to the immobilization, but also to the location of the skin graft and the type of skin used.

When Li got to Boston and New York to see some well-known dance medicine specialists, all remarked how well she was doing. She was given new exercises involving props to roll along the bottom of her foot to loosen tissue.

In May 2000, she performed Melissa Fenley's *Chair Dance*, choreographed after Fenley herself had been injured. Li had known the choreographer earlier, and the two connected again through the injury. Fenley had called Li in the hospital, and Li then traveled to New York for Pilates sessions and to work with Fenley.

Various leaves from academic teaching in fall of 2000 and spring of 2001 allowed her to work on her choreography as well as rehabilitation—both activities contributed to her physical as well as emotional recovery. She also took the time to undergo formal somatic training (in Pilates). Li had a fall 2000 season at Danspace in St. Mark's Church in New York, which included a new solo that would eventually become part of her widely acclaimed full-length work, *Venous Flow*. In April 2001, her company performed the full work; Li danced her solo, having just given birth the month before to son Jacob. By summer 2001, Li was teaching class again. It was important for her to rehabilitate away from classes and other academic responsibilities, as it often is for professional dancers taking physical therapy away from company studios: "I wasn't prepared to face students who didn't know me or understand that I had an injury or difficulties with balance. Now, I can almost have a sense of humor about it all."

Li's recent choreography, an ambitious work using Bach's suites and concertos, includes a few solos for herself. In fall 2003 she performed the piece as one of the dancers in her ensemble—dancing steps that had been designed for her completely mobile dancers: "It was interesting to be put in a position of doing the steps that I hadn't ever expected to do—it was a breakthrough in my performing. Even today, the accident generates ideas for my choreography, perhaps none better than in *Venous Flow*."

Louise Nadeau

Louise Nadeau's expressive dancing, solid technique, and dependability are her trademarks (see Figure 40). She trained in Massachusetts and New York, including a stint at the School of American Ballet, and worked with the Basel Ballet and Kansas City Ballet before joining the Pacific Northwest Ballet (PNB) in 1990. She was promoted to principal in 1992. Nadeau has been featured in numerous major roles at PNB: a princess, a sugar plum, a village heroine, and many characters in Balanchine ballets.

During 2003, a case of Achilles tendinitis brought on by rehearsing for Balanchine's *Tchaikovsky Pas de Deux* sent her on a temporary hiatus from classes and rehearsals as she rehabilitated from the injury. Says Nadeau, "You can test your limits in practicing a piece, but you always need to remember technique. The *Tchai Pas* was very demanding." As noted in *Balanchine's Festival of Ballet*, this is a "display piece, based on the music and the maximum gifts of virtuoso performers . . . [Balanchine] comments that a dancer did not know if she'd be able to do the piece again, but she did 'again, and again and again, and better!'"[158]

Nadeau performed the *Pas de Deux* in the PNB spring 2003 program and then allowed herself 4 months away from dancing to rehabilitate. This included missing a gala inaugural performance in PNB's new performance hall (Seattle's Marion Oliver McCaw Hall), so as to fully recover before rehearsing for *Swan Lake*, which premiered shortly thereafter:

Figure 40 Pacific Northwest Ballet's Louise Nadeau in arabesque. To execute an arabesque correctly, the dancer must coordinate postural control with arm and leg movements. (Photo by Angela Sterling)

My Achilles tendinitis was clearly an overuse injury in rehearsing for *Tchai Pas*. There are many fast-tempo landings from échappé and other moves. I guess in rehearsal I tried to attain some ideal aesthetic for the speed—I sacrificed what I know to be proper technique (rolling down carefully, through the foot), and then needed to rehabilitate. I tried to rush [recovery]; I wanted it to happen faster, but you must listen to the injury and let it dictate how much time it takes to heal.

Dancers often rehabilitate away from the company studios, halls, and offices. "There are wonderful physical therapists at PNB, but I found that it was necessary to leave the building. I had to rehabilitate away from other ballet dancers because it was too painful not to be able to take class. There was just too much self-imposed pressure of seeing what I was not able to do. Being there would have been too distressing and would have handicapped the healing process."

Nadeau was fortunate to find a physical therapist with a background in dance, who could work with her on regaining and developing proprioception lost with the injury: "I found a wonderful physical therapist with experience in dance. Mostly what we worked on was trunk stability exercises. Really what we focused on was core strengthening—nothing for my ankle for quite some time. The point work was the last to come back."[159]

Nadeau was back in form in sufficient time for her appearance as Odette/Odile in Kent Stowell's newly designed *Swan Lake*. In a review of her performance, I wrote, "In the duel role of Odette/Odile—a role challenging for the artistic interpretation required to portray the sweet Odette and beguiling Odile—Louise Nadeau, partnered with Christophe Maraval, stands apart in the Act II pas de deux. Nadeau's breathy upper body and expansive moves, together with the pair's superb aerial lifts, filled all the music. Their counterbalances—as she throws herself backwards, her hands sweeping the floor—are daredevilish."[160]

Nadeau acknowledges the lasting value of her rehabilitation, "I think my work is even better than before in that I feel much stronger and more balanced. I would think, 'how can this benefit my ballet? My turnout?' The exercises I was doing did not use turnout. But the trunk strengthening and proprioception work applied to everything I did, and can do now."

3
Technique and Training

WHAT IS TECHNIQUE?

"Technique" is the way in which dancers use basic physical movements in class or performance. In casual usage, the word has come to mean a style of dance movement or movement vocabulary, referring to how (and where) a dancer has trained. Technique can be based on the style and conventions of the seventeenth century, folk traditions, principles of releasing and resisting against gravity, and even biomechanics.

Technique is often codified and associated with a particular teacher or choreographer: for example, Cecchetti, Bournonville, Balanchine, Hawkins, Graham, Cunningham, or Luigi. The origins of the different techniques vary with the dance idiom. Conceptually, they represent branches of a tree, rather than steps of a ladder, with no one technique necessarily more "advanced" than another.

Is there one technique that is easier or safer to dance? This is a difficult question to answer. Each style has its adherents and its skillful practitioners. Some researchers maintain that for dancers trained in a particular style (from an early age), who continue to perform in that style with adequate physical facility, risk in performing should be minimal.[1]

Good technique, rather than luck or chance, allows dancers to balance at will, pirouette quickly, turn in the air and in time to the music, be an attentive and graceful partner, lift cleanly, and perform a pas de deux with precision timing. As dancer Risa Steinberg, formerly of the José Limón Dance Company, who also has worked with Annabelle Gamson, says, "[It's not that] I am lucky, but I work well." Or, as the late Erick Hawkins once said, " . . . [we] must obey rules of kinesiology—you just don't practice practice, you practice theory"—meaning that the dancer should not move a particular way out of habit.[2] Rather, the dancer should move with a thinking body, using deliberate moves based on movement principles that seem to be right for both the dancer and the dance. For example, dancers sometimes may have to question time-honored rituals in technique class, such as beginning the class with a grand plié; research shows that there may be excessive external movement of the kneecap at the bottom of the movement. Thus, grand plié in training should be used with caution.[3]

Good technique helps to minimize injuries and maximize career longevity. Some would argue that good technique is of primary importance in keeping dancers injury-free. According to dance educator Stuart Wright, "The simple fact is that virtually all dance injuries result from faulty technique. Technical correction is the best means to prevention and treatment."[4] Though perhaps an overstatement of the case, Wright's point is nevertheless well taken. Dancers rarely have perfect alignment; thus, harmful compensations in the weight-bearing joints are likely to occur (see Chapter 2).

It is widely acknowledged, for example, that poor technique in forcing hip turnout in ballet is the single largest factor contributing to overuse injuries of the lower extremities.[5] Dancers with poor technique may compensate by flexing and slightly abducting the hip, so that the Y-ligament is relaxed to allow for more apparent hip rotation (stressing the hip ligaments and posterior vertebral elements of the lumbar spine), by rotating the knee, especially in plié, and by pronating the foot. The dancer then may grip the floor with the toes to straighten the knees and maintain turnout, causing tight hamstrings and hip flexors which, in turn, can lead to snapping hip and patellofemoral problems. Thus, learning proper turnout in technique class and avoiding compensations at a young age are critical to maintaining healthy knees, spine, hips, and feet.[6] Even among professionals, maintaining good technique is a key factor in injury-free dancing especially when fatigued or when the intensity of rehearsal and performance increases (see Chapter 2 profile of Louise Nadeau).

Acquiring good technique is, for many dancers, a continuous process.[7] It begins early in training, for example, by receiving feedback about the correct landing from a jump, to ensure that weight is placed fully and equally on both feet when landing. An attentive teacher plays an important role in this process. American Ballet Theatre principal Julie Kent credits her understanding of technique to her teacher, Hortensia Fonseca, at the Maryland Youth Ballet School:[8]

> I think learning how to dance on point is the single most important thing in the training of a dancer. You really have to know how to support your body weight with your foot, to stand on your toes, not just sink into the shoe or let the shoe hold you up. [My teacher] was very careful about the age she would put the girls on point—often we would wear the shoes for 15 minutes at a time, just do half point in the shoes to get the strength in the ankle to the feet, to the toes.

TRAINING FOR TECHNIQUE

Dancers train to acquire the technique needed to perform movement efficiently and correctly, i.e., with good alignment. (Admittedly, there is the occasional "natural-born dancer" —see Chapter 1 discussion.) Taking class on a regular basis (once or twice a week for beginning students, more for advanced) is only a first step. Whether in class or with personal coaching, a dancer needs to become a "thinking body"[9]—to train mindfully and to dance seamlessly. Dancer-choreographer Bill Evans (see end-of-chapter profile) even incorporates time for mindful reflection in his technique classes. He urges dancers to appreciate fully the importance of technique:

> In studying technique, the dancer needs to be fully engaged, so that [even in class] the dancing is an expression of who you are; your vision of the work is [what constitutes technique]. In class you need to continue with that, for there is nothing more personal and complete than your movement. Most of the communication we have with others is about how we express ourselves. So I ask students in almost every class to reflect on some experience.[10]

These ideas also can be framed in more scientific terms and study, as indeed Evans has done with colleagues from the University of New Mexico by positing some ideas about the efficacy of training at the barre in performing a développé devant for transferring skills to the center.[11] Although contested,[12] these ideas profile the possible limitations of the barre and the optimal balance between barre and center in a ballet class. The researchers suggest that barre work may be more appropriate for training the gesture leg than the standing leg, which showed a significant difference in electromyographic activity between barre and center work, so that exercises for placement and stability of the standing leg should be emphasized more in center work. Students and teachers should be open to such new ideas and find ways to either validate or dismiss them for their own work.

Another interesting research application can be found in considering Martha Graham's technique. Those who have taken Graham classes know that central to the technique is the stylized abdominal contraction, with the head moving backward in hyperextension and the arms reaching forward, wrists hyperextended. Casual observation in class reveals that the lower torso takes on a concave form when performing a contraction. To execute the movement correctly and safely, there should be no anatomical variations (especially in the lower spine) that would interfere with the range of motion required to perform the movement. Verbal cues by the teacher indicate to the student that the abdominal musculature first "releases" and then "contracts." Teachers also might use terms such as "hollowing" or "scooping" the abdominals and advise students to exhale so that the muscles needed to support the spine are engaged.

Provocative research advises reconsideration of the use of exhalation (especially in dynamic movement), and the role of muscles other than the transversus abdominis (a popular one to consider in dance),[13] as a stabilizer of the spine. In barre work, hollowing or curving the spine—flattening the lumbar curve, known as "tucking"—for extended periods of time does not offer the stability dancers need for proper dynamic alignment[14] (alignment when moving).

Such research applications are particularly useful for teachers. But, besides being open to new ideas coming from research,[15] teachers and dancers alike need some intuitive, if not formal, knowledge of movement mechanics and physical analysis tools. Otherwise, dancers may be attempting to achieve an arabesque line—challenging for even professional dancers (see Figures 5 and 13), but their muscles may not be sufficiently strong or their neuromuscular patterning developed enough to allow for proper and safe execution of the movement. Injuries may result.

ANALYTICAL TOOLS FOR TECHNIQUE

Obviously, there is far more to understanding dance than performing a physical analysis of component movements. As physicist and author Kenneth Laws says, " . . . ballet cannot be 'reduced to a science.' But the world of dance is large and complex, with many windows through which one can both perceive and illuminate . . . the view through the window of physical analysis will enhance, not detract from, an appreciation of this art form [and] contribute to the advancement of the art and skill of dance."[16]

In her foreword to Laws' new work, *Physics and the Art of Dance*, Francia Russell, co-artistic director of Pacific Northwest Ballet, notes that, "though we work hard to give the illusion of defying natural laws, gravity for instance, physics applies to every movement we make and must be taken into consideration."[17] She also observes, however, "that technique is only a tool—a beautiful and essential tool but not the ultimate goal. In the end it is the illusion that counts, the character, musicality and intense personal involvement of the dancer that creates a performance."[18]

Laws explores how physical movement principles can be applied to dance, and he urges dancers and dance educators to think analytically as well. Such an analytical framework is not foolproof; there are no guarantees that the analytical dancer is the more successful one, or even the more consistent. Just knowing the physical principle does not mean that you can embody it and perform it consistently (how this transfer occurs is an interesting question in itself). Likewise, to argue for a more scientific understanding of dance movement is not to deny the equally important artistic dimension of movement that dancers bring to their art. Dancers do not need to know the name, origin, and insertion of every muscle in the body. However, it can only improve performance and health to know, for example, that a tight hip flexor, such as the psoas, pulls the lower spine into hyperextension, interfering with the correct alignment of the pelvis and lower body joints, because this muscle is attached to all the lumbar and the lowest thoracic vertebrae.

As *Journal of Dance Medicine & Science* co-editor Karen Clippinger notes, "the inspiration, passion, and spirit [of the dancer should] not become a slave to the technologically-derived data, but rather . . . the technology [should be] used to advance the potential expression of dance," whether it involves biomechanical or physical analysis, application of experimental research findings,[19] or self-help electronic monitoring devices. She further warns that information should be applied in a way that does not "unduly limit the artistry of the dancer or the given dance form, but rather allows the dancer to more readily meet artistic goals with less stress and greater longevity."[20]

The dancers whose stories are profiled in this book have, for the most part, been self-taught in principles of human structure and movement. For them, and for many in dance, it is technique in the broad sense—information gathering, problem solving—that is of interest and that helps in their understanding of serviceable technique. Bill Evans has had formal training (in kinesiology as well as somatic disciplines), whereas dancer-choreographer Donald Byrd and master ballet teacher Cher Carnell (see end-of-chapter profile) represent a more intuitive knowledge base. This suggests that many paths lead to similar general principles of movement.

Thus, if technique can be considered as the full discovery and mastery of basic principles of movement, then evaluation of technique should involve an analytical perspective, looking at the physical principles at play, as well as a structural/functional evaluation using biomechanics as well as somatic disciplines.

Analyzing Movement Using Physical Principles

Human movement has been studied as a science for more than two millennia, beginning with the work of Aristotle. Today, "biomechanics" generally concerns itself with principles and laws of mechanics applied to the function of living organisms, usually using quantitative data. Biomechanical study often involves two- or three-dimensional high-speed filming of a particular movement and subsequent video analysis. According to educators Yiannis Koutedakis and N. C. Craig Sharp, the discipline came into its own in the 1970s, when coaches wanted to analyze the technique of current sports champions to search for methods to train others.[21] It is an important component of the larger study of "kinesiology," which includes both qualitative and quantitative analysis of human movement and requires thorough knowledge of the neuromuscular system.[22]

One of the first full-length works in the field of dance kinesiology was published in 1984 by Schirmer Books. The strength of *The Physics of Dance* lies in the clear and nontechnical terms that author Kenneth Laws uses to describe how physical laws affect dance movement. In a more recent work, *Physics and the Art of Dance*, Laws discusses, among other topics, the biomechanical processes used to control the leg in fouetté turns, giving the "correct" technique and showing how the number of turns can be three times greater with proper technique than when mistakes are made. Similar analysis could focus on factors affecting the height of a vertical jump in adolescent classical ballet dancers[23] or the development of normative kinematic data of the passé in highly skilled dancers. These data could be used to compare injured with noninjured, or novice with experienced, populations of dancers to determine rehabilitation outcomes or the result of training.[24]

Analysis of movement using physical principles allows both teacher and dancer to observe movement clearly, describe it accurately, and derive other principles that help in the understanding of human movement. It is with this idea, and the hope that students may advance toward becoming their own textbook, laboratory, and teacher, that consideration of questions such as the following can help.[25]

- You're in rehearsal trying to perform a double tour en l'air, landing in fifth position, but you can only get around one-and-a-half turns. If you cheat some—begin the turn with the feet ever so slightly apart—the double turn is much easier. (For this movement problem, note that an increased distance allows for double the torque, or "turning force.")
- You're in ballet class, watching the first group perform their entrechat six. The older, taller dancers can't seem to stay with the music. Your turn is next, and you perform the movement easily, and in time to the music. Perhaps you know, even with less experience and strength, that it takes much less effort to cause a slightly smaller leg (yours!) to move rapidly around the hip joint. (Note that the inertial resistance of the smaller leg to such beating movements is much less.)[26]

The following discussion of several common dance movements is meant to introduce the reader to the language and the power of physical analysis.

Plié

The plié is a movement central to most dance forms. It is one of the first movements taught in technique class; anatomically, it is one of the most difficult to execute. Understandably, it is one of the most controversial—at least from fifth position, and at the beginning of a class. To perform it correctly, students must pay attention to the proper alignment of the hip, knee, and ankle joints. As students begin the plié, the legs must be aligned so that a straight line could be drawn from the hip socket through the knee and ankle joints to the second toe—points that lie in the same plane, and continue to do so throughout the plié (Figure 41). This means that the knee should not protrude in front of the toes as judged from the side. For the deeper grand plié, spine (and knee) stability is required. Some research showing excessive external movement of the kneecap at the bottom of the grand plié suggests that in training the movement should be used with care.

Figure 41 The pelvis, hips, legs, and ankles should be well aligned, with no rolling in on the inside edge of the foot, and with weight equally on both feet. (Photo by Angela Sterling)

Arabesque

To execute an arabesque correctly, control of the gesturing limb, as well as the torso, is necessary. For example, in Figure 42 the movement involves the coordination of postural control with upper (arms) and lower (legs) extremities and requires balance. Students frequently focus their attention on control of the gesture limb, but mastery of torso control is what distinguishes professionals from novices.[27] In terms of a physical analysis, the center of gravity must lie on a vertical line that passes through the foot at the floor. The dancer's base is less than a square inch for a dancer on point.[28] The dancer balances, maintaining the center of support under the center of gravity by making very small (hardly noticeable) "wavering" motions. Those subtle body shifts act to apply the appropriate horizontal force from the foot against the floor so that there is a corresponding force from the floor back on the body. This corresponding force moves the center of gravity back to the position above the support that allows for the regaining of balance.

The closer a dancer is to a mastering a balance, the slower will be the fall away from that position; she seems to balance "forever." The dancer who can balance by subtle movements means that she (or he) is very sensitive to balance and movement and is able to sense small changes in position—in other words, the dancer has good proprioception.[29]

Pirouette

Understanding the mechanism by which a torque (a twisting force) is exerted against the floor can enhance dancers' ability to control any turn performed on one leg. A torque is exerted by the body on the floor to initiate a pirouette. The reaction torque of the floor on the body actually causes the body to start turning.[30] To execute a successful pirouette, a dancer must stretch vertically, exerting a force on the floor equal to one's body weight while reaching for the ceiling through the top of the head. The dancers are actually exerting a torque against the floor by pushing in a horizontal direction with one foot and the opposite direction with the other, with some distance between the feet.

The more vertical the body, the easier the turn because for a given magnitude of angular momentum (or quantity of angular motion), if the moment of inertia is small (i.e., the mass of the body is close to the rotation axis), the rate of turn will be relatively large and hence less effort will be required to produce the movement. An off-center mass will wobble around the rotation axis, creating an unstable situation (Figure 43). If the body is not well aligned (i.e., part of the body is "off-axis," as when the arms are held too far forward), centrifugal force will tend to increase the body's distance from the axis of rotation. This means that the supporting leg also will move around the rotation axis, turning with a wobble. As a result, the turn is not smooth and is more difficult.

Jumps

Many aspects of jumps can be submitted to physical analysis, for example, the "floating" illusion during a traveling jump such as a grand jeté. In this illusion, the dancer appears to hang in mid-flight, floating horizontally near the peak of the jump before beginning the descent. The dancer appears almost to defy gravity, in part because the vertical motion of the body is quick at the beginning and end of the jump, but slow near the peak. (According to equations of projectile motion, one half of the total time the body is in the air is spent within one quarter of the height to the peak of the jump.) Control of body shape when in flight can enhance this illusion even more (Figure 44).

Once the magnitude and direction of the initial velocity upon leaving the floor are determined, the shape of the parabolic trajectory followed by the center of gravity can be predicted. Although the dancer cannot change this trajectory in flight, the relative position of the body's center of gravity (indicated by "O" in Figure 45) can be changed by controlling the body configuration.[31]

For example, lifting the arms and legs near the peak of the jump (Figure 45) causes the position of the center of gravity in the body to rise. If that rise and subsequent descent of the center of gravity relative to the body coincides with the rise and fall of the center of gravity in its trajectory in space, then the head and torso can actually move horizontally for a short time, creating the illusion of floating.[32] Researchers have made the point that the height of the jump is not completely dependent on the depth of the preceding plié, since a very deep knee bend can cause a mechanical disadvantage at the knee joint.

Lifts

Lifting involves a partnership between two or more dancers—a partnership that involves trust and responsibility. In this example, we are assuming that the person lifting is male and the person being lifted is female. The woman trusts that her partner will control her descent to the floor. Likewise, the man expects that his partner will carefully time her jump so that part of the upward impetus comes from the push-off for the jump, not solely from his

Figure 42 Students at the Nancy Whyte School of Ballet (Bellingham, WA) practice mastery of torso control in an arabesque. (Photo by Angela Sterling)

Figure 43 A dancer's well-aligned center of mass will result in an even turn, this includes keeping the arms close to the body, to stay "on-axis." Dancers are, from left to right, Jessica Dill, Jenelle Keiper, Kelen Laine, and Laura Tucker. (Photo by Angela Sterling)

strength. The woman must maintain a vertical body configuration to assist as much as possible in the lift.

Each partner has a responsibility to develop the coordination that will allow both dancers to use their strength effectively in supported poses. If each partner is not sensitive to the timing, balance, and strength needed to successfully execute a lift, injuries may result. As stated by Kenneth Laws:

> Controlling a nonrigid weight equal to perhaps three-fourths of [the male's] own weight can be tricky and demanding. For high lifts, his back takes substantial compressive stress, particularly in the lumbar region when its curvature is exaggerated. Since the woman's weight is often borne by the man's hands, the position of the hands is important in avoiding unnecessary stress. If his arms are not vertical (especially in a sustained lift), there is substantial torque in the shoulders with possible muscle or tendon injury.[33]

Figure 44 Control of body configuration (e.g., raising the arms) when in grand jeté flight can enhance a "floating" (in mid-air) illusion, as demonstrated by Pacific Northwest Ballet principal Kaori Nakamura in Peter Martin's *Fearful Symmetries*. (Photo by Angela Sterling)

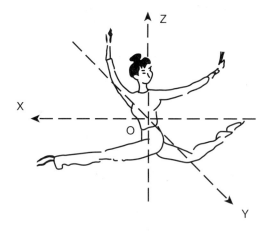

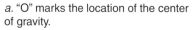

b. The relative position of the center of gravity is changed by lifting the arms and legs toward the peak of the trajectory, creating the illusion that the head and torso have moved horizontally.

a. "O" marks the location of the center of gravity.

Figure 45 "O" marks the location of the center of gravity. The relative position of the center of gravity is changed by lifting the arms and legs toward the peak of the trajectory, creating the illusion that the head and torso have moved horizontally. (Adapted from Lei Li and Kenneth Laws, "Physical analysis of Da She Yan Tiao" in *Kinesiology for Dance* 11/4 (1989): 10, 11 and *The Physics of Dance*. New York: Schirmer Books, 1984, p. 35.)

The vertical lift is decidedly easier to accomplish if the woman who is being lifted does not have to reach a stable equilibrium position during the lift, or if the arms can be brought in, thus reducing the torque in the shoulders. Otherwise, large torques (approximately a force of 1,100 pounds in the muscle-tendon system of each shoulder) can possibly result in injury.

When the choreography requires that the lift be "held," the combined center of gravity of the two people must be directly over the area of support. For example, in Figure 48, the woman is at rest, held aloft by her partner, and thus the force he exerts is almost entirely vertical. Close to the peak of the lift, the lifter should fully extend the arms and legs, thus increasing the force they can exert (Figure 47).[34]

Also important to the success of the lift is the proper positioning of the hands and the distance between the two partners. In the straight vertical lift, support is provided with the heel of the hand directly underneath the rib cage, so that the base of the rib cage receives much of the vertical supporting force (Figure 46), rather than with the fingers and thumbs squeezing between the ribs and the hip bones.

Experienced partners know how to move so that the full weight of the woman is not supported by her partner's thumbs, which leads to sprains and strains. Flexing rather than extending the elbows renders the torque in the shoulders small, for in general the distance between the two partners should be less rather than more. If the lift is initiated at too great a distance, there is a large torque at the hip joint exerted by the muscles attached to the lower back. Too much separation forces the man to use his upper back and shoulder muscles to support the lift, thus adding stress to the spine. Ideally, the large muscle groups of the hips and legs (the gluteus maximus and quadriceps, respectively) should be used, together with the shoulder flexors and elbow extensors.

Structural and Functional Analysis

As discussed in Chapter 2, there are any number of anatomical variations and biomechanical factors that limit the dancer's ability to perform a movement correctly. The following are a few examples of such constraints that some dancers may face in the foot, ankle, and hip.[35] Dancers usually have to find outside expertise—a health professional, therapist, or coach with training in anatomy and kinesiology—to assist in evaluation of the structural variation. Also, functional constraints such as weak, tight muscles and muscle imbalances must be considered.

Foot and Ankle

Several common anatomical variations in the foot and ankle predispose a dancer to injury. One example is the presence of a small bone, the os trigonum, at the back of the talus (affecting barely 5 percent of the population). When fused with the talus, it appears as a

Figure 46 Vertical lift with Gael Lambiotte and Sabine Chaland of the Dutch National Ballet. The center of gravity is in the same vertical line as her partner's, and thus the force he exerts is almost entirely vertical. (Photo by Angela Sterling)

Figure 47 Close to the peak of the lift, the lifter should fully extend the arms and legs, thus increasing the force they can exert. (Photo by Angela Sterling)

protrusion. If separated from the talus, it appears as a separate bone. Whether fused or not, its presence can sometimes restrict plantar flexion. As dancers assume a full-point position, soft tissue irritation and inflammation may occur. Some dancers with this condition may be asymptomatic or may compensate for pain by sickling the foot to appear higher on point. Unfortunately, this overstretches the outside foot and ankle tendons as the foot rolls out. Dancers who have a high instep and somewhat rigid structure may also have a tendency to roll their feet to the outside, overstretching the outside tendons.

Hip: External Rotation

As discussed earlier, external rotation at the hip is desirable in most western dance forms, but classical ballet in particular emphasizes "perfect turnout" (see Figures 14 and 15). However, one would need an imperfect anatomy to achieve a perfect turnout of 90 degrees at each hip. Usually no more than 60 to 70 degrees can be derived from external rotation at the hip, with the remainder achieved at the expense of forcing outward rotation of the knee, as well as the foot and ankle.

A number of structural factors influence the amount of external hip rotation that is possible, including the angle of femoral anteversion (rotation of the femur in the hip socket), orientation of the acetabulum (a cup-shaped cavity relative to the head of the femur), elasticity of the anterior hip capsule, and flexibility of the muscle-tendon units that cross the hip joint.

Dancers frequently compensate for inadequate hip turnout by winging or rolling in on the ankle. Instead of turning out at the hip joint, they overutilize the outside leg and ankle muscles to achieve the turnout. The same compensation occurs in second position demi-plié: the foot is forced to stretch along the inside border, which strains the structures of the medial foot and knee.

Rolling in on the ankle is usually accompanied by adjustments in the pelvis. The pelvis may be tilted so that the natural curve of the lumbar spine is exaggerated in an anterior pelvic tilt or flattened in a posterior pelvic tilt, known as "tucking." A physical therapist can correct the alignment by adjusting the position of the pelvis and reducing the motion at the foot (Figure 48). Dancers should avoid the tendency to "anchor" the foot and rotate from the knees in a plié position.

Karen Clippinger has outlined a series of tests for flexibility and range of motion.[36] Since proper measurement is essential for accurate results, she uses a goniometer—a device that measures the angle between different body segments (Figure 49). The test requires that subjects lie on their back with both hips extended and knees straight, externally rotating one leg from the hip joint. The end point of the stable arm of the goniometer must be in contact with the midpoint of the kneecap.

The number of degrees that the femur can be outwardly rotated from this starting position is measured in positive degrees.[37] Some experts recommend a minimum of 60 degrees (in each hip) for classical ballet dancers; the typical nonathletic adult has about 45 degrees. Experts note that dancers who have 60-degree external hip rotation (i.e., the minimum) may still lag in internal hip rotation, lacking even the 45 degrees of normal hip rotation of the general population. Thus, dancers also should work on enhancing their internal hip rotation in barre or introductory exercises in technique class.

Hip: Extension

Hip extension is a vital part of many moves in dance, including tendu derrière and arabesque. Dancers must avoid tilting the top of the pelvis forward, which slackens the iliofemoral ligament and hip flexors and hyperextends the lower back. This compensation places stress on the lower spine and slackens the structures that actually should be stretched. Rather, the hip flexors should allow free movement to the back without substituting back extension.

EXPERIENTIAL TOOLS FOR TECHNIQUE

Certainly, the application of experiential tools—in the form of visualization training and numerous somatic therapies or disciplines[38]—to dance technique of various sorts is as old as dance itself. Although the use of visual imagery arguably can be traced back tens of thousands of years,[39] recent roots of such work are found in music educator Heinrich Kosnick's "psychophysiological" methods with "directed will." These methods were used by Kosnick to promote musical skills in his students.[40] The work of Mabel E. Todd, author of *The Thinking Body,* also describes the ability of the body to change in response to will (referred

Figure 48 Physical therapist Sydney Anderson corrects Alona Christman's alignment by adjusting the position of the pelvis from an anterior tilt, with feet rolling in to a more stable and neutral position. (Photo by Angela Sterling)

to as "structural hygiene"). Contemporary researchers and practitioners of visual imagery approaches were mentioned in Chapter 2 and are also cited in this chapter.

Central to the somatic disciplines is a view that human beings are self-aware and self-responsible for technical and rehabilitative work.[41] Included in such study are relaxation techniques to reduce muscle tension and movement explorations directed toward whole body awareness.[42] Visualization techniques focus on refining sensory awareness by incorporating anatomical and other imagery to improve alignment. Donna Krasnow of the University of York has organized her work in a system called C-I (conditioning with imagery) training, as discussed below. Dancer and professional movement imagery specialist Eric Franklin presents an overview of the roots of imagery for alignment and somatic disciplines in *Dynamic Alignment Through Imagery*, in which he includes consideration of Ideokinesis, Skinner Releasing Technique, Alexander Technique, Feldenkrais Technique, Body-Mind Centering, autogenic training and functional relaxation, and Rolfing techniques. Several of these techniques are discussed in this chapter. Other approaches, like the therapeutic work of Anna Halprin, could be included as well.[43] Pilates work, which is used in training the

Figure 49 A goniometer is a device that measures the angle between different body segments. (Photo by Angela Sterling)

body for technique as well as for rehabilitation and conditioning, is discussed in both Chapters 2 and 4.

Visualization Techniques Applied to Alignment

Many emerging concepts of posture and alignment use ideas about dynamic alignment as presented by the theorists and somatic educators F. M. Alexander, Irmgard Bartenieff, Moshe Feldenkrais, Mabel Todd, and Lulu Sweigard. In their work, alignment is considered an on-going process of neuromuscular postural responses occurring on an unconscious level—either statically or dynamically. Contemporary dance educators such as Eric Franklin are continuing the work. Franklin, with more than 20 years' experience as a dancer and choreographer, is founder and director of the Institute for Movement Imagery Education in Lucerne, Switzerland. As an educator, Franklin is particularly gifted at synthesizing information from anatomy, biomechanics, physiology, physics, and somatic disciplines (Feldenkrais, Alexander, Body-Mind Centering, etc.). He presents a good discussion of using imaging techniques to improve posture and alignment, together with possible exercises.[44]

Certainly, proper alignment should be stressed throughout a dancer's training; class is one important opportunity dancers have to work on it. In rehearsal and performance, the dancer must be sufficiently strong and technically aware to be able to "hold on" to his or her dynamic alignment. How can visualization and somatic disciplines help? Training need not be extensive; perhaps as little as 15 minutes three times a week for 3 weeks can result in improved alignment.[45] As Donna Krasnow and her colleagues note, "posture is a dynamic process of ongoing neuromuscular adaptations on an unconscious level of recruitment, and [somatic] training can alter or modify these unconscious neuromotor patterns."[46]

Students and faculty at the University of Oregon have attempted to quantify the effectiveness of somatic training through a controlled research design, looking at its effect on pelvic tilt and lumbar lordosis, two important aspects (and thus measures) of skeletal alignment[47] during quiet stance as well as dynamic dance movement. The somatic training involved anatomical imagery, relaxation techniques, and attention to body-mind integration (mentioned also in Chapter 2).[48] The researchers found that improvement in alignment can be made with somatic training, although there is some day-to-day alignment variability.[49]

Somatic Disciplines in Dance

Somatic disciplines, known also as body therapies, have given dancers a new vision of human movement for retraining and reeducating the body, for rehabilitating it from injury, and for enhancing the quality of performance. It was Martha Myers, dance educator and former dean of the American Dance Festival, who promoted the idea of "body therapies" as an umbrella term for the amalgam of movement education styles and philosophies based in gymnastics, neurology, physiological psychology, Eastern philosophies, principles of François Delsarte and Jaques-Dalcroze, and even the martial arts.[50] Many focus on poor muscular habits in technique and training or early developmental patterns of mobility that predispose the dancer to injury.

Such somatic disciplines help dancers to identify areas of neuromuscular tenseness and inefficient movement patterns (poor alignment) and to be spatially aware of body parts (Figures 50 through 53). This enables them to sense, for example, when the shoulders are lifted or the knees locked. One has to recognize the locus of tension—the source of poor movement habits—before there can be any correction or adjustment. Otherwise, the new habit superimposed over the old will create further distortions and harmful movement patterns.

Almost all the somatic disciplines emphasize movement patterns rather than individual movements because muscular action does not occur in isolation. Further, different parts of the same muscles are often responsible for different actions, some of which are evident only through electromyographic recordings of the neurological components of the muscle fibers. Also, as discussed in Chapter 2, supra-organizations of muscles exist in the distinct but extensive fascia webs of the body. Distant parts of the body (the neck, the feet) are, quite literally, connected to each other. Thus, it is not surprising that it is a challenge to correct inefficient or harmful movement patterns once they have become ingrained.[51]

Where does the student begin? The first edition of *Finding Balance* featured four of the more common somatic disciplines known as body therapies—Bartenieff Fundamentals, Ideokinesis, Alexander Technique, and Feldenkrais—and the reader is referred to that edition for a discussion of them. What is exciting is the development over the past 10 to 20 years of rehabilitative somatic disciplines. New approaches to rehabilitation, body reeducation, and conditioning based on such therapies include the foundational work of movement analyst, educator, and occupational therapist Bonnie Bainbridge Cohen. This approach, called Body-Mind Centering, serves as the basis of the manual therapy work developed by health professional William Weintraub.[52] Mentioned in Chapter 2 for its role in tendon and ligament rehabilitation, the system involves the exploration and repatterning of

Figure 50 Some somatic disciplines help dancers to identify areas of neuromuscular tenseness by recognizing primal movement patterns. Here, Kristin Torok demonstrates components of a Bartenieff Fundamentals movement pattern involving cross-lateral, body-half, and core-distal patterns. (Photo by Angela Sterling)

Figure 51 A Bartenieff Fundamentals movement pattern involving core-distal work and emphasizing flexion. (Photo by Angela Sterling)

neuromusculoskeletal systems that support movement.[53] Another example of movement reeducation and conditioning is Lulu Sweigard's body work, upon which Eric Franklin bases many of his ideas (mentioned earlier in this chapter), and the development and expansion of Alexander Technique, which also forms the basis of Thomas Myers' work as discussed in Chapter 2.

Figure 52 Kristin Torok demonstrates the distal movements in a Bartenieff Fundamentals movement pattern. (Photo by Angela Sterling)

Figure 53 Bartenieff Fundamentals sequence continued. (Photo by Angela Sterling)

Ideokinesis

Lulu Sweigard developed visualization techniques as "ideokinesis"—the conceptualization of movement with the purpose of promoting a balanced skeletal alignment and greater efficiency in movement. Building on the work of Mabel Todd and writing in *Human Movement Potential: Its Ideokinetic Facilitation*,[54] Sweigard showed how the initiation or inhibition of impulses to specific muscles is made possible by visualizing correct movement patterns. Such visualizations can be used to correct alignment and other problems. Change is subcortically controlled so that students need to concentrate on envisioning movement occurring within their body (as in a "perfect" plié), without contributing any physical effort to its performance.

Sweigard further refined Todd's ideas concerning the "hook lying," or constructive rest position as a training position for mental imagery. Sweigard proposed nine lines of action that had the most impact on the alignment of the entire body. These included lines of movement that individually lengthened the spine downward, shortened the distance between the mid-front of the pelvis and the lowest thoracic vertebra, narrowed the rib cage, lengthened the central axis of the torso upward, and others. The purpose of the nine lines of movement is to release tension and muscle tightness, improve alignment and weight transfer during locomotion, and achieve stability (i.e., the ability to maintain good alignment). The imaging exercises, in particular, help to balance muscle action around the joints.[55]

As is clear in Sweigard's work, Ideokinesis is learning to use the mind's eye in the service of altering muscular patterns. It is both art and science. A good teacher of visualization techniques should have a firm concept of good skeletal alignment based on anatomy and biomechanics, knowledge of typical faulty alignment, the ability to determine where and in what direction movement is needed to bring the skeleton into correct alignment, and the ability to note alignment problems in the habitual movement patterns of students. Most importantly, the teacher must be able to design meaningful and workable images to which the student can relate. The image should also be developed with words, such as *imagine, visualize, as if, watch,* and *pretend.*

The purpose of the constructive rest position (a position used for reducing muscle strain and balancing the muscles before imaging movement)[56] is to help the body to get rid of unwanted tension and allow the mind to be calm and focused. The position of constructive rest is a hallmark of many somatic disciplines in learning the art of "nondoing." Sweigard's rich images help to reduce strain and improve neuromuscular coordination in daily movements. Irene Dowd, building on Sweigard's work, and Rebecca Dietzel, a student of Dowd's, offer imagery for complex dance movements. For example, in an arabesque, Dowd encourages students to imagine having eyes in each vertebra and seeing the skin cells of the back opening to look into a huge mirror, visualizing that the arabesque is supported from behind the body.

In the constructive rest position, the image of the "empty suit" is used for locating and directing imagined movement in the body.[57] The trousers of this suit are imagined to be supported at the knees by the crossbar of a hanger extended from the ceiling; the arms of the coat rest across the chest and front of the coat. The suit is disheveled. Movements are then described to straighten out the suit. One of these images is: "Watch the upper part (thigh) of the trouser leg collapsing together as its knee is supported over the crossbar of the hanger."[58]

Ideokinesis offers enormous possibilities for developing ideas on dynamic alignment. Eric Franklin, in his work as founder and director of the Institute for Movement Imagery Education in Lucerne, Switzerland, has synthesized and expanded upon ideas of Barbara Clark, Joan Skinner, F. M. Alexander, Moshe Feldenkrais, and Bonnie Bainbridge Cohen.[59] Franklin's work advances the idea that images in the mind can alter the physiology and neuromuscular behavior of the body. His work reminds all of us that we are natural-born imagers. Recognizing that imaging is an ability often lost by the time we reach adolescence, he provides suggestions for ways to realize our human movement potential—professional and novice dancer alike. Likewise, teachers can learn to use such imagery to become more effective in their teaching. One of Franklin's recent works is *Pelvic Power: Mind/Body Exercises for Strength, Flexibility, Posture, and Balance for Men and Women.*[60] It focuses on exercises for core stabilization applicable to contemporary, classical, and world dance forms.

Alexander Technique

Originally developed for actors, the Alexander Technique was originated by F. Matthias Alexander as a way of improving "the use of the self." Psychophysical unity is at the core of this use. The technique has been a part of the program at the Theatre Center of the Juilliard School since its opening in 1968.[61]

Alexander hypothesized that in each of us there is an inherent "integrating mechanism" that provides for coordination if allowed to operate without interference. This mechanism he called "primary control," which he described as an active, buoyant, supportive use of the spine. He observed, "I discovered that a certain use of the head in relation to the neck, and of the head and neck in relation to the torso and other parts of the organism . . . constituted a primary control of the organism *as a whole.*"[62] The head is thus balanced freely and easily on the spine, activating the muscles along the length of the spine.[63]

A key element of the Technique is the concept of "inhibition." By becoming consciously aware of movement patterns, a person can then choose to organize more efficiently (in dynamic alignment) and move more freely. Once students are aware of inefficient movement patterns (e.g., "locking" the knees), they can learn to direct themselves toward more functional movement.

Jerry Sontag, publisher and editor of Mornum Time Press,[64] is himself a teacher of the Technique and committed to publishing works on the topic. In *Thinking Aloud: Talks on Teaching the Alexander Technique,*[65] he presents a series of lectures by Walter Carrington, who first studied with Alexander in 1935 and joined his training course in 1936. Carrington, who emerged as a teacher-lecturer of the Technique, provides insights through his lectures into its masterful teaching and general applicability. Perhaps more well known is the work of Michael J. Gelb as discussed in *Body Learning: An Introduction to the Alexander Technique.*[66]

In general, teachers of the Technique assist students through light, delicate hands-on work and verbal cues to activate their primary control. The Technique is traditionally taught one-on-one, since touch is such an important part of helping students find the buoyant support of the primary control. (Teachers study for 4 years to learn to communicate with their hands, as Alexander did.) Eventually, the student is able to activate conscious control (i.e., find the support independently) without any direction from a teacher.[67]

The Alexander teacher helps students discover tension-free movement patterns ("free," "embodied," "ease of movement"), preferably individually, but when necessary also in groups (as is the case at the American Dance Festival, where the Alexander Technique has been taught in groups for close to 20 years). Martha Myers notes that the change in students' movement has been dramatic. Once students become familiar with the Technique and recognize that this is indeed the "real stuff" (i.e., technical training), they find their discoveries exhilarating: "[The students] become more aware of themselves and of others around them, and this learning feeds directly into technique, improvisation, and composition classes. Students who've studied Alexander Technique find it easier to spot [when turning], and the improved coordination reverberates down the spine and into other movements."[68]

As with the other somatic disciplines, following the Alexander Technique is as much a way of living as it is a therapeutic intervention. Robertson Davies, a longtime Alexander student and practitioner, says that "improving the use of the self" is a lifelong commitment to reflection and improvement[69] that can have far-reaching applications. For example, dancer, physical therapist, and Alexander teacher Deborah Caplan applies the technique to conditioning work. Caplan studied the Technique with her mother, who was a certified practitioner in the 1940s. Caplan writes, "I do not believe in giving strengthening exercises to the neck . . . because most of the time such exercises just increase muscle tension and pain. Good use is, in itself, the best form of exercise for this area."[70] Many dancers would agree that there is no point in strengthening if poor use results in misaligned joints and overworked muscles.

Depending on the practitioner with whom one works, the somatic disciplines can be enormously helpful—even for virtuoso dancers. The dancer may need to budget for lessons, but group sessions can be arranged so that costs are divided among the participants. For dancers who are ready to break harmful movement patterns and let go of inappropriate solutions to dance movement problems, the lessons are well worth the investment.

SELECTING A TEACHER

Many of the ideas discussed in this chapter—what is good technique, how to analyze dance movement, and which somatic disciplines facilitate dynamic alignment—are puzzles that dancers spend a lifetime trying to solve. In a real sense, dancers are lifelong learners. The selection of good teachers or coaches to facilitate that learning is part of being a dancer. No one teacher or approach is going to do it all.

Kenneth Laws himself, while highlighting the singular value of physical analysis, also acknowledges that a mere understanding of the mechanical principles that apply to dance—for example, in achieving the balances in the Rose Adagio of *Sleeping Beauty*—does not necessarily make the balances any easier. "To what extent are dancers [even] aware of the physical principles that govern the way rotations [turns] occur?" asks Laws. " . . . dancers have learned exactly how to perform the movements by experience, instruction, trial, error, and observing others . . . unconsciously [using] mechanical principles that are usually applied to wheels, gyroscopes, and planets."[71]

So, dancers use a variety of approaches to learn what they need to know in order to understand technique. At the same time, they must develop an intuitive feel for technique, which often comes via a positive learning environment (i.e., studying with a well-respected teacher or practitioner who appreciates the presuppositions, biases, or history the student brings to an instructional setting). Key, however, to that setting is the persona of the teacher —she or he plays many important roles in the dancer's life: mentor, coach, critic, healer, friend.

Thus, dancers should be critical and selective consumers.[72] This may be difficult, especially in places where selecting a good teacher might mean long commutes and considerable expense. Still, it is worth it to find a teacher who can explain *why* a step needs to be done in a particular way. Dancers need teachers who challenge them in terms of their individual abilities, who help them to develop their creative expressive talents, and guide them in sustaining the motivation and passion to dance. As a Limón technique teacher once said to me, "You move across that floor as if it were your time. Believe me, as you get older, *no one* cares if you move or not except you."

Furthermore, a good teacher, besides being competent and knowledgeable, should facilitate the guided self-discovery so important to the growth of the student as dancer and artist. This is as important for little ones new to dance as it is for seasoned students (Figure 54 through 56). In a safe and nurturing environment, students will learn to develop movement that is aesthetically pleasing as well as anatomically sound, eventually becoming their own teachers, their own therapists. Clearly, there is more to dance than learning steps.

Kitty Daniels, chair of dance at Cornish College of the Arts in Seattle, and a longtime ballet instructor in Bill Evans' Summer Institutes of Dance, shows how dance teachers can bring dance science to the studio. Her work illustrates how teachers can blend analysis with intuition, kinesthetic experience, and conceptual understanding. The exemplary ballet barre that Daniels teaches focuses on torso stabilization and hip turnout, with stabilization of the pelvis during level changes (plié and relevé), of the supporting side during leg gestures (tendu, dégagé, ronde de jambe, and développé), and of the pelvis and spine during arm movements. Daniels gives teaching cues and imagery based on the anatomical principles of turnout throughout the class. Use of anatomical imagery greatly enhances the class. Also effective are teachers who can work with verbal, visual, and kinesthetic learning styles.[73]

Younger dancers must be able to recognize and avoid a teacher who is long on criticism, short on clear explanations, and who humiliates students repeatedly. Rather, they must look for teachers who are intelligent, experienced, gracious, and focused on the learning process —lifelong learners themselves. Perhaps the best way to identify good teaching is to reflect on the exercises that are taught, by asking, for example:

- Is each exercise purposeful?[74]
- Is the teacher well informed on the movement intent? (Does it make sense to begin a ballet class with grand plié?)[75]

Figure 54 A positive learning environment should be provided early, with easily understandable technique, conditioning with stretches as demonstrated by Emily Allaway (above), aerobic activity in class (leaps and jumps, Figure 55), and time for creative work (Figure 56). (Photo by Angela Sterling)

Figure 55 A positive learning environment allows time for aerobic activity by dancer Ian Allaway. (Photo by Angela Sterling)

Figure 56 A positive learning environment is critical to the growth of the student as dancer and artist. Erika Yonally, Marena Salerno Collins, and Emily Allaway (left to right) demonstrate. (Photo by Angela Sterling)

- Does our work in the center and at the barre make sense? (Why stretch the hamstrings at the barre by overflexing the torso, bringing the head to the knee instead of stabilizing the torso by pressing the lower back into the leg; exercises should emphasize spinal extension rather than flexion—for we spend much of our lives resting/slouching/relaxing in spinal flexion with the same muscle repeatedly tightened or stretched)?[76]
- Are stretching and movement well integrated? (Why does a modern dance class emphasize swings in the early segments of the class and exercises with hip flexion to the neglect of stretches for the often tight hip flexors?)[77]

The explanation for the way exercises are taught should not be, "Because we've always done it that way," or "Because the teacher says so." As Erick Hawkins said, "You have to act on some *principles* of movement."[78] It is the teacher's responsibility to point out to the student exactly what those principles are and how they should be applied. The movement must make anatomical, physical, and kinesiological sense. Otherwise, it may serve no useful purpose other than as a harmless (or not-so-harmless) diversion.

Dancers are relying more on practitioners of somatic disciplines for assistance in technical training. Perhaps as a result, the therapies are appearing in more school curricula, so that younger professional dancers are exposed to them. Students learn somatic disciplines in performing arts high schools, in colleges and universities, and at dance institutes and festivals. They are becoming part of a more inclusive educational setting and process.

Dancer Jan Hyatt, at age 68, has perhaps summed up the feelings of many dancers:

As a dancer, you simply need to take responsibility for your body. You need to have intelligent training and you need to be connected with your physical instrument. You need to listen to it and not abuse it. It's designed to move—to abuse it when it's your instrument of expression just for special effect is stupid. It is not luck that prevents injuries; rather, it is being sentiently connected to what's going on with your body when you are moving. "I am a body," not "I have a body." You must think this not just in technique class but at all times. You can't be abusive with your body one day and make up for it the next. You must study with someone that has true body awareness.[79]

Hyatt did just that, traveling 30,000 miles in one year, between Meadville, Pennsylvania, and Cleveland, Ohio, to study with Kelly Holt and Kathryn Karipides at Case Western Reserve University. Others do not need to travel as far.

Another example of a teacher benefiting from multidisciplinary study is massage therapist and dance educator Noa Spector-Flock. Growing up in Israel, she was exposed to many new approaches in physical education and modern dance. She found (and selected) teachers in a number of disciplines, including her mother's practice of astrology-influenced yoga, study with Katia Michaeli (an Alexander teacher and a former dancer with Mary Wigman), 5 years of study in Feldenkrais movement awareness, and directed study with Bonnie Bainbridge Cohen. Spector-Flock thus brings a synthesis of all this work to her conditioning programs. Her programs are discussed further in Chapter 4.

PROFILES

Bill Evans

Bill Evans (Figure 57) acts as a powerful magnet, attracting dancers and others from all walks of life, of all ages and physical abilities. People flock to his classes and workshops for his breath-supported modern dance and rhythm tap techniques—technique that is sound and, in many ways, commonsensical, yet produces dramatic results in terms of performance quality and career longevity. Says Pam Paulson, a past president of the National Dance Education Organization, "[Evans'] approach to technique with its sense of honesty and wonderment resonates with audiences and students alike. He has found the confidence to do what he knows is right for his body, his spirit, and what fits him emotionally."[80]

Evans approaches many tasks with a passionate enthusiasm, not least the touring of the work based on that famously fluid, exuberant technique. From 1976 through 1983 and in 1985–1986, he toured for an average of 40 weeks per year, performing more than 100 times per year. The Bill Evans Dance Company (BEDCO) toured as the "most booked company" in the United States for 2 years running. His summer teaching institutes included venues as diverse as San Jose, Seattle, Bellingham, New London, Tempe, Port Townsend, Dallas,

Figure 57 Bill Evans in Evans' *Dances for my Father.* (Photo by Kevin Elliff)

Meadville, Winnipeg, Atlanta, Colorado Springs, Bloomington, Kent, Albuquerque, Edmond (Oklahoma), Santa Fe, Indianapolis, Muncie, and Las Cruces and Puebla in Mexico—more than 75 sessions in total. For several years, Evans' school of dance in Seattle was the largest contemporary dance training center on the West Coast.

In some ways, Evans is something of a dance "crossover" enigma. In 1997, he played Drosselmayer, co-choreographing a *Nutcracker* for New Mexico Ballet. This longtime modern dancer has impressive ballet credentials, as a soloist at Utah Civic Ballet under the directorship of Willem Christensen, and in New York performing with Oleg Briansky Ballet and the New York City Opera Ballet. But there is no doubt that his real love is modern dance, dance that allows the dancer, "to find the inner connectivity to support the outer expressivity."

For Evans, creating a dance technique and teaching methodology has been the major undertaking of his life since 1968. As early as 1965, when he was an apprentice to the Harkness Ballet in New York, he realized that his body was mostly "wrong" for ballet, although he loved the formality and musicality of classical technique. He did not have a tight fifth position, he could not wing (evert) his gesturing foot, his knees would not straighten (hyperextend). Still, he tried.

It was during some time off from Repertory Dance Theatre (which he had joined in 1967), when he began to explore ranges of movement, patterns of breath support, and body awareness of specific muscle groups that he discovered greater freedom of movement and appropriate conditioning for muscle balance and tone. Says Evans,

> I started to develop a highly individual way of structuring a class, and perceiving what was important within it. I sensed that I needed to work deeper in the body. I hadn't yet studied anatomy and kinesiology, but I intuited that I needed to work frequently in full flexion at the hip joint. I discovered the psoas, and other deep and smaller muscles close to the bone. I stopped overworking my quadriceps and gluteals and started working more synergistically, more democratically, and to allow a full range of both femoral and scapulo-humeral rotation. Because Laban/Bartenieff specialist Peggy Hackney joined my dance company in 1976, I experienced [first hand] the application of Laban theory and how it could enhance my dancing, teaching and choreography before I learned the theoretical framework of Laban/Bartenieff Movement Analysis (LMA) in a formal way.

As Evans notes, "my thorough study of LMA helps me make connections to the larger world. For me, Bartenieff Fundamentals has become a spiritual practice." Evans earned certification from the Laban/Bartenieff Institute of Movement Studies in New York (1992–2003).

Evans eschews dance that emphasizes rigid and unnatural lines and placement and extreme positions. His technique today is an amalgam of knowledge of anatomy, kinesiology, and movement repatterning, building on Irmgard Bartenieff's Fundamentals and Rudolf Laban's theories of Effort, Shape, and Space Harmony as foundations. His studies with Peggy Hackney, Janet Hamburg, and Karen Clippinger, and of Bonnie Bainbridge Cohen's trademarked Body-Mind Centering, have helped to build that foundation.

Today, at age 64, he performs solo concerts of rigorous modern, tap, and jazz movement. For conditioning, he practices Bartenieff Fundamentals and his own modern dance technique and rhythm tap several times a week. Says Evans,

> These practices are the key to my health and longevity as a dancer because they allow me to move my body through its full range of movement and expressive

possibilities in a low-impact way. I often perceive that my contemporaries are be-coming more neurotic as they age while I am becoming more serene. But I work as much as anyone. I'm just more internally focused and efficient in how I move. Bartenieff Fundamentals incorporates the developmental movement patterns through which the brain is developed and through which healthy body-mind bal-ance is maintained throughout our lives. My tap dancing has provided great car-dio-vascular conditioning for me. And at age 45 [Evans believes that his peak dancing was between 45 and 50 years of age] I started to run every day, and lift weights every other day, with yoga-like stretches three times a week.

For young dancers . . . Bartenieff work is absolutely key. It can make such an as-tounding improvement in kinesthetic awareness in younger people—necessitating less movement re-education to do later on. Young dancers need access to patterns of fundamental movement based on the body's needs. Unfortunately, many teach-ers feel compelled to give young dancers a barrage of "steps" to keep them enter-tained, rather than attending to their life-long needs to understand healthful, regenerative movement in its most basic forms. One of the first texts we require in the dance program at University of New Mexico is Peggy Hackney's *Making Connections: Total Body Integration Through Bartenieff Fundamentals*. For some of our students, it becomes a "bible" that they carry with them several days a week, reading and rereading it in their spare time.

Passing on what he has learned is very important to Evans:

Students challenge me and thrill me and give me the chance to pass on what I have learned. Teaching allows me to gain a measure of immortality as students choose to embody my work. I think it behooves a good teacher to [foster] environments in which students can take risks and explore the sensual and intuitive as well as the cognitive—without being criticized too soon or inappropriately. The more I teach, the less I intervene and the more I encourage students to engage in open inquiry and make personal meaning of such exploration.

Evans also believes that "positive attitudes towards ourselves are tremendously important in achieving efficient and expressive dancing." Says Evans,

One of my major goals in the first semester that students spend with me is facili-tating a process by which each dancer gets to know that she is ok. Many dancers come to us with low self-esteem. They are preoccupied with all the ways they do not measure up to some perceived ideal. Some dancers can't even articulate any-thing that is "right" with them. I think it's our job as teachers to help them realize that one can be a beautiful, expressive, and successful dancer with a less than "ideal" physical body, whatever one might consider that to be.

This fits with Evans' belief that dance is primarily an activity of the human spirit, and that it requires a healthy, well-functioning body, but not a body of any particular shape or size. Evans urges dancers to, "be grateful for the body with which you were blessed and fulfill its possibilities to the greatest degree by finding informed, caring and generous teachers."

Cher Carnell

Cher Carnell (Figure 58) is a peripatetic dance teacher as well as performer. She has directed academies, chaired a department of dance, and served as an artistic director or guest faculty at over two dozen different schools, companies, and associations of dance. She has performed as a principal with Ballet Met, Santa Barbara Ballet Theatre, California Ballet Company, and Wisconsin Ballet Company, with soloist stints at Theater an Der Wien in Austria, Milwaukee Ballet Company, San Diego Ballet Company, Arizona Ballet Theater, Louisville Ballet Company, and guest spots elsewhere.

Reflecting on her performing career, Carnell says,

> I was always a big fish in a small pond, continually moving to a slightly larger pond. For me, dancing was always about opportunities. In order to dance Giselle, Odette, Swanhilda, Raymonda, or Sugar Plum, I had to move on—dancing those roles was a lot more rewarding than being a merliton or a cygnet. I always had to find the jobs, and would audition in person for the fun of it. With the exception of Arizona Ballet (which folded), I've always had a job when I auditioned for the next.

What is surprising is that, as a performer, she was never first cast in principal roles, but in rehearsal she would land a featured role.

> Every time I danced a principal role, I was never first choice, but I got it once rehearsals began. I remember for the Santa Barbara Ballet, I was an understudy for

Figure 58 Cher Carnell. (Photo by Angela Sterling)

Giselle, but 3 or 4 weeks into rehearsal, I was moved up to first cast. It was my performance ability and emotional force that got me the role. My whole career I never did a real entrechat six. I just had so much confidence that nobody counted what was happening at my ankles. I suppose that one of my main assets was that I was a very quick study. I could learn a role in a day.

Perhaps it is not surprising that she has taught everywhere she has danced, for Carnell also is a master teacher with singular zeal, focus, and attention to detail. For Carnell, teaching always went hand in hand with performing:

I always taught company class wherever I was performing—babies through professionals, and I still love it to this day. Sometimes it was tough doing both. I might have quit dancing one year sooner . . . the last year of performing was less fun, but I was in excellent performance shape. You need that last year to get tired of the pressures of performing. And then I realized that dancers tend to assume audiences really care who's doing *Sugar Plum*. Frankly, they adjust more easily than dancers would like to believe.

Carnell appeared last as Odette with the Twin Cities Ballet in Monroe, Louisiana, stopping in her prime, at age 30, to assume the chairpersonship of a university dance department.

What's appealing about the university teaching is that you're often dealing more with modern dancers and don't need to bother about "perfect" ballet technique. There's a certain freedom to focus more on dancing, and less on technique. For me, personally, I made up for lack of technique and an ideal dancer body with élan, aplomb, presence, and my port de bras.

Carnell moved to Bellingham, Washington, in 1996 to raise her family, and continues to teach.

Dancers must be highly intelligent and quick—the body-mind connection is imperative. I like teaching technique to the individual. Technique is the foundation, it's the tool. Dancers have to have the tools to build the shelves—for example, finding the functional turnout that works for their bodies, rather than striving for an unreachable ideal.

Carnell structures her class in much the same way as many other ballet teachers, but her exercises are purposeful and rich with imagery:

One good thing about images is that if you can deliver them effectively, they will live forever in the student's memory—for example, saying "plié as if you're smashing peas before each piqué turn," rather than just "use your plié." I'm teaching teenagers now, and must use a whole different batch of images—a favorite is, "you're doing that combo as if your mother made you!"

The following are some thoughts and verbal cues from Carnell for individual movements of technique class.

Pliés generate warmth, the deep bend gets warmth into the hip sockets, which is why they are first in class. Adults forget that pliés are a stretch — children will happily stretch into a plié. The more advanced the dancers get, the tighter and more controlled it becomes. I ask the dancers to think of themselves as a half-inflated rubber cushion, letting the rest of the air out and in — very buoyant. Or, as in the old Prell commercial — being that sinking pearl.

The purpose of tendu is to find the bottom of the foot (i.e., to wake up the bottoms of the feet, of the toes). A well-crossed tendu is vital to the shape of the leg when dancing. Similarly, the *degagé* connects the foot to the leg and turns them into a single unit, which is so crucial to, say, petite allegro. You can have a couch potato degagé or a Jackie Chan degagé or somewhere in between. The alignment must be such that you feel that you are sandwiched between two sheets of paper.

The movement ronde de jambe is as much for the supporting leg as for the working leg. Dancers need to start finding the connection all the way up to the supporting arm and leg, as if you were making a near-perfect crystal-clear circle in a sandbox—half circles drawn with the tip of the big toe.

Teaching pirouette is one of her strengths. It also is one of the gender battlefields of ballet:

As a company teacher, I was always encouraging the boys to be more like the girls, who tended to get carried away with neat and tidy turns, and the girls to be more like the boys and blast it out—exuding raw, uncontrolled energy. Both genders can learn a lot from each other.

Technically, Carnell teaches the pirouette, moving from fifth front to fifth front "because you cannot cheat," and with many strategies for getting people to spot and get their arms out of the way—to avoid the huge wind-ups and arm-flinging that throws the turner off balance.

One thing I'd notice when I was a company teacher was that I could see who was going to make the pirouette just by looking at their feet. If they were tense in the feet, they couldn't make the turn. Rather, dancers need to turn calmly. With each revolution there should be a sense of going higher and higher, more than simply thinking "head, head" for spotting.

For Carnell, the purpose of barre is to warm up the body, to prepare it for center work— and for dance:

Dance—the word seems so obvious, but there is a category of people who are attracted to ballet for the barre and are not comfortable when it comes time to dance. Most people prefer one part or the other—people who get through barre so they can dance and vice versa. The combination always starts with music as a foundation and is something to get you on your legs—like tendu grand battement, followed by adagio, a pirouette, a second pirouette combination, a warm-up jump, petit allegro, and grand allegro. Sometimes you should do an entire class on pirouettes and delve into it, but usually the body needs the full complement of exercises as in a well-balanced meal. At any rate, classes should provide a lot of movement. You can take classes from teachers who talk so much that the students don't even move.

For me . . . individualization is imperative. Students are people who have different abilities and the teacher must be realistic and observant. One dancer may be thinking about a career in musical theater, so you need to keep that goal in mind for her—where she's headed and what she needs to work on. Another might be a gifted modern dancer. This boy might really have a chance; you need to help students set goals for themselves in the class.

Donald Byrd

Donald Byrd (Figure 59) has enjoyed a long and varied career as a dancer and choreographer, with exposure to many different techniques, training styles, and performance venues. He has danced with Twyla Tharp, Karole Armitage, and Gus Solomons jr. He has choreographed close to 100 works—for his own company, for major modern dance companies, including the Alvin Ailey American Dance Theater, Dayton Contemporary Dance Company, Philadelphia Dance Company (Philadanco), Cleo Parker Robinson, Dallas Black Dance Theater, and Phoenix Dance in Leeds, England, and for classical companies, including Pacific Northwest Ballet and Oregon Ballet Theatre. Mr. Byrd has also choreographed for numerous stage productions, receiving a Bessie Award in 1992.

Keeping things in perspective and maintaining your own standards is the key to longevity in dance, Byrd believes.

It's hard for dancers—they are so self-absorbed and self-critical. I can remember being hired by Twyla Tharp and fired within a month. It was the most difficult time in my life—I had low self-esteem issues about my dancing, even though people said my dancing was good. Yet being hired by Twyla was a validation of sorts—fame by

Figure 59 Donald Byrd. (Photo by Adam L. Weintraub)

association. So, when I was let go, it forced me to look at why I was doing what I was doing, and to look at my place in the dance world.

Byrd replaced the irrational "I'm no good" with the more productive attitude, "I'm only interested in dancing for people whose work is interesting and to which I can make a contribution; I know what I have to offer." Byrd began to tell himself that an audition was not to get a job but to see if he was interested in the work. If the style didn't suit him, he wouldn't do it.

> This is the only way to survive in the dance world—you have to be your own person. You can't wait for someone else to tell you you're doing a good job. It's the only way to emotionally survive and find some balance and not be victimized or brutalized by the profession.
>
> If someone confronts you, then you have an understanding when it's truthful and when it's not. So dancers need this emotional placement as well as physical. It's helpful to make it bigger than the dancer, to say — I'm trying to make a contribution to the art form so it's not about me. When we put ourselves at the center of the universe, it's too much of a burden.

Byrd has directed his company, Donald Byrd/The Group, since 1978, and now serves as artistic director of Dance Spectrum in Seattle. He has a vision of the theater as a place where a profound intellectual and visceral experience occurs. Thematically, much of his work emphasizes social concerns such as isolation, community, culture, and gender. He believes that life is indeed complex and there is no one way of looking at the world.

The same holds true for dancers' obsession with body image and type:

> Dance is demanding—for the physical part but also how dance deals with ideals. Dance is full of unrealistic demands, but the pressure is still on. In choreography— in the last 20 years, more demands have been placed on the body. The moves are more extreme and there's less time to learn how to do them. Still, the worst is the notions of perfection, achieving the ideal that doesn't even exist in the world. I look at some beautiful mover like Sylvie Guillem—how many dancers would have the combination of technique and artistry that she has? But, she probably doesn't think she's perfect either.
>
> I think it's hard to get away from. Most dancers have a really, really negative self-image. Even if they have the most beautiful body, they're still hyper-critical. There're certainly images of bodies that are built around race, too—ideas that a dancing body is to look a certain way regardless of race and ethnicity. I think a lot of it comes from the hyper-critical teachers that comment on body and the kids never forget it. It's brutal.

So, how can dancers realistically evaluate the way they look and dance without being so critical that they actually hate themselves? Byrd says he's done it the wrong way to himself, listening only to his own negative talk: "One day I heard myself saying this stuff, and that's what kills you, ultimately." He argues that one way to fight the negative images is for dancers to gain confidence with and experience in as many different techniques, styles, and teachers as possible:

> The exposure to different ways of thinking is important, especially to study a non-Western dance form. I studied Indonesian dance for 6 years and it made me think

about the body differently. It contributed to appreciation of correct placement of the body in terms of maintaining health. A lot of dance techniques are similar but decisions about movement are made based on aesthetics, and those different explorations are important.

Byrd likens experiencing a variety of styles and teachers to getting a liberal arts education —"the more you're exposed to, the better dancer you are." He believes it's worth investing the time to do this—it helps to develop a point of view that is the sum of many different perspectives. In dance (as with most other things) there's no one truth or absolute truth, but many different truths. For Byrd, training at places like the Cambridge School of Ballet, London School of Contemporary Dance, and Alvin Ailey American Dance Center and with teacher Mia Slavenska helped him form his very inclusive views.

It's important to have a teacher you can trust. I learned the most about technique from Mia Slavenska. I completely transformed my body studying with her. Many dancers have one particular teacher who really trained and supported them. Then there're other teachers that teach you different things as you move along in your professional life. The body is really smart—it truly is a thinking body—and carries all sort of information to touch and transform us. A good teacher helps you realize that.

Kelen Laine

From the time she was three, Kelen Laine has taken ballet class (see Figure 43; Laine is in the background center) and also participated in soccer and gymnastics. Now, 11 years past that first ballet class, she is a very active 14-year-old, enthusiastic also about snowboarding and horseback riding, which she was first exposed to in a summer camp.

Piano is her other passion. Both Suzuki piano and ballet come relatively easily for her. "It's never really been a big struggle to do both," she says. Laine's favorite ballet roles have been character parts, "where I can do more acting, and show my emotions."

With the increasing demands of all her activities, she is now taking a break from ballet:

Performing is my favorite part of ballet because you get to present what you've been working so hard on. Rehearsals are fun. The hardest part is the physical stress. The stress is emotional and physical. It's a big time commitment and doesn't leave you much time to do anything else. Once you're in the company, there are even more rehearsals. You're cast in more ballets. The first year in a company is just a huge time commitment [2003 was Laine's first year]. I've been doing this since I was three. Right now I'm going to relax—I need to figure out what I want to do.

Gus Solomons jr

Gus Solomons jr (Figure 60)—company dancer, artistic director, choreographer, dance critic, feature writer—is also a faculty member at New York University's Tisch School of the Arts, where he has the opportunity to teach young artists some of his craft. Teaching requires special skills, he knows: "Teachers need experience, patience, compassion, and rigor. A good teacher knows how to demand everything from the student and have them give it, but not intimidate them into obeying. I remember Martha Graham would slap her dancers regularly."

Figure 60 Gus Solomons jr. (Photo by Tom Caravaglia)

Solomons should know. He was in the Graham Company (1964–1965)—and also in the companies of Pearl Lang (1962–68), Joyce Trisler (1963–1966), Donald McKayle (1961–1964), and Merce Cunningham (1965–1968). As an artist in residence, he has taught in Tanzania, Poland, France, Russia, and Argentina and throughout the United States. He has TV performances and video projects among his credits, as well as numerous dance theater performances. His choreography is performed by dozens of companies, and his dance reviews appear regularly in *Dance Magazine* and other publications.

Solomons believes dance is a demanding profession, but that dancers can find their way when they feel overwhelmed, if they take one step at a time.

> Dancers tend to beat themselves up. They have a strong will and a strong drive to succeed so they don't give themselves leeway to fail. They need to realize that it is not possible to be in complete control.
>
> As a student at MIT [Solomons holds a Bachelor of Architecture degree from the Massachusetts Institute of Technology], I'd study architecture and still perform in nine shows at the same time—burning the candle at both ends. Dance demands everything—it is a physical discipline but also requires persistence, courage, and a certain amount of luck. For the most part, my parents supported me. My father had gone to MIT and as long as I got my education, I was ok.
>
> When you're young, you just have to have the desire to dance—and persistence. Dancers need to keep healthy and learn as much as they can about their instrument. Many of the injuries that I had were due to ignorance. But what's out there for young people today is so much more than what I had when I was learning to dance. It's worrying to think that there are whole generations of dancers who were trained poorly and are now teaching. There was so much we didn't know . . . So we ended up hurting ourselves a lot. That misuse doesn't happen any more.

> At Tisch, we are training elite dancers. My responsibility is to teach a breadth of what their needs will be. So, as a teacher, you have to keep up with the latest improvement, like being a doctor.

Solomons has had only one serious injury in his career—a fall in an airport, resulting in torn quadriceps muscles and tendons. With physical therapy, a positive attitude, and a belief that the body can heal itself, Solomons recovered. Complementary and alternative health care help dancers today, he believes: "Today, there is recognition of alternative modalities such as yoga and other body work of all sorts. Dancers today understand the benefits of a good massage."

Solomons credits his training at the Boston Conservatory of Music, studying with Jan Veen, and Wigman training, for allowing him to "see the music regardless of the style of dance. I'm dancing on momentum now [he reported in the *New York Times* in April, 2003, for an article on sustaining a dancing career despite the limitations of age]. You can do more on momentum than on muscles." Solomons says he always wanted to dance but had little formal training when he was young. He'd go to the movies and watch the hoofers on screen, and "when I was around twelve-ish, I had a little tap, acrobatic, and ballet training, and then some training in college."

Solomons considers that his architecture training at MIT helped him to see relationships in space, at least early on in his dance career. Or perhaps it was his innate ability to visualize space that helped him in his architecture degree. At any rate, he had many opportunities to dance. "I could dance Graham and Cunningham 40 years ago because I saw what was happening in relationship to space rather than what the muscles were doing. Then, technically, I learned a lot of things about dance. What I do now is not technical dancing but presence—and communication about the essence of a idea."

What does he think, then, about the perennial question: Are dancers born or made?

> I think it's both. You can teach a young resilient body to do anything. What the dancer does with that skill—whether they are able to communicate—makes the difference as to whether or not they'll be a dancer. To dance is really a combination of real desire and passion—if someone needs to communicate and has the equipment he'll find a way to do it.
>
> Some students come to Tisch with ballet training since they were two, but nothing else. They can do all the tricks, but when they get into a modern dance class, they learn that dance is not only about ballet but about moving and the world opens up for them. They have to have the appetite for it.
>
> What I see more and more is that the people who don't have the instruments are being selected out. But what about the emerging Martha Grahams? What would happen to the Graham dancers then if they were auditioning now? They would be selected out of a technique class in a heart beat.

To Solomons, longevity in dance is about developing and maintaining a point of view:

> I always raise the question of why, what's driving the dancer? How does this piece look differently than the piece before? And, as long as I'm active in the field, that's what I do. I don't know why I'm curious, but if you're not curious, you may as well just stop. That and maintaining a sense of humor—maybe that's part of being curious. Most dancers don't become world famous, so you do whatever you choose to do because you've empowered yourself, you have stamina—and then you should never have trouble finding a job.

Today, Solomons directs Paradigm, a project of Solomons Company/Dance. He is currently dancing with Carmen de Lavallade and Dudley Williams. All three dancers have been making dance history for 40 years or more: Solomons, who performed in the 1960s for Merce Cunningham in featured roles; Carmen de Lavallade, who originated roles for dance greats like Alvin Ailey and Donald McKayle; and Dudley Williams, who to this day takes center stage among dancers in their 20s.

> With Paradigm, it's easy in a way. My dancers are grown up. They know how to use themselves well—and we're commissioning other choreographers' work, which is interesting for us. Many of these choreographers are younger. If there's something in their work that interests me and that can translate into something other than technical [tricks], work that does not need to be athletic but has the intensity—we can use it. We simply don't have access to certain tools—to jump or rebound. So what is it about their work that will translate to us?

Solomons advises that, if you have the appetite, you need to find ways to make the profession work for you:

> Everybody now has multiple careers, so it's not a big surprise that most of the students at Tisch are now at least double majoring—in dance and something else. Younger dancers understand that they'll dance while they're still resilient.
>
> It never occurred to me when I started that I wouldn't dance forever—I have constantly reinvented myself so I could still dance. But I had to find ways of doing it effectively—to weigh my desire against my means, and the pain of doing it.
>
> The 'world of dance' doesn't necessarily mean only performing—although my main interest is in performing. So, it's important for me to find ways to continue to perform. Maybe not in dancing, but in acting or other theater work. Something in me needs to perform.

To achieve prominence in so many facets of the field is quite an accomplishment. In 2000 Solomons was recognized with a Bessie Award for his contributions to choreography and dance. As he notes, "age need not be a limitation. It is a resource of life experience and dance craft that enriches performance beyond technical virtuosity."

Solomons says that, throughout his career, he has never had enough money to realize all the big ideas he had, but it didn't matter.

> I know a lot of people who wring their hands about not having enough money for this project or that project and then they end up doing second-rate work rather than just figuring out what to do with what you have. If you have 10 yards of fabric and your idea calls for a million, then what you need to do is find out how to make the 10 yards eloquent.

What Solomons is saying is, don't throw away the good because you can't have the best:

> If you wait for inspiration, then you get rusty. If you look at the greatest art, the greatest genius—Merce [Cunningham], Pablo Picasso, Igor Stravinsky, George Balanchine—they didn't wait for the right moment, they were just working. When

the inspiration did come, they were ready. They had all the tools there, they'd been practicing for this moment. It's like going to the studio every day, no matter what —and once there, you'll never fail to learn something. It's awfully hard to get up and go, but it's a preparation for making the dances you thought you could never make.

4

The Fit Dancer
Conditioning the Body for Strength, Endurance, and Flexibility

Dancers would seem to be among the fittest of athletes. Yet strength[1] and endurance[2] deficits abound, despite their "almost pathological hyperflexibility."[3] For some dancers, becoming—or staying—fit is a question of finding the time and other resources to do so.[4] Technique class by itself cannot provide the conditioning needed for optimal fitness and injury-free performance. Dancers need "supernormal" strength to perform demanding choreography, lift another dancer, or whip out turns à la seconde (with the leg lifted to the side) for 16 measures of music, not to mention the flexibility needed to achieve the aesthetically desired line of many ballet or jazz movements.[5]

Dance kinesiologist Karen Clippinger notes that "the aesthetically desired line of many dance movements such as a large jump . . . or jazz lay-out requires both great flexibility and strength . . . intricate pointe [work may] require fine neuromuscular coordination [synchronous working of muscles during complex movements]. Each of these necessary components [of fitness] should be adequately stressed and developed in dancers' training programs."[6]

Why is fitness important in dance? The possible effects of fitness can be looked at in a number of ways. Fitness provides strength, power, and stamina as well as resistance to injury. This enables dancers to better deal with the demands of dance training and performance. On another level, fitness enhances the function of energy pathways involved in the execution of various exercises and dance routines, perhaps improving the capacity for fast dance moves and those requiring power (explosive moves), together with a greater and specialized muscle mobilization. Fitness also involves neural conditioning.[7]

In the words of former American Ballet Theatre principal Cynthia Harvey, fitness has been a lifelong endeavor for her:

> [A]s I was warming up for a rehearsal, Rudolf Nureyev came up to me and said in a wistful tone, "I wish I knew as much about dance and the body as you do when I was your age." I understood what he meant. It was by no means merely a compliment and I felt it my duty to continue the process of education so that I would have no regrets during my career. That was over 20 years ago, and I was fortunate to have had

a long career . . . I can say to a young dancer today, that I too wish I knew what they now know, due to their good fortune in having access to [muscular training information, for example], no longer is it a mystery as to why there appears to be soreness following a performance, when the same activity during rehearsal may seem to have little or no effect . . . armed with knowledge and understanding, you are empowered.[8]

Dance classes cannot take care of all the necessary components of fitness, so dancers must supplement their technical training with other activities. For example, a conditioning program for hip flexor strength could help increase dancers' extension à la seconde (to the side; Figure 31), especially in the extreme ranges of hip flexion. The therapeutic intervention for this could be a conditioning program for just 6 weeks, with the dancer practicing a modified leg raise (see Figure 61).[9]

The possibilities for improving performance by conditioning are considerable. Conditioning is particularly important for young dancers, who need to realize early on that the body is the dancer's only instrument and needs to be well taken care of.[10] Conditioning can help.

Surprisingly little published data exist on the benefits of physical fitness for dance training and performance.[11] In contrast, studies proliferate showing why fitness is important to athletic performance. Fortunately, dance medicine and science specialists are stepping forward, and thus books like *The Fit and Healthy Dancer*[12] are being published. Some of the information in these publications draws heavily from sports sciences. As educators Yiannis Koutedakis and Craig Sharp note:

> The prospect of the application of physiology and movement science to dance promises to enhance not only performance, but also safety . . . The scientific analysis of nutrition, strength, and cardiorespiratory demands of elite athletes has increased our

Figure 61 To strengthen hip flexors, a conditioning program for just 6 weeks, with the dancer practicing a modified leg raise, may be effective; Alona Christman demonstrates. (Adapted from Gayenne Grossman and M. Virginia Wilmerding, "The effect of conditioning on the height of dancer's extension in à la seconde," *Journal of Dance Medicine & Science* 4/4 (2000): 117–121.) (Photo by Angela Sterling)

understanding of the stresses placed upon the body in a great variety of sports, and in so doing has improved training techniques, enhanced performance, and helped to decrease the incidence of injuries. The application of these scientific analysis techniques to dance may reap similar benefits.[13]

Just as the preceding chapter asked how the science of physics is of practical importance to the dance profession (and drew heavily on physicist Kenneth Laws' work in exploring the question), in this chapter and the next we ask, "How is the science of exercise and sports of practical importance to dancers?" Studies now being conducted suggest that the fit and healthy dancer also is a top performer, less vulnerable to injury, and needing less recovery time when injuries do happen.

This is not to say that dancers need to become walking encyclopedias of exercise science, able to define "muscle function," "cardiorespiratory fitness," "overuse injuries," or "osteoporosis" at will. However, dancers can benefit greatly from the application of physiology and movement sciences to reduce injuries and to prevent burnout (i.e., overwork or overtraining syndrome, which afflicts dancers during periods of increased commitments to class or performance, when there is little time for recovery from physical activity).[14] In many ways, then, fit dancers work less hard than those who are unfit.[15]

This chapter covers conditioning in three important areas of fitness: muscular strength, cardiorespiratory endurance, and flexibility. There are other areas not considered here in any depth: body composition (discussed briefly in Chapter 5), anaerobic as well as aerobic capacities, muscle power and endurance, joint mobility, and balance or proprioception (discussed in Chapter 2).[16] Good conditioning programs will not produce undesirable bulk, make dancers slower, or reduce their flexibility, but will rather make them less vulnerable to injuries, perhaps illness, and maybe even better stage performers.[17] The examples presented here by no means include all the exercises and regimens dancers may want to try, but they do typify a breadth of effective conditioning regimens based on principles of dance science and the physical demands of classical ballet and contemporary dance. Those exercises that emphasize trunk or core stability are useful for most forms of social and world dance as well.

STRENGTH

Strength, or the maximum force that can be exerted in a single all-out effort, is important for the execution of many dance movements.[18] Strength training also may improve dance performance, enhance body composition, and reduce injury rates.[19] For young dancers, however, excessive loads may be damaging to the immature skeleton.

Much less is known about strength training for performance for adolescents than for adults. Certainly, the anatomical and physiological changes occurring during the adolescent growth spurt directly affect strength training and development (as discussed in Chapter 2). Rapidly changing proprioception and coordination must be taken into consideration when giving training guidelines. Caution must be taken to avoid injury to an immature musculoskeletal system, especially around the epiphyseal growth plates. In contrast, exercise to improve endurance can be safely practiced, as long as conditioning programs meet the criteria for intensity, frequency, and duration and the dancer is in good health. Note that the dancers should consult a physician or other primary healthcare professional before beginning any exercise, fitness, or health regimen.[20]

As mentioned in Chapter 2, the young dancer who experiences a rapid increase in height often has, in effect, longer and heavier limbs exerting increased biomechanical demands but inadequate muscle recruitment and strength to control them, putting him or her at risk for spinal injuries. Perhaps because of this, many specialists have been cautious in issuing guidelines for training. It is not even clear what are the most important contributors to strength in adolescents. Certainly, muscle size is a factor, but strength differences also may arise from the level of neurological maturation and the ability to activate a greater number of motor units within a muscle. This may be especially true for the preadolescent child.

As will be a theme elsewhere in this chapter, training efforts targeted at core stability are especially important for protection for the developing spine, literally providing the dancer with a solid core from which the limbs work, i.e., a "center."

How is strength training important in injury prevention? There is evidence that, for example, psoas (or other hip flexor) strengthening for greater hip movement may result in less harmful compensations.[21] Also mentioned was the role of the hip flexors in extending the leg to the side à la seconde. These muscles are also important in passé, développé, and grand ronde de jambe. Figure 62 illustrates some of the compensations dancers make when they do not possess sufficient strength to sustain a grand battement en avant. The dancer in the foreground is flexing the knee of her working (raised) leg; the dancer behind her (far right) is leaning backward, "cheating" by flexing the spine to achieve the look of high extension (hip flexion). To avoid such compensations, muscles must be sufficiently strong

Figure 62 Gigi Berardi, Mirabel Cruz, and Brenna Bond performing Saga Ambegaokar's *Moss*. Dance requires flexibility (flexing or extending the hip, thus raising the leg to a desired height) as well as strength (the ability to maintain a position against the resistance supplied by gravity). When dancers do not possess sufficient strength to sustain a grand battement, they will compensate by flexing the lower spine and the hip joint (as well as the knee), thus engaging the more powerful hip flexors instead of abdominal and lower-back muscles. Note also the varying degree of hip turnout of the dancers. (Photo by Bill Owen)

and flexible, and movement must be adequately coordinated to support the lifted weight. A conditioning program focused on hip flexors may help to achieve this.

In brief, dancers must have sufficient strength and flexibility for a sustained, full-height extension à la seconde (Figure 63); muscular power, or the ability of a muscle to exert force with speed, as in a rapid grand battement[22] (Figure 64); and muscular endurance, or the ability of a muscle to sustain a contraction or to contract repeatedly against moderate resistance, for example, in performing grands battements in rapid succession.

To do all this, is the training gained in class enough? For many it is not. Muscular strength, flexibility (including neural involvement), and power can be increased with conditioning programs. As researchers Gayanne Grossman and M. Virginia Wilmerding note, "The intent of a dance class is to develop the movement vocabulary of a specific idiom . . . and, therefore, it is not within the scope of class to provide adequate time for the development of strength, endurance, and flexibility for all muscle groups."[23]

Figure 63 Dancers must have sufficient flexibility for a full height extension à la seconde, and strength to maintain it; Sabine Chaland of the Dutch National Ballet demonstrates. (Photo by Angela Sterling)

Figure 64 Dancers also need muscular power (the ability of a muscle to exert force with speed), as demonstrated by Sabine Chaland. (Photo by Angela Sterling)

What can dancers do to achieve this strength? Former New York City Ballet principal Daniel Duell encouraged the dancers he directs to lift free weights. Duell says, "Dancers dance hard for 10 or 15 years and then fall apart physically. Strength training is necessary to prevent this."[24] Lifting free weights is just one way to train for strength. There are others: programs that, for resistance, use only body weight, or wall racks or machines, or belts and bands.

The types of training programs that are best suited to dancers' needs are discussed throughout this chapter. One general rule that applies to any regimen is that the dancer knows what the intent of each movement is and which muscles are being worked and why. The first thing is to determine the goal for doing an exercise or movement, including proper positioning of the body and stabilization of nonmoving body parts.

The following are specific questions to ask when considering a particular exercise, irrespective of whether it makes use of one's own body weight or machines, bands, or any of the various types of weights that are common in resistance training:[25]

1. What is the goal?
2. What are the joint motions?
3. What muscles are being used to create movement at the joints?
4. What is the appropriate path of motion?
5. What is the normal range of motion at the joint?
6. What is the active range of motion at the joint?
7. Is the overload effective in terms of the amount of resistance?
8. Is the direction of force or resistance in direct opposition (or as close as possible) to the movement pattern?
9. Is the body well stabilized?
10. Can the movement be performed correctly with the necessary stabilization maintained throughout the exercise?
11. How can the exercise be modified to make it safer/more effective?[26]

For example, in performing a "supine decline plank" with a stability ball or resistaball (Figure 24), the dancer first identifies the body parts to be strengthened—legs, hips, torso. The joint motions involved are hip extension (to achieve the plank), with stabilization at the shoulder girdle, spine, hips, legs, and ankles after the initial lift. The primary muscles strengthened are the gluteus maximus and hamstrings. The major stabilizing muscles—at least a dozen—include muscles in the torso and legs. The range of motion involves maintaining a neutral lumbar spinal position throughout the exercise. If the dancer is sufficiently strong, this is an excellent exercise for stability. The exercise is deceptively simple: just lift up, extend the hips, and breathe. However, maintaining the plank on the balance ball is an additional challenge.[27]

Core (or spine and pelvis) stabilization is really a goal unto itself. In fact, it is a focus of most of the exercises presented in this chapter. It is obviously important for the back not to buckle and move under forces that otherwise would compress or stretch sensitive structures in the spine. Instability of the spine, or an excessive range of abnormal movement with little or no protective muscular control, is quite different from hypermobility. Many dancers have hypermobile spines, meaning an excessive range of motion but with complete muscular control. The main characteristic of stability, then, is control of the entire range of motion of a joint. Such stability is even more challenging to maintain during dynamic alignment, when the body is moving.

Note that all conditioning exercises and programs presented in this chapter should be preceded by an adequate warmup, at least 10 minutes on a stationary bicycle or other exercise machine, light running in place, or performing movements requiring a change in level (e.g., as in nonimpact aerobics). Training sessions should be accompanied by static or slow stretching to reduce muscle soreness. Some coaches recommend waiting about 6 hours before stretching, since it is a form of recovery that may be counterproductive to the strengthening work.[28]

Warming Up

To dance, one has to be ready to move. The muscles have to be ready. The nervous system has to be ready. The dancer has to be focused on the activity at hand. The movement possibilities for warmups are enormous, and dancers often spend a lifetime discovering them for themselves.

Warming up is technically the preparatory period before the start of the main dance activity. Some dancers enjoy it; others consider it drudgery, a routine they must or should perform. Most dancers, however, realize that a good warmup is important for reducing the stress of rapid or sudden movements of the joints and for general health and injury prevention. A good warmup can also serve to control muscle soreness and enhance mechanical efficiency, not to mention relieve stress and, ultimately, prolong a performing career.

The ritual of warming up is centuries old. Yiannis Koutedakis reports how, in ancient Greece, covering the body with olive oil, indulging in massage, and using light exercise equipment typically were employed before athletic competitions as well as theater performances.[29] This preparation was considered to be part of the entire physical effort.

Is warming up merely ritual? Although there seem to be few scientific reports confirming the relationship between warming up and injury prevention, it is generally recognized that warmup, and the temperature increases that accompany it, have positive effects on aerobic fitness, flexibility, muscular strength, and power. There is, however, little agreement on the appropriate intensity, type, duration, or place of warmup.

Dancers usually warm up before every class, rehearsal, or stage performance. The length of time and the intensity of the warmup will depend on their level of fitness, class and performance demands, and individual preferences. As dancers get older, their warmups get progressively longer. The 15- to 20-minute routine of younger years becomes 30 or 45 or 60 minutes long. Perhaps younger dancers should also take more time and care to warm up, heeding the words spoken to me once by Erick Hawkins: "Of all the early people in Martha [Graham's] company, only Merce [Cunningham] and I warmed up, and I warmed up more than Merce and I am dancing more."[30]

Important benefits of warming up are to rehearse skills, focus on the upcoming performance, and relieve pre-performance anxiety. Getting both the body and mind ready is vital. Mental preparation might, in fact, be the more important part of preperformance activity.

In a good warmup, the dancer increases the core temperature of the body (which changes mechanical characteristics of muscle fibers, functional properties of the nervous system, and the efficiency of the cardiorespiratory system), the heart rate and thus blood flow to the muscles, muscle elasticity, the breathing rate as the diaphragm muscle warms up, and fluid movement into the joints. In addition, the warmup should increase the sensitivity of the nerve receptors.

The warmup can last anywhere from 5 minutes to 2 hours, although 20 to 40 minutes seems reasonable for most dancers. A basic problem is staying warm throughout class or performance. Cooling down can happen when teachers give many corrections during class, dancers are rehearsed in groups, or performers have to wait their turn to dance on stage. Eventually dancing "cold" will catch up with even the younger dancers. But older dancers (here I mean 40-something and above) will probably have to keep moving to keep their core temperature slightly raised.

At the end of class or performance, the cool-down is vital—a transition from dance to more pedestrian activity. If nothing else, abrupt cessation of exercise can lead to muscle soreness and cramping, hence the need to take approximately the same amount of time as with warmup, to slow down movements, stretch, and eventually come to rest.

The following suggestions are a primer for what should be done in a warmup.

A Warmup Primer

1. What: Increase the core temperature, heart rate, blood flow, breathing rate.

   How: Walking, prancing, gentle jogging (springing rather than running), knee bends —anything that involves a change in elevation of the body. Even moving the arms, large arm movements with no flinging, will increase the heart rate; nonimpact aerobics could be especially valuable for this. Although the general maxim, "Do not stretch to warm up, warm up to stretch," should be followed, once you are warmed up there still may be some problem areas (e.g., in the calf muscles) that are especially tight and need to be stretched before attempting vigorous movement. Studies show that active warmups (with some mild stretching) seem to produce the greatest benefits in terms of raising the body's core temperature and increasing overall flexibility.

2. What: Lubricate the joints, increase movement of fluid into the joints, although not to the point of overuse.

   How: Flexing and pointing the toes, circling the ankles. Movement of the torso in all directions. Shoulder rolls and drops, arm circles, gentle neck circles (side-to-side).

3. What: Focus on the performance; relieve emotional stress and anxiety. Try not to fixate on the tight costume, the slippery floor, the clumsy partner.

   How: Laughing, singing, meditating. The literature is rich with work on specific methods that enable performers to focus on rehearsal and performance.

4. What: Practice neuromuscular patterning, coordinating movements and patterns that produce balance, timing, and muscular control needed for performance.

   How: Repeating movement with attention to dynamic alignment. A ballet barre reinforces required neuromuscular patterning, especially for complex allegro work. Almost all the ballet dancers and many of the younger modern dancers I speak with usually do some barre as part of their warmup to establish the patterning of movement in the muscles, if nothing else. Another good warm-up is 20 to 25 minutes of C-I (conditioning with imagery) Training, performed in various positions on the floor, which borrows from many somatic disciplines.[31]

Strength Training Using Body Weight for Resistance

For some dancers, using their body weight for resistance is sufficient in conditioning. This includes the floor work of Kathryn Karipides; the core stabilization program of Stuart McGill (Figures 65, 66, 67, and 68), emphasizing muscular endurance as well as strength (maximal loading); many forms of yoga[32] (Figures 69 and 70); Pilates Method floor work (Figures 71 and 72); and GYROTONIC® and GYROKINESIS® Methods (Figure 73). Each is discussed in turn. Note that discussion of the somatic therapies presented in Chapters 2 and 3, including Ideokinesis and Alexander Technique, is also relevant to a discussion of conditioning approaches.[33]

Karipides Floor Work
Retired as chair and professor of dance at Case Western Reserve University (CWRU), Kathryn Karipides continues to practice a regimen she developed that uses body weight as resistance for strengthening. Karipides bases her strengthening methods on the muscle balance principles of Scandinavian gymnastics for "training and conditioning that does not sacrifice basic movement principles for a particular style of dance."[34] Her 30- to 45-minute

daily movement regimen maintains the body strength and mental fortitude that, as she says, "keeps [her] injury free." The work helps her to evaluate her dynamic flexibility, coordination, and agility.

Karipides draws on three main sources of movement systems and styles: Emily Andrews (a practitioner of Niels Bukh gymnastics who worked at CWRU), Erick Hawkins, and early modern dance pioneer Hanya Holm. Andrews, a former director of physical education at CWRU, was a devotee of the gymnastics system developed by Bukh, which was based on "Danish gymnastics" and is freer in style and range of motion than that allowed by standard Swedish gymnastics.[35]

Karipides credits Erick Hawkins for expanding her free-flowing movement vocabulary and Hanya Holm for her introduction to a creative kinetic vocabulary. Much of Hawkins work is a logical progression from the Bukh gymnastics work ("continuous work proceeding from one exercise to another without stopping [in which] unison need not be stressed . . . extension without tension").[36] Karipides accepts this and adds, "There are universal physical truths that can't be denied, whether you call it gymnastics or a particular form of dance. Much of modern technique has added quirks and cosmetics, and it's easy to focus on these rather than the basis of the movement—the strength of the pelvic muscles and the alignment of the torso."

The movement Karipides has developed emphasizes agility (the ability to make changes in position and movement quickly), imagery (the ability to imagine fluid shapes and forms that actually affect movement and balance between different muscle groups), and opposition (no body part is ever inactive as one knee flexes, the other is extended, always in opposition, and engaging the entire body), and clarity.

Core Stabilization

Core stabilization has been much written about in the literature. For example, University of Waterloo professor Stuart McGill conducts research on problems of lumbar function, low-back injury mechanisms, tissue loading during rehabilitation programs, and injury-avoidance strategies.[37]

McGill presents evidence that muscular endurance (as opposed to strength) is more protective of the spine. He further deconstructs sacred cows such as breathing-on-the-exertion in strength training, arguing, for example, that core stabilization is important during all phases of breathing. He discusses how some exercises are better than others for training and impose lower loads on the spine. For example, traditional sit-ups with the knees bent cause supine loading conditions that greatly elevate the risk of injury; in fact, sit-ups can produce compression levels close to the National Institute for Occupational Safety and Health (NIOSH) action limit. There is little evidence that they increase back health; the same is true for toe touches. All of these can cause core instability. Rather, there are far better ways of challenging the abdominal musculature and imposing lower lumbar spine loads. Stabilization exercises thus need to emphasize the grooving, or establishment, of dynamic complex motor patterns, without imposing unduly large loads on the spine. Such grooving also should include normal breathing; the spine and pelvis need to be stabilized during all phases of breathing.

Note, however, that although a stable spine with a neutral pelvis is desired in upright stances, there is no ideal sitting position. Certainly, the hips and knees bent at 90 degrees with a neutral spine is ideal, but not many people can hold this for longer than 10 minutes! The ideal sitting position is really one that continuously changes, thus preventing any one tissue from experiencing too much strain. Tissue loads can then migrate and thus reduce the risk of overtaxing any single tissue. Therefore, it is important to vary the sitting position—getting out of the chair or off the floor; just maintaining a relaxed standing posture for 10 to 20 seconds (with the back extended) can relieve stress.

Dancers (as well as the general public) also should avoid strenuous exercise just after rising in the morning, especially movement that involves full spine flexion or bending, given the increased tissue stresses that result. This stress is due in large part to fluid shifts and disc expansion that occur at night. For much the same reason, dancers should avoid exertion after prolonged flexion (like sitting in rehearsal!), instead spending at least some time standing upright before attempting more strenuous exertions.

Core stabilization exercises can be performed every day (this is more than the three-times-a-week recommendation for strengthening in general). Combining such a program with cardiorespiratory work, in particular fast walking, is effective in terms of strength gains. More repetitions of less demanding exercises will enhance endurance.

For any task, the order and type of loading should be considered, and demand on tissue should be varied. Variable positions, and postures, are thus critical, especially for dancers who spend much time watching rehearsal, waiting to perform, or repeatedly practicing a movement. The key to safety is variety. So, moderation in all things applies to much of biomechanics—and dancers' work in general!

Such exercises require abdominal bracing or core stabilization (a term preferred by many dancers and somatic educators) and a neutral spine throughout the movement. In stabilizing, the dancer activates the abdominal muscles, neither hollowing nor pushing out, activating all three layers of the abdominal wall (external oblique, internal oblique, transversus abdominis). Positions should be held for 7 to 8 seconds, with the dancer increasing repetitions rather than the duration of each hold. The dancer can begin with a warmup and the cat/camel motion (Figure 65) to reduce viscous stresses. Slow lunges to stretch the hip flexors also are advised (Figure 66), with the dancer maintaining a stable spine throughout.

Since the various abdominal muscles have different functions, several different types of exercises are needed to challenge them in all their roles. For example, a curl-up exercise will activate all portions of the rectus abdominis. The following three exercises and their progression are recommended for a basic core stabilization program. As mentioned above, lung ventilation should become independent of the exercise exertion, since the spine should be stabilized whether one is inhaling or exhaling, except for extreme efforts needed for power weight lifting.[38] A goal is to train the motor system so as to stabilize the spine during dynamic performance.

Exercises for abdominal muscles as part of a basic core stabilization program include:

- Curl-ups for the rectus abdominis (Figure 67).
- Variation of the side bridge for the obliques, transversus abdominis, and quadratus. (see Figure 34; this is an advanced version).
- Leg and arm extensions leading to progressions of the "birddog" (Figure 68) for the numerous back extensors. For the curl-up (Figure 67), start supine on the floor, with the hands supporting the lower back. The back should not be flattened, which removes the elastic equilibrium. Bending one leg with the knee flexed to 90 degrees helps to prevent the lumbar spine from flattening. Lift the torso so that the motion is confined to the midthoracic or thoracic area (upper part of the torso); there should be no flexion of either the lumbar (lower back) or cervical (in the area of the neck) spines. The tongue can be placed on the roof of the mouth behind the teeth, which

Figure 65 Core stabilization: Positions should be held for 7 to 8 seconds. The cow/camel movement can be used as a warmup to reduce the viscous stresses of prolonged sitting. Here, the first part of the exercise is demonstrated by Alona Christman. (Photo by Angela Sterling)

Figure 66 Core stabilization: Lunges are a good exercise for challenging strength, endurance, balance, and mobility in the lower torso and extremities. To spare the back, an upright torso should be maintained. This psoas stretch requires the torso to be laterally bent, away from the extended hip. (Photo by Angela Sterling)

Figure 67 Core stabilization: Curl-up for the rectus abdominis: more advanced, with the elbows lifted so as not to raise the shoulders. (Photo by Angela Sterling)

helps to promote neck stability patterns. Advanced forms of the exercise involve raising the elbows an inch or less and then placing the fingers lightly on the forehead.

Isometric exercises for the neck can relieve any neck symptoms experienced during curl-ups. Recommended exercises include those with the hands placed on the forehead, resisting neck flexion effort; the side of the head, resisting cervical side flexion; and the back of the head, resisting cervical extension—all of which help to strengthen and stabilize the neck.[39]

In the side-bridge, the knees and hips are flexed (more so if the spine and pelvic muscles are weak), so that most of the body (above the knees) is in the same plane. In all of these variations, the forward foot should be on the floor in front of the other foot. For those who are less strong, a modified bridge, either standing or lying on the floor, barely raising the legs off the floor or even just barely taking the weight off the legs, can be effective. Place the free hand on the opposite shoulder or, for more load, along the side. Straightening the legs increases the difficulty of the exercise. Higher levels of activation are reached with transferring from one elbow to the other (one side to the other) while stabilizing the abdominals, or placing the feet on a labile (unstable) surface, like a resistaball or gym ball. An advanced form of side-bridge is to lift the top leg, while maintaining a stable spine (Figure 34).

For the leg and arm extensions leading to progressions of the "birddog" (Figure 68), begin with the hands and knees on the floor—the hands under the shoulders and the knees directly under the hips—then raise one leg and the opposite arm, simultaneously. Neither the arm nor the leg should go past horizontal (i.e., they should be in line with the spine). To progress, the dancer should not rest after each repetition but make the transition more continuous, sweeping the floor with the hand and the knee.

Such exercises have various progressions, which are explained in more detail in McGill's *Low-Back Disorders*, as well as in work by Dixie Stanforth and colleagues at the University of Texas.[40] Adding a resistaball or any labile foam surface (a wedge, perhaps) is desirable in that it incorporates proprioceptive challenge and more complex, skilled spinal action (Figure 23).

Figure 68 Core stabilization: Leg and arm extensions leading to progressions of the "birddog" for the back extensors, avoiding raising the arm or leg past horizontal. For further challenge, after extending the normal birddog position, to repeat the exercise, brush the floor with the hand and knee before extending again (rather than putting full weight on either). (Photo by Angela Sterling)

Such exercises serve as the foundation of a basic strengthening program. Yet, because of the fascial connections and force transmission among the shoulder musculature, the spine, and the abdominals, exercises involving larger movement patterns are needed as well, examples of which are given in the Pilates and GYROKINESIS® exercises that follow. All exercises presented in this chapter should be undertaken only after any restrictions in soft tissue have been addressed (see Chapter 2).

Core control or stability is a function of several muscles. P. Hodges and C. Richardson and colleagues in Australia have identified the transversus abdominis as a major postural control muscle.[41] Another postural control muscle group is the deep abdominal muscles or the multifidi, which have a disproportionately larger number of muscle spindles (in the lumbar spine) than any other muscles in the lower torso.[42] The multifidi thus serve as a great source of kinesthetic feedback in core awareness, the loss of which can show an asymmetrical recruitment of the multifidi on the affected side of the body, leading to a decrease in core awareness and control.

In fact, the lumbar multifidus has been shown to be the most important stabilizer of the lumbosacral junction, providing more than one-third of the stability contributed by muscle contraction.[43] Almost all muscles play a role in stability, but their importance varies. Focusing on one muscle (e.g., the transversus abdominis in abdominal hollowing) can lead to overflexion of the lumbar joints and passive tissues, especially among beginning students. More advanced students can perform hollowing moves with a neutral spine. Exhaling enables recruitment of the transversus abdominis, but abdominal stabilizing activates it together with the internal and external obliques. Researchers conclude that abdominal bracing (or core stabilization) is superior to hollowing in terms of achieving core stability, with the abdominal wall neither hollowed nor pushed out. Such movements activate all muscular layers of the abdominal wall. The various abdominal muscles—the rectus abdominis, external and internal obliques, and transversus abdominis—may work independently as well as together. Thus, several different types of exercises would be needed to challenge them in all of their roles.

Yoga (for Strengthening and Stretching)

Yoga is probably one of the oldest and most widely known disciplines that offer conditioning for the body, mind, and spirit.[44] More commonly regarded for its flexibility benefits, already flexible dancers can realize substantive strength gains with yoga using just body weight for resistance. The practice of yoga poses, or *asanas*, is more than physical exercise; it is a spiritual practice. According to one ancient text, the *Gheranda Samhita,* "There are eighty-four hundreds of thousands of Asanas described by Shiva. The postures are as many in number as there are numbers of species of living creatures in this universe."[45]

Some basic ideas emerge in the writings on yoga:

- The body is an instrument of attainment.
- The yogi masters the body by the practice of asanas.
- The yogi performs asanas to develop complete equilibrium of the body, mind, and spirit.
- The body, mind, and spirit are inseparable.[46]

Dancer Lori Brungard speaks of the rebalancing that comes with the practice of yoga.[47] Yoga, millennia old, conditions the body as well as the mind. The different approaches include Ashtanga, Iyengar, Jivamukti, Kundalini, and Sivananda. Hundreds of poses are designed to refresh, renew, realign, and heal body tissues. For almost all practitioners, the spiritual dimensions are as important as the physical. Examples of multipurpose poses (strengthen and stretch) are the warrior and triangle poses, given in Figures 69 and 70.[48] Dancers may want to avoid yoga poses that overstretch knee and ankle ligaments.

Pilates Method Floor Work

Joseph H. Pilates (also discussed in Chapter 2) developed a series of exercises to enhance muscle control, proper breathing, and biomechanical and postural stabilization, as well as overall strength and muscular endurance. The Pilates system is perhaps best known by its machine-based exercises. Yet many dancers also condition just by using their body weight for resistance.[49] The focus of all Pilates work is on concentration, control, precision, and fluidity of movement.[50] Examples of floor exercises are given in Figures 71 and 72.

Pilates—Man and Method

Almost 75 years have passed since Joseph and Clara Pilates opened their studio in New York, intended for those who wanted to learn and teach a program of health and fitness enhancement. With all the popularity and accessibility of work involving the Pilates Method early on, it might be overlooked that it was the performing arts community that frequented the Pilates studio for this unique "exercise therapy" (originally called "contrology").

Within the past 40 years, since Pilates' death, this popular conditioning and rehabilitation approach has become widely known. Promoted in magazines as varied as *Lear's, Vogue, Newsweek,* and *Cooking Lite* and widely available in gyms, hospitals, universities, and private studios across the country, movie stars, sports icons, and dance students alike are enjoying

Figure 69 Yoga poses for all-body conditioning. Warrior II, as demonstrated by Alona Christman. (Photo by Angela Sterling)

Figure 70 Triangle: The palm of the right hand may be placed along the outside of the left ankle. (Photo by Angela Sterling)

Figure 71 Pilates: Kristin Torok demonstrates the Hundred, knees flexed, feet on the floor. (Photo by Angela Sterling)

Figure 72 Pilates: The Teaser. (Photo by Angela Sterling)

the benefits from the training system. The utility of the approach has also been recognized by dance companies (Boston Ballet, Pacific Northwest Ballet, San Francisco Ballet, and Houston Ballet, among others), many of which have facilities on site for dancers. Others have facilities close by: New York City Ballet sends its dancers to Westside Dance Physical Therapy, and the Cleveland Ballet to the Cleveland Clinic Foundation Dance Medicine Division. Facilities in universities with dance departments abound. In short, Pilates as an approach has been well received, with more than 175 dance departments and 120 dance companies using the method.

GYROKINESIS®

The goal of GYROKINESIS®[51] floor work is to promote core stability and overall flexibility. Since the work includes supine, prone, and seated exercises as well as mat-work, dancers who need to work in a partial or non–weight-bearing status can easily do so. According to practitioner Kristin Torok, "The approach works especially well for dancers, since much of the movement is three-dimensional, and includes full range of motion—simulating actual dance." The exercise in Figure 73 shows the multiple planes of movement utilized.[52]

Figure 73 GYROKINESIS® movements emphasize fluidity, connectivity, and rhythm, as demonstrated by practitioner Kristin Torok. (Photo by Angela Sterling)

STRENGTH TRAINING USING INCREASED RESISTANCE[53]

Dancers are necessarily concerned with stabilizing their core, that is, their pelvic and abdominal muscles, for safe movement of the torso as well as for meeting aesthetic requirements by maintaining a compact and sturdy body. Some dancers prefer the variety offered by using increased resistance and the relatively quick fitness gains it offers. Using increased resistance makes sense: over time specific bodily adaptations to a given amount of resistance will occur (the key is knowing when that point in conditioning has been reached). The body adapts precisely to what is demanded of it; unless the demands or stress on the body are increased and varied, no increase in strength will occur.

A General Adaptation Syndrome (GAS), first described by Dr. Hans Selye, provides a framework within which a strengthening program using weights may be designed for dancers.[54] The theory states that whenever any stressor (including productive stress such as exercise) is experienced by the body, adaptations are made (after an initial response of shock or alarm) so that future exposures to the stressor will be less disruptive. Over time, a strenuous workout program results in specific and quantifiable bodily adaptations. It should be remembered that adaptations to strength training also occur at the neural[55] and metabolic[56] levels.

Thus, strength-training programs should:

- Begin gradually to ease through the shock or alarm phase of GAS.
- Be varied in content, intensity, and duration of workouts for constant improvement.
- Include occasional breaks from the routine to change the stressor input to the body and to avoid damage to the tissues.[57]

Dance educator Karen Clippinger points out that,

> . . . overload criteria indicate the importance of careful class design to provide the appropriate magnitude and progression of overload. If class demands are too similar day to day, there will be insufficient overload for the desired improvement. [On the other hand, dance] teachers and students . . . are notorious for noticing a weakness or problem and wanting it changed immediately . . . This approach utilizes too extreme an overload applied for too short a time . . . Careful selection of an appropriate mode of progressively increasing overload in small increments over several months is often necessary to achieve the desired gains.[58]

In addition to overload, specificity is important in designing training programs. Optimal gains may require a training overload similar in intensity and duration to the goal movement. For example, performing slow tendus has little relation to building the strength needed for fast grands battements; many of the same muscles are used, but the velocity and hip joint angle are quite different and there is a different recruitment of muscle fiber types.[59]

One consideration in specificity is the type of resistance used. For example, elastic resistance, in the form of bands, tubes, or other material, allows the dancer to strengthen with resistance when performing actual dance moves. Other forms of resistance include free weights—whether dumbbells and barbells in a gym or cans of soup and other household items. Stationary machines use weights or springs to provide resistance.

Besides overload and specificity, two other principles apply to training regimens: reversibility and individuality. Basically, training gains are reversible, owing to injury, aging, illness, or inactivity. The duration of training (the longer the training period, the slower the detraining) is just one of several factors that affect the rate of reversibility.

Lastly, because of the unique physical, physiological, and psychological characteristics, not to mention injury history of each dancer, it is imperative that training programs be individualized as much as possible. Thus, the utility of mimicking successful training programs elsewhere is questionable, as is establishing a single conditioning program for an entire dance company.[60] In a very real sense, dancers can be their own best teachers and therapists in developing a personal training program, which is why dancers' access to information (and resources) is important. Before starting a conditioning program, a medical evaluation is important. Such an evaluation provides a baseline against which later fitness gains can be measured. Furthermore, such a practice is a good habit for children and adults alike, since many illnesses and diseases, if detected early, have a better chance of being successfully treated.

The principles given above can be applied to a strengthening program in dance.[61]

The easier workout may begin with two sets of 10 repetitions (reps),[62] then move to three sets of 6 reps, and eventually to three sets of 10 reps, with enough stamina to do three or four more per session, at least two times per week for each major muscle group of the body.[63] The weight lifted should feel comfortable and somewhat challenging; otherwise, technique may suffer.[64]

The number of reps performed in the program, however, should vary with the movement exercise. For example, the larger muscle groups should be worked fewer reps than the abdominals and smaller or single muscle groups.[65]

Paramount to safe and effective strength training is that correct technique in lifting should never be sacrificed for higher resistance (lifting more weight). Even a minimal hiking of the hip when lifting the leg to the side can have a dramatic effect on the way the muscles are used. Correct technique also involves core stability, maintained on inhalation as well as exhalation. The dancer should control the movement through its full range, rather than rely on the momentum of the movement. Also, to enhance flexibility, the muscles should be worked throughout their full range of motion. This is relatively easy to do with free weights. This does not mean that the movement always has to be performed slowly.

The speed of the movement is part of the intensity component of a training program. The speed with which the movement exercises are executed affects the way the body adapts to them. If the muscle groups being exercised are used "explosively" in the movement (such as large jumps) the dancer is training for, then the specific movement exercise should be performed quickly. This also assists in neuromuscular learning, or training the nervous system. In addition, it helps to prepare the tendons and other connective tissue to withstand the large forces and accelerations required in the jump.

Usually, when it becomes possible to lift the current resistance for a greater number of repetitions in the set, the resistance must be increased. This does not mean that the weight must be increased consistently; on a 3-days-a-week program it would be best to have one heavy, one light, and one medium training day. Remember that some type of variability must be incorporated into any training program if progress is to result. Runners, for example, run different distances at different paces (intensity) from day to day. Otherwise, total adaptation of the body occurs and no event is sufficiently specific to result in strength gains.

Larger muscles should be exercised first because smaller muscles tend to fatigue more readily. For example, if the goal is to develop leg and hip strength using free weights or conventional resistance machines, leg presses and other lower-body exercises should be performed first. The rest of the movement exercises should be put in a specific order so that single-joint movement exercises come last.

Above all, the individual needs of the dancer must be considered in designing any conditioning program. Exercises that closely replicate movement demands of the dance form should be used. It is clear that many dancers are not interested in body building and muscle definition per se. Rather, they are more concerned with the strength increments needed for the repertory or movement they are dancing, which may vary throughout the season.

In view of their functional needs, dancers should train in cycles: strength training for a given period of weeks (this also can be done between rehearsals), followed by stamina and general fitness conditioning, perhaps preparing mentally and emotionally by reading, reviewing videotapes of other performances, or working with coaches. This planned and organized variety is referred to as periodization of training.[66]

A sampling of types of strength training is discussed below. Specificity of training should be one important guide.[67] Beginning with elastic resistance, mentioned also in Chapter 2 as a favorite tool of rehabilitation, I then briefly look at resistance machines and free weights, the type of equipment one is more likely to find in a conventional gym (examined more extensively in the first edition of *Finding Balance)*. Finally, I discuss popular forms of strengthening, with an emphasis on core stability—in particular, Pilates Method. Although the machines used in Pilates are similar to standard resistance machines in principle (the speed of movement is constant), they also are different and are discussed in greater detail later.

Elastic Resistance

A number of elastic bands and tubing are commercially available for conditioning programs. The resistance is usually determined by the thickness of the band. Bands of different thickness can be used individually or in combination for greater resistance. This form of resistance exercise also can be used to develop increased range of motion. For more, see Noa Spector-Flock's excellent *Get Stronger by Stretching with Thera-Band,*[68] which describes a specific program with Therabands, use of the band, rationale for the product (which is the exercise band endorsed by the American Physical Therapy Association), forces produced, how the bands compare to free weights and complement Pilates work, and precautions for starting a program. Another program, developed by dance kinesiologist Judy Gantz, outlines a similar program for strengthening, and is described and illustrated in the first edition of *Finding Balance.*

One of the main advantages of using elastic bands or tubing for resistance exercise is its variability. Training can easily include all three mechanical conditions of muscle contraction (see Appendix A: Anatomy Basics); it also delivers a variable force when the band or tubing is stretched.[69] Unlike most machines, the speed of movement during the muscle contraction also can be varied.[70]

Precautions should be taken when doing resistance work with elastic bands or tubing:

- Exercise care in performing high-resistance work and consult a physician before starting a conditioning program (especially for trainees with hypertension problems).
- Perform abduction and adduction movement exercises with the band tied above the knee joint (especially for trainees with a history of knee problems).
- Perform exercises through the full range of motion of the joint or, at the very least, the end-point of the ROM to be exercised should be considered.
- Take care in estimating the starting amount of resistance that is desired.
- Use a starting length of band or tubing approximately equal to the length of the limb segment being worked (e.g., a 12-inch forearm length requires a 12-inch length of band for shoulder external rotation).

- Begin the movement with a slight stretch on the band.
- Maintain correct alignment, especially in standing exercises, at all times. When bending the knees, the dancer can visualize an imaginary line running from the hip to the center of the knees, then to a point on the side border of the second toe; in sitting, the dancer needs to be on top of the sits bones, with the head extending as a continuation of the back. Shoulders should be broad and not elevated. Knees and elbows should not be locked.[71]
- Increase resistance by proceeding to the next color of band or adding additional bands or tubing.[72]
- Breathe evenly while performing the exercises.[73]

To these guidelines, Spector-Flock adds: work simply, work deeply, work evenly. In short, be aware.[74] Spector-Flock's program consists of work for the center of the body, the lower body, the upper body, as well as various warmups. She also addresses the special needs of dancers, demonstrated in Figures 30 and 31. Ballet barre exercises could consist of tendus (being careful to move from the hip joint, spreading the toes and going through demi-point, repeating en croix), dégagé, frappé (for example, with a wrapped foot sur le cou-de-pied), développé (using the barre hand to increase the tension on the band as the leg extends; see Figure 31), and grand battement, with the torso staying as stable as possible.[75]

For dancers, the pattern of resistance should match that which is demanded in dance; typically, the exercises are performed in three sets of 10 reps for 3 days a week. The intensity—the amount of resistance worked against the band—should be varied for strength gains to occur: one day should be heavy, one medium, and one light. Dancers should start slowly with the exercises before pushing for heavier resistance work loads.[76] For all these exercises, place the band around the midfoot area. Either dorsiflex, plantar flex (Figure 25), invert, or wing the foot, feeling the muscles working in the specific leg area.

Resistance Machines

Some would argue that isokinetic training in which a constant speed of motion is maintained is especially useful in rehabilitation to restore motor performance skills such as running and jumping. Yet in a general conditioning program there are other considerations. Exercising at a constant movement speed (as opposed to exercising with acceleration, as with free weights) means that no acceleration is present, and in this sense it is not specific to real-life dance movement patterns. However, the advantages offered by the machines—convenience, safety control, training at high speeds—outweigh the disadvantages, especially if strength-training programs use a combination of free weights and machines.[77]

Undoubtedly, the machines are easy to use; resistance is adjusted merely by changing the position of a metal pin or pushing buttons on a digital readout. Compared to free weights, machines are often preferred in large facilities because of their convenience and their safety features.[78] (A sample strengthening program using Cybex machines is given in the first edition of *Finding Balance*.)

Free Weights for Resistance

Free weights, usually barbells or dumbbells, are often recommended for strength training in dance because they require dancers to balance both themselves and the weight, rather than allowing the machine to do it. This results in greater muscle coordination during the exertion phase of a movement. Free weights also permit a freer range of movement; machines are more limiting in this respect. Some machines have good two-dimensional range of movement, but they do not imitate freely moving bodies accelerating in three-dimensional space.

Since muscle groups are not worked in isolation in dance, a sample strengthening program should emphasize multiple-joint exercises. These are often called "total body" exercises, since many joints and muscles of the body are involved. Two examples are:

1. *Push jerk*: hip and leg extension (explosive strength or power). This exercise begins with hand-held weights resting partly on the shoulders. Bend the knees, then thrust the weights straight upward with quick knee and hip extension. Lastly, the weights are caught and held steady overhead with the knees bent, which straighten for final support.[79]

2. *Lunge*: hip and leg extension. This exercise can be performed with either hand-held dumbbells or a barbell held on the shoulders behind the head. With the dumbbells, grip strength is also developed, especially as the load is increased. The movement begins from a parallel standing position; vertical alignment is maintained throughout by isometric contraction of the spinal erectors. Move one leg forward in a lunge and lower the body toward the floor so that the lead knee is approximately over the lead foot at the lowest part of the lunge. Reverse the movement by pushing up and back with the lead foot. It may take several small backward steps to return to the original parallel position.

Advanced trainees can perform 5 to 10 consecutive lunges on the same leg before alternating sides. For dancers, it is probably best to alternate legs to avoid fatiguing the muscle. As a variation, the barbell can be held on the front of the shoulders and clavicles. Also, the movement can be completed by stepping forward with the leg. As with all exercises with free weights, dancers must be very careful to maintain good vertical alignment throughout the movement, especially when increasing the intensity of the workout (heavier weights or higher reps).

As more and more professional companies offer weight-training facilities and dancers are able to afford the time and money to work in private studios and gyms, dancers will become more comfortable with using free weights. Kent Stowell, co-artistic director of Pacific Northwest Ballet, says[80]: "Weight training in professional ballet is no longer the exception, it is the norm. Our new studios will have a strength-training room complete with Pilates and Universal machines, barbells, and dumbbells. Dancers need to train with the free weights, especially to meet the demands of the abstract and modern ballets in our repertory."

Pilates

Pilates technique has been used by dance pioneers such as Ruth St. Denis, Ted Shawn, Martha Graham, Helen Tamiris, Hanya Holm, Pearl Primus, and George Balanchine. It is one of the most common methods of strength training used by professional dancers today.[81]

As mentioned earlier, Joseph H. Pilates originally designed his work using spring tension as the resistant force to work against to build strength. Several pieces of equipment incorporating the spring tension followed, including the popular "Universal Reformer," a sliding horizontal bed on which the dancer may pull or push against a metal bar or leather straps (it was said to look like a giant sliding mousetrap). The resistance is provided by detachable springs (these are color-coded; different colors and different numbers of springs can be

Figure 74 Former Pacific Northwest Ballet principal Lisa Apple demonstrates Pilates exercises using the universal reformer. In the "Twist" of the "side-sitting series," Apple rotates around her spinal column, activating the oblique abdominal muscles, moving against a stabilized torso. (Photo by Angela Sterling)

added for resistance). Many dance movements, such as plié, relevé, développé, and batte-ment, can be performed in turned-out and parallel positions with the machine (Figures 74 through 78).

Other parts of the Pilates program feature core stabilization (for which many dancers use the technique unassisted by machines), for Pilates himself believed that core control was at the heart of controlling human movement. This continues today to be a major feature of the work. Studies are underway to clinically verify the efficacy of the exercises.

A typical Pilates conditioning program might occur in three phases. First there is assisted movement with the use of springs, with a focus on isolating the movement in question in-dependent of the pelvis or spine. The work, in principle, emphasizes more efficient use of deep, stabilizing muscles (transversus abdominis, multifidi, internal and external obliques). The second phase might include dynamic stabilization or challenging the newly acquired mobility or stability in a functional and gravity-dependent environment. This is achieved by decreasing the base of support or increasing the length of the levers in order to increase the difficulty of the movement or exercise. The third phase might consist of functional reeducation in both a foreign (with the spring-resistance machine) and a familiar (jump-ing unsupported in the studio) environment, with the final goal of becoming autonomous of the movement. The Pilates Universal Reformer exercises are well suited for multijoint, multidimensional movement and can be progressively modified, moving from the Pilates Reformer to weight-bearing exercises in class.

Figure 75 Pilates: In the "Hug-a-Tree" exercise, Lisa Apple begins with the arms extended to the side, and then draws them in, as if "hugging a tree." The tendency is to lean forward. Instead, the stable core should keep the body upright. This exercise also works the latissimus dorsi and other back extensors. (Photo by Angela Sterling)

Figure 76 Pilates: "Eve's Lunge" or the "Hamstring stretch I," side view, can work both the hamstrings and hip flexors, depending on how vertical the spine is, and the positions of the foot on the floor and of the front leg. (Photo by Angela Sterling)

Figure 77 Pilates: In the "Swan," either facing front or with a twist to the side, the back extensors are fully engaged. (Photo by Angela Sterling)

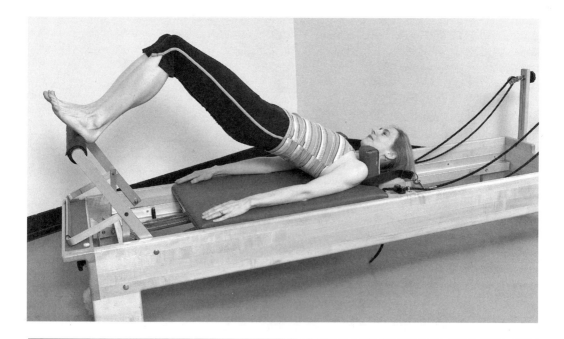

Figure 78 Pilates: In the "Bridge," Lisa Apple begins with her spine on the mat, peeling off the surface very slowly against a stable spine. (Photo by Angela Sterling)

ENDURANCE

Cardiorespiratory endurance in dance refers to the uptake, transport, and utilization of oxygen to release moderate levels of energy from (primarily) carbohydrates and fats.[82] It is not clear that stamina enhances dance performance, but it does assist in decreasing recovery time between movement sequences and increasing anaerobic endurance (exercise or energy pathways of muscle that do not require oxygen, useful in, for example, sustained jumping lasting more than 10 seconds), in part because the muscles are trained to use fat and spare glycogen stores (see Chapter 5 for further discussion).

Given the increasing demands of choreography, both physiologically and in the variety of the skills required, it is not surprising that dancers may fall short of the strength and stamina required. Rather, dancers tend to resemble strength athletes physiologically.[83]

But dance is intermittent in nature, and rehearsal periods may be insufficient to allow for the fitness gains needed for the increased demands of performance. Studies have shown differences in the possible endurance training effects of different parts of class—warmup and center work in a modern class[84] and barre and center work in a ballet class.[85] Thus, there seems to be a difference in the intensity at which training (dance class) and dance performance are conducted,[86] which is related to class size and the amount of verbal instruction given between exercises. It may well be that class needs to be modified or supplemental training added to accomplish the conditioning needed.

Much of dance itself takes place in intervals of several minutes followed by varying periods of rest. The movement is either moderately intense with a strong isometric component during adagio dancing, or it is a highly intense, brief-duration exercise, such as jumps or leaps (Figure 79). Sometimes this highly intense exercise must be sustained. In the original staging of *Annie Get Your Gun*, Daniel Nagrin was required to run and jump for 2 $1/2$ minutes with one 4-second break, ending with 16 continuous jumps in place, 12 of them split-jumps—a sustained endurance event by any standard.

Dance movements, thus, can be categorized according to the length of work and the power required. Most dance (for example, the movements listed in Table 3) would not be considered true "endurance work," lasting at least 15 or 20 minutes in which the dancer maintains a heart rate of 55 to 85 percent of maximal heart rate.[87]

The heart rates of dancers during performances of classical ballets such as *Swan Lake* and *La Bayadère* have been measured by researchers.[88] They found that the longest single period of nonstop dancing was 7 minutes and that the overall performance demands tended to fall into the category of "interval work": 2 to 3 minutes of intense activity followed by 2 to 3 minutes of rest. For such work, dancers use both intermediate and short-term energy systems. For intense activity (say, 30-second bursts), energy must be generated very rapidly, much of it in an oxygen-deprived (anaerobic) muscular environment.[89] To train the short-term energy system, activities must be selected that engage the muscles needed for power movements.[90] This usually involves strength training that increases the intensity of overload during maximum bursts of effort.

Although most dance cannot be characterized as true, uninterrupted endurance exercise, continuous movement performed for more than 2 minutes (as in Nagrin's solo mentioned above) will use energy from aerobic as well as anaerobic energy systems. This work requires dancers to have a highly trained oxygen transport or aerobic energy system and a well-conditioned heart and vascular system that can circulate large quantities of oxygenated blood for relatively long duration. The weak link in oxygen delivery in normal populations (unless one has a respiratory disability) is the cardiovascular, not the pulmonary, system. For elite endurance-trained populations, the limiting factor is seen at the

Figure 79 Dance is characterized by short-burst activities as seen in movements performed by Pacific Northwest Ballet's Olivier Wevers in José Limón's *The Moor's Pavane*. (Photo by Angela Sterling)

Table 3 Duration and Power Requirements of Dance Movements

Exercise	Duration (seconds)	Power
Tendu en croix	30	Moderate intensity
Rond de jambe with allegro component	60	Moderate intensity
Combination with grand battement	30	Maximum short-burst
Combination with jumps	30	Maximum short-burst

muscle cell level, where energy is produced.[91] Dancers also usually try to maintain low body fat, and endurance work may be essential to fat breakdown.[92] For discussion purposes in this chapter and unless otherwise stated, "endurance" refers to cardiorespiratory, not muscular, endurance.

Dancers must be able to sustain physical activity with little fatigue, especially since fatigue is an important factor in the causation of injury. In training and rehearsal, dancers become easily fatigued when, for example, their technique is incorrect (e.g., sickling the foot in relevé) or inadequate (e.g., landing from a jump without loading weight on the heel); when they have not had enough fluid (i.e., at least 64 ounces per day) or calorie intake (see Chapter 5); and when they are stressed or overloaded with training and performance demands.

Fatigue is a way of life for many professional dancers. One way to minimize fatigue is to condition the heart and blood vessels for efficient delivery of oxygen to the working muscles, possibly reducing muscular fatigue pain. A case in point is work with Twyla Tharp.

Much of the movement Twyla Tharp choreographs could be classified as endurance exercise. The rehearsals should have almost a training effect for the dancers, especially when the company runs two demanding pieces such as *Sue's Leg* and *Four Down Under* back to back. Much of the choreography of Laura Dean, Molissa Fenley, Danny Smith/Joanie Shapiro, Lynne Taylor Corbett, and others is also "aerobic." It is continuous, moderate exercise for at least 12 to 15 minutes.

Endurance Conditioning

Class and Rehearsal

What training do dancers receive to be able to dance at a moderate intensity uninterrupted for 15 minutes or more? Often the training is in class or rehearsal itself. As mentioned above, rehearsal periods are often short and do not allow enough time for physiological demands to meet the aerobic power requirements of performance. As researchers Steven Chatfield and William Byrnes suggest, advanced and professional dancers—without any supplemental training—seem to have above average aerobic capacities when compared with the general population (40 to 50 milliliters/kilogram of body weight/minute [ml/kg/min]).[93]

Studies reviewing the literature on physiological responses to dance training report a maximal oxygen uptake for female and male dancers of about 45 to 55 ml/kg/min, respectively, with more typical oxygen requirements ranging between 16.5 and 18.5 ml/kg/min at the barre and 20.1 and 26.3 ml/kg/min in center work for females and males, respectively.[94] Other researchers have noted that dancers spent almost 50 to 90 percent of the dance class within a training zone (60 to 90 percent of an individual's maximum heart rate),[95] depending on the level of skill of the dancers and size of class.[96]

According to Chatfield and Byrnes, using rehearsals of the performance for conditioning guarantees the specificity, if not the overload, needed for increments in endurance. The energy systems involved in the performance will be targeted in the training, as will the specific muscles and reflex patterns used for the performance. As these authors report:

> First, imagine a 20-minute piece that requires all dancers to be on-stage for the entire time. [The] steps [elicit] a steady state heart rate near 160 beats per minute . . . In the second piece there are two contrasting dynamics: One is explosive, utilizing jumps, leaps, kicks, lifts, and throws which elicit heart rates of up to 200 beats per minute for 30 to 45 seconds; the contrasting dynamic lasts 60 to 135 seconds and is a smooth, calm series of sustained, stationary, slow motion gestures allowing the dancers' heart rates to recover to below 100 beats per minute. These two dynamics continually alternate throughout the piece. The cardiorespiratory demands of these two pieces are antithetical. Rehearsing for one piece would not condition a dancer to perform in the other.[97]

Supplemental Aerobic Training

The concept of training specificity involves measures of performance that are specific to training modes. For example, if a piece of choreography requires a dancer to run for 2 minutes, drop to the floor, return to standing, and jump backward for 30 seconds, the best way to train for the requisite endurance is to rehearse the specific movement.

However, supplemental training also can be beneficial to improvement of the dancer's overall endurance.[98] For example, adding swimming to dance training can "improve overall endurance [and] offer the physiological and aesthetic benefits of breathing with less labor during performance . . . [In addition, the swimming adds] very little risk of musculoskeletal injury during the supplemental training."[99]

Certainly, the time demands of dance training limit how much exercise outside of dance can be managed. Strength training and flexibility need to be emphasized as high priorities in conditioning programs for dancers. Nevertheless, to the extent that the training does not interfere with the dancer's timing or cause injury (e.g., when jogging "toed-out"), endurance exercise also should be encouraged in dance training. A widely accepted exercise recommendation by the American College of Sports Medicine is for 20 to 60 minutes of aerobic exercise performed 3 to 5 days a week.[100] However, as Karen Clippinger points out, many of the protective health effects of exercise may be derived from less regular, vigorous programs.[101]

Exercising 3 days per week for at least 20 minutes is a good starting regimen in a supplemental conditioning program. To vary the program, the frequency (from 3 to 5 days), duration (up to 60 or more minutes depending on the intensity), and intensity (up to 85 to 90 percent of maximal heart rate) can be increased. These components of the program—frequency, duration, and intensity—are considered separately below. Whatever the aerobic activity chosen, it must provide an adequate overload to the heart and vascular system, and it must develop the aerobic capacity of the specific muscles that are worked—usually the larger leg muscles.

It is not *continual* progression, but *varied* progression that is important in conditioning. Dancers are not training to run marathons but to increase stamina in class and performance. Being able to dance at a lower heart rate may allow the dancer to concentrate on the more artistic aspects of the performance.[102] Progress need not be immediate, but rather can be slow and steady. This is especially important given the time constraints on dancers. Most dancers may not be able to squeeze daily 30-minute workouts into their training schedule.

- *Frequency*: Of the three training components, there seems to be most agreement about the frequency of exercise. The trainee should work out at least 3 times a week. However, Yiannis Koutedakis and Craig Sharp note that two training sessions per week may yield acceptable levels of fitness.[103] Also, "more" is not necessarily "better." Exercising 5 or 6 days a week does not necessarily produce greater cardiorespiratory gains than exercising 3 days a week; some strength gains depend heavily on the intensity and duration of the exercise. One exception to this may be flexibility, for which daily work is effective.

  This is not to say that the program must be all or nothing. If dancers have time to work out only one or 2 days a week, that still may be worth the effort; an extra day or 2 might eventually be worked into their busy schedules. Above all, it is very important for dancers to feel that this is not just "something else" that must be added to their already overfilled training regimen. Likewise, if dancers want to exercise 5 or 6 days a week, although the rate of improvement in cardiorespiratory fitness may not be sustained, the calorie expenditure resulting from the additional exercise may be worth the time commitment.

- *Duration*: There is some debate over this component of conditioning. If 15 minutes is good, is 45 minutes better? It depends. In the case of "fat burning," light continuous exercise seems most effective (see Chapter 5).

    Bouts of short, moderate exercise might help to promote fitness; studies have shown that three 10-minute jogging workouts a day, 5 days a week for 8 weeks (at moderate intensity) increased the aerobic capacity of participants.[104] Bouts of short, intense exercise also may be helpful: fit individuals who run approximately one mile as fast as possible 4 days a week will require only about 30 to 45 minutes of total exercise time per week. The fitness gains, however, may be dramatic owing to the intensity of the exercise.

    There also is some question about whether or not the activity needs to be continuous to see a training effect. Clippinger comments on the health effects of dividing exercise into several 10-minute sessions, perhaps throughout the day.[105]

Clearly, the exercise does not have to be long-duration to show fitness gains. Nevertheless, dancers must be very careful if they engage in high-intensity/high-impact endurance activities such as running or jogging. Injury might result if they have any structural or muscular imbalance (e.g., patellofemoral problems or muscular imbalance of the hip rotators).

- *Intensity*: Some published studies indicate that high-intensity exercise—exercising at high target heart rates—results in better fitness gains and higher caloric expenditure if it is intermittent.[106] Previously, it was thought that exercise must be continuous in order to show a training effect (i.e., the heart muscle must be subjected to continual stress and not allowed to "relax" during the training bout). However, intermittent exercise—alternating high-intensity movement with moderate- or low-intensity work—may result in greater fitness gains.[107]

    Another interesting finding comes from a fitness study of healthy men and women that appeared in the *Journal of the American Medical Association*.[108] Ever since its publication, dozens of newsletters and magazines have reported that people do not have to be marathoners to greatly improve their fitness level. The study found that of the five groups of people categorized according to fitness levels, the least-fit group derived the largest benefits from moderate exercise—walking briskly for 30 to 60 minutes every day.

    Few dancers would qualify for inclusion in the least-fit group of study participants. Nevertheless, future studies probably will show that for individuals at a moderate cardiorespiratory fitness level, moderate-duration and moderate-intensity exercise is effective in realizing fitness gains. For maximum gains, the National Academies Institute of Medicine issued fitness guidelines in 2002 with an exercise target of at least 60 minutes each day of moderately intense physical activity.[109] What does this mean for dancers? Walking on a regular basis is probably the best exercise. Cycling and swimming, as low-impact cross-training, also should be considered.

Some Considerations in Selecting Training Modes

- *Running*: Dancers should be careful if they select a weight-bearing endurance exercise such as running. Their muscles must be sufficiently strong to support the exercise (e.g., for running, the inward hip rotators must be strong enough to prevent "toeing-out," a cause of injury).[110] Dancers can check for this by imagining a line that runs down their chest and extends between the legs and the feet. As they run, their feet should be on each side of and parallel to the line—not toed-out. In addition, proper athletic shoes that provide shock absorption, flexibility, and support should be worn.

- *Cycling*: Dancers often fear that they will develop "big thigh muscles" by cycling. This may be true if they cycle with heavy resistance. To concentrate on cardiorespiratory conditioning rather than muscle strengthening, they need cycle only with light resistance applied (see section on strength training). Dancers with patellofemoral problems should cycle with no more than 15 to 20 degrees of knee flexion.

- *Swimming*: It may be, as is sometimes alleged, that swimming "works the wrong muscles for dance" in terms of balancing the strength of all the large muscle groups, or that relatively higher body fat percentages are maintained by swimming compared with other aerobic training activities. However, these problems are unlikely for dancers who swim at low-intensity levels. Many dancers enjoy the recreational as well as conditioning aspects of the sport. Swimming is particularly useful for rehabilitation when there has been an injury to the lower body and weight-bearing exercise is contraindicated. Movements that might stress the lower back muscles (e.g., the butterfly stroke) should be performed only when supporting musculature is sufficiently strong. I highly recommend a guide to fitness swimming published by Human Kinetics.[111]

- *Walking*: With hand weights or without, walking is a safe and enjoyable endurance exercise.[112] Compared with other aerobic training modes, it is certainly easier on the knees and lower-body joints—especially if there are no steep inclines to walk down (deceleration can irritate some of the connective tissue in the knee). A number of studies have shown that substantial caloric expenditure can be achieved with certain walking regimens. This low-intensity exercise with long duration will demand a large percentage of its fuel as fat rather than as glycogen or "stored" carbohydrate; thus, walking may produce positive fitness gains in terms of fat loss.

- *Nonimpact aerobics*: Dancers should also consider nonimpact aerobics for endurance training as well as for developing creativity and expressiveness. This exercise combines numerous movement forms and rhythms with various visualization techniques. Shoes need not be worn. Training heart rates are achieved by frequent changes of level and continuous, active use of the upper body. This technique should not be used by individuals with knee or shoulder disabilities.[113]

- *Other indoor and outdoor training modes*: There are other forms of endurance exercise (jumping rope, using an elliptical trainer, canoeing, cross-country skiing, and so on) that could be included in a program. There are also other factors in the fitness program to consider, such as training to condition a particular muscle-fiber type.

Assuming that dancers do not have the time to stroll for 2 hours in the local foothills or city park, or find some snow, strap on the cross-country skis, and go touring for 40 minutes, what would a cardiorespiratory conditioning program for dancers look like? Dance researchers Robin Chmelar and Sally Fitt offer an answer. They have combined the principles discussed above into some very workable exercise guidelines.

For example, Week One/Day One to Two starts off with 15 minutes of exercise (all of which should be low-impact or non–weight-bearing, e.g., walking, cycling, swimming, in intervals of 3 minutes at 60 percent of the maximal heart rate and 2 minutes at 70 percent. The interval set is thus 5 minutes, which is repeated three times for a total 15-minute workout. Two minutes are added for the 17-minute bout on Day Three. As the fitness level increases, the workouts gradually become longer. The program includes variations in frequency, duration, and intensity.[114] Each exercise bout should be preceded by a warmup and concluded with a "cool-down" that is essentially the reverse of the warmup, resulting in a gradual decrease in body temperature.

FLEXIBILITY

Flexibility is defined as the range of motion around a joint or set of joints, without undue stress to the muscles or tendons.[115] It involves both muscle flexibility (how supple and pliable muscles are) and joint mobility (the active range of motion).[116] Thus, flexible dancers should be able to move their joints through the required range of motion without unduly stressing muscles and tendons; this assumes that there are no serious anatomical restrictions, muscular limitations, or restrictive adhesions.[117] Further, numerous neural reflexes influence how muscles respond to stimuli, suggesting a neurological contribution to stretching.

Researchers speak of both static and functional flexibility.[118] Static flexibility is the range of motion produced statically without using the momentum of the movement itself. Of particular interest to dancers is functional flexibility, or the ability to move a joint with little resistance during actual dance movements. Flexibility is usually achieved through stretching, a specific form of exercise designed to increase or maintain flexibility.

For functional flexibility, much is required of dancers in terms of strength and neuromuscular coordination. For example, to perform a side leg extension (see Figure 63), sufficient strength is needed to raise the large weight of the leg. The timing of external rotation of the hip (stabilizing the torso and "dropping" the hip) and extension of the knee (raising the knee high before beginning to straighten the leg) are also very important to achieve the desired height.[119] Also, visualizing the elements of complex movement patterns during relaxation may produce neural activity that results in a "rehearsal" effect to successfully stretch muscles or perform endurance choreography.[120]

Traditionally, stretching exercises have been purported to be a necessary part of a warmup and injury-prevention program in dance and sports. However, it is now clear that one should warm up to stretch, not the other way around.[121]

There also is some debate about the relationship between flexibility and injury prevention. Beyond moderate flexibility, there is probably no further injury-prevention effect.[122] Extreme flexibility, on the contrary, may be associated with unstable joints[123] and higher risk of injury to connective tissues, especially if muscle and structural imbalances and other risk factors are present.[124] Flexibility has a more general protective function, increasing the range of possible skills and maintaining a healthy musculature.[125]

Extreme flexibility, or hypermobility, can, in fact, be a risk factor in injury, as discussed in early chapters. These terms refer to a range of motion in excess of the accepted normal motion in most of the joints; in contrast, "laxity" refers to the instability of a joint.[126] Excessive joint laxity can be a result of hereditary, congenital, or past injury conditions.[127]

Joint laxity is a two-edged sword, allowing for 180-degree turnout but predisposing the dancer (or contortionist or athlete) to injuries in general and stress fractures in particular. Ballet dancers with joint hyperlaxity need to perform strengthening exercises to be able, for example, to support point work.[128]

Thus, extreme flexibility should not be a goal for dancers, since there is a tradeoff between strength and power, and flexibility. Dancers need the power for strength and turns as much as they need the flexibility for extensions in adagio work.[129] Dancers should be mindful, then, of the balance needed in muscle flexibility and joint stability. Researcher Craig Phillips discusses a "stretching curve," where optimal flexibility is reached at the peak of the curve and further stretching can possibly damage or compromise the function of neural structures, resulting in muscle stiffness and a loss of flexibility, hypermobility (to the detriment of proprioception), and even strength deficits.[130]

More significant benefits of flexibility are its influence on technique and on muscle properties. For technique, good flexibility allows dancers to avoid the pathogenic compensations they often make when structural limitations restrict flexibility. Certain mechanical properties of muscle, such as peak-force development and speed of contraction, may be enhanced by rigorous stretching, although not so rigorous that muscle cross-bridges are permanently broken, potentially enhancing speed and efficiency during performance.[131] Stretching also can increase proprioceptivity (i.e., the ability of neural system components to sense position and placement) and serve as a biofeedback mechanism to reduce pre- and postperformance stress.[132]

Much of the difficulty in achieving flexibility is individual and genetic in nature; therefore, flexibility should be approached on an individual basis. Stretching techniques are part of a dynamic pedagogy, changing constantly.

Ever since Herbert A. De Vries published his paper on static stretching in 1962,[133] this mode has been widely used in technique classes of all dance idioms. Research now shows that proprioceptive neuromuscular facilitation (PNF), which involves a contract/relax procedure, probably yields the greatest increases in flexibility over time. These gains, however, may not be long-lasting.[134]

Stretching Techniques

What limits flexibility? One of the greatest resistances to stretch comes from the fascial sheath (a sheath of connective tissue support; see Chapter 2) that covers the muscle.[135] Certainly, the dancers' skeletal physical limitations, emotional state, and ability to relax,[136] as well as environmental factors, such as room temperature, also influence the range of flexibility. In general, the joint capsule and articulations account for about 47 percent of flexibility, tendons and ligaments about 10 percent, muscles and fascial sheaths about 40 percent, and skin about 2 percent. It is the muscles, fascial sheaths, and skin that should be emphasized in any stretching technique, not the relatively inelastic connective tissue. Also, different dancers may find different body parts more or less flexible at different times. Flexibility is not necessarily a general body characteristic but, rather, is specific to a particular joint and joint action, reflecting genetic variation, activity patterns, and the specialized mechanical strains that the individual has imposed on his or her connective tissue.[137]

Static stretching, also known as stretch-and-hold, is a low-force, long-duration method. Usually the position is held anywhere from 30 to 60 seconds. In the stretch, the muscle is held in a position of elongation greater than its resting length. There should be a stretching sensation, but no pain.[138]

Slow stretching involves a gradual lengthening of a muscle group, but the stretch is not held. When the muscle is in a maximally stretched state, it is then released. This can become a more "static" technique if the terminal position is sustained. Combining slow stretching with static methods for certain muscle groups, in particular, the hamstrings, can be effective.

Ballistic stretching depends on the speed and weight (momentum) of the moving body part to lengthen the muscle. An example of a ballistic hamstring stretch would be a leg swing from a back lunge position to the front and return to the starting position, with repeats. The problem with ballistic stretching is that the force generated from the fast stretch to lengthen the muscle operates against a protective (stretch) reflex contraction of the same muscle group. This combination of opposing forces may result in muscle tears and injury. Some research shows that ballistic stretching may be as effective as static methods for increasing flexibility,[139] especially dynamic flexibility,[140] yet there may be residual muscle soreness and some connective tissue trauma.[141]

Proprioceptive Neuromuscular Facilitation (PNF) *stretching* is derived from a clinical rehabilitative program and has since been applied to dancers and other athletes in training.[142] This method of stretching, exemplified by two types—hold-relax and contract-relax—can be done passively or as active-assisted exercises. This method basically uses active motion and isometric work to improve flexibility and enhance motor learning.[143] Possible benefits claimed for the method include large gains in flexibility, greater strength and balance of strength, improved stability about a joint, and prevention of injury.

A typical PNF approach involves placing the muscle group (e.g., hamstrings) to be stretched in an elongated position; gradually contracting the muscle group isometrically until a near-maximum effort is obtained (e.g., in a supine position, lowering the leg to the floor against resistance provided by a partner or an elastic band); sustaining the contraction for 4 to 10 seconds, followed by relaxation of the muscle group;[144] returning the leg to the beginning position, then stretching further (i.e., static stretch of the muscle).[145]

Arguments against PNF stretching include that it is too complex, it is too risky (the stretching actually occurs with more tension in the muscle), and it takes considerable time, especially in a class situation.[146] There also are concerns about a partner's assistance, namely, that the person assisting with the stretch should be well informed about the technique and the correct alignment that must be maintained throughout the stretch (watching especially for "cheating" during the contraction phase) for both partners.

In addition to static, ballistic, and PNF techniques, stretching can also be categorized according to who or what is responsible for the range of motion. In passive stretching, the motion is performed by a partner or special equipment (e.g., traction). In active stretching, motion is accomplished solely by the activities of one's muscles; there is no outside resistance or assistance. Intermediate forms of the exercise also exist: passive-active stretching and active-assisted stretching.

Relying mainly on passive stretching is not advised because the dancer will develop mainly passive flexibility, which is not very useful in performance. Dancers must also be careful when using passive stretching to avoid extreme and rapid stretch (see Jan Dunn profile in this chapter), possibly activating the stretch reflex, as discussed above for ballistic stretching.

Flexibility can be developed at any age given the appropriate training; however, the rate of development and potential for improvement is not the same at every age.[147] For adolescents, there are special considerations, as discussed in Chapter 2.[148]

Stretching Programs

Some general principles apply to all methods of stretching:

- Flexibility training sessions should be preceded by a warmup of at least 5 to 15 minutes—whatever is needed to increase the body temperature 1 or 2 degrees.
- It is especially important for dancers to be relaxed, since the ability to reduce muscle activation (i.e., to relax certain muscles so that others are able to stretch or activate) is critical to successful stretching.
- Effective stretching requires a relatively quiet environment, a passive attitude, relaxed breathing, and a reasonably comfortable position.
- Exercises can be performed with the eyes closed to help concentration and visualization of the correct performance of the exercise.
- Frequency and duration of the stretching program must be varied so that progressive adaptations result. (The routine stretching done in ballet class and other dance forms is hardly sufficient to result in any improvements in flexibility.)
- Stretching three times a week is probably adequate to maintain flexibility. The less flexible dancer should try to stretch at least five times a week.[149] Dancers with particularly tight muscle groups should stretch several times a day, especially after class when the muscles are warmer and more pliable.
- Train, don't strain.[150] Use pain as a guide to differentiate mild discomfort from overstretching.

The duration of the "hold" phase of static (10 to 60 seconds[151]) and PNF techniques also needs consideration, in addition to the length of each session and number of stretching exercises used. It may be difficult for beginning students to sustain a stretch for more than 10 seconds without "pulsing" or "bouncing," in which case monitoring the time and giving verbal cues may help.

There are many warnings that dance researchers, educators, physical therapists, and kinesiologists give to dancers regarding stretch programs. Perhaps none are so cogent or vociferous as those of Judy Alter: do not bounce, lock (hyperextend), arch the lower back or neck, swing, do fast exercises, or "overbend" a joint.[152] These can be expanded:[153]

1. Do not hyperflex the knee or neck.
2. Do not hyperextend the knee, lower back, or neck.
3. Do not apply a twisting force to the knee (see discussion of torques in Chapter 3).
4. Avoid holding the breath (on inhalation) during the stretching exercise.
5. Avoid overstretching any joint so that the ligaments and joint capsules are overstretched.
6. Avoid stretches that place acute compression forces on spinal discs.

A number of stretching exercises are questionable and should be avoided or modified.[154] These include the following:

- Stretches using excessive flexion of the lumbar spine (e.g., in a standing hamstring stretch, leaning over as if touching one's toes with unsupported lumbar flexion; back muscles relax, leaving the unsupported ligaments and vertebral discs of the spine to support the weight).
- Stretches using excessive flexion of the knees (e.g., in the double-leg inverted hurdler's stretch or in deep knee bends).

- Stretches using excessive hyperextension of the lower back and cervical spine (e.g., as in a back-arching abdominal stretch, possibly causing impingement on the nerve, compression, and even herniation of the disc and myofascial trigger points).
- The yoga "plough" (the dancer is supine with the legs extended over the head, feet touching the floor; this is inappropriate because large compressive forces may be placed on the cervical spine).
- The hurdler's stretch (the rear foot is usually flared out to the side, placing stress on the medial aspect of the knee and overstretching the medial ligaments, not to mention causing increased strain on the lower back).

Some stretches are useless rather than dangerous, often because there are "weak links" in the "stretching chain" that prevent the desired muscle group from stretching. For example, tight hamstrings (the "weak link") may prevent a dancer from actually feeling a stretch in the lower back musculature, or the reverse.

Although many of these exercises are potentially harmful, dancers still may be asked by choreographers to perform some of the movements. What should dancers do? First, determine whether or not the movement is actually risky, then decide whether or not to perform the choreography. If the decision is to perform, dancers can then begin to condition the body to be able, at least partially, to withstand some of the stresses that the movement places on the body. Conditioning for this purpose emphasizes strengthening (e.g., neck and upper back musculature for many jazz movements) and training to maintain good alignment (e.g., of the upper torso joints), but can also include some flexibility work (shoulder and shoulder-girdle muscles).

Many of the exercises considered dangerous are problematic partly because they do not allow for individual anatomical differences. In a clinical setting, in which the correct execution of the movements is supervised, some of these "dangerous" exercises, modified, may actually be quite useful.[155] Three examples are toe-touching stretches (Figure 80), the prone quadriceps stretch,[156] and the modified hurdler's stretch.

In the prone quadriceps stretch, proper alignment of the knee and hip joints is maintained by the dancer holding onto the foot with both hands. The stretch can be increased by allowing the thigh to come off the floor, taking care not to pull down on the foot and hyperflex the knee. In the modified hurdler's stretch, the rear foot is not allowed to flare to the side, which would result in overstretched medial ligaments. Also, the external rotation of the hips is maintained. By pressing forward, increased strain on the lower back is avoided.[157]

As with all exercise regimens—and flexibility programs are no exception—the dancer must vary exercise/training components if increases in flexibility are to be made. For flexibility work, this usually means increasing the duration or the frequency of the session or the intensity (perhaps by using different stretches) until acceptable flexibility is achieved and can be maintained.

Conditioning and Class

The reader might be asking: "This is all well and good, but how can I fit it all in?" Can regular dance classes provide at least some of the conditioning? They could, by creatively increasing the "work" and decreasing the "rest." Karen Clippinger argues that a fitness goal can be achieved by add-on choreography, having portions of the class where less verbal feedback is given and movement is more continuous (some teachers do this already: "Today we're going to do an aerobics barre"; see Chapter 3 profile of Cher Carnell) and, in across-the-floor movements, working with larger groups and different spatial arrangements (a

Figure 80 Modification of potentially harmful toe-touching exercises. (Photo by Angela Sterling)

group of four in a diamond rather than just one or two students going across the floor at a time, and use of circuit formats with "stations" that the students go to, moving continuously).[158] Figures 30 and 31 shows how Therabands can be used in barre exercises, for conditioning. Exercises for the anterior lower-leg muscles also can be incorporated into exercises at the barre (Figure 18). Whether in class or rehearsal, daily practices must have a balance between physical activity and recovery.[159]

Yet caution should be used in considering conditioning approaches. Karen Clippinger notes that "care must be taken when new 'fads' arise to not necessarily throw out past approaches in favor of theoretically attractive approaches, which have not necessarily been given adequate clinical or research evaluation."[160]

At the same time, new ideas (or very old ideas, resurfacing) emerge all the time. Attendance at conferences in dance medicine and science is one way to keep abreast of current work in a variety of areas. For example, research showing the effects of imagery and imaging techniques on dance technique (e.g., alignment) can be applied to conditioning programs as well[161] via an integrated program of fitness and dance technique.[162] Eric Franklin's excellent *Conditioning for Dance* provides full-body conditioning programs based on current research in this area.[163]

In Donna Krasnow's writings and training videos she makes a convincing case for C–I training to improve muscle balance, support neuromuscular repatterning, and assist in the transfer of training (e.g., between the quadriceps and hamstrings—strengthening the hamstrings and increasing flexibility in the hip flexors).[164] Neuromuscular patterning and motor recruitment can be enriched with images—for example, using a cue of visualizing the inner thighs "gathering" or being drawn together like magnets to encourage hip adductor use and inhibit quadriceps overuse, or, in a hip flexion floor series, visualizing the sacrum weighted and heavy on the floor upon flexion, and then the spine lengthening along the floor as the abdominals continue to activate during the return of the leg to extension. Such powerful imagery also creates an environment for relaxed and effective stretching and also aids in the transfer of skills from training to performance.[165]

Despite our increased understanding of the importance and the techniques of conditioning training, challenges remain in actually implementing fitness programs, particularly for professional dance students (who may face faculty resistance, scheduling challenges, or a lack of space and equipment). Some of this resistance may be overcome once the effects of increased fitness levels are more fully appreciated.[166]

PROFILES

Jan Dunn

Jan Dunn (Figure 81), a dance medicine and Pilates specialist based in Denver, Colorado, is widely known for her dance medicine seminars and the role she has played—together with other pioneers in the dance education field, such as Martha Myers, Janice Plastino, and Ruth Solomon—in establishing the field and practice of dance medicine in the United States.

Dunn served as the founding chair of the National Dance Association's Committee on Dance Science and Medicine, and she was on the staff of the American Dance Festival (ADF) in Durham, North Carolina, from 1984 to1991 as assistant dean and workshop coordinator. For almost 10 years she served as president and then executive director of the International Association for Dance Medicine and Science, and she continues to serve on the board of directors of the organization. She also originated the *Dance Medicine/Science Resource Guide* (now published by J. Michael Ryan Publishing Co.). One of her current positions is dance medicine trainer for the Cleo Parker Robinson Dance Company in Denver, as well as guest faculty at the University of Colorado-Boulder department of dance. Dunn explains how dance medicine has evolved:

> Injury rehabilitation and conditioning for dance is a vastly different scene for young dancers today than when I was dancing. In the United States, now there are dance medicine specialists—not everywhere, but in hundreds more places than earlier. At the very least, dancers today know that working with a healthcare team that is familiar with dance is critical to rehabilitation and conditioning.
>
> For example, in Denver we have at least two terrific dance medicine physical therapists and three or four orthopedic physicians who know dance medicine very well. Today, dancers expect to deal with physicians and therapists who can help them address faulty technique issues. Dancers also have a large support system network available [see the *Dance Medicine/Science Resource Guide*]. Gone are the days of dancers thinking there is no one out there who can understand, or help.
>
> In the early 1980s, in professional conferences related to dance, I can remember being in breakout sessions and talking about the need for integrating dance medi-

Figure 81 Jan Dunn. (Photo courtesy of the *Pensacola News Journal*)

cine and science-type of courses into university curricula. Now, 20 years later, you can find them easily. It happened in the academic world a lot faster than we thought it would. It's the same thing with the growth in the *Resource Guide*. Originally, it was just a three to four page specialist list that we handed out at the summer ADF festival. And here we are 15 years later, with hundreds of people listed worldwide.

Dunn herself trained as a dancer:

I can remember never wanting to do anything else except be a ballerina. I started taking ballet classes intensively when I was 10, every day after school. So, up until my late 20s, I performed as a classically trained ballet dancer. I was lucky because my ballet teacher was so many years ahead of her time. She had had the experience of going on point too early with Cechetti technique and had many injuries as a result. So, she developed an interest in anatomy and kinesiology. At age 10 or 11, I can remember her dragging out the anatomy book. She also promoted what we would call today a floor barre. This was unusual training in the 1950s.

Dunn recalls never having a serious injury until age 26, when a jazz teacher in New York City pushed her down in a sitting hamstring stretch:

I felt it rip but I was young and stupid. I could barely walk, much less dance. That injury was never rehabbed, so it healed with lots of scar tissue. It affected my back and sacroiliac joint. It took me years longer to recover than it should have, and it played a major role in the various body issues that I currently deal with, as an "aging dancer"!

In Florida, Dunn met the person who first got her interested in dance medicine—Heather Shepley, who had been on scholarship at New York City Ballet. After switching to contemporary movement and attaining a masters degree in dance, she started a dance degree program at Pensacola Junior College that Jan Dunn eventually took over. It was at an ADF festival in Durham where Dunn was introduced to Martha Myers and anatomist Irene Dowd.

> Contemporary dance is where my heart really lay. It appealed to me philosophically and politically [from a feminist perspective], and at age 30, I found the movements "felt right" on my body—classical ballet did not. My first modern technique class was a Limón class. At ADF, I discovered teachers Betty Jones and Martha Myers, who were significant mentors to me.

Dunn has served as a dance faculty member at Connecticut College, Colorado College, the Academy of Colorado Ballet, Florida State University, Hartford Ballet, and Washington University in St. Louis. She says that Pilates is often the preferred form of conditioning for dancers.

> It's true that Pilates is not the only form of conditioning for dance. It is, however, an ideal form for dancers because it emphasizes eccentric vs. concentric muscle conditioning, and muscle balance. It is perfect for achieving the strong, long, and lean look so desirable in dance. It's also good because many Pilates trainers are former dancers and can develop a conditioning program specific to certain dance moves. For example, Florida-based Polestar Pilates Education has an entire dance-specific Pilates training program, aimed at addressing typical muscle imbalances in dance.
>
> If Pilates is not available or dancers prefer GYRATONIC® or to go to the gym and work out with a trainer, they need to be careful that the trainer knows something about dance. For both Pilates and GYRATONIC®, an aerobic component of training (achieved by going through the routines accurately but quickly, or by an outside aerobic activity) should eventually be incorporated for a total conditioning program.

Murray Louis

For Murray Louis (Figure 82)—dancer, choreographer, artistic director, and writer—dance is vital: "I've never thought of dance as being just a part of my life. I've always known it as my entire life. With that overwhelming commitment, it is understandable how all of my values and perceptions have always emanated from a dance compulsion."[167]

Louis calls himself a "natural-born dancer" because he was self-taught, having never taken a dance lesson before the age of 20. Louis began a lifelong association with Alwin Nikolais in 1949, founded a dance company in 1953, and heads the Nikolais/Louis Foundation for Dance—established after Nikolais's death in 1993. Louis has created over 100 dance works, including dances choreographed for the Royal Danish Ballet, The José Limón Dance Company, The Hamburg Opera Ballet, The Scottish Ballet, The Berlin Opera Ballet, and The Cleveland Ballet.

At the age of 78, Louis attributes his longevity to the power and the health-sustaining philosophy inherent in dance—to move "without resistance," that is, never "forcing the movement." As he explained in an interview for the first edition of *Finding Balance*:

Figure 82 Murray Louis. (Photo by Nan Melville)

I dance only one piece on a program today and choreograph more for my company. I don't want to leave this profession crippled and bitter, as is the case with so many of my colleagues. But I must admit I look forward to not having to warm up and maintain my standards of performance someday. I hear there is a life after dancing.

For Louis, dance—although not necessarily performing it—is a lifelong career. He finds out what to do through honest discussion with his "interior person."

This is how I do it. I discuss everything with the interior person in me and see what my limits are. Those limits have become clearer as I've become more mature. It began years ago when I was reshaping my body and I'd say 'why am I doing this?' and the inner me would say, 'wait, you'll see.' And, after about 5, 6 years, I had a whole new body and mind; both are absolutely related. Every 7 years the entire cell system in the body is rejuvenated. I've discovered that my life goes in 7 year cycles. I look differently, I think differently, I create differently, I respond differently. I ask 'what cycle is this?' and just accept it, just go with it.

Louis has learned to make the transition to less dancing gracefully: "I no longer want to do just a solo. If the audience can't see me when I was at my peak and could accomplish anything I wanted to do, then they're not seeing Murray Louis. So I write today and think today. I'm getting paid back for all those years of work, and, I'm in good health."

Louis himself has written about the life cycle of dancers: "The physical intensity of the profession places not only a strain upon the body, but upon the psyche as well . . . Dancers as a rule, start early and train during their teens, arriving at the starting line at 20 and finishing at 40. Of course there are many exceptions to this timetable."[168]

The cycle of some dancers is like that of certain flowers, he writes:

> They have a blooming season. The young dancers bloom very early—as with the tulips they too bloom early and once and then that's it for the season. They can have no sense of what a chrysanthemum is, for that's a fall flower. Just like, once the blooming season is over, the chrysanthemum has no idea of what the spring flowers are like. It's just nature's timetable.
>
> Like a flower, a dancer does not last for all seasons. There is summer, fall, winter. Dancers must find another physical outlet for their physical capacities. If you are creative, Louis says, begin to write, to paint . . . whatever gives you satisfaction.

Louis realizes that, for many, dance is a compulsion—the 21-year-old dancer is like the young puppy who has no other choice but to behave as a frisky puppy. The only real sadness of retirement from performing, he notes, is to know there is no other occupation in the world that can possibly "bring you up to those heights, back to the gods, as only the dance can. This, whether you realize it or not, is the real tragedy."[169]

Hardly sitting around himself, he continues to head the Nikolais/Louis Foundation for Dance. As he noted in a *Dance Magazine* article,[170] he had to prioritize the process of preserving Alwin Nikolais' legacy. This meant, eventually, closing the school, disbanding the company, and completing a book on the philosophy and pedagogy of the technique, *Nikolais/Louis Technique: The Unique Gesture* (forthcoming Routledge Press). He also forged a partnership with the Ririe-Woodbury Dance Company to mount a program of seven pieces that had never been presented together before. The program, under Louis' direction with Alberto (Tito) del Saz, was performed by the Ririe-Woodbury Dance Company. It premiered in Salt Lake City in September 2003, toured, and played at The Joyce Theatre in New York for a week in October that same year. It then toured into February and March of 2004, with performances in France and Italy.

How does he participate in dance now?

> I find alternatives. For the physical, I do a warm-up and then try dancing a solo piece. I stop when I fall on my bottom and think, "not bad." Almost got through it. I also read a great deal. I make myself write 2 hours every day . . . getting all the Alwin-Nikolais notes together, and sending everything off to archives in Ohio. I spend time with my companion, and he knows nothing about dance but marvels at everything. I walk a great deal every afternoon. I work out at a local gym 3 days a week, where I perform 40 minutes of my regular dance stretch. When summer comes, I attack my garden on Southampton on Long island and I don't stop until I "break a sweat."

With some of the tulips performing his *Deja-Vu*, a witty piece with a 16-measure grand plié, this chrysanthemum still enjoys—as he puts it in *On Dance*—the "exhilaration of exhaustion," the "radiance of sweat," and the "passion of stretching," with his inner self listening very carefully to "the eloquence of silence as the next gesture awaits its cue."[171]

Figure 83 Gary Galbraith of the Martha Graham Dance Company in Graham's *Night Journey.* (Photo by John Deane)

Gary Galbraith

Gary Galbraith (Figure 83) is good at dealing with transitions. He needs to be, as he holds down two high-profile positions at the same time: principal dancer with the Martha Graham Dance Company (he's been with the company since 1993), and artistic director and associate professor of dance at Case Western Reserve University (CWRU) in Cleveland, Ohio (since 1999).

Galbraith accepted the tenure-track position and became artistic director of Mather Dance Center (his partner, Karen Potter, a dancer affiliated with Erick Hawkins for 15 years and now director of the dance program at Case, accepted a second faculty position) at a time when the future of the Graham company seemed tenuous, at best (the company was virtually in suspension from 1999 to 2001 during prolonged legal battles over copyright and the authority to perform Graham's works). Galbraith and Potter had been courted by the then CWRU dance heads, Kelly Kolt and Kathyrn Karipides, who were soon to retire. Accepting the position was a difficult choice for Galbraith; still, he was able to remain active as a volunteer in the Graham company's struggles, helping to rally support, drafting memos and press statements, while at the same time embracing the security and prestige of an academic position at his alma mater.

Galbraith has two degrees from CWRU: one in biomedical engineering with an interest in biomechanics (what he says would be considered dance medicine, or close to it, now) and an MFA in dance. His undergraduate degree included a liberal dose of dance technique classes as electives, supplemented by forays to New York City in the summer to take technique class.

After completing his MFA in dance at Case, Galbraith took class in New York City for a few months, joined the José Limón Company in 1990, and then the Martha Graham Dance Ensemble, a training ground for Graham dancers, in 1991. The Erick Hawkins–based technique he had studied at CWRU served him well throughout his early performing career, although he acknowledges that one of the reasons he had to leave Cleveland was to find his own path:

> When I left school, I wanted to find my own way. For me, there was no one prescribed technique or way to dance. It was a hard, even exciting time for me. Even though I was with the José Limón company for a short period of time, I still faced another set of transitions when I went to the Graham company. I've thus had to retrain significantly twice in my career. In addition to the physical retraining pertaining to style and technique, one's aesthetics must also be reexamined.

Galbraith adds: "It was an interesting and strange time to make a transition into the Graham company. Not only was I making personal/professional adjustments, the entire Graham organization was also undergoing a change in leadership following Martha Graham's death."

In his career with the company, he has danced such prestigious principal roles as Jason in *Cave of the Heart*, both the Husbandman and the Revivalist in *Appalachian Spring*, and The Christ Figure in *El Penitente*. Galbraith also has been featured in new ballets created for the Graham Company, including Robert Wilson's *Snow on the Mesa* and *But Not For Me* by Tony Award–winning choreographer Susan Stroman. Lucinda Childs choreographed a duet on him which was premiered by the Graham Company and which he later premiered in Cleveland.

At first, managing both academic and professional positions wasn't difficult:

> At the beginning, the then dean of arts and sciences [at Case] was very supportive and very excited about having a professional dancer on the faculty. He had worked out an arrangement for me to take a leave when I had professional responsibilities to perform with the Graham Company. So, in my first year at Case, I had to take a spring semester off to do a Graham tour in spring 2000. After that, there was a suspension of the Graham Company's operations for 2 years, and no problem then balancing the two—I focused on my work with Case while playing a key role in uniting the dancers during the company's suspension.

Since the Graham Company resumed operations, the balancing act has become more demanding:

> Especially for the senior people in the company, it was important for us to work collectively to maintain the work of Martha Graham. The company is now up and running again. I'm told that we'll have a lot more bookings this year and can look

forward to real positive growth. And, there's also a new dean at Case who seems enthusiastic and positive about the celebrated dance program and its future. So I remain excited about my dual passions (or my dual career).

Very few performing dancers in a major modern dance company need to worry about putting together a tenure-application package as does Galbraith. Obviously, Galbraith believes in the world of academic dance, being both a product of it and a teacher in it.

What would he say to young people, trying to make a decision about pursuing a degree in dance vs. training outside academia with professional dancers? It depends on the individual and the level of education, he says. At the graduate level, Galbraith works with professional dancers as well as recently minted baccalaureates:

> I work with people who have been dancing and performing and creating and are now at a point when they want to re-evaluate, to revisit their own relationship to their craft, or perhaps they are looking at the training they need to compete for academic positions. There are also those who, like I . . . have finished undergraduate work and are compelled to get more time in, more experience in an academic setting. Also, in the conservatory environment within the dance program at Case, we support the dancers in their constant discovery and education. There is probably no other time in your life when you can have such a concentrated learning experience. One of the beauties of the graduate academic process and experience is that you can commit to such a course of study without the immediate pressures of finding a job [especially students with graduate assistantships].

There are different considerations for those who are finishing high school and wondering about how to move forward:

> It's quite an individual choice. Still, I feel it is important to get an education. Sure, you can go off to New York City and sustain odd jobs early on and easily. But you have to figure out how to juggle different jobs, unless you're one of the rare few who can get a dance position right away. But when you get older and certain things change or you get tired with the scut work, unless you have an education there may not be a lot of opportunities for you. Education is going to be something very helpful in that regard. On the other hand, those who go straight through, they have to ask themselves—when am I going to start my professional career, when I'm 23, 24? For me personally, after my undergraduate degree, I wasn't ready for performing and touring, I wanted more time for study.

Galbraith, a master performer and teacher—who recollects that, at one time, he had "zero interest in teaching or in looking for a MFA degree program"—highly values his graduate education at Case:

> When I was younger, the only thing I wanted to do was perform, perform, and then perform some more. Later on in life, when choreography was more of an interest, I realized that I had the life experience; I knew what I was talking about so I could actually practice my craft. For the teaching, I found that that only comes from being exposed to fantastic, magnificent teachers in my life. To really teach, as opposed to just regurgitating what I've been taught, that comes from personal professional experience—it took me 10 years to come to this.

5

Nutrition, Weight Management, and Diet for Dance

Diet is critical to good performance and to a long dancing career because food is the main source of fuel for muscles, body fluid replacement, and the other nutrients needed for fitness and health. An inadequate diet may trigger injuries[1] and prolong rehabilitation.[2] While many dancers are concerned about diet and nutrition, those with disordered eating are obsessed by it. In pursuing ill-conceived diets, some dancers eat too much of certain nutrients —too much protein, too much fat—while depriving the body of much-needed carbohydrates.[3] Iron, calcium, folic acid, and vitamins C, B_{12}, D, and E are some of the essential nutrients that dancers commonly lack in their diets.[4] This self-deprivation is in line with a belief in "success at any cost."[5]

Nutrient imbalances, especially of calcium and iron, are clearly a problem among dancers,[6] particularly for women. Postmenopausal and amenorrheic dancers produce less estrogen and are at high risk for osteoporosis (adult bone loss in which the bone becomes porous), especially those with a dietary history of calcium deficiency. Osteoporosis can begin early in life and progressively worsen with prolonged calcium deficiency (Table 6); exercise may help to slow the rate of bone mass loss.[7] Many dancers take mineral and vitamin supplements, but these may be neither complete nor balanced for a dancer's particular needs.

Apart from nutrients, it appears that dancers often consume far less than the recommended energy intake of 1,900 to 3,000 kilocalories per day (see Table 4).[8] Various studies of female athletes report an average energy intake of 2,159 kcal/day, which is close to the recommended value of 2,200 for sedentary or lightly active women.[9] However, in studies of dancers, an average daily intake of 1,400 to 1,900 kcal is more common.[10] More recent studies report a similarly low intake, with values for professional female dancers averaging 1,600 kcal/day and many female dance students ingesting less than 1,500 kcal/day, with some even as low as 550 kcal/day (Table 4; for comparison with values in the table, the recommended dietary intakes for females is reported to be 2,200 kcal/day for ages 11 to 14).[11] It should be recognized, however, that studies using self-reporting to measure food intake may be unreliable, with subjects often underreporting (or overreporting) their consumption, especially if there is a stigma attached to excess (or deficits) of the kind or amount of food.[12]

Table 4 Summary of Caloric Intake Among Adolescent and Adult Dancers

Study[a,b]	Population	Daily Calorie Intake Mean (range) kcal[c]
	Professional/Adult	
Fogelholm et al. (1996)	Female ballet dancers (Netherlands)	1,548 (721–2,217)
White (1982)	Female adults—Ballet West (Utah)	1,282 (722—2,043)
Calabrese et al. (1983)	Female adults—Cleveland Ballet (Ohio)	1,358 (550–2,115)
Cohen et al. (1985)	Female adults—American Ballet Theatre (New York)	1,673 (977–2,361)
Hamilton et al. (1986)	Female adults—four national ballet companies (United States)	1,894 (650–3,758)
Cohen et al. (1985)	Male adults—American Ballet Theatre (New York)	2,967 (1,739–4,104)
	Dance student/Adolescent	
Mittleman et al. (1992)	College female dancers	1,640 (941–2,488)
Bonbright (1989)	Female students—professional schools (Washington, DC)	1,584 (642–2,611)
Benson et al. (1985)	Female students—professional schools (California)	1,890 (700–3,000)
Clarkson et al. (1985)	Female students—professional schools (Massachusetts)	1,776 (784–2,513)

[a]Some of these data have appeared in Priscilla M. Clarkson, "An overview of nutrition for female dancers," *Journal of Dance Medicine & Science* 2/1 (1998): 32–39, and Robin Chmelar and Sally Fitt, *Diet for Dancers* (Pennington, NJ: Princeton Book Co., Publishers, 1990). Note that the range in energy Recommended Dietary Allowances (RDA) for females is 1,900 to 2,200 kcal and for males is 2,300 to 3,000 kcal.

[b]See also Bright-See et al., "Nutrition beliefs and practices of ballet students," *Journal of the Canadian Dietetic Association* 39/4 (1978): 324–331; A. P. Kvasova, "Evaluation of a balanced diet for students at a ballet school," *Higiena Sanitariya* 39/8 (1974): 27–29; and K. D. Mittleman, M. Keegan, and C. L. Collins, "Physiological, nutritional, and training profile of university modern dancers," *Medical Problems of Performing Artists* 7/3 (1992): 92.

[c]A calorie is a unit of energy; a calorie or kilocalorie equals 1,000 calories.

Researcher Jane Bonbright has calculated that approximately 15 kcal/lb/day (kilocalories per pound of body weight per day) is needed for the body to function under normal circumstances.[13] Dancers must add at least another 200 to 300 kcal/day to meet class, rehearsal, and performance energy demands. Roughly, a consumption of two-thirds the recommended level is considered adequate, yet dancers, according to their food record reports, are not ingesting even this amount.

Dancers deficient in calories are easily tired and are more susceptible to infections and injuries such as stress fractures.[14] Many dancers' energy consumption is even lower than their basal metabolic needs—the minimum amount of energy needed to sustain the body's vital functions.[15] The resting or basal metabolic needs usually represent about 60 to 70 percent of the recommended daily intake.

As discussed in Chapter 4, dance is low in the range of energy expenditure compared to other athletic pursuits; it consists of short bursts of strength, power, and stamina rather than sustained endurance exercise. Dancers know that they must be careful that their energy intake is in balance with their energy expenditure[16]; they believe that counting calories is the only way to maintain a slim look in dance. However, the source of the calories, the timing of consumption, and the type and amount of exercise dancers get affect weight loss and gain.

Balancing food intake with caloric expenditure is especially challenging when dancers are between seasons or shows and training is less intense. There is still pressure to maintain a lean look during this time, putting dancers at risk for restricted or disordered eating. Amenorrhea[17] and osteoporosis,[18] together with eating disorders, form a condition known as the Female Athlete Triad. This condition can ruin a promising career in professional dance.[19]

Disordered eating can take one or more forms. These include: food restriction; bingeing; purging; extended fasting; use of diet medication, diuretics or laxatives; and dissatisfaction with one's body and a distorted body image.[20] Eating disorders lie on a continuum, with many dancers falling in a subclinical category of "dancer disordered eating," which is characterized by a preoccupation with body weight and shape and restricted intake.[21] In the most extreme form of disordered eating, dancers may suffer from clinical or diagnosable anorexia nervosa and/or bulimia nervosa.[22]

THE YOUNG DANCER: DIET AND HEALTH, GROWTH AND DEVELOPMENT[23]

The making of the ballerina starts at a young age, and with it often comes some of the unhealthful eating practices that permeate the dance world. Researchers note that even a moderate level of training—8 hours a week—is enough to trigger young dance students to start controlling their caloric intake in the hope of becoming a "ballerina."

Young dancers may feel pressure from teachers, directors, and peers to conform to an ultra-lean body type. The need for control in the highly competitive world of dance helps to foster disordered eating. In companies where there is little acceptance of a fully developed woman's figure, young girls approaching puberty, which produces physical transformations in weight and secondary sexual characteristics, find it especially difficult to attain a thin, prepubescent form. Even normal growth and development is viewed as aberrant. For example, adolescents who mature on time (menarche at age 12.9 years) may tend to have a worse self-image of their bodies, higher psychopathology, and rate being attractive as very important; their figures are fuller earlier in a world that is rife with sylphlike forms. The weeding-out process is in full swing.

Trying to conform to an ideal look, which is unattainable for most, dancers restrict calories, even though weight goals are best reached by adding exercise to the diet. Eating disorders, including severe food restriction, fasting, excessive exercise, binge eating, vomiting, and use of laxatives, are widespread among young dancers. Poor nutrition and subsequent menstrual problems can result in lowered bone density just as the average young person is attaining almost half of her skeletal mass, struggling with the demands of technique, and trying to conform to a perceived ideal body shape.

As researcher Judy Sonnenberg notes, eating disorders are complex and are certainly not limited to the young—or to dancers. Sonnenberg reports that 0.5 to 1 percent of adolescent and young adult women suffer from anorexia nervosa and an additional 1 to 3 percent suffer from bulimia nervosa.[24] The rate of bulimia among males is estimated to be about one-tenth the rate of females. Others find a range of 3.5 to 7.6 percent of anorexia nervosa among ballet dancers.[25]

How does such aberrant behavior happen in the otherwise beautiful world of dance, and in ballet in particular? For younger children in a beginning ballet or creative movement class, dance usually is a highly positive experience and gives a boost to their self-esteem (Figure 56). Yet by the time dancers reach adolescence, with the rapid changes it brings to their bodies, their self-image is deteriorating and they distrust even normal patterns of development. This attitude can have lifelong consequences; a body image (and dissatisfaction with oneself) formed in early adolescence and early adulthood (without intervention) may well last a lifetime.

Psychologist and former dancer Linda Hamilton has reported widely on the incidence of dieting, disordered eating, and overt eating disorders as well as on the related psychological profiles of dancers. In Hamilton's view, adolescents often focus exclusively on the competitive and career pressures in dance, rather than exploring other skills and support resources outside the dance world. They identify primarily with the values and standards of professional dance—in other words, a lean look and unwavering focus. In this world view, healthy eating may be just a distraction. The dancers' commitment to dance is huge, as is their will to succeed, but in a world that is profoundly self-absorbing. If an aspiring dancer is defeated in attaining her or his career goals, it can produce a real identity crisis.

However, there is much that can be done to support young dancers as they move through adolescence, Hamilton believes. A dance support team—family, friends, teachers, and therapists—can personalize the care that young dancers receive. Individual attention seems to be critical to the prevention and treatment of eating disorders. Ballet dancers, in particular, may benefit from broadening their perspective on dance by exploring other forms such as contemporary and jazz dance, perhaps in an international dance exchange program. Anything that gets them to think beyond their imperfect bodies in the "perfect" world of dance can help: volunteering in any realm outside their immediate dance environment, service learning in particular. Seeing options in performance, career, and beyond is beneficial; changing their attitudes and goals to more realistic ones is the key to career satisfaction.

Damaging self-images and eating behaviors are learned in response to sociocultural pressures. According to Linda Hamilton, anorexia nervosa seems to be more prevalent among aspirants in environments who have not gone through a stringent selection process. Those who make it through more competitive training are perhaps the more "naturally thin ones," in the words of Larry Vincent. This concern is echoed by Marika Molnar, director of physical therapy services for the New York City Ballet, who encourages teachers and other members of the "team" to assist young dancers in understanding normal growth and changes at puberty, including weight gain, and then finding their way to natural body weight. This process would mean that the team would support only that which is "normal, healthy, and attainable for each dancer individually," in the words of Judy Sonnenberg. Reaching that goal is a long time coming in dance. Dance teachers thus should help young dancers to challenge dance norms; doing this involves talking and being frank with students about body-image issues, promoting healthy attitudes, and being a good role model (see Chapter 5, Catherine Allaway profile, for more discussion).

If such self-criticism can be minimized, however, dance can be a positive experience for young people. Young dancers are entering one of the most beautiful and challenging of art forms. From a physical perspective, dance is beneficial in developing balance and coordination; it may even positively influence bone mineral density. Researchers Karim Khan and colleagues note that ballet is often started at an early age, when physical activity may allow children to maximize peak bone mass.[26] Certainly, primary amenorrhea, low body weight, low energy intake, low calcium intake, and eating disorders can negatively influence bone mineral density, but dance, when not associated with abnormal eating behavior or prolonged menstrual disturbance, can be a positive lifestyle choice that can aid in decreasing osteoporosis in later life. Dance should be a positive formative experience for youths and adults alike.

Yet even dancers who do not show any signs of disordered eating often are preoccupied with food. A diet mentality is pervasive in dance and in our society at large: food becomes an obsession. People may eat virtually nothing all day, only to eat with abandon in the evening.[27] Once a "forbidden food" is eaten and the dieter has "failed," even more "forbidden foods" are eaten. Stringent practice quotas may be self-imposed, specifying how many calories are to be expended each day. To make it worse, dancers may have gotten the "forbidden food" all wrong (e.g., all fats are bad). As discussed later, dancers (and the American public at large) have learned to favor "low-fat," high-sugar snack foods, avoiding high-fat foods at all costs. This behavior leads to excess sugar consumption, which does not help in achieving weight control.

Dancers need a more realistic attitude toward food. Of course, it is frightening to acknowledge that the "controls" one has been using are not working: tight clothes, daily weighings, or labeling foods as "good" and "bad." The way to gain control of the obsession is to relinquish the notion of diet (calorie restriction) and return to normal eating habits, trying to follow the guidelines given in this chapter and letting the body's physiological hunger cues govern what and how much is eaten.

Part of setting realistic weight goals is understanding the concepts and principles of diet and nutrition. Also important is setting fitness goals that include regular aerobic exercise. Proper exercise, combined with a moderate food plan (approximately 1,400 to 1,600 kcal daily—for a limited time and assuming sufficient exercise to preserve lean body mass—with 25 to 40 grams of fat) can result in weight loss without compromise to a dancer's health.[28] As part of this, dancers need good sources of information about macronutrients (carbohydrates, fat, protein), water, micronutrients (iron, calcium, and so on), and the use of vitamin and mineral supplements, snack foods, and fluids in general. Even more critical is learning to give up the guilt that surrounds so much of their eating and to increase enjoyment from food within a healthy lifestyle of balance, variety, and moderation.[29] Taking the time to gain a basic understanding of nutrition from reliable sources is an important first step.[30]

ENERGY NUTRIENTS AND WATER: A PRIMER

Carbohydrates

Carbohydrates contain carbon, hydrogen, and oxygen in a specific ratio of two hydrogens to each oxygen.[31] All carbohydrates, whether in a disaccharide or polysaccharide form, must eventually break down in digestion into glucose for energy metabolism.[32] A small amount may be stored as glycogen, and some carbohydrates that are resistant to human digestive enzymes are excreted from the body. Besides serving as the body's primary energy nutrient (and usually the only energy source for the central nervous system), glucose facilitates the complete breakdown of fat. Each gram of carbohydrate provides about 4 kcal of energy.

Monosaccharides and disaccharides are both sugars. Foods containing these sugars include brown sugar, corn syrup, honey, and white grape juice. Excessive amounts can result in body fluids being drawn quickly into the intestinal tract and blood glucose levels dropping. Thus, the type of carbohydrate consumed—and whether it is consumed during before, or after, a class or rehearsal—can affect the degree of carbohydrate concentration in the body. The term *Glycemic Index* (GI) indicates the extent to which a particular food item causes glucose to increase in the blood after the food has been consumed.[33] Foods with a high GI, for example, baked potatoes, refined pasta, vanilla cake with frosting, and certain soft drinks, are associated with a large insulin release (and subsequent drop in blood sugar) and should be avoided, at the very least immediately before a performance.[34] Foods with a low GI (for example, high-fiber foods such as beans and certain grains) seem to have less effect on blood sugar.

Physiologically, people's blood sugar responds differently to low- and high-GI foods. The response is related to many factors, including age and activity level, the amount of fiber and fat in the food, how refined (i.e., processed) the food is, what else was consumed with the food, how it was cooked (e.g., baking vs. boiling a potato), and how quickly the food is digested. Each person is different in terms of response. Thus, it is very difficult to devise and use a standard GI for foods that can apply to everyone (which is why dieticians prefer to use "grams of carbohydrate" rather than a GI for nutritional planning). (See "Achieving a Balanced Diet" in this chapter for further discussion.)

Cellulose and polysaccharides such as pectin make up the fibrous parts of plants and are thus sources of dietary fiber. They are common in leaves, roots, seeds, and other plant structures. A single polysaccharide (starch) unit can consist of thousands of sugars strung together, such as in breads and other grains, beans, and potatoes. These foods are referred to as complex carbohydrates. However, many health professionals prefer looking at the distribution of carbohydrates throughout the day, in meals and snacks, when attempting to manage blood sugar levels, rather that distinguishing between "simple" and "complex" carbohydrates. For example, table sugar (sucrose) has less effect on blood sugar than some "complex" carbohydrates such as potatoes.

Glycogen is a polysaccharide of particular importance in energy management. It is usually stored in the liver, where it is transformed from glucose in a process called "glycogenesis." It is also found in the muscles, totaling an average reserve of up to 3 percent of muscle cell weight (less than one pound). When glucose is needed to maintain blood glucose levels, liver glycogen is reconverted to glucose in a process called "glycogenolysis." This glucose is then available for use by the working muscles.

When glycogen is depleted through dietary restriction (or exercise), glucose synthesis, or "gluconeogenesis," occurs by breaking down protein and other nutrients from muscle tissue. Thus, adequate carbohydrate intake is essential in limiting the use of body protein (muscle) as an energy source. Recall that maintaining muscle mass is critical to a healthy (and relatively high) metabolism. The implication here is that with restricted eating, muscle tissue will be mobilized to provide glucose, resulting in a loss of lean body mass—something dancers want to avoid!

Fat

Fats are compounds that contain carbon, hydrogen, and oxygen. Each gram of fat provides about 9 kcal of energy. Fats are particularly dense in calories. According to the American Heart Association, each of the following contains 0.1 kcal, or 100 calories, the last three being "fatty" items: 20 stalks of celery, one medium potato, two cups of fresh strawberries, six ounces of white wine, one apple, eight large potato chips, one tablespoon of butter or margarine, and two-and-a-half teaspoons of oil.[35]

Triglyceride (glycerol and fatty acids cojoined) is the most abundant fat in the body. A fatty acid is saturated if each of the carbons is bound to hydrogen. Some food items that contain saturated fatty acids are butter, red meats, coconut oil, and palm oil. Unsaturated fatty acids are found in plant foods; they liquefy easily and tend to be liquids at room temperature. Examples of monounsaturated fatty acids are olive and peanut oils. Examples of polyunsaturated fatty acids (two or more double bonds along the main carbon chain) are corn and safflower oils. The omega-3 fatty acids are highly polyunsaturated fats. They are found in the oils of marine fish such as mackerel, salmon, sardines, and herring and in plant products such as walnuts and soybeans. They are referred to as "good fats," touted for the cardiovascular health they promote.[36] Other important roles for fat are protection of vital organs and insulation of the body against external thermal stress. Clearly, dancers need to ensure that they daily consume sufficient amounts of this important nutrient.

Fat represents a more compact or concentrated form of stored energy than glycogen. When glucose is stored as glycogen, 2.7 grams of water are required for each gram of glycogen (on a dry-weight basis). This is one reason that there is an upper limit to the amount of glycogen that can be stored when athletes "glycogen load."

Protein

Protein contains nitrogen as well as carbon, hydrogen, and oxygen. Protein supplies energy but has other roles, which include building blood, scar tissue, enzymes, hormones, and antibodies and maintaining fluid and salt balance.[37] Each gram of protein provides about 4 kcal of energy. Proteins consist of amino acids, eight of which are considered essential (essential amino acids, or EAAs) because they must be obtained through the diet.

Although a brain cell is only about 10 percent protein, muscle cells may contain more than double that amount. Although resistance exercise encourages an increase in muscle size and protein content in exercised muscle, simply eating larger amounts of protein does not. In order for muscle cells to increase in size, a demand must be put on them (i.e., they must be made to work). Protein cannot be "pushed" (force-fed amino acid supplements) into the cells; it must be "pulled" in—unlike fat, which is easily stored in the body when consumed in excess. Thus, for dancers and others, there is no advantage to eating excess protein, and doing so may ultimately be stressful on the kidneys.

The RDA for protein is sufficiently high to cover most athletes' needs, but, not unlike most Americans, many athletes and dancers consume too much protein.[38] What athletes and dancers should focus on is sufficient calorie intake: to eat enough protein-sparing calories in the form of carbohydrates—so that protein is not mobilized as an energy source.[39] This is important because, otherwise, lean body mass decreases.

Some dancers may take amino acids (e.g., protein powders) as supplements to meet dietary deficiencies and as ergogenic aids to build muscle, promote fat loss, and provide energy. However, there is little or no evidence that amino acid supplements will help them achieve these goals. Furthermore, the supplements are expensive.

The proteins contained in food can be classified as complete or incomplete, depending on their amino acid composition. An incomplete, or lower-quality, protein is deficient in one or more of the EAAs. Foods predominant in the nonessential amino acids (NEAAs) should be consumed in larger amounts or complemented by foods high in the EAAs. For example, in wheat-based diets, the wheat must be consumed in portions larger than that which the American population would consider "normal" or consumed in combination with foods high in EAAs (for example, low-fat dairy products). It makes sense, of course, that plant foods such as grains contain less of the EAAs than animal foods. For example, other animals have an oxygen-transport systems similar to humans; thus, we have to eat fewer animal products to accumulate the requisite amino acids for the production of compounds like hemoglobin, common to many animals. This is not to say that the amino acids needed to produce hemoglobin cannot be derived from consumption of plants; it is just necessary to eat more and a greater variety of plants. This is yet another reason why dancers (especially those avoiding animal products) need to consume sufficient calories daily.

It is relatively easy to make complete proteins by combining different food groups[40]: the legume group—beans (black, fava, kidney, lima, pinto, and so on), peas (black-eyed, chick, split), peanuts, and lentils; the grain group—barley, corn, oats, rice, wheat (wheat germ, sprouts), flours, and cereals made from these grains; and the nut and seed group—

almonds, cashews, walnuts, pumpkin seeds, sesame seeds, sunflower seeds, and so on. The following combinations make complete proteins:

- Legumes and grains: rice-bean casserole, corn tortilla and beans, peanut butter sandwich
- Legumes and nuts or seeds: blended dips with garbanzo beans, lentil casserole
- Legumes and low-fat dairy products: cheese sauce for bean dish, enchiladas
- Grains and low-fat dairy products: cheese sandwich, sandwich with milk, rice pudding, pasta with cheese, pizza
- Nuts or seeds and low-fat dairy products: cottage cheese–nut croquettes
- Small amounts of meat, poultry, or fish and plant proteins

Cereals should be eaten preferably in their whole-grain, low-sodium form.

When are our eating habits wasteful (i.e., amino acids are not used to build protein)? Amino acids are wasted when they are consistently consumed in excess of the RDA. Since protein cannot be stored as such, it is readily broken down and metabolized or stored for energy. However, an excess of anything is bound to get anyone in trouble, whether it is red meat alternatives such as chicken or even carbohydrates. (If eaten in large enough quantities, substantial amounts of protein and sodium can be consumed, and insulin levels can be adversely affected.) In short, dancers should be eating a balanced diet.

Water

Daily water intake is essential for good health and performance. It is essential for thermoregulation and for weight management. Very few dancers manage to consume the recommended 64 fluid ounces of water daily. According to the National Research Council, "The normal rate of turnover of water per day approximates six percent of total body weight in the adult . . . The body is equipped with a number of homeostatic mechanisms . . . that operate to maintain total body water within narrow limits."[41] For an adult requiring about 2,000 kcal/day, water consumption should be about 2,000 ml (2 liters), or about eight glasses of water per day.

For adequate hydration, 16 ounces or several glasses of fluid should be consumed one or 2 hours before exercise, another 10 to 15 ounces 15 minutes before exercise, and 3 to 6 ounces every 10 to 20 minutes during exercise, whether or not one feels thirsty.[42] This may not be completely practical for class, but can be readily accomplished in rehearsal. Dehydration occurs long before thirst is experienced. Dehydration can impair physical performance as well as mental function.[43]

One adaptation to dehydration is sodium retention (the sweat becomes more diluted) as kidney production of the hormone aldosterone is increased. Repeated bouts of dehydration may cause the body to become more efficient at storing water in excess of the sweat loss, resulting in greater rehydration and "water-weight gain."[44]

Elizabeth L. Snell of the National Ballet School of Canada refers to water as a "liquid asset."[45] Physical therapist Suzanne Martin notes that "how [dancers] manage nourishment during intense dance periods will leave telltale signs. They need to know how to balance the right foods and fluids to look and perform their best."[46] As mentioned above, Martin notes that dancers can lose up to 2 liters per hour during intense physical activity. With the body compensating at best for only one liter of lost fluid per hour, rehydration is critical.

ENERGY EXPENDITURE: A PRIMER

Energy expenditure is a function of three factors: basal (BMR) or resting (RMR) metabolic rate, muscular activity, and assimilation of food (referred to as specific dynamic action/effect, dietary-induced thermogenesis, or thermic effect of feeding).[47]

The BMR is frequently misused to denote RMR in discussion of human thermoregulation. The RMR (representing 60 to 70 percent of energy expenditure), together with the thermic effect of feeding (representing another 10 percent), constitute what is called "resting energy metabolism."[48]

Muscular activity is the most variable component of energy expenditure and can constitute 20 to 30 percent of the daily total through physical work, involuntary activity such as shivering and fidgeting, and purposeful physical exercise. Assimilation of food or the thermic effect of feeding refers to the heat released when consuming energy nutrients; carbohydrate, fat, and protein have different thermic effects. For example, the digestion of protein increases the metabolic rate substantially because the liver expends considerable energy processing the amino acids.

Of the three factors, RMR represents the largest use of internal energy resources. The beating of the heart, inhaling and exhaling of air, maintaining body temperature—these energy needs must be met before any calories are used for the other two factors.

There are many factors, in turn, that influence RMR.[49] These include age (the younger the person, the higher the RMR), height (the taller the person, the larger the surface area, the more heat is lost from the surface of the skin, and thus the higher the RMR for maintaining body temperature),[50] sex (males have higher RMRs than females owing to the presence of male sex hormones and to the higher percentage of lean body mass, since muscle tissue is highly active, even at rest),[51] health (fever increases the RMR of cells), fasting and/or constant malnutrition (RMR is lowered owing to loss of lean body tissue and the degeneration of body organs), and glandular secretions (such as the increase in RMR when epinephrine is released in response to stress).

Estimates of RMR can be made by using a nomogram,[52] which provides a simplified method for computing surface area based on height and weight. Take, for example, a woman about 5'6" tall and weighing 125 pounds. To determine her surface area, she would use the three scales of the nomogram to approximate 1.64 square meters, and then multiply 1.64×35 (38 for males) kcal/m²/hr $\times$ 24 hrs to determine the daily RMR—approximately 1,378 kcal daily just to sustain vital functions.

If the dancer's caloric intake is so low (less than 1,100 kcal) that basal metabolic needs are not being met, what adaptations does the body make? Besides becoming less active, which is usually not an option for dancers, one obvious change is that RMR decreases (i.e., the metabolism "slows down"), and thus the need for calories declines. This is in large part due to the mobilization of lean body tissue as a source of energy and is thus highly counterproductive to weight loss.

RECOMMENDED DIETARY ALLOWANCES AND DIETARY REFERENCE INTAKES: NEW GUIDELINES ON DIET

New information on nutrition in the last 10 or so years has led the Food and Nutrition Board of the Institute of Medicine, a part of the National Academies, to issue new guidelines on diet. Since World War II, Recommended Dietary Allowances, or RDAs,[53] have been the basis for almost all federal and state food and nutrition programs. Now, nutrition guidelines have been expanded to include indicators of good health and the prevention of chronic disease, as well as possible adverse effects of overconsumption, and to be more specific about age and sex. The new guidelines are called Dietary Reference Intakes, or DRIs (although they are sometimes still stated in terms of RDAs). These are reference values, as opposed to recommended or even desirable intakes.

A series of reports prepared over the past few years jointly by American and Canadian scientists provide authoritative new recommendations for vitamins, minerals, and macronutrients that include carbohydrates, fiber, fat, fatty acids, cholesterol, protein, and amino acids. The recommendations also link energy consumption in the form of calories to energy expenditure and advise on both the exercise and calorie intake needed to maintain a healthy body weight. Adults and children, the group advises, regardless of weight, should spend one hour a day in moderately strenuous activity, which is double the minimum recommendation of the 1996 Surgeon General's report (and somewhat more stringent than information presented in Chapter 4).

Recommendations for the major vitamins and minerals are summarized in Tables 5 and 6. (The recommendations are expressed in RDAs, intended as goals for individual intake and "set to meet the needs of almost all (97 to 98 percent) individuals in a group."[54])

An underlying assumption of the determinations is that food selections will be made from a wide variety of choices. This is to ensure that nutrients that are known to be required, but for which no recommended or reference intakes have been established, are consumed in sufficient quantities. Under no circumstances should the reference values be used as justification for reducing habitual intakes of nutrients. Likewise, they are not meant to be satisfied by overconsumption of vitamin and mineral supplementation or by megafortification of single foods. When vitamins and minerals are indicated for supplementation, they are meant to supplement a somewhat robust daily diet—not a carton of yogurt, half a sandwich, a salad, and an apple.

The body will adapt to occasional periods of nutrient deprivation. This is why, in estimating dietary adequacy, it is acceptable to average intakes over a 5- to 8-day period. However, nutrient supplementation on a regular basis is not recommended. One of the main reasons for this is that macronutrients (protein, carbohydrates) cannot be supplemented in adequate quantity. Carbohydrates are required in large amounts (accounting for at least 50 percent of total calories, and closer to 65 percent during heavy training and rehearsals[55]), as is protein (approximately 40 to 60 grams per day, or 12 to 15 percent of total calories).

As some food scientists note:

> While significant progress has been achieved in developing technological approaches to particular micronutrient deficiencies . . . the attempt to devise technological solutions to macronutrient deficiencies such as protein entails problems of a completely different magnitude . . . macronutrient deficits (whether protein or protein-calorie) require consumption in relatively large, daily quantities. As a result, the medical-type intervention [supplements as "medication"] as a response to macro-deficits is rendered totally inappropriate. Protein or protein-calorie interventions can only be conceived to be what they actually are, [i.e.] sources of food, with all of the social, cultural, and economic preferences and constraints that this involves.[56]

Supplements cannot be treated as medicines, as drugs, as a shot of this, or a hit of that. Dancers must adopt a new paradigm of eating, not "I need some vitamin A or thiamine or protein," but "I need to eat enough calories to meet my nutrient needs." Adequate calorie intake—with sugar and alcohol restricted and assuming a wide variety of foods—should ensure adequate intake of nutrients.

RECOMMENDED INTAKES OF ENERGY NUTRIENTS

Key points of DRI recommendations for macronutrients and for calories[57] are as follows:

- *Carbohydrates* should constitute 45 to 65 percent of calories (including sugar and starches).[57] However, dancers should note that the new recommendation of percentage calories for carbohydrates represents, in part, somewhat of a reassessment of the relative roles of carbohydrate and fat in the diet (see following).
- *Dietary fiber* is the residue of plant food resistant to human digestive enzymes. For children and adolescents, the daily requirement for dietary fiber can be determined by adding 5 to their age. So, a 10 year old would require 15 grams daily; a 17 year old would require 22 grams daily. For the 17 year old, the 22 grams could be achieved by eating a bowl of oatmeal, peanut butter on a slice of multigrain bread, an apple, and a garden burger with corn on the cob. Women 50 years of age and younger should consume about 25 grams of fiber daily, and men 38 grams (adding a bran muffin and additional fruit to the list for adolescent females raises the total to the needed 38 grams). The recommendation includes dietary fiber consumed directly, for example, in grains (found in oats, wheat, unmilled rice, barley, and so on) and consumption of functional fiber synthesized or extracted from plants shown to be of benefit to health. In addition, typical plant sources of fiber include fruit (apples, oranges, and peaches), vegetables (corn, squash), and legumes (baked beans). Another distinction has to do with the fiber's solubility, with water-soluble fibers such as pectin and guar gum that are present in oats, beans, peas, and fruits reputed also to lower blood cholesterol and the risk of type 2 diabetes.
- No more than 20 to 35 percent of caloric intake should be in the form of *fat*.[59] A typical recommendation has been that fats in the diet should consist of 10 percent polyunsaturated, 10 percent monounsaturated, and no more than 10 percent saturated. Recent guidelines as DRI recommendations give the following:
- No upper limits are set for *saturated fat* (commonly found in foods such as butter and coconut oil) *or trans fatty acids* (commonly found in foods that are processed or cooked with polyunsaturated oils at high temperatures, as in many fast food franchises), since any amount can bring increased risks. These fats have no known disease-prevention role and are not required at any level in the diet. The general recommendation is to eat as little of these substances as possible while still having a diet containing all important nutrients.
- Two kinds of essential *polyunsaturated fatty acids* must come from food, since the body cannot make them: alpha-linolenic acid (an omega-3 fatty acid) and linoleic acid (an omega-6 fatty acid). The Adequate Intake (AI) of alpha-linolenic acid per day for female adolescents and adults is 1.1 grams (1.0 grams for females 9 to 13 years of age), and for male adolescents and adults, 1.6 grams (1.2 grams for males 9 to 13 years of age). The daily AI for linoleic acid is 12 grams for women aged 19 to 50 years and 17 grams for men aged 19 to 50 years; the AI for individuals outside the 19 to 50 year range is slightly less. These beneficial fatty acids are found in milk, nuts, avocados, olives, flaxseed, soybeans, and safflower, canola, and corn oils.

Table 5 Adult RDA for Vitamins

Vitamin	Function	RDA/AI[a]	UL[b]	Food Sources
		Fat Soluble		
A	Required for normal vision, gene expression, reproduction, embryonic development, immune function	700 µg/d (women), 900 µg/d (men)	3,000 µg/d	Liver, dairy products, fish, darkly colored fruits, leafy vegetables
D	Maintain serum calcium and phosphorus concentrations	5 µg/d (age 19–50 yr), 10µg/d (age 50–70 yr), 15µg/d (age > 70 yr),	50 µg/d	Fish liver oil, flesh of fatty fish, eggs from hens fed vitamin D, fortified milk, fortified cereals
E	Metabolic function not yet identified; major function seems to be as antioxidant	15 mg/d	1,000 mg/d	Vegetable oils, unprocessed cereal grains, nuts, fruits, vegetables, meats
K	Coenzyme during the synthesis of many proteins involved in blood clotting and bone metabolism	90 µg/d (women), 120 µg/d (men)	ND[c]	Green vegetables, brussel sprouts, cabbage, plant oils and margarine
		Water Soluble		
C	Cofactor for reactions requiring reduced copper or iron metalloenzyme, and protective antioxidant	75 mg/d (women), 90 mg/d (men) .	2,000 mg/d	Citrus fruits, tomatoes, potatoes, brussel sprouts, cauliflower, broccoli, strawberries, cabbage, spinach
Thiamin (or B$_1$)	Coenzyme in metabolism of carbohydrates and branched-chain amino acids	1 mg/d (women), 1.2 mg/d (men)	ND[c]	Enriched, fortified, or whole-grain products (breads, mixed foods whose main ingredient is grain, ready-to-eat cereals)
Riboflavin (or B$_2$)	Coenzyme in various redox reactions	1.1 mg/d (women), 1.3 mg/d (men)	ND[c]	Organ meats, milk, bread, fortified cereals
Niacin (or B$_3$)	Coenzyme or cosubstrate in many reduction and oxidation reactions (i.e., required for energy metabolism)	14 mg/d (women), 16 mg/d (men)	35 mg/d	Meat, fish, poultry, enriched and whole-grain bread, fortified ready-to-eat cereals
Cobalamin (or B$_{12}$)	Coenzyme in nucleic acid metabolism; prevents megaloblastic anemia	2.4 µg/d	ND[c]	Fortified cereals, meat, fish, poultry

Table 5 Adult RDA for Vitamins (Continued)

Vitamin	Function	RDA/AI [a]	UL [b]	Food sources
Folate (or folic acid, folacin)	Coenzyme in the metabolism of nucleic and amino acids; prevents megaloblastic anemia	400 µg/d	1,000 µg/d	Enriched cereal grains, dark leafy vegetables, enriched and whole-grain bread, fortified ready-to-eat cereals
Pantothenic acid	Coenzyme in fatty acid metabolism	5 mg/d	ND [c]	Chicken, beef, potatoes, oats, cereals, tomato products, liver, kidney, yeast, egg yolk, broccoli, whole grains
Biotin	Coenzyme in synthesis of fat, glycogen, amino acids	30 µg/d	ND [c]	Liver, smaller amounts in fruits, meats

[a]RDA = Recommended Dietary Allowances; AI = Adequate Intakes; may be used as goals for individual intake. Ages 19–50 (values for 9–13 and 14–18 age categories may be slightly lower; values for the over-50 age group are usually the same).

[b]UL = Tolerable Upper Intake Levels. Maximum level of daily nutrient intake likely to pose no risk of adverse effects.

[c]ND = Not Determinable, due to lack of data; source should be only from food to prevent high levels of intake.

Source: Food and Nutrition Board, Institute of Medicine (Washington, DC: National Academies). *Dietary Reference Intakes: Vitamins.* Based on several Food and Nutrition Board, Institute of Medicine publications: *Dietary Reference Intakes for Calcium, Phosphorous, Magnesium, Vitamin D, and Fluoride* (1997); *Dietary Reference Intakes for Thiamin, Riboflavin, Niacin, Vitamin B6, Folate, Vitamin B12, Pantothenic Acid, Biotin, and Choline* (1998); *Dietary Reference Intakes for Vitamin C, Vitamin E, Selenium, and Carotenoids* (2000); *Dietary Reference Intakes for Vitamin A, Vitamin K, Arsenic, Boron, Chromium, Copper, Iodine, Iron, Manganese, Molybdenum, Nickel, Silicon, Vanadium, and Zinc* (2001).

Table 6 Adult RDA for Minerals and Trace Elements

Mineral/Element	Function	RDA/AI[a]	UL[b]	Food Sources
Calcium	Essential in blood clotting, muscle contraction, nerve transmission, bone/tooth formation	1,000 mg/d (age 19–50 yr) 1,200 mg/d (age 50–70 yr)	2,500 mg/d	Milk, cheese, yogurt, corn tortilla, calcium-set tofu, Chinese cabbage, kale, broccoli
Copper	Component of enzymes in iron metabolism	900 μg/d	10,000 μg/d	Organ meats, seafood, nuts, seeds, wheat bran, whole-grain products, cocoa products
Fluoride	Inhibits dental caries, stimulates bone formation	3 mg/d (women), 4 mg/d (men)	10 mg/d	Fluoridated water, teas, marine fish
Iodine	Component of thyroid hormones; prevents goiter, cretinism	150 μg/d	1,100 μg/d	Marine origin, processed foods, iodized salt
Iron	Component of hemoglobin and numerous enzymes; prevents microcytic hypochromic anemia	18 mg/d (women) (age 19–50 yr) 8 mg/d (men)	45 mg/d	Fruits, vegetables, fortified bread/grain products, meat, poultry
Magnesium	Cofactor for enzyme systems	310–320 mg/d (women) 400–420 mg/d (men)	350 mg/d[c]	Green leafy vegetables, unpolished grains, nuts, meats, starches, milk
Manganese	Involved in formation of bone, and in enzymes for amino acid, cholesterol, and carbohydrate metabolism	1.8 mg/d (women) 2.3 mg/d (men)	11 mg/d	Nuts, legumes, tea, whole grains
Phosphorus	Maintenance of pH, storage and transfer of energy, nucleotide synthesis	700 mg/d	4,000 mg/d	Milk, yogurt, ice cream, cheese, peas, meat, eggs, some cereals and breads
Zinc	Component of multiple enzymes and proteins; involved in regulation of gene expression	8 mg/d (women), 11 mg/d (men)	40 mg/d	Fortified cereals, red meats, certain seafoods

[a]RDA = Recommended Dietary Allowances; AI = Adequate Intakes; may be used as goals for individual intake. Ages 19–50 (values for 9–13 and 14–18 age categories may be slightly lower; Values for the over–50 age group are usually the same).

[b]UL = Tolerable Upper Intake Levels. Maximum level of daily nutrient intake likely to pose no risk of adverse effects.

[c]UL for magnesium does not include intake from food and water.

Source: Food and Nutrition Board, Institute of Medicine. *Dietary Reference Intakes: Elements. Elements.* www.iom.edu/includes/DBFile.asp?id«eq»7294. Based on several Food and Nutrition Board, Institute of Medicine publications: Dietary Reference Intakes for Calcium, Phosphorous, Magnesium, Vitamin D, and Fluoride (1997); *Dietary Reference intakes for Thiamin, Riboflavin, Niacin, Vitamin B6, Folate, Vitamin B12, Pantothenic Acid, Biotin, and Choline (1998); Dietary Reference Intakes for Vitamin C, Vitamin E, Selenium, and Carotenoids (2000);* Dietary Reference Intakes for Vitamin A, Vitamin K, Arsenic, Boron, Chromium, Copper, Iodine, Iron, Manganese, Molybdenum, Nickel, Silicon, Vanadium, and Zinc (2001).

- *Protein* should account for 10 to 35 percent of daily calories for adults.[60] Adults should consume 0.8 grams of protein for each kilogram (2.2 lbs) of body weight; this varies for younger individuals—0.95 grams for each kilogram of body weight for ages 4 to 13 years, and 0.85 grams for each kilogram for ages 14 to 18 years. So, an adolescent dancer weighing about 54 kg (about 120 pounds) could consume a small bowl of oatmeal with soy or cow's milk, a peanut butter sandwich, snacks of yogurt and a handful of nuts, and two pieces of cheese pizza for dinner to meet the generous daily protein requirement of 46 grams.
- There is little evidence that muscular activity increases the need for protein disproportionately to calories. If athletes need additional protein, it is in ample supply in the extra calories consumed in high-carbohydrate foods.[61]

In sum, recommended intakes for the general population are:

- Carbohydrates: 45 to 65 percent of total caloric intake
- Protein: 10 to 35 percent
- Fat: 20 to 35 percent

Researchers Robin Chmelar and Sally Fitt recommend similar though somewhat tighter ranges of intake levels for dancers:[62]

- Carbohydrates: 55 to 65 percent of total calories
- Protein: 15 to 20 percent,
- Fat: 15 to 25 percent

DIET AND WEIGHT CONTROL

For the purposes of weight control, Robin Chmelar and Sally Fitt outline diets consisting of approximately 20 percent protein, 20 percent fat, and 60 percent carbohydrate. Part of the rationale for this is empirical: many female dancers have difficulty losing weight with protein intakes of only 10 to 15 percent and fat intakes below 25 percent, especially on low-calorie diets.[63]

Of vital importance is that dancers not go for long periods without food, say, 4 to 6 hours, which can cause the insulin response to "overshoot" and produce a dramatic drop in blood glucose levels, followed by a craving for carbohydrates.[64] Such large swings in blood sugar that result from hours of not eating should be avoided. One way of doing this is to eat smaller meals (and snacks) throughout the day, perhaps a light snack of yogurt, fruit, and cereal 45 minutes before class and a similar snack after class, with the rest of the day's meals consisting of lunch, midafternoon snack, dinner, and evening snack.[65] If it is difficult to eat before class, a more substantial meal can be eaten after class.

The Importance of Carbohydrates

For the general population—and dancers are no exception—most of the calories in the diet should come from carbohydrates because foods high in carbohydrates also contain ample amounts of vitamins and minerals. As long as dancers consume enough varied carbohydrates (and water), many nutrient needs should be met. This may be a tall order. Bonbright has reported that even when dancers consumed close to their RDA for calories (83.7 percent of the RDA), the RDAs for biotin, zinc, linoleic acid, copper, iodine, and chloride were not met. Almost all dancers were deficient in the other vitamins and minerals studied, with the exception of vitamins B^2, B^1, C, B^3, A, K, and B^{12}, sodium, and chromium.[66]

The body needs carbohydrates to provide a continuous supply of energy to the cells. The carbohydrates in food eventually break down in digestion into sugar units or glucose. Glucose is one of the two major fuels used by the cells for energy (the other is fatty acids). Glucose is usually the only fuel source for the brain and central nervous system. Glucose levels in the blood are maintained by periodic eating of foods containing carbohydrates and by release of glucose from stored glycogen.

During exercise, glycogen is metabolized anaerobically—for example, providing the energy for a short, vigorous floor combination (lasting between 2 to 5 minutes)—and aerobically, for example, providing the energy for more endurance exercise, with continuous movement more than 5 minutes in duration.[67] The other major fuels used by the cells for energy are muscle triglycerides, which are broken down into fatty acids that are metabolized to produce energy for muscular contraction. Under certain conditions (see discussion of endurance exercise in Chapter 4 and the next section on feasting and fasting) triglycerides are broken down in adipose tissue and the fatty acids are then released into the blood to be carried to muscle cells.[68] A small percentage of glucose can be obtained from amino acids (the "building blocks" of protein) in muscles and other tissue proteins; this percentage dramatically increases during carbohydrate deprivation and is counterproductive to dancers' long-term weight management goals.

Feasting and Fasting

The brain alone requires about 400 to 600 kcal each day as glucose. Even at rest, it consumes about two thirds of the total circulating blood glucose. What happens when dancers deprive their bodies of calories and, in particular, carbohydrates?

In the first few days of a fast, tissue protein provides most of the needed energy, the remainder coming from fat reserves (see Figure 84). The loss of protein can usually be controlled by exercise and carbohydrate consumption.[69] Yet without adequate carbohydrate

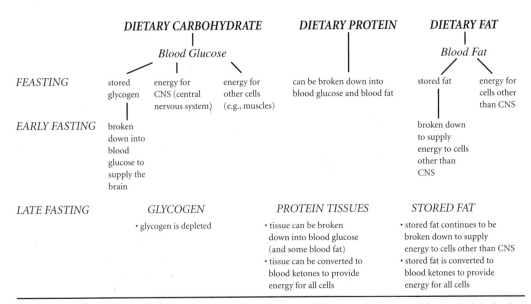

Figure 84 Energy flow in feasting and fasting: energy balance in feasting (excess calories), in early fasting (calorie deprivation), and in late fasting (severe caloric deprivation). [Adapted from E. M. Hamilton, E. N. Whitney, and F. S. Sizer, *Nutrition: Concepts and Controversies.* 3rd ed. (St. Paul, MN: West Publishing Co., 1985).]

intake, death would inevitably result were it not for a specific metabolic adaptation: ketosis. In ketosis, the body converts fatty acid (fat) and amino acid (protein) fragments into ketone bodies, a fuel alternative to glucose, allowing the body to survive an extended period of starvation or "self-induced" starvation. If ketone bodies are produced in excess of what can be excreted in the urine, however, they can accumulate in the blood, leading to "acidosis."

The adult body thus adapts to a carbohydrate deprivation/starvation situation by mobilizing amino acids (which decreases muscle mass), degrading the organs (in particular, the liver), and decreasing resting or basal metabolism. This is obviously helpful for people who are trying to survive a famine situation; it is exceptionally counterproductive to dancers who want to "lose weight" quickly and permanently. The body begins to need fewer calories because fat tissue requires considerably fewer to maintain itself than does muscle. Moreover, because certain organs begin to waste away, the body is not capable of performing as much work and therefore requires fewer calories for daily maintenance. Thus, dancers trying to lose weight by restricting calories will not be successful (in the long term); the body adapts to restricted calories by needing less.

How Do Diets "Work"?

Low-calorie, low-carbohydrate diets work in terms of short-term weight loss. In fact, some hospitals administer very low calorie diets (VLC), 400 to 800 kcal/day: a "modified fast," in which the patients are strictly monitored; five-pound losses per week are common. But these diets do not work in terms of long-term weight management. Most of the weight loss seen on the bathroom scale is from mobilizing protein and water. Approximately 75 percent of the weight lost during the first week of the diet is water, with the rest coming mostly from muscle tissue. But where is the water coming from?

With a low-carbohydrate intake, the body must use its meager stores of glycogen for fuel. When glycogen is depleted, so is the water stored with it. Muscle itself is about 70 percent water, so that breaking down glycogen and muscle tissue results in water loss (referred to as "weight loss"). However, when refeeding starts, the body replenishes its glycogen stores and deposits fat first, so that the first weight regained is water (for the storage of glycogen) and fat. This is why starvation dieters regain weight with a greater proportion of the regained weight as fat.

Another risk is that, with repeated or "yo-yo" dieting, the fat or adipose cells adapt by becoming increasingly efficient at storing fatty acids. Thus, it is even harder to lose weight during the next dieting bout or to maintain the loss of those 7 or 10 pounds for any extended time period. Of course, dancers with rigorous work schedules have an activity level high enough to force the body to use fat as an energy reserve, but their slim, lithe bodies may belie a large percentage of internal fat, possibly as an adaptation to repeated dieting bouts. Nevertheless, dancers continue to diet on-and-off. In one study, Bonbright found that 37.5 percent of the dancers interviewed dieted five or more times a year for 12-day periods.[70]

Fortunately, the body is "smart." We do not have to precisely calculate percentages and weights for the appropriate amount of protein, fat, and carbohydrates in our diet—to some extent. Excess calories as protein, fat, or carbohydrates are readily converted to fat. Interestingly, the energy cost of storing carbohydrates as fat is greater than, for example, that of storing fat as fat. Alternatively, if the diet is deficient in carbohydrates, protein and fat will eventually be converted to ketone bodies.

Fat Mobilization

It is easy to become fixated on day-to-day weight fluctuations on the scale. However, dancers' primary interest should be their body composition—the relative amounts of fat and muscle. Dance is known as a "low-body-fat" profession, with female professional dancers ranging from 11 to 16 percent body fat and male professional dancers ranging from 5 to 11 percent.[71] These figures are low compared with values averaging more than 12 percent for men and 20 percent for women,[72] in the general population although some average estimates are as high as 15 percent for men and 30 percent for women.

How is it possible to reduce the percentage of fat in the body? How can fat be mobilized as an energy source? It is thought that the best way is through low-intensity exercise. This light exercise applies just the right amount of stress to energy systems so that the slow lipolysis ("fat-splitting") process can take place.

During exercise intensities demanding more than 50 to 60 percent of the maximal oxygen uptake, muscle glycogen is the major fuel—its depletion coincides with the time of physical exhaustion. However, as the duration of the exercise increases to several hours, more than 50 percent of the energy is supplied by fat. Blood glucose also increases in importance as an energy source during prolonged exercise.[73] For example, by the end of the day a mail carrier will have used 90 percent of his or her energy as fat. Just sitting in a chair or sleeping—both considered "light" activity—will cause a large percentage of the fuel to be mobilized as fat.

The total amount of fuel used in "light" activity, however, will be low compared to the amount used in intense activity, such as repeated jumping. For the jumping activity ("moderate" to "heavy" exercise), energy requirements are higher. Although a smaller percentage of the fuel will be derived from fat during the exercise, especially if it is of short duration (glycogen and circulating blood glucose are used first), total fat mobilized after exercise may be substantial and the physiological effects of such exercise may be more long-lasting.

There are at least three reasons for this. First, for up to 8 hours after exercise, the body's metabolic rate, and thus its need for calories, remains elevated. Second, because exercise that sufficiently stresses the body's musculoskeletal system may result in muscle accretion and thus an increase in lean body mass, the body's metabolic rate remains slightly elevated, assuming that the exercise is rigorous. More energy is required to maintain a gram of muscle than a gram of fat, but more energy is also required to build the protein. Synthesis of protein is energetically expensive; several hours after exercise, protein synthesis increases and remains elevated up to 24 hours.[74] Third, glucose tolerance is increased for several days after vigorous exercise, partly owing to the increased glucose uptake by muscle in order to replenish glycogen stores.

Energy In, Energy Out?

It is relatively easy to find information on how many kcal one can "burn" during a specific exercise. For example, for a 123-pound person, the following energy expenditures could be expected:[75]

Archery:	216 kcal per hour
Badminton:	324 kcal per hour
Swimming, backstroke:	570 kcal per hour
Dance technique class:	200 to 300 kcal per hour

However, such charts are virtually useless unless one is more specific about sex, weight, and other variables. Worse, such charts feed our society's obsession with the "quick fix": "I ate a brownie, so now I'll get on an exercise bike for 45 minutes to work it off."

Physiologically, the only given in terms of "burning" energy is that phosphorus-containing energy compounds (called adenosine triphosphate, or ATP) must be broken down to release energy. If one wants to manipulate the fuels (fat, carbohydrate) from which ATP compounds are formulated, the body must be conditioned in terms of number and size of mitochondria (the cell's "powerhouse" unit), oxidative enzymes, and muscle fiber type.

In addition, the duration of and nutritional intake before exercise determine which fuel source will be most easily mobilized. For example, consuming glucose less than an hour before exercising encourages the body to use glucose rather than fat as a fuel source, all other factors being equal. Again, biophysical and chemical inertia take over in determining how much fat is "burned."

The bottom line is that if calories are going to be somewhat restricted (not to fall below 1,400 kcal daily, mostly in the form of carbohydrates), the individual has to engage in daily endurance activity for at least 30 minutes to restrict muscle loss. Thus, only through balanced food intake and daily endurance activity will the effects of severe caloric deprivation —the metabolic changes that result from the loss of muscle and organ tissue—be reversed.

ACHIEVING A BALANCED DIET

Good news: fat is not necessarily bad! As Geoffrey Cowley writes in *Newsweek*,[76] "The USDA's famous Food Guide Pyramid, first published in 1992, is now widely viewed as flawed [primarily because it] introduced the notion that some foods (fats) required more moderation than others (carbohydrates)."

Walter Willett and his colleagues at the Harvard School of Public Health have revised the pyramid (called the "Healthy Eating Pyramid") to emphasize calorie-rich vegetable oils. The pyramid downgrades refined rice and even potatoes and upgrades fats, tropical oils, and eggs.[77] The USDA pyramid faltered by implying that all fats are dangerous and most carbohydrates are safe. Hence, the general public—and dancers especially—have gone on a feeding frenzy of low-fat carbohydrates, to the exclusion of fat and protein. But a diet rich in refined carbohydrates dumps considerable glucose into the bloodstream; insulin is released to empty it into cells. But cells bombarded with insulin become increasingly resistant to it. As a result, there may be increased risk for fat weight increases, type 2 diabetes, and cardiovascular dysfunction.

So, throw out the low-fat muffins and bring on the avocados? The idea here is that the oils found in fish, nuts, and vegetables have protective properties and that cereal grains have "all the nutritional value of table sugar when milled into flour."[78] This means that meals should consist mostly of whole grains and protective oil and fats, with refined carbohydrates used sparingly (Figure 85). The less preprocessed the food is, the better—raw broccoli or coarse, chewy bread. Daily exercise (which forms the base of the "Healthy Eating Pyramid") also is critical.

Should the Food Pyramid Be the Food Square?

Perhaps none have flattened the food pyramid base so strikingly as Diana Schwarzbein and Nancy Deville, as discussed in the popular book, *The Schwarzbein Principle*.[79] The authors explain the importance of balanced meals in terms of physiology and biochemistry. For

Figure 85 A healthy diet that is balanced and varied, including "good fats." (Photo by Angela Sterling)

Schwarzbein, how the body uses carbohydrates (sugar) is determined by the ratio of insulin to glucagon—two hormones produced in the pancreas, whose job is to regulate nutrient distribution. Briefly, glucagon causes the liver to release sugar, which raises the levels of available blood sugar. Insulin, on the other hand, causes nutrients (proteins, fat, and sugar) to unload from the bloodstream and be stored in cells, thus balancing blood-sugar levels. So, eating a mixed meal of proteins, fats, "nonstarchy" vegetables, and carbohydrates (Schwarzbein's four food groups) provides a balanced insulin-to-glucagon ratio. In addition, the Glycemic Index(GI)[80] of the meal is lower. This also was one of the principles Harvard's Willett used in redesigning the pyramid.

Here is an example: If eating a potato alone, the GI of the meal is higher than eating it with salmon, kale, and a salad. This is because carbohydrates enter the blood much faster than proteins and fats, causing insulin release. Excess carbohydrates will be stored as fat. Thus, eating protein and fat actually lowers the insulin-to-glucagon ratio (since, with a balanced meal, the secretion of insulin is lower and glucagon is higher). So, food eaten will be used either to rebuild the body or directly as energy, rather than stored as fat.[81]

So, a narrower base makes the pyramid a square. This is not dissimilar to the three-decades-old (and somewhat contested) Atkins diet that also argues that carbohydrates, not fat, are the cause of obesity in the American population.What all this suggests is that balance, variety, and moderation (in this case, of refined foods) is the most prudent way to eat.

The general public will not shed pounds and pounds on this diet, but following some of the basic principles may reduce the amount of overeating (of low-fat, high-calorie foods) rampant in this country. The real question here is, how much of this applies to athletes and dancers? Most athletes and dancers should be consuming a high-carbohydrate diet (high in fiber and other nutrients and low in sugar) in order to balance energy stores needed for optimal performance. Balancing the carbohydrates with protein and fat[82] makes sense.[83] The idea here is that diets for dancers should be neither low-fat nor low-carbohydrate, but full of foods high in nutrients that taste good and satisfy hunger.

RECOMMENDATIONS FOR A BALANCED DIET

- Practice balance, variety, moderation.
- Choose a diet from a variety of foods.
- Try to eat foods in their most natural state.
- Avoid foods that contain human-made, damaged fats (trans-fats), harmful food additives, and/or excess sugar.
- Avoid processed and high-sodium meats.
- Limit refined grain products.
- Limit sugar and desserts.
- Limit alcohol consumption.
- Avoid processed snack foods.
- Avoid condiments that contain sugar and chemical additives.
- Do not smoke. (See "A Cautionary Note: Dancing and Tobacco Do Not Mix.")

Choreographing Meals

The spacing and scheduling of meals is sometimes a problem for dancers. As ABT's Cynthia Harvey says, "Most of the time, I really don't eat three meals a day, although I know that when I do I'm better off. In fact, I went to a nutritionist who told me I'd be better off eating six tiny meals a day for my metabolism."[84] This advice is well taken. The three-meal daily diet is a result of cultural conditioning, not physiological necessity.

Dancers are busy, they are constantly working. They take class, rehearse, perform, teach class, and tour. As one dancer said, "When I tour, my diet is anything but sublime." In colleges and universities, students go to class, choreograph, rehearse, perform, take notes, sit for exams, write papers, dance more, and study. It is hard to find time to eat. As a result, dancers consume excess carbohydrates (sugary foods) and processed (junk) foods. They grab whatever they can, usually foods high in fat and salt. Former Pacific Northwest Ballet soloist Melanie Skinner takes exception to this behavior. She prides herself on being a gourmet cook, eating small meals throughout the day and sitting down to a hearty meal at night (see Chapter 5 profile). Of particular importance is breakfast; those who skip this important meal are at risk for sharp drops in blood sugar and increases in physical cravings—often met by sugary foods, and resulting in further cravings.

For most dancers, it is difficult to schedule full meals consisting of a varied diet. Yet, the body is unforgiving: if at least 900 carbohydrate-rich kcal are not consumed on a daily basis,[85] the body will compensate by degrading dietary protein and muscle tissue for the needed glucose, no matter what the dancer puts into or purges from the body. The result is that dancers lose lean body weight.

Table 7 Foods High in Calories from Carbohydrates and Relatively Low in Saturated Fat

Hot Cereal: small amounts of peanut butter, sunflower seeds, wheat germ, or dried fruit.

Toast: whole-grain breads spread with nut butter.

Salads: low-calorie salads are converted into full meals by adding low-sodium cottage cheese, garbanzo beans, sunflower seeds, vegetables, chopped walnuts, tuna fish.

Soups (all low-sodium): hearty lentil, split pea, minestrone, barley.

Sandwiches: hearty, dense breads (such as thick-sliced sprouted whole grain) with tuna salad, bean spreads, or lightly spread with nut butters.

Snacks: fruit yogurts, sandwiches.

Timing Is Everything

As discussed earlier, eating most of the daily calories at one time rather than spacing meals throughout the day can result in large swings in blood glucose levels, intense hunger contractions, and overconsumption of foods high in sugar.[86] This is something dancers want to avoid. For preperformance meals, dancers usually prefer to eat light meals one to 3 hours before performing, saving a bigger meal until after the performance.[87] Dancers also should drink plenty of water.[88]

After long periods—up to 6 hours—without food, blood glucose levels drop dramatically.[89] Stomach contractions intensify concurrent with a craving for carbohydrates. It is thus better to eat a full sandwich for lunch than try to do without food altogether. What dancers should not do, but usually do, is eat practically nothing—a little salad, a half bagel, some yogurt—generally thinking of food all day long but resisting eating until hunger is so great that they will eat anything in sight. This usually means eating something high in sugar for rapid satiety.

When the body is deprived of food, it seems to call upon every psychological and physiological mechanism at its disposal to get itself to eat. A one-meal-a-day schedule will certainly increase appetite. Dancers pass up food they really want in order to keep their weight down, and then "pig out," eating beyond satiety. This is part of the obsession with food, insulin levels notwithstanding. Instead, what dancers should focus on is how to distribute their caloric intake throughout the day. To this end, there are certain foods that dancers should incorporate into their diet that are high in calories from carbohydrates, yet low in sodium and somewhat balanced in terms of fat and protein (Table 7). Recall that, for maintaining blood sugar levels, achieving balance within and among foods eaten in a meal also is important.[90]

A CAUTIONARY NOTE:
DANCING AND TOBACCO DO NOT MIX

According to the American Lung Association, more than 400,000 Americans die each year from diseases caused by smoking— one in five deaths in the United States. Morbidity is also high, with increased incidence of respiratory diseases, potential retardation in rate of lung growth and the level of maximum lung function, decreased physical fitness, and unfavorable lipid profiles. Smoking produces chronic irritation of the respiratory lining, and the carcinogens in cigarette smoke effect cellular and molecular changes that greatly increase the risk for lung cancer.[a] Such changes are particularly noticeable in individuals who began smoking as adolescents (individuals who started smoking before the age of 15 have four times the risk for lung cancer as those who began smoking after 25 years of age). Negative effects include cardiovascular diseases, diabetes, cancers of the respiratory tract, osteoporosis,[b] and emphysema.

Further, cigarette smoking may adversely affect one's appearance, as well as injury recovery—two items of concern to dancers. Smoking results in premature facial wrinkling and graying of the skin. It also affects the synthesis of collagen needed for healing. Decreased blood flow to the extremities compromises the healing of foot blisters and sores. Smoking also is associated with a higher risk of spinal disc disease and complications following many surgical procedures.

The American Lung Association estimates that one-third of children smokers will die of smoking-related illnesses. The prevalence is particularly high among adolescents (with over one-third currently using cigarettes, half of that number frequently). Tobacco use is associated with a lower self-image and self-esteem than for peers, the belief that tobacco assists in weight control and other useful functions, peer and sibling use, and lack of parental involvement as adolescents face the challenge of growing up.

The incidence of smoking among dancers, even young dancers, is believed to be high—many smoke cigarettes as an intended form of weight control. Although smoking does seem to cause a 3 to 10 percent increase in resting metabolic rate, the effects on metabolic rate are temporary and decline within about 24 hours of the last cigarette, upon which weight gain begins immediately. There are certainly safer ways to increase the metabolic rate—building muscle mass through strength training and regular endurance exercise are but two.

It is estimated that a smoker costs an average employer about $4,000 per year in additional medical costs and days away from work. Smoking is serious business. Others should not profit at the dancer's expense.

Sources: Adapted from "Teenage tobacco use," *Journal of Dance Medicine & Science* 3/3 (1999): 113–114. American Lung Association, *Trend Report on Cigarette Smoking* (1999); Centers for Disease Control and Prevention, "Incidence of initiation of cigarette smoking—United States, 1965–1996," *Morbidity Mortality Weekly Report* 47/39 (1998): 837–834; Karen S. Clippinger, "Smoking in young dancers," *Journal of Dance Medicine & Science* 3/3 (1999): 115–125. See also http://www.lungusa.org/tobacco/teenager_factsheet.html.

[a]Karen Clippinger reports that since 1987, more women die each year from lung cancer than from breast cancer. Smoking also increases the risk for cancer of the pancreas, kidney, urinary bladder, stomach, and cervix.

[b]A serious concern for dancers who already struggle with inadequate calcium intake, stress fractures, and the Female Athlete Triad.

PROFILES

Kent Stowell

Kent Stowell (Figure 86) and Francia Russell, husband and wife and co-artistic directors of Pacific Northwest Ballet (PNB), serve as role models for the dancers in their company. They danced as soloists in a very influential company, the New York City Ballet, and Stowell also danced as a principal elsewhere. Russell is highly regarded for her staging of Balanchine ballets worldwide. Stowell not only directs but also choreographs for PNB. Their skill and artistry in directing PNB have earned the company both a national and international reputation.

Figure 86 Pacific Northwest Ballet's Kent Stowell in rehearsal. (Photo by Angela Sterling)

While running a major ballet company, attending to dancers' development as technicians and artists, creating and rehearsing new works as well as Balanchine classics, and developing an audience for dance in Seattle, Stowell and Russell have raised a family of three boys —one of whom currently directs the Oregon Ballet Theatre.

Stowell, reflecting on his own career, contends that companies now take care of their dancers in ways that were unheard of in the past:

> Forty years ago, [New York City Ballet] was practically the only place to earn a living [in ballet]. American Ballet Theatre was on and off, and Ballet Russes had folded. You could get work with the opera [as Stowell had done in the 1950s, with San Francisco Ballet]; most companies offered a spring performance and a Nutcracker season. Things are different today—major regional companies such as PNB and Miami City Ballet, San Francisco Ballet, Boston Ballet, Houston Ballet started to take hold in the community. Operating budgets expanded as did 401K plans, health insurance benefits, and the availability of physical therapy—all these amenities have helped to shape the lives of our artists today in such a different way.

A theme of food as more than fuel, as part of a balanced life, runs through Stowell's observations:

> Along with that, we are a different country, too—there's a sense of discovering food . . . not just as a fuel additive but as nourishment in so many ways. Many dancers need quick gratification. But as you grow older, your tastes change. Just as Mozart is not a young person's first choice for music—it's an acquired taste, it is the same thing with food.
>
> When Francia and I lived in Europe [in the 1970s, Stowell as leading dancer and choreographer with the Munich Opera Ballet, and then as ballet master, choreographer, and co-artistic director—with Russell—of the Frankfurt Ballet], Francia did a lot of the cooking. After we moved to Seattle [in 1977], Francia did more of the child care and I did more of the cooking. When we'd come home from work, I'd fix dinner. Part of the nutrition of our family was to reconnect with each other. It was important for the boys to observe this process of preparing food. Even their buddies would come over and ask, 'what's that?' referring to the exotic leftovers. Our children grew up with a full sensory sense of life—it brought our family together. Now, all three of our children cook.
>
> What happens in Ethan's restaurant [referring to son Ethan Stowell's Seattle restaurant, Union] is what happened in our house all the time: people gathering, enjoying food, and there're important spiritual values that go with that. Meals are a time when families rebond and rekindle relationships. Certainly, there are lots of people in our profession who love cooking. There's a certain amount of craft and a certain discipline in cooking and presenting food.

A candlelight dinner, as was the rule with Stowell's family, may not be in the cards for every dancer. But Stowell hopes that, at the very least, his dancers have a nourishing meal—if only to "give them a sense of life, somehow." He feels providing information is the key; PNB keeps a nutritionist on staff to advise dancers on healthy eating.

> A lot of dancers smoke and that's destructive—they feel that they need to do it. They know what they're doing is not healthy—smoking and eating junk food. Finally, they get to a stage where they have to come to grips with themselves . . . knowing that they're not going to dance forever. We've often thought of having a cooking course for the dancers so that they learn to cook things tasty and delicious, good for their health, and nourishing. We've even thought of having our son, Ethan, come in for classes.

Stowell believes that the benefits for dancers of food and cooking go far beyond nutrition:

> Besides eating a healthier diet, dancers discover other things about food . . . Where do you get this kind of fish, what to do with a Jerusalem artichoke or pureed ham. Or, that this is a wonderful olive oil, and this wine goes with this dish. Mr. Balanchine thought that thinking about something else other than ballet meant you were in trouble, although he himself had a penchant for cooking Russian dishes. But we've always encouraged our dancers to think about other things, if for no other reason than it makes them more interesting performers.

Dancers start at such an early age, and sometimes at 17 or 18 they're cast in a major role but they don't know how to do laundry or cook a meal. Dancers need the basic elements required to maintain a life. It's hard to tell them to do differently, when they're devoting their lives to it. But when dancers have children, things change. Having three children to raise gave us perspective. Getting to a soccer game on time was just as important as running a ballet company. Raising our children helped us to focus on things other than the frustrations at work. And the dancers can see this, that our relationships with our children are important, as are our relationships with the community. We are solid citizens but, in a way, surrogate parents. In a sense, we're a mom and pop ballet company.

Times have changed from when we were young. Growing up as a dancer, there was a belief that to give you the power on stage, in the 50s and 60s, dancers needed to have a steak before a performance. Steak, ice cream, and tea—that's all we knew about nutrition. It's different than the carb packing you hear about today. The idea of nutrition as a lifestyle or direction to enhance your career didn't exist then. Neither did physical therapy—everyone was on their own when injured. All the things that have shaped PNB—the health care and nutrition—are the things we didn't have as dancers but perhaps should have had.

Catherine Allaway

Catherine Allaway (Figure 87) is a rebel. Her strong will about how to subsist at meal times in a tree-planting camp in northern Ontario ("I will not eat Twinkies") grew from an equally strong attitude as a ballet dancer who refused to destroy her body and a former ski champion who would not be deterred by a knee injury (she continued to coach).

As a young girl growing up near Sault Ste. Marie, Ontario, she seemed to have a promising career ahead of her as, first, a gymnast and, second, a skier. Allaway took gymnastics for 8 years (between the ages of 4 and 12), and competed for 3 years on a provincial tour. She

Figure 87 Catherine Allaway. (Photo by Gigi Berardi)

took ballet for 4 years, between the ages of 10 and 14, starting with two classes per week, then up to six classes per week during the school year. Summer session was almost full-time. Now as a tree planter in her late 20s, she uses what she learned about technique in ballet and ski racing to keep herself injury free: "It's so great, knowing what your body is capable of—and having the feeling of being an athlete in whatever sport you're in. To be really good at something is an incredible thing. And to put all your focus into how your body works is a valuable lesson. It teaches you what you are capable of."

Her training lessons included learning to define goals and coming up with a step-by-step training program and preparing for performance. Says Allaway: "Once you've been on stage a number of times, you get used to being in front of people and being observed and criticized. In class, you're told to drop your hip a bit lower and extend—and you do it."

> In tree planting, I experiment with the way I can use my body in handling the equipment and terrain. It's the best drug-free rush out there—a working body. But you need to find balance in your work—and there're many parts of ballet that apply to everything, including tree planting. In ballet, you know that some girls worked their butts off and got all the parts. Same thing with tree planting—some tree planters can make over $10,000 in a summer, but I'm not going to destroy my body just to do that.
>
> A really good part of ballet is the focus, and the attention that you get. Even if you decide you don't have a future, you can know that it was all well-placed energy, with teachers and coaches helping you along the way—that's the great part of any intense sport.

Allaway recently finished her undergraduate degree at McGill University. It took her a while, and in-between terms she planted trees for eight summers.

> To stay as healthy as I am, and to be able to do the job, nutrition is important. The tree planting draws a random crowd of people, with lots of university students—all of whom have a different idea of how to eat. But the tree planting is a great leveler—although they may have grown up with processed single cheese slices on Wonder Bread or macaroni and cheese or Hamburger Helper, in a high-performance situation—like ballet or tree planting—you have to have good nutrition.
>
> We really need calories—that's our biggest problem. So, there's plenty of soup, homemade bread, and salads. Many are vegan or vegetarian, and there's options available for them. I grew up with fresh, unprocessed, homemade breads and baked goods—always with fresh ingredients—and it made such a difference to my health.

Allaway reflects on her ballet training, classes, and classmates:

> When you're 12 or 13, you don't know what other people are eating at home but I was sure that the people I was dancing with were not getting a careful diet—Twinkies and wonder bread. At the same time, in dance class, people are telling you you're too fat.
>
> What are your options, then? Eat less or eat nothing, but the junk foods that people are eating are not giving them the required nutrients. Those of us who are conscious about what we are eating can't understand what it's like for others.
>
> I think about the very first time I was put on a diet in gymnastics. I was 10 years old. I was told to eliminate all carbohydrates, which I did—and that's certainly bad advice for a 10-year-old. I wasn't obese by any stretch of imagination—I was just pretty solid.

It wasn't until I was 13 years old and ski racing that I got good advice about diet. I was doing a lot of team travel, and we'd go away for a week at a time, in a van. Traveling, it's hard to get good food into you. The temptation is to stop at McDonald's or chow down on a bag of potato chips to get through. Instead, we had lots of good food—a container of chopped up vegetables and fruit. We were considered athletes and had to think like athletes. Our training program included consciously thinking about what you put into your body the week before.

This was such a big difference from the mind set at my ballet school. At school, our classes were set for 6:00 or 7:00 in the evening, right around dinner time. This meant that a lot of dancers were skipping meals or not showing up for family meals. There never was any mention of good things to eat, just what *not* to eat. We knew we weren't supposed to have potato chips but we didn't know what to eat.

But the more time you spent at the studio, the more you realized people were going across the street to eat fries and gravy, and throwing them up before the next class. Or, just sneaking candy bars.

It's a really hard transition to make—maintaining an elite athletic body compared to just fitting in at school. At least in ballet, you've got a body that's approved of by peers because most likely you're slimmer than kids in your class at school. Skiing is different.

Skiing creates a body that is not at all the fashion ideal because you have really big legs, so a higher percentage of girls out of the ski-racing group were really sick. Many were dealing with bulimia, others became exercise fanatics—they couldn't leave the gym. They'd do several hours daily on a Stairmaster. It was a problem, especially for those who didn't know anything about nutrition—what a nutrient even is or what nutritional requirements even are. The chances, then, that someone will make a good decision are really remote. Not because they're not intelligent, but it's not something that's even important to 14-year-olds. Basic biology in high school comes a little too late.

What I found was that a lot of people who have had eating disorders do become interested in the science and biology of their disorders, and nutrition—but it comes too late. In dance, once you started developing a curvy body, you had to be very good if they were going to keep you around, and the fact that the instructor was rail-thin didn't help the situation. She was the one who told you were fat!

There was a lot of competition. In preparing for auditions for the National Ballet School, you simply wouldn't be cast in certain pieces. Everyone knew if there was a great piece of music, it would be saved for so and so. There were definitely people who were deemed more promising than others. Competition between dancers was encouraged, even though dancers weren't interested in competing against each other. Competition to be the most thin as well as the most dutiful—who was willing to be the most compliant, to do whatever it was you were asked.

The instructor would tell the students that they were too fat and that they had to be thinner by next week. How else to deal with it? Many bulimics didn't know any other way to cope with what was being demanded. There also were plenty of anorexics, but it was harder to tell what was going on with them—you'd never know if someone was eating while you weren't looking.

I stayed healthy, but I did get "fat." But because I was doing other sports where there were girls who were muscularly built—in fact, more weight gave you a bit of an advantage because you wouldn't get thrown around so much on a rough race course—there were options for me as to what I could do, what my body was good for—compared to others in ballet who'd done just that for 5 to 6 years and didn't know what they'd do otherwise. Many had hoped for a future in the big world of dance. I guess it just wasn't big enough.

Not all the studios there were like this, and there were certainly good dancers at all the studios, but [the one I attended] was considered to be the most serious studio, the 'best studio,' with more placements, more opportunities for competitions, more opportunities for dancers to be seen. But to show your dedication, you had to be thin. If you wanted to have a future as a real professional dancer, you had to make sacrifices, which started with starving yourself.

I felt like saying to some of the others, "Do something where you're not looking in a mirror—some other physical activity with less focus on your body."

Allaway raced in 1989 in a precompetitive league, and competitively when she was 13 and 14. At 15, she attended the National Ski Academy in Collingwood, Ontario. A serious knee injury—a torn anterior cruciate ligament—at the end of the season meant the end of her competitive racing career. She coached for 3 years after that, and some of her students are now on the Canadian National Ski Team, destined for the Olympics in Torino in 2006. And that feels good.

Jenifer Ringer

As a little girl, Jenifer Ringer (Figure 88) always loved to dance. "I'd shut myself into my bedroom and turn on the record player and dance for hours," she says.

For such an ardent dancer, becoming a principal with New York City Ballet might seem like a dream come true. But Ringer's path has been fraught with trying times: "In achieving my dream of becoming a ballerina, I hadn't factored in the more difficult aspects—especially the fatigue or stress level. I just loved dancing, especially the romantic and lyrical ballets."

Raised in Summerville, South Carolina, and known as a tomboy, Ringer grew up in a close-knit family. At 10, she took her first ballet class. At 14, she landed a summer scholarship at the School of American Ballet, and soon enrolled in the regular academic year course. In October 1989, she joined NYCB as an apprentice. As is typical with many maturing 16-year-olds, her body was becoming more "feminine," more curvy, and she was overcome with self-doubt. Still, she was invited to join the corps in January 1990, in part for her exceptional musicality, radiant quality, and technical skill.

> From that first ballet class, I thought, 'this looks really interesting.' I absolutely loved it but thought of it as extracurricular. I had the opportunity to dance *Serenade* at the Kennedy Center (with the Washington Ballet)—that was my first real professional experience and I said to myself, 'I think I want to do this for a living.' When I was made an apprentice in the New York City Ballet at 16—they only took a few of us that year—I was thrilled. It was one of the biggest thrills of my life even though my parents were then transferred away from the city, so I was alone.

Ringer soon found the corps members to be the hardest working dancers in the company —in large part due to the number and technical difficulty of the ballets. She incurred a few minor injuries (an ankle sprain) with the load that comes with being one of the more used corps members. It was at that point that she started to have emotional problems. She was often unhappy with herself, and suffered from low self-esteem: "I started to lose a little bit

Figure 88 New York City Ballet's Jenifer Ringer in Jerome Robbin's *Four Seasons*. (Photo by Paul Kolnik)

of the joy in dancing. I did start in my 20s to have some eating disorders. I had a more womanly body and I was still having a hard time dealing with the changes."

Ringer was promoted to soloist in 1995, at 21. She notes: "I remember thinking, 'now I'll be happy and all my problems will be solved. But I was so dependent on ballet and ballet masters and mistresses to give me self-esteem, it was impossible to find. So I started gaining a lot of weight and couldn't really perform. It got to the point that the one thing bringing joy was unavailable to me. A back injury at the time just made matters worse."

Ringer was sidelined for 9 months with the injury. She decided that the best thing was to leave the company at the close of the 1997 season. "I hadn't much danced in 1996, and the company and I decided that I should leave with no guarantee that I'd be able to return." Ringer notes that, as a policy, NYCB doesn't grant leaves of absences, but it is usually very generous when a dancer wants to return. "I had to go, it was too painful to dance. I hated everything having to do with dance. I wore huge clothing and baseball caps over my eyes."

She worked as a secretary at her church and taught the NYCB workout throughout the city. She completed her undergraduate studies at Fordham University and began taking class with Nancy Bielki—as just another dancer. "Even though I was 40 pounds overweight,

I realized I was beautiful just like this. I decided I wouldn't look in the mirror. Towards the end of the year [1997], James [Fayette] asked me to do *Nutcracker*—I could hardly find a romantic tutu to fit into." A tutu was found, and Ringer danced onstage for the first time in several years. Her disordered eating diminished and she started to lose weight. By mid-1998, she had returned to company class, and in January 1999, she was back onstage.

> Even now, I say my affirmations over and over, reminding myself where my self-esteem comes from. Those first few classes, coming back, were hard. I was absolutely terrified. I had to talk myself through it and tell myself over and over, 'you're beautiful the way you are.' I knew that I was a good dancer. I had a right to be there. What was meant to happen would happen—I was willing to walk away if I had to.

Ringer was promoted to principal at NYCB in January 2000. She married Fayette in July of that year. She is known for her romantic interpretation and dramatic partnering (especially relishing pas de deux with Fayette), whether it be in Peter Martins' full-length *Sleeping Beauty* or George Balanchine's *La Source*. Ringer has been featured in numerous Balanchine works, as well as in major works by Jerome Robbins, Peter Martins, Robert La Fosse, and Christopher Wheeldon.

> I wouldn't change the path I took. If I had stayed the way I was, I would have been too self-involved. The injuries and even the weight gain enriched me as a person, helping me reaffirm what my priorities are. It gave me increased confidence in myself as a person, and the knowledge that I could function as a non-ballet person. The hiatus also helped me find James [Fayette]. I see myself on stage with the principals I admired as a corps dancer—Darci Kistler, Wendy Whelan, Kyra Nichols, in *Liebeslieder Walzer,* and I can't believe I'm on stage with them.

And what is her advice for young people?

> It's hard to grow up in the ballet world. It's easy to stay in an adolescent stage mind set. I love ballet, but I also know that it is not going to fulfill me as a person. Young people need to have a life outside ballet, with outside interests, and to have confidence in themselves as unique individuals. The ideal ballerina is something every little girl wants but feels she will never be. My advice? Love dancing and enjoy it. Work hard and pursue excellence, but do it keeping in mind that your value as a person cannot come mostly or completely from ballet.

Ringer doesn't know what her weight is because she doesn't weigh herself any more: "I think I'm 115 pounds in performance weight, but I'm not even sure of that number. I don't weigh myself any more—it's too damaging. If I weigh an extra pound . . . maybe it's due to salt. I don't really know. What I do know is obsession is not productive." Ringer notes, "My [spiritual] faith . . . continues to be the main thing, along with support from James [Fayette] and my family, that helps me to maintain a more healthy attitude towards myself and the ballet world. When I constantly 'affirm myself' it is to remind myself that my worth comes from God and not from ballet."

Melanie Skinner

It would be hard to imagine a more enthusiastic dancer than Melanie Skinner (Figure 10). A soloist with Pacific Northwest Ballet since 1994, who retired just this year to assume a position as ballet mistress of the Evergreen City Ballet in Auburn, WA. Says Skinner,

> I take my job on a day-by-day basis. If I find myself lagging a bit, I'll watch performance videos—William Forsythe's company or the Paris Opéra Ballet, and then I want to work even harder. The key to longevity is to find the challenge, what's new in the work.

Growing up in Delaware, Skinner was close to 10 before her mother allowed her to take a ballet class:

> I had begged my mom to take ballet since I was four and then she finally let me take it. She wanted me to start a little later so I could appreciate it and fully know what I was doing. By the time I got to junior high, I was trying to keep up with both academics and dance and I needed to be exposed to better teachers if I wanted to be a professional dancer.

When Skinner was 13, she attended a summer course at the North Carolina School of the Arts. By 15, she was at the school full-time:

> From the first day, I loved the school. It was great going to a school where people are so diverse—musicians and actors—and where I finally fit in. As a teen, you want to fit in and in my small town I just didn't. In North Carolina I had a lot of friends —as well as great teachers and training. I remember Melissa Hayden, and especially Sanchon Cordell.

Skinner also took summer courses at the School of American Ballet (SAB) in New York City. At 17, she was invited to take the SAB year-round course, and did so hoping to get into New York City Ballet (SAB is a training school for the company). She completed her last year of high school via correspondence. Typically, students moving from the school to the company are selected after performing in a graduation workshop.

> That was such a crucial year for me. But I was injured right as I was being cast in the workshop where Peter Martins [the artistic director of NYCB] views the company. Landing from a jump, I sprained my ankle. It was a Grade 3 sprain. The doctors said it would have been better if I had broken my foot.

Skinner rehabilitated with a lot of physical therapy and exercises to build up the muscles in her foot and lower leg. It took 4 months for her to get back to class.

> I was devastated then, but things have a reason for happening. If not for the accident, I may never have come to PNB or met my husband. It took a year for the scar tissue to heal, but it took longer to emotionally recover. I've had several other injuries since then. One recent injury was a torn hamstring—I missed my first *Nutcracker* performance in 10 years. But mostly, I've been lucky. I attribute it to what you're born with—I have a pliable, resistant body.

Skinner also is well endowed in another respect:

Luckily, I don't have to watch my weight. My mother weighs about 115 and she is 5'10"—I attribute my staying power in dance to not having to struggle with what I weigh or how I look. Everywhere I've been I've seen young dancers struggling. When you're surrounded by mirrors, it's inevitable.

Skinner got a wake-up call regarding this in an SAB summer course when she was 14.

That summer everyone was talking about how fat they were and there I was, a string bean. But I dieted anyway and when I came home I was so skinny that my mother said she'd pull me out of ballet if I didn't change my image. 'Don't let other's neuroticism get to you,' my mother said. I've seen a lot of careers ended with poor nutrition. I have a healthy diet so I have strong bones and am relatively injury-free.

After the sprain healed, Skinner auditioned for a PNB summer course. After dancing on scholarship in the summer and fall, she joined the company as an apprentice. She entered the corps a few months later, in 1990.

Although it was a shock moving from New York to Seattle, I immediately loved it. My mother joined me after a few months—she's always been very supportive. I really respect my mom a lot because she was not a stage mother—and I always had her support. She would drive me 30 miles to ballet each way—60 miles every day, and she never complained.

I think a lot of how you draw on internal resources is how you're raised. Having good parents and good values, and knowing that my mom did not put pressure on me helped me to be level-headed. It's especially hard as a teenager, but learning to 'let go' is a life skill. I have it even today. I'm one of the most dedicated people I know. But at the end of the day, I can walk away from work and enjoy my home and my husband — I rely on him now for perspective.

Another way that Skinner relaxes and unwinds is by cooking. Skinner says that Seattle is a great place to cook. She can do dinners "pretty fast" and, on weekends, make them more elaborate. When she is performing, her husband does the cooking. Skinner's other hobbies include hiking and reading and writing, as well as taking an occasional college course.

I'm taking a creative writing course now. I might have a little bit of a talent for writing. I like to write short stories. But cooking is my main love. Especially on the weekends, or when the company's off, I like to take my time and shop at Pike Place market—I love its seafood. I also love to read cookbooks and watch cooking shows.

Cooking runs in my family. My [older] sister was a chef. When I was 17 and living by myself in New York, I got into it—the cooking was soothing. Since I've been married, the cooking is more enjoyable—cooking for two. The whole process of cooking is therapeutic. Part of the therapy is the creative part, I like to experiment and add spices. I love the presentation.

With her strong technique and breezy demeanor, Skinner was a natural for much of the PNB rep—including works by William Forsythe, Lynne Taylor-Corbett, and a lot of Balanchine (PNB co-artistic directors Kent Stowell and Francia Russell are former Balanchine company members). At the time of writing (fall 2003), Skinner was in rehearsal with PNB dancers for a Balanchine centennial repertory:

I'm really looking forward to the Balanchine rep. I've danced one of the principal roles in *Divertimento No. 15*—the role that was choreographed for Tanaquil Le Clerc. I also performed it in London at Sadler's Wells with PNB, which was great. I always find something new and interesting to work on in his ballets. *Agon*, too, is in my top three favorite ballets of all time. I love the simplicity of the lines and the complexity of the music—it's patting your head and rubbing your stomach at the same time.

Skinner's practical, positive attitude marks her professionalism: "What sets apart professional dancers is their inner drive to strive for better technique. Ballet is hard and challenging but dancers need to focus on their attitude, daily. One time my turns are really on, the next day I have to work harder to meet a goal. I'm constantly trying to improve or maintain my technique." Skinner shows the same professionalism in her teaching at the Evergreen City Ballet in Auburn, WA, and in striving to meet career goals—attaining an undergraduate degree, continuing with her teaching and coaching of young women in ballet, and some day, developing a nonprofit organization that "introduces underprivileged children to the arts."

6

Finding Balance
What Does It Take to Succeed in Dance?

What does it take to "succeed"—that is, to accomplish something significant in dance? Some of the stories and source materials offered in Chapter 1 suggest that the world of dance is severe, all-consuming, and inhabited by perfectionists. Indeed, as Donald Byrd (see Chapter 3 profile) notes: "Dance is demanding—for the physical part but also how dance deals with ideals. Dance is full of unrealistic demands, but the pressure is still on . . . the worst is the notions of perfection, achieving the ideal that doesn't even exist in the world. "

The message of this book, however, is that dancers do not need to obsessively self-analyze and criticize themselves in order to sustain a career in dance. The stories of the dancers profiled here attest to this. What dance actually demands of one person is not the same as what it demands of another. The challenge (a competition, a long rehearsal, cutbacks in pay, a difficult partner) may be the same, but how each dancer responds is highly individual. A dancer's approach and personality play a large part in how the dancer responds to difficult and stressful situations.

Some researchers argue that there may be a natural-selection process for personality in much of dance, perhaps favoring those who are born with a particular personality.[1] Others argue the opposite, stating that there is little evidence for the existence of "a dancer's personality," although they admit that the study of dance itself can have an influence on the development of personality.[2]

In an informative study of professional and preprofessional dancers, researchers Ruth Solomon and colleagues explain,

> The folklore of the dance world holds that student dancers evolve into professionals simply by virtue of hard work and perseverance. [All the dancer needs is] training and enough time to allow the inherent talent to emerge . . . Unfortunately, this way of thinking does not take into account the part played by the dancer's personality in promoting (or retarding) his or her career.[3]

In their studies of professional dancers and students, the researchers found that both men and women had a narrow, internal focus of attention as well as high levels of self-assurance, competitiveness, and a need for control. There also was evidence of a tendency to avoid conflict. They note that, with such a strong focus on sense of self, the dancer may feel little need to change the behavior of others and gives in to authority. Yet psychologist Linda Hamilton cautions against "blaming the victim" and points to the tremendous impact of verbally abusive teachers on dancers' psyche.[4] Says dancer Gus Solomons jr, speaking from his long experience in dance (see Chapter 3 profile): "Dancers tend to beat themselves up. They have a strong will and a strong drive to succeed so they don't give themselves leeway to fail . . . [yet] it is not possible to be in complete control."

Researcher Stanley E. Greben notes,[5] "As a group, dancers tend to be intelligent, multi-talented, and highly motivated . . . [being] goal directed toward their career from an early age."

He notes that dancers have the ability to concentrate their attention on a particular task, follow through, and not miss any details. This suggests good analytical and planning skills.[6] Cirque du Soleil's Paul Bowler would agree, having transferred some of his intense focus and attention to detail to a secondary occupation: real estate (see end-of-chapter profile). For Bowler, both theatrical performance and real estate brokering require concentration, consistency, and reliability.

A POSITIVE SELF-IMAGE

One thing is clear: to sustain a lifetime in dance, dancers must enjoy the challenges dance poses. This is not something that students find only on day one of an audition class in high school, but rather something dancers learn as children from their first teachers—their family. Pacific Northwest Ballet dancer Melanie Skinner notes (see Chapter 5 profile),

> . . . a lot of how you draw on internal resources is how you're raised. Having good parents and good values, and knowing that my mom did not put pressure on me, helped me to be level-headed. I'm one of the most dedicated people I know. But at the end of the day, I can walk away from work and enjoy my home and my husband —I rely on him now for perspective.

Adds Gus Solomons jr (see Chapter 3 profile), "For the most part, my parents supported me [in my decision to pursue dance]. My father had gone to MIT, and as long as I got my education I was ok."

This is not to say that all dancers' parents were supportive—especially initially—of their children pursuing a career in dance.[7] But it is true that dancers who thrive are able to see challenges and obstacles as opportunities.

A case in point is Catherine Cabeen, who dances with Bill T. Jones (see Chapter 2 profile). For Cabeen, injuries provide an opportunity, making her "a better dancer because it gives me an opportunity to work on my technique . . . I become more conscious of alignment and it puts my ego in check." To help deal with the injury, Cabeen draws pictures, reflecting on the possible imbalances in her body that predisposed her to injury. Such a calm, rationale approach to dealing with a potential setback in one's dance career is critical to achieving longevity in dance performance.

This fits with the findings of psychologist Linda Hamilton.[8] She notes that just as with body type (where some dancers seem more suited to certain types of dance), certain personal qualities also give an advantage to dancers. For one, being strongly motivated is a big advantage because then dancers can train even when faced with distractions and temporary setbacks. Hamilton also notes that dancers who have a desire to achieve and are, by nature, optimistic also are resilient—they can bounce back from setback and injury.

Perfectionism, as a personality trait, can be either adaptive or maladaptive. Gifted artists ("perfectionists") can have high standards, which helps to advance their careers, but not to the point of being overly self-critical. Then, the drive for perfection puts too much pressure on the dancer, as do irrational beliefs. More likely, the dancer that replaces an irrational belief—"I must have a flawless performance"—with a more rational one—"I've been rehearsing for weeks, I'm going to do my best, and I know that's good enough; this is what a performance with 6 weeks of rehearsal looks like"—is going to fare much better. Then, when the unexpected happens (a few missed cues, say), the dancer's reaction will be calmer and less self-critical.[9] Pessimism and depression (and self-sabotage associated with excessive struggle for an ideal) are counterproductive in that they limit one's ability to cope with the everyday stresses of dance.[10] Rather, developing effective coping skills can help a dancer handle competition and boost personal self-esteem. However, this may come easier to some dancers than others.

Hamilton's advice is to set goals that are specific and include improving motivation and reducing stress. (Visualization as part of anxiety management helps develop the focus and awareness needed in the practice of somatic disciplines, discussed in previous chapters.) Thus, dancers should set specific but challenging and attainable goals for their performance (e.g., completing a tour jeté with good alignment) rather than outcome goals that are not under the dancer's control (i.e., getting a specific job). In a sense, practicing mental skills is as important as developing physical skills.[11] Such cognitive control, in terms of dancing, would mean being able to focus one's attention on what one is doing rather than being distracted by negative thoughts or constant worrying. A variety of techniques can help dancers accomplish this task, such as "thought-stopping" (for example, stopping the negative thought by flicking a rubber band on your wrist and silently saying "stop") and disputing negative self-talk, using facts, logic, and reason. Practicing at a time when no major life change (in careers or training) is occurring is most effective. Working with a psychologist who focuses on mental skills training—or performance—is most helpful.

Hamilton makes quite clear that the key to dealing with the various challenges in dance is to gain cognitive control by focusing on what you can control such as your attitude and good health habits as opposed to factors actually outside one's control—how you're cast, what costume you'll wear, the audience's response, an acute injury. Understanding that you have little control over such external factors helps in optimizing performance potential.

Much the same is reiterated in Nancy Shainberg's *Getting Out of Your Own Way: Unlocking Your True Performance Potential.*[12] Shainberg advises the dancer to think about process not product (outcome) and to see mistakes as part of the learning process.[13] The hypercritical dancer needs to practice cognitive anxiety management (changing thought processes) to counter self-defeating thoughts (negative self-talk).[14] Donald Byrd fashions himself to be a master of this. (See Chapter 3 profile referring to his firing by Twyla Tharp and his development of cognitive control.) For Byrd, dancers need emotional as well as physical placement. Much the same sentiment is echoed by Murray Louis (see Chapter 4 profile).

Catherine Allaway (see Chapter 5 profile) says it this way, "Do something where you're not looking in a mirror—some other activity with less focus on your body." For example, Pacific Northwest Ballet co-artistic director Kent Stowell (see Chapter 5 profile) takes great pride in his cooking of fine food, and encourages dancers to do the same.

New York City Ballet principal Jenifer Ringer would agree: "Young people need to have a life outside ballet, with outside interests, and to have confidence in themselves as unique individuals. My advice? Work hard and pursue excellence but do it keeping in mind that your value as a person cannot come mostly or completely from ballet."

ESPECIALLY FOR YOUNG DANCERS

As mentioned earlier, practicing making good choices early in life will be critical to maintaining the level-headedness needed by teens and young adults. For most dancers, valuing challenge, cultivating creativity, and building self-esteem is a lifelong process—something that good dance training encourages. Dance training should be part of a young person's education in the process of becoming an adult. It helps young dancers to achieve the realistic goals of developing strength and coordination, staying fit, and expressing themselves. Dance training shouldn't be viewed as a ticket to placement in a nationally recognized dance company.

Developing and maintaining a positive self-image in dance is challenging. But it is absolutely essential to dancers' good health, especially at puberty and during adolescence. Young dancers need to accept their rapidly changing bodies and continue to get pleasure from dance, as well as enjoy a feeling of success and achievement. Since the perfect body in dance does not exist, students need to learn to work within their limitations. Teachers and the healthcare team (discussed in Chapter 2) can help them to set goals—little ones, near-term ones—and avoid pushing beyond the body's limitations. Part of the team approach is to help modify perfectionist tendencies and to make the studio experience less goal-oriented and competitive. The team also can encourage a problem-solving approach to dealing with challenges, reinforced with injury prevention training and annual health screenings and assessments.[15]

Admittedly, dance is demanding—especially if one's heart is set on joining a high profile ballet, modern, or world dance company (an outcome over which one has little control; see above). But the rewards of staying with it are enormous—assuming one finds balance by goal setting, focusing on working with limitations, and trusting oneself to make good decisions.

Good decisions begin with diet and training related to one's "look." Even in nondance populations, according to Susan Bordo, ideas about body image are fed by "fantasies of rearranging, transforming, and correcting, *limitless improvement and change . . .* "[16] Bordo asks, "When did 'perfection' become applicable to a human body? The word suggests a Platonic form of timeless beauty—appropriate for marble, perhaps, but not for living flesh."[17] If dancers find themselves unwilling to conform to an impossible ideal in any one particular dance form (or school or company), there are many others to try. Indeed, as Donald Byrd notes (see Chapter 3 profile), experiencing a variety of styles, teachers, and performance settings is like getting a liberal arts education: "the more you're exposed to, the better dancer you are." Says Byrd: "The exposure to different ways of thinking is important, especially studying a nonwestern dance form. A lot of dance techniques are similar, but decisions about movement are made based on aesthetics, and those different aesthetic explorations are important for developing a healthy body image."

Even as a principal dancer at New York City Ballet, a mark of great success in the dance world, holding to common sense and rational belief systems is critical to staying power in dance.

Dealing with ideals of body image is but one of the many challenges young dancers face. They need the full set of information and resources to solve the many physical and emotional demands they encounter. Finding such information is a lifelong process.

LIFELONG LEARNERS:
HOW THE SCIENCE OF DANCE INFORMS THE ART

The dancers profiled in this book consider themselves to be lifelong learners. Yet, there is so much information to digest, how does one choose the best practice? One important principle is that the science of dance medicine, dance technique, and dance conditioning can inform the art of all dancers and dance students who have ever faced challenging physical, emotional, or psychological problems—which is the vast majority of us, irrespective of our dance idiom. The essential information on recognizing, treating, and preventing injuries, as well as managing a life in dance, can be summarized in a handful of principles. They are:

- Practice—in the form of endless repetition of dance movements—does not necessarily make perfect (as discussed in Chapter 1).
- Dancers need to work with limitations, and in so doing recognize their strengths (Chapters 1 to 5).
- Pain is a warning sign; it is important not to ignore pain and to change beliefs and values that promote acceptance and ignoring of injury (Chapter 2).
- Being injured is an opportunity to learn and become more sensitive to the warning signs of pain (Chapter 2).
- Mistakes are a critical part of learning; emotions play a major role in affecting the growth and functioning of brain structures (Chapters 2 and 3).
- Dance is a multidisciplinary practice, so try to access medical and health information using as many disciplines as possible (Chapters 2 to 4).
- The brain-mind connection is important; this includes practicing imaging and visualization and related somatic disciplines or any technique that works for the dancer (Chapter 3).
- Challenging unreasonable behavior may be necessary, including questions about technique class itself: for example, why begin a technique class with a grand plié in fifth position? Consider all valid and justifiable alternatives (which, understandably, is difficult for beginning students) (Chapter 3).
- The particular health practitioner is as important as the kind of practice—if not more so; practitioners experienced in dancing or in working with dance client populations are valuable (Chapter 3).
- Learning is most effective with respected teachers and in supportive learning situations where the dancer feels safe (Chapter 3).
- The science of dance can inform the art—for example, how to find balance when turning, how to create the illusion of floating in air, how to increase the height of a leg extension (Chapter 3).
- Conditioning is particularly effective when it mimics dance moves and involves varied progression (avoiding goals of fast, dramatic change) (Chapter 4).
- Certain dietary practices (e.g., restricting calories or over- or under-consumption of macronutrients) are counterproductive to long-term weight management (Chapter 5).
- The science of dance is fraught with controversies and challenges, healthy debate, and multiple interpretations (as is the art of dance); this is another way of saying that there is no one truth but multiple truths. However, good ideas and good practices often converge.[18] Good and effective practice is often multidisciplinary.

Thus, many roads lead to the same path. Often, there is no one right answer. This rang true for me when once I took a self-defense course. For 6 weeks, we studied all sorts of moves and strategies. At the end of the class, I noticed that there did not seem to be any summary, conclusion, or even parting words of wisdom. I asked, "So, if we're in a threatening situation, what do we do?" The teacher said, "Run." I said: "I knew that before I took the course!"

This is precisely the point. Even though I had been given a lot of information, the teacher was saying: use your intuition—always.

Good teachers know how to encourage their students to use their intuition. It does not matter how much and how good the information available to a young dancer is, she or he needs to have an intuitive understanding of it to really be able to use it. Dancer Catherine Cabeen (profiled in Chapter 2) gives an example of a favorite teacher, Christine Wright, who helps her students intuit anatomical understanding:

> My one teacher has an amazing anatomical understanding of the body. She'll stand with you at the barre and give you all this information—but once you step away, she wants you to let go of all [of it] so you can feel it in your body. She encourages you to have the experience of dancing instead of getting caught up in any intellectual right and wrong . . . it is really moving to me when I work with a teacher who knows all the nitty gritty details [of anatomy, kinesiology, and the rest] but focuses more on actually feeling something when you dance—to dance like you're singing some beautiful note.

So, dancers need to use their intuition, trusting themselves. An appetite for lifelong learning helps to feed their exploration of what is undeniably the best profession in the world. At least, many of the dancers profiled here think so. Two thirds of them are still performing. Others have sought a different niche in the world of dance and have used their skills that were developed in dance training in other ways.

WORKING WITH LIMITATIONS

All of the dancers profiled in this book have found their place in dance by recognizing limitations as well as strengths. These artists, however, are interested in more than just what to substitute for split leaps in their choreography. They are more concerned with what is being communicated. As dancer David Zurak (profiled in Chapter 1) notes: "For me, I am not drawn to displays of high extensions or multiple pirouettes so much as to how connected a dancer is. Seeing a beautiful dancer who's connected perform—that's when I really feel something."

Wendy Perron, profiled later in this chapter, has worked with limitations and challenges throughout her professional career. "This is my body, one must be intelligent about it. If the pleasure stopped, I would stop. If I'm not enjoying it, I won't do it. This is one of the reasons that I have lasted so long . . . you must keep the joy alive." Perron has done just that. (As of this writing, she continues to enjoy dance as editor-in-chief of *Dance Magazine*.) In fact, every dancer in this book has learned to work with limitations—to set goals, to make adjustments, and to adapt.

FINDING ONE'S PLACE IN THE WORLD OF DANCE

The individuals profiled in this book have found their place in the world of dance. Some are creating their own niche with a dance form or style of moving and are directing their own companies: Elizabeth Streb, David Parsons, Li Chiao-Ping, Bill Evans, Gus Solomons jr,

Donald Byrd, Pat Graney. Others have found other avenues to express themselves in dance or movement or sports: Kellen Laine, Jan Dunn, Catherine Allaway, Wendy Perron. The world of dance is indeed broad.

These dancers have all, at some point in time, seen beyond the hard work and competitiveness to realize the great satisfaction of dancing. As researcher Stanley Greben puts it,[19]

> Dance is one of the most complicated sources of pleasure in work. The dancer has aesthetic and kinesthetic pleasure from the use of the body, a sense of mastery or control in that use, and the pleasure of working with a group or company of others, as well as the gratification of a beautiful visual and musical environment. Performance also yields the pleasure of fantasy through story and of imagery through characterization. Furthermore, the dancer, like all performers, has the satisfaction of the attention and applause of the audience.

In an interview about his 2003 movie, *The Company*, depicting the behind-the-scenes life of the Joffrey Ballet of Chicago, director Robert Altman discusses "the melancholy of young lives sacrificed in the name of this most exacting, underappreciated and ephemeral of art forms."[20] But I don't quite see it that way, and neither does dance writer Ann Daly, who, in a commentary for public radio, "No More Starving Artists," said, "Even the most subversive [artists] I know want a living wage, health insurance, and affordable housing . . . Money . . . can be the creative means to increased personal autonomy . . . Leading universities are setting up whole institutes to study how to transfer profit know-how to nonprofits."[21]

This is not a bad idea, for, as a report from the National Endowment for the Arts (NEA) documents,[22] the financial health of nonprofit dance companies is often tenuous. The NEA reports that the number of nonprofit dance companies grew by 93 percent in the period 1987 to 1997, but that NEA funding for dance companies fell from an average of $5.7 million between 1988 and 1995 to $2.7 million in 1996.[23] Overall, declining government and business support for dance companies curtailed growth in unearned income—contributions, gifts, and grants. Due in part to this decline, companies had to increase their earned income (ticket sales). The 1990–1991 economic recession hit nonprofits hard, and the report estimates that it took ballet companies nearly 6 years to recover from the recession, more time than for modern and ethnic companies, with their better adaptability to budget constraints due to shorter planning periods, fewer large and complicated sets, smaller administrative staffs, and other characteristics that may give them more flexibility in budget cuts.[24]

The challenges that nonprofits face, especially in times of declining public and private grants, is huge. Elizabeth Streb (see Chapter 1 profile) acknowledges the difficult economic times, saying that "We always feel like we've won a gamble when something comes in—you have to make a game out of it." Some dancers and directors (for example, Li Chiao-Ping, see Chapter 2 profile, and Bill Evans, see Chapter 3 profile) have full-time academic positions at universities to serve as their main economic (and creative) livelihood. Others are in transition, for example Pat Graney (see end-of-chapter profile).

One innovative northern California-based company, Moving Arts Dance, directed by Anandha Ray, has extended itself to touring worldwide (with three concerts and master classes in Byelorussia scheduled for the 2003–2004 season), serving as cultural ambassadors of the United States.

Clearly, earning an adequate income in dance is important. But one also needs satisfying work in terms of a productive creative environment, good peers and colleagues, and reasonable work hours and conditions. One does not need all four pieces of the puzzle in order to have a "good job;" having at least two would suffice as a minimum. Most dance professionals wouldn't want to sacrifice a good working environment and job satisfaction for income. Says Murray Louis,[25]

> Because dancing is not a lucrative profession and has a limited income-producing period, nature has wisely arranged for it to occur at a time in life when people are least concerned with middle-age security: at a time when youth is inured against injury, unconcerned with acquisition, when the word "age" has not, as yet, become a part of their vocabulary, and before they have their feet caught in the glue of economic responsibility . . . There is no right or wrong in the many ways people deal with the present and the future.

CAREER TRANSITIONS

For at least 30 years there has been some recognition of the need to support dancers retiring from performing, as discussed in *The Fit and Healthy Dancer*.[26] Centers in Great Britain and the Netherlands were the first to formalize assistance for making the transition to another career. Support from national dance transition centers today, such as Dancers' Career Development in London and Theater Instituut Nederland in Amsterdam, may include financial assistance for retraining as well as psychological counseling and mentoring. In 1993, the International Organization for the Transition of Professional Dancers (IOTPD) was founded at the University of Lausanne under the sponsorship of the United Nations Educational, Scientific, and Cultural Organization (UNESCO). The organization's objectives include securing accident and illness insurance, career counseling, supplemental accident insurance, and provisions for medical care, and academic education.

Other well-known centers include the Dancer Transition Resource Centre of Canada, which is a national organization with administrative offices in Toronto and regional representatives in Canadian cities with dance companies. The Centre offers personal counseling as well as legal, business, and accounting advice, career guidance of various forms, and seminars on topics specific to career transition.[27]

In the United States, Career Transition For Dancers (CTFD), with offices in New York and Los Angeles, is a national service organization that assists free-of-charge current and former professional dancers with information and skills development in the form of individual career counseling, educational and entrepreneurial scholarships, seminars, workshops, and a reference library with a toll-free line to provide dancers in the United States and Canada with one-on-one career counseling and professional referrals. The organization, through various outreach efforts, also offers services throughout the United States. The numbers are impressive: to date, CTFD has provided more than 2,600 current and former professional dancers with more than 35,000 hours of career counseling and over $1.7 million in scholarships for course work in higher education and specialized certification programs as well as start-up money for business ventures. The organization's annual operating budget of about $936,000 is supported by private individual, corporation, and foundation grants. Alexander Dubé has been active with the organization since its inception in 1985, becoming executive director in 2001. Dubé notes that originally the organization provided services mostly to mid-career artists. Such artists now represent about one quarter to one third.[28]

For Dubé, many dancers' transitions are success stories. He says,

> Former Dance Theatre of Harlem principal Virginia Johnson, who now is editor-in-chief of *Pointe* magazine, is one of our biggest success stories. We've assisted dancers

who were interested in starting businesses of all sorts, including music production companies, clothing design, interior design, horticulture, architecture, and photography.[29] We've assisted dancers in moving into positions as vice presidents of financial institutes, researchers in marine biology, and professionals in health and medicine—nursing, physical therapy, chiropractic. The career transitions run the gamut—A through Z, accounting to zoology.

That does not necessarily mean that making the transition is easy. For many, dance is more than an occupation or profession—it is a calling. Any loss or change of work can be a threat to the dancer's sense of identity as a performing artist. Loss of work, also, literally means loss of financial security and the support networks of peers.[30] CTFD Counselor Lauren Gordon notes,[31]

> At first, it is daunting and very difficult for the dancers to overcome their fears of exposure, of failure, of not fulfilling dreams. They think that nothing else will be as compelling. They have a fear of not bring able to fall in love again with another career, and this holds them back from moving on. But dancers in transition need to "go where the warm is"—this is a great saying that means that they really need to find something that stirs their interest. To do this, it helps to start with the belief that transition is normal and inevitable. In terms of coping strategies, we identify other parts of their life where they've gone through personal changes—the death of parents, a divorce, the shock of 9/11—overcoming adversity and loss. People then realize that what they fear is the fear of the unknown and not feeling prepared. We try to identify for the dancers coping strategies that they have practiced in the past that have helped them work through feelings of loss, fear, and uncertainty.

Gordon also notes that the average age of the client is decreasing: "Dancers are coming in younger and younger. There is so much they can do while they are still dancing and enjoying successful careers. We're here to help them identify what tools and skills they can start developing early on."

CTFD offers numerous seminars, workshops, and networking events. For example, free Career Conversation" seminars offered in 2003–2004 included "The Dance of Networking/Mentoring," "Dancers & Taxes," "How to Find Teaching Jobs," "Interviewing 101," and "Embracing the Fear of Transition." CTFD also offers monthly support group meetings and specialty meetings such as "the diamond group" for dancers in their 50s and 60s who want to continue having fulfilling careers and to serve as mentors for those younger. Says Gordon: "We're glad to offer a place where people can meet with each other and talk. They want to continue to keep the focus on dancing. But many want to take a course or two while they're still dancing."

It is becoming more common for dancers to earn college credits while they are still performing. To do that, dancers need to find universities and colleges that are willing to offer classes to accommodate dancers' schedules (for example, in New York, finding courses that are scheduled on Monday evenings when most theaters are dark). Numerous programs exist; for example, CTFD publicizes the LEAP (Liberal Education for Arts Professionals) program, through St. Mary's College in San Francisco, which is accessible via correspondence and is currently offering programs in San Francisco and Los Angeles.

Another example is Pacific Northwest Ballet's partnership ("Second Stage") with Seattle University (see Carrie Imler profile in Chapter 1) and Fordham University's "Dance On" program in New York.[32] Researchers attribute the success of the Fordham

University program to various tuition reductions (dancers used their personal income, which ranged from a low of $18,500 to a high of $110,000 annually, to cover much of the tuition), geographical proximity to campus (most of the dancers had performed with the New York City Ballet, which is adjacent to Fordham University at Lincoln Center), and scheduling of classes at convenient times. Another factor is that most of the students came from the same professional company, and thus have familiar (and supportive) colleagues in the program. Gordon notes that a number of major dance companies have some partnership program in place.

As mentioned earlier, taking classes for college credit also can be a restorative escape from the intensity of performances and rehearsals. Says Elizabeth Streb (Chapter 1 profile), "I go to class a few times a week and feel refreshed. Besides, you have to do it. Just as scholars have to know Greek, Latin, and German, say, movement practitioners probably should know about math and physics." Carrie Imler, who was promoted to principal at Pacific Northwest Ballet just 2 years ago, takes university classes so she can do something different with her mind: "Incorporating something else in my life, something new like university classes, is perfect for me to take my mind away from the pressures of training and rehearsal. The classwork and assignments develop another dimension of you as a person. I also enjoy using a different section of my brain rather than just using it for learning choreography."

KEEPING THE DESIRE TO DANCE ALIVE

Staying power in dance is very much about desire and appetite. Gus Solomons jr (see Chapter 3 profile) advises that if you have the desire to dance, you need to find ways to make the profession work for you. Cirque du Soleil artist Paul Bowler (see end-of-chapter profile) performs "to do something I love. I was born a show-off and now I'm able to perform in one of the best companies in the world: Cirque. All the hard work is worth it—not just to please others but to please myself. I don't ever want to be performing just for the money."

Katherine Karipides of Case Western Reserve University in Ohio expresses the sentiments of many dancers when she said, "I have spent so many years learning and maturing, why throw it all away now?" She would continue to perform as long as she continued to improve, and as long as the "joy [was] there."[33] Today, her dancing includes a weekly technique class in addition to daily conditioning. Risa Steinberg (featured on the book cover for the first edition of this book) says quite simply, "you have to want to do it. As José [Limón] said, `you must be wanting and willing."[34]

If the desire to dance is there and dancers truly want to work, then they will need to forge their own aesthetic, with confidence and perseverance. This won't come easily. Finding balance is a lifelong process. It involves accepting the person that you are and the dancer that you will become and being open to a lifetime of learning and self-discovery. Dancers on half-toe use many small, subtle movements to find balance even though they look like they're holding a position. So, too, do all dancers practice a similar balancing act throughout their lives—with daring, agility, and grace.

The desire to be part of the dance world lasts a lifetime. The "retired" dancer who has hung up her point shoes for good or the Graham performer who no longer wears the familiar husbandman garb in a popular ballet is easily spotted in a dance audience. They're the ones clapping long after others in the audience have stopped. Perhaps Erick Hawkins summed it up best, "I just love it more—I take more delight in art, in poetry, in painting."

Hawkins was one of George Balanchine's first students at the School of American Ballet, Martha Graham's first leading male dancer, and the creator of an aesthetic that saw only beauty and possibility in dance. It is love of the art form that kept him dancing on stage (for 50 years without serious injury) and, as once he told me, that kept him applauding in an audience to bring a performer back for her fifth and sixth curtain call.

What dancer or former dancer doesn't do the same? As the desire to keep dancing is reinforced by audience acclaim, so the determination to stay active in the world of dance continues to be driven by love of dance, dreams, and a solid sense of self—strong enough for a lifetime in dance.

PROFILES

Jamie Farquhar

Jamie Farquhar (Figure 89) is known as something of a dancing phenomenon in his native Prince Edward Island (PEI) and more widely in Canada. The 20-year-old Farquhar, renowned for the speed and symmetry of his step dancing and his relaxed style, was the first Islander to place nationally in step dancing, at the age of 13. Farquhar appears to dance "from the knee down," a blend of Irish hard-shoe and traditional step dancing. This dance form is unique, with a relaxed body but "all fire from the knee down," according to Farquhar's teacher Judy Mac Lean.

Farquhar holds over 60 first-place prizes and five provincial titles, and has appeared several times on the front page of regional newspapers (including a formal commendation by the PEI legislature). Farquhar was asked to perform in opening ceremonies in May 2003 in New York City for a Canadian tourism convention. He wowed 300 invited American journalists with a reel. More recently he has performed at a number of CD launches and other benefits on the island.

Farquhar is now enrolled in Mount Allison University in Sackville, New Brunswick, where he is majoring in psychology and is planning to pursue a career in either psychology or family law. During the academic year, his dancing is confined to featured roles in productions of the Musical Society (he was awarded "Rookie of the Year" in his first year). He balances academics with running and other physical activity besides dancing, and plans to continue dancing:

> Dancing is something I want to keep on doing. I am still going to accept offers to dance—in summer, on breaks, when I can fit it into my schedule—and someday I want to try my hand at teaching dance. I don't plan on stopping anytime soon, for I know people who are dancing into their 40s and 50s and older on the Island.

Farquhar recognizes that his particular dance form is outside the main professional stream:

> It's sort of hard for step dancing. There's not really a defined arena for the art form. Ballet has the Royal Winnipeg, but for step dancing, there are no companies. You see it at a variety show or a concert. There's *Riverdance*, but that's a completely different style of dancing for me. It's not the style you see around here.

His participation in dance has evolved in recent years, and now he is thinking of dance more in terms of a continuing passion than a career:

You never know how far it's going to take you, and what invitations to accept, assuming you have the time. The performances now are more a way to explore whatever you're about for that moment [rather than a career move]. I feel differently now than I did 5 years ago. Then, if someone said, "We have a show," I'd step right in. Five years ago dancing was a huge part of my life . . . you don't see anything past it. But today my goal is to find a career that I'm happy in, although dance will always be a part of my life. I'm always going to be a dancer even though I'm not pursuing a career in it.

Figure 89 Jamie Farquhar trained with Prince Edward Island's Judy Mac Lean. (Photo by Alanna Jankov)

James Fayette

In his early years, New York City Ballet principal James Fayette (Figure 90) never set his sights on one particular goal in dancing, much less a particular professional company. He began his ballet training at age 5 in his home town of Ridgefield, Connecticut. "Being a professional dancer and joining New York City Ballet was not something that I was striving for —rather, I danced because I enjoyed it. A preschool movement teacher told my mother that I had some talent and my mom made me go."

Fayette danced until he was 12 or 13, when, in junior high school in a small town, he got teased:

> I said that I wanted to quit but my parents wanted me to learn a life lesson. They encouraged me to go on—they didn't want me to be a principal but just not to quit due to peer pressure. I started to take summer classes away from home for 4 weeks in the summer. So, there I was, surrounded by beautiful women—ballet became interesting to me for other reasons! But at 15, I went to the School of American Ballet and it was all very serious. I was surrounded by competitive dancers.

Fayette says that being surrounded by this level of semi-professional dance changed the way he thought about dancing. He started to see ballet as a real art form and to think of himself as a professional dancer. He became an apprentice with New York City Ballet in the fall of 1990, having spent 5 years at the School of American Ballet. He was then invited to join the Company as a member of the corps de ballet in the spring of 1991. Fayette was promoted to the rank of soloist in the spring of 1997 and to principal in May 2002. He notes that persistence helped, in part, to get him where he is today.

> Persistence, sticking with it, is just part of my character I think—my parents' influence and just the nature of dancing have given me an incredible discipline in my life—which carries over into other things, like courses at Fordham University [Fayette refers to a partnership of learning between the NYCB and Fordham]. Taking courses with over 30 dancers, it was very competitive.

Persistence is what he needed to perfect the featured roles he's danced in George Balanchine's *Brahms-Schoenberg Quartet, Cortége Hongrois, Firebird, The Four Temperaments, The Nutcracker* (Cavalier, Herr Drosselmeier, and Hot Chocolate), *Kammermusik No. 2, A Midsummer Night's Dream, Prodigal Son, La Sonnambula, Tschaikovsky Suite No. 3, Vienna Waltzes,* and *Western Symphony*; Peter Martins' *Fearful Symmetries, Morgen, A Schubertiad, The Sleeping Beauty, Swan Lake, Them Twos,* and *The Waltz Project*; Jerome Robbins' *Dances at a Gathering, Glass Pieces, Interplay, In the Night, Moves,* and *Watermill*; Miriam Mahdaviani's *Correlazione*; Kevin O'Day's *Badchonim (Merry-makers)* and *Huoah*; and Richard Tanner's *Ancient Airs and Dances*. This partial list does not include roles he originated in works by Peter Martins, Kevin O'Day, Lynne Taylor-Corbett, and Christopher Wheeldon.

Says Fayette, "Every role that you dance is extremely important whether a character role or the prince of the ballet ... Dancing with my wife [Jenifer Ringer] gives me the most pleasure ... there's a level of synergy that we can achieve when you're dancing with someone comfortable and inspiring, ... that you just can't achieve in other partnerships." He mentions this personal and professional partnering with NYCB principal Jenifer Ringer as providing a foundation and needed balance in his life:

Figure 90 New York City Ballet's James Fayette in Lynn Taylor-Corbett's *Chiarascuro*. (Photo by Paul Kolnik)

NYCB is great because it is so intense—50 ballets in a season! But you can get too caught up in it and become anxious and tentative. I keep myself grounded in my marriage, my family, and my faith. I keep a positive attitude about my work. I dance for the best company in the world and it's the best job in the world. The City Ballet team is huge. Everyone is so committed to the mission of NYCB, it's amazing to get so many people inspired to work as hard as they do. The only downer for me personally is that you have to retire when your body says it's time.

Fayette feels a responsibility to give back to the company, and so he started working with the Dancer's Committee his second year in the company and took over a leadership role a few years later. The Committee aims to help with dancer frustrations and dancer-administration communication issues. Fayette also sits on several committees of the American Guild of Musical Artists (AGMA)—on the dancers' committee, the board of governors, and on a health and pension fund committee.

> [I'm trying to] make NYCB and the union work its hardest for the dancers. This parallels my formal education in economics. I would like it to carry over to help dancers manage their lives and their money. Dancers can make a good salary, but it's only for a short time.
>
> I'm lucky I've never had a major injury [other than a knee injury at 16]. I've only missed two performances in my professional career . . . Still, dancers eventually have to make career transitions, and it's very key that they make decisions early on in their career. So, at NYCB, I've tried to bring in long-term financial planning, and push through some simple things such as flexible spending accounts, better salaries, and larger pension funds. Being a dancer is such an intense job that you forget about your responsibilities to yourself financially. For me, personally, I derive some satisfaction from being able to help dancers, irrespective of rank . . . and also learn more about challenges management faces . . . to keep the lines of communication open. Communication is what dancers do so well on stage.

Besides pursuing an undergraduate degree at Fordham University, Fayette regularly takes a group of dancers to Manchester, Vermont, for benefit performances and has led a performing tour of northern Italy. He has recently begun guest teaching at various ballet schools. "Ballet will be a part of my life for 10 years after I retire. Whether I'm involved with the AGMA union as a member of staff or in work with a financial firm—dancers need to be taken into the modern world. Sometimes it seems we're stuck in the nineteenth century."

Paul Bowler

Thirty-seven-year-old Paul Bowler is a former Olympic gymnast who has earned numerous awards and titles. Since 1999 he has performed "The Aerial Cube" in Cirque du Soleil's Las Vegas production of *Mystère*. Twice nightly, Bowler spins a 6-by-6 feet metal-framed cube while performing a ballet of aerial maneuvers 60 feet in the air. Bowler first performed the act in Cirque du Soleil's *Alégria*, but the massive *Mystère* theatre allows him to literally soar to new heights, accentuated by his sleek costume and the lighting that illuminates the cube in the dark, cavernous theatre.

The goal of a Cirque performer is not just to perform a quadruple somersault," says Pavel Brun, a former Cirque artistic director, "but to treat it as some manifestation of a spiritual, inner life." Adds Brun:

> The ideal performer, then, besides being highly skilled and passionate, should also be hungry for such transformation. Like in dance, the goal is not the fouetté turn or the arabesque, per se, but to have a language, a conversation, with the audience. Likewise, the artists evolve so that the audience sees the musicality and the artistry, understanding it in the context of the entire show, rather than seeing it as a single trick—achieving harmony, despite the demanding work that is being asked of them.

One performer who has achieved such harmony is Bowler, working with Cirque du Soleil since 1997. Bowler says,

> You have to be absolutely fabulous to capture someone's attention, especially when you're moving in a cube—it's like a frame and everyone's watching. Who wants to see just a gymnast? What is unique about Cirque is that it takes a [regular] gymnastic act and turns it into living art. I'm constantly developing as an artist.

Bowler's act is risky as well as spectacular, with its high-speed overhead aerial work, sweeping across the stage and into the audience with nary a safety net in sight. Yet safety is a primary concern of Cirque's—there are emergency procedures for every act of every show. For "The Aerial Cube," if the motor jams, foot and hand loops are lowered immediately. There's an on-call physiotherapist and massage therapist. There are plenty of financial safety nets available, too—Cirque performers are well taken care of.

Cirque du Soleil extends to its employees the same attention it lavishes on its productions. Benefits and working conditions are generous and include some profit-sharing. Performers' annual earnings can range from an apprentice rate of $30,000, to $250,000 for a veteran who owns creative rights to original choreography. On tour, performers receive state-of-the-art medical care and physical conditioning support, with physical and massage therapists on staff. Says Brun,

> The original intent of Cirque du Soleil was to provide infrastructure and support for the artists so that they could concentrate with their souls and brains on their creativity, performance, and growth. So Cirque remunerates the performers so that they can afford good lodging, food, and health maintenance—either on the road, or in the residence shows.

A reality check about a performer's longevity came to Bowler recently in the form of a shoulder injury that required a complete reconstruction:

> I was just training a little differently and moved my arms too fast. It was an unfamiliar movement and I ended up tearing my subscapularis completely off the humerus, I damaged the rotator cuff muscles, and the joint capsule. I was just trying some variation of flying; I can't believe all the damage I did. Cirque's response was typical. I had full medical backup throughout. I was injured at 7 P.M. By 9 A.M. the next day, I was at the specialist's office. I had an MRI at 11A.M. and the diagnosis by 2 P.M. that same day. The doctors told me I'd never be able to come back to the show. I knew I would. I needed surgery to reduce adhesions in the joint capsule. I rehabbed for 2 hours a day every day for 6 months. I started with 2-pound weights, and then progressed to heavier weights. Today, I've fully rehabbed. I have no fear of reinjury; I'm stronger than I ever was.

He's happy where he is in his career.

> I'm fortunate to do something I love. I was born a show-off and now I'm able to perform in one of the best companies in the world—Cirque. All the hard work is worth it—not just to please others but to please myself. I don't ever want to be performing just for the money.
>
> Ten years from now, I'll be retired from everything. Five years from now, if my body doesn't want to do the show any longer, I won't. But I would have retired too soon if I had let the shoulder injury stop me. Whether or not I perform should be

my choice. I don't want the choice to be made for me. Ideally, I'd like to do the final show of *Mystère*—I want to outlive the show.

Yet Bowler is already starting the transition to his next big act: real estate. Cirque performer by night, realtor by day? He argues that both are challenging because they require extreme concentration, consistency, and reliability, which he developed early on through the discipline of gymnastics. "If I mess up on stage, say, drop the cube, I can't blame anyone else except myself, that's the being responsible part. In real estate, too, if I drop the ball, forget to send the fax, whatever, it's my fault. You own up to it. There's also a professionalism expected in both real estate and Cirque performing."

At the time of this interview Bowler had been working with an understudy on "The Aerial Cube," training him personally by breaking down the act into steps, just as Bowler was taught. Says Bowler: "It will take him 25 times before he gets it right. Right now, he's just a gymnast with a cube." His advice to young people? "Take your professional sport—or art—to the limit. So, you're working 35 hours per week for zero financial gain? Still, take it to the highest level while you can. Don't give up."

Pat Graney

Pat Graney (Figure 91) has created over 40 major works since 1979. Her trademark humor and irony can be found in pieces such as *Tattoo*—an exploration of the concept of women and "genetic memory," delving into the personal memory of childhood and family she first introduced in *Faith* and *Sleep*, the two earlier pieces in the trilogy. Her achievements have been recognized with awards, including a John Simon Guggenheim memorial fellowship for choreography in 1995.

This uncompromising artist is known for her edgy full-length works, combining community activism with dance making. For example, she bristles at the possessive term, "my dancers": "Perpetuating the ownership idea is not good—the financial situation for dancers just becomes more difficult if you don't treat them professionally. I want to empower dancers. Mine is a humanistic concern—I am training dance artists not dancers." Even the progressive Graney admits that it's difficult not to become obsessive about body image in dance. She says that the women in her company, aged 32 to 46, are "skinny."

> When I stopped dancing 4 hours a day, I gained weight. Of course it's hard for me. I've always been a big person, and that's not what the culture admires. I've said to myself, ok, this is my kind of programming. I'm not doing any more diets so I gained 40 pounds. But now, I have changed my eating habits, eating more fresh food, which is good because I'm such a sugar addict. I'm really moving towards the idea of health and away from the idea of losing weight, so that there's no fear motive in why and what I eat. I'm finally taking charge of my own cultural icon. I'm trying to let myself find a natural way to be, knowing that in rehearsal I see that my dancers are a size zero—I look like the Incredible Hulk next to them . . . especially in the work they're doing on point (for *The Vivian Girls*).

Graney is not as hard on her dancers as she is on herself. A woman in the company had just given birth, and was worried about her looks. I said to her, "the only thing that's an issue is strength, not weight. Weight for me is a nonissue. We'll change the company costumes, if we have to."

Graney is an artistic director who "walks her talk" in many ways. Her work with incarcerated women and girls—as in her prison project, *Keeping the Faith*—has expanded from its base in Gig Harbor, Washington, to Cincinnati and Phoenix, with talk of adding San Antonio and New York. The first international phase of the project will take place as part of the International Dance Festival in Dublin, Ireland, in May 2004. Graney has a lot to be proud of, with her "Prison Project"—which, besides dance-based activities, has expanded to a performing arts series and a theater program in the prisons. At one point there was talk about making 2 days a week "arts days" in the prisons. According to Graney, this represents a major institutional change in the history of treatment for incarcerated people, and is commensurate with decreases in repeat offenses.

Other projects, though, are in transition. And Graney, at 49, especially questions the financial prognosis for nonprofits in this country. As for her own organization, it's a challenge to maintain—for she admits to having big, wacky ideas and to a time-consuming choreographic process.

> In the past 2 years, I've lost all my staff. It forces you to look at what is possible and what is going to drive you out of your mind [in handling all the jobs in running a company]. I'm now on the work schedule I had in my 20s—where I'm doing it all . . . It's a harsh reality for young dancers, and I'm one of the mid-career artists who is "making it" [referring to the high profile of her troupe as a touring company and to her access to grants].

Graney is always working on developing an audience for dance—and dancers for the audience. She worries about what is being presented, the choices young people have in the work they can see.

> I find I'm doing a lot of work with really young people these days. It's quite refreshing. I also mentor early-career dancers and make sure that their names get out there as well. I'm really interested in curating some work of younger dancers, really

Figure 91 Pat Graney. (Photo by Liz Roth)

interested in hip hop as an art form, the performances of transgender men and women. I get more concerned about presenting work, and access, and about cultural policy and how dancers are viewed. To talk about arts policy at a national level is important to me. Still, I find dance is a field dominated by people of privilege. Dance has always maintained its strings to the patronage system—other than popular dance. Just look at the NEA report [*Raising the Barre: The Geographic, Financial, and Economic Trends of Nonprofit Dance Companies,* 2003] or data from Dance/USA. Other than, say, Rennie Harris's leading work in hip-hop, there's not a lot of artistic directors out there developing a popular audience for dance.

As the NEA report suggests, this is a difficult time for dance nonprofits—especially for mid-career artists like Graney, who finds that "my work has never been better but I'm spending more and more of my time—up to 75 percent—on administration." And that doesn't count set and costume construction.

Private donations have been down, following the vagaries of the stock market, and that adds to the difficulties. Graney is concerned with the unreliability of funding for longer projects: "The money for staff and a managing director is there at the beginning but not the end of a project," she laments.

However, she is ever the optimist, able to see the world in several ways:

Admittedly, these hard times have put me in an amazing place—leading me to new things. I can move on, without beating myself up about it. It's an amazing period of transition for me. I've come to the realization that for me, in western culture, I need to remove myself from it to figure out what's going on, to do the work I want to do. But the typical kind of nonprofit you must direct doesn't allow it to happen. I can make a faster work but it's not the kind of work I want to do. So, I ask myself if I want to just curate the work of younger artists. Or, take advantage of the opportunities out there for choreographer-scholars in residence at colleges and universities [such as with the New England Foundation for the Arts "Choreographers on Campus" project].

Lately, Graney, the community activist, reformer, performer, humorist, and populist, has been immersed in production for the premiere of *The Vivian Girls*, based on the watercolor art of Henry Darger. Not surprisingly, the work involves ideas about a heroic dream life where even those who have been through the most harrowing of experiences survive to triumph or, at the very least, accept the world as a place where fairy tales often go awry and fitting in becomes a matter of scale.

Wendy Perron

Wendy Perron was touring with her company when I interviewed her in 1990 for the first edition of *Finding Balance.* She spoke about the traits that had served her so well in dance, and about wisdom: "As I get older, I realize that there's a certain authority that comes with maturity."

Even at a younger age, she was "somewhat defiant," in what she would and would not do in a technique class. Injuries early on taught her about her own limitations (primarily due to disc degeneration in her lower back) and how to work with them. I wrote about her balancing performance schedules, choreographing, obligations to family and friends, and organizing in the peace movement. And, through all this, somehow finding a way to keep the joy alive in dance.

Perron says that when she's watching a performance, she still feels like a dancer looking across the stage lights.

> I have dreams, and in them I'm a dancer—turning and jumping and doing whole combinations. In one of these dreams, my leg was in a in a very low attitude devant, and I remember asking myself why I couldn't get it higher. It was the first dream in which I wasn't all powerful; maybe in my consciousness, I was starting to accept my physical limitations.

Perron's creative work, her service to the profession, and her social and political commitments are strands that run throughout her life. Yet perhaps she has embarked on her most high-profile performance to date: editor-in-chief of *Dance Magazine*.

For Perron, finding balance by recognizing limits began early on, "As soon as I got to New York City in 1969, I was very interested in a lot of things. I didn't go to dance classes three times a day because I didn't want to burn myself out." But now?

> Being editor-in-chief [of *Dance Magazine*] really does obliterate everything else. The job has its own momentum. This job is flooding me! But still I find the time to exercise and sleep and be with my family. There are a lot of demands on me now. People are always asking me to come see their concerts. My old friends say, 'you must come!' But what I need to do is to find ways to say no. My husband is a big ally in this and tells me when to say no, he keeps me in balance.

Adds Perron,

> It helps to prioritize by keeping a calendar. If I can put things on the calendar in advance, I can schedule around it. Looking at my calendar is almost a kind of meditation. It prepares me for how big a day I'm going to have and what I'm going to do. Certain times are really intense—like the first week I had this job. I couldn't rehearse, I couldn't go out at night . . . I just had to dive right into it.

The rehearsal she mentions is her choreographing of a solo for former American Ballet Theatre principal Martine van Hamel, presented at Jacob's Pillow in July 2004. She observes, "This might be the last choreography I do for a long while. It's a good time to be working together. If I had had the editor-in-chief job 6 months ago, though, I wouldn't have committed to this." She recognizes her limitations:

> I've always had to be aware of what I could and couldn't do at a certain age. Especially now, I find I need to build in rest time into my 10- to 12-hour workdays. I have to pay attention to my body; otherwise, the work takes a toll. So, I try to be careful about sleep and drinking enough water. For my back, sometimes, I'll just lie down in the middle of my office. Or, watching a performance, I'll stand up to give my lumbar discs a break. I recently realized that my metabolism at this point is faster than my bones and discs [will allow], so I have to continuously slow down.

Perron plans on continuing with service and scholarship in the world of dance. She says,

> I also realize that there are still certain things that are really important to me. It's the reason I do panel discussions, so I will make time. Still, for other tasks, I need to find people who can replace me. I feel fortunate to get offered to do panels and talks that I'm really interested in. I'm looking forward to moderating a panel on

modern dance legacy at Hunter College [in New York]—I'm very interested in dance history, but then there are other events that I won't be able to do. It's the same thing with writing. I might think there is a moving story I want to write but probably won't write it. Maybe I'll need to keep a list of articles and essays I want to write for the future. These are all the things that I love to do—and I'll find the time for them, eventually.

A
Anatomy Basics

Connective tissue consists of bones, ligaments, tendons, and fascia, all of which create form, transfer mechanical force, and provide support; they return to their original shape to varying degrees after deformation. Connective tissue consists of a large extracellular matrix (fibers and ground substance) and a wide dispersion of cells (fibroblasts that synthesize and maintain the fibers and the ground substance). The fibrous component of the matrix is primarily collagen, with a tensile strength approaching that of steel.

Bones are the densest connective tissue and can withstand high compressive loads. Bone consists of cells in a matrix of ground substance and collagen fibers. Minerals (in particular, calcium phosphate and carbonate) constitute almost two thirds by weight of adult bone and give the bones hardness and rigidity. It is the collagen in the intracellular material that gives the bones resistance and toughness. More than 200 bones form the supporting framework of the body (Figure 92).

Ligaments serve as the "pulleys" of the body, securing the joints—connecting bone to bone, limiting joint motion, and otherwise stabilizing the joint.

Tendons are fibrous cords or bands that anchor a muscle to a bone, transferring the force of the muscle to the bone. Both ligaments and tendons have high tensile strength. They consist of almost parallel rows of collagenous fibers.

Both ligaments and tendons have relatively little direct blood supply. (This suggests yet another reason why smoking is hazardous to health: smoking, which contracts the blood vessels, also affects these tissues and may be an important factor in overuse injuries such as Achilles tendinitis).[1] Tendons blend with muscles at one end and meet their bony attachments on the other end. Tendons transmit forces from muscle to bone. Ligaments stabilize joints, guide movement, and prevent excessive joint motion. Ligaments and tendons are both particularly adapted to the stress of tensile loads. They have a fairly balanced combination of brittleness (resistance to force) and ductility (capacity for deformation without failure).

Fascia is the connective tissue layer that separates, connects, and surrounds our muscles and organs, thus forming compartments. Some refer to a fascia "web" or "net."

Muscles allow us to move various parts of our body. They are large bundles of innervated fibers, with every fiber (in skeletal muscle) acting as a small contracting machine that can

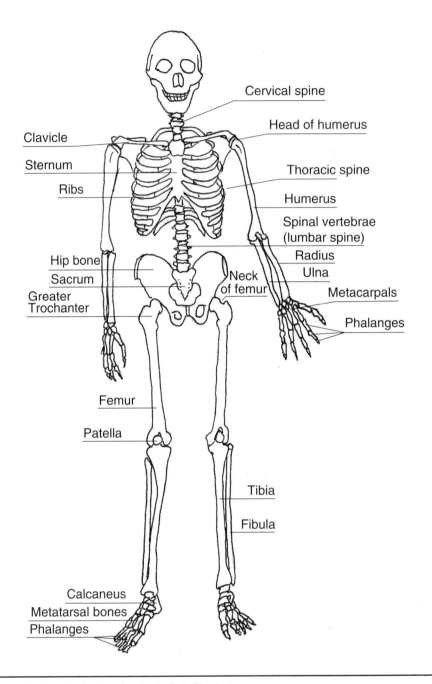

Figure 92 Human skeleton, anterior view. (Drawing by Emily Rhoades)

exert a shortening force on the bones to which it is attached. Three types of contraction result in movement and are referred to in the text: concentric (shortening of the muscle fibers),
eccentric (lengthening of the muscle fibers, against resistance), and isometric (no change in
the muscle length). Eccentric literally means "away from the center" and describes a muscle
action such as slowly lowering your arm with a hand-held weight. The muscles are still

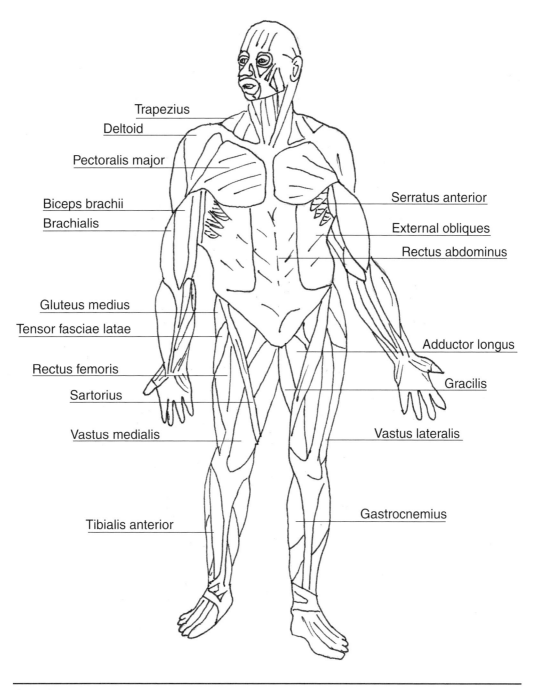

Trapezius
Deltoid
Pectoralis major
Biceps brachii
Brachialis
Serratus anterior
External obliques
Rectus abdominus
Gluteus medius
Tensor fasciae latae
Adductor longus
Rectus femoris
Gracilis
Sartorius
Vastus medialis
Vastus lateralis
Gastrocnemius
Tibialis anterior

Figure 93 Muscles, anterior view. (Drawing by Emily Rhoades)

lengthening but are contracting to break the fall of the weight. Many injuries in dance (and sports in general) are more likely to occur during the eccentric phase of muscle contraction (for example, in plié, where the quadriceps lengthen, contracting just enough to break a fall). Figures 93 and 94 show many of the muscles referred to in the text.

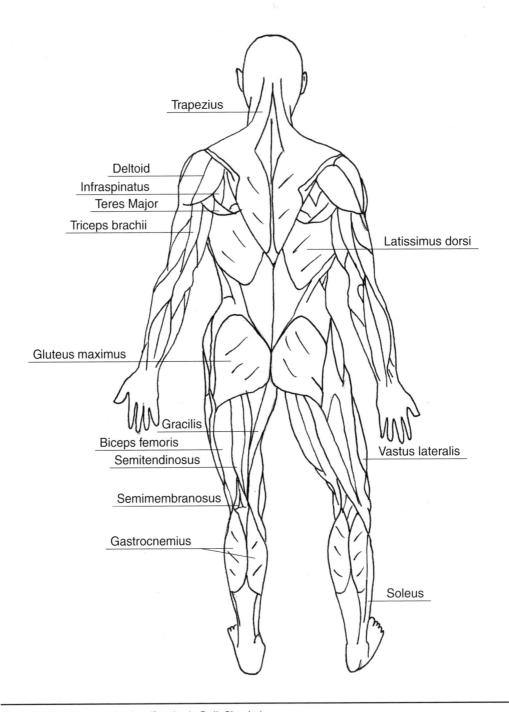

Figure 94 Muscles, posterior view. (Drawing by Emily Rhoades)

Sources

Jeanne Achterberg, *Imagery in Healing* (Boston: Shambhala Publications, 1985), and Eric Franklin, *Dynamic Alignment Through Imagery* (Champaign, IL: Human Kinetics, 1996), p. 3.

William Weintraub, *Tendon and Ligament Healing: A New Approach Through Manual Therapy* (Berkeley, CA: North Atlantic Books, 1999).

B

Dance Flooring

Dance floor construction and surfaces can predispose dancers to injury, compromising performance and even the longevity of dancers' careers. Many injuries of the lower leg, such as "shin splints," inflammation of the tendons of the ankle, and stress fractures of the foot and leg, may be directly attributed to dancing on a hard surface, i.e., a surface with poor shock absorption. Likewise, surfaces that are too soft, with too much give and too little resiliency, can lead to increased fatigue and chronic injury, requiring the dancer to push off harder for jumps. In addition, if the dancer has structural imbalances, such as a rolled-in arch, landing from a jump on a soft surface will increase the chance of injury. This is because the ground reactive forces are decreased and the flooring does not sufficiently stop the excessive motion resulting from such arch anomalies.

If dance floors do not absorb the shock from aerial landings—which can be at least triple the forces that pass through the foot or ankle—the shock is transmitted to the dancer's bones. Repeated landings can then result in microtears to tendons and in chronic inflammation.

Besides shock absorption and resiliency, floors also need to neither deform permanently under pressure nor be excessively springy or rigid. Besides the construction of the floor, the angle of the floor and its surface are important factors in injury. For example, rosin—the sticky distillate of pine pitch commonly used on ballet floors—can be a hazard, with its irregular and uneven patches over the floor surface.

Dancers, dance teachers, and dance directors need to know what constitutes acceptable construction for dance floors to properly evaluate a performance environment. To a certain extent, some of that can be done without expensive measuring instruments. Friction can be determined by actually dancing on the floor; resilience or give is more difficult. Physicist Kenneth Laws suggests that what is needed is something like a standard steel ball to be dropped from a height of 4 feet. The height of the bounce is then being measured. This at least mimics the relative give of the dance floor.

How does one determine if a floor is too hard? At the very least, one can rap on the floor with one's knuckles or the heel of a shoe. A resilient sprung floor will give off a hollow dreamlike retort since the rapping is amplified by the air space. A hard floor, one with a concrete base, will sound like a sharp click when you tap the floor since there is no air space to create resonance.

Studies are needed, however, on the actual external and internal forces acting on the dancer's body upon impact with the floor. This would contribute to the establishing of meaningful standards, ones that can encompass the requirements of a male contemporary dancer in bare feet as well as a classical dancer on point.

Widely accepted, however, is the idea that the ideal stage or studio floor (for injury prevention) is a floating or suspended system with either a hardwood or vinyl surface (sometimes called Marley) that has good shock-absorbing qualities, has some give under impact, does not deform permanently or easily dent, and is not springy (trampoline-like) or unforgivingly rigid or hard. In addition, dance floors should provide good traction or surface friction (although allowing for needed slide) and a uniform surface. However, sprung floor systems—both permanent and portable—are also available that do not use metal springs or rubber pads and can be laid on top of existing floors (even carpet) without preparation. Cushioned vinyl surfaces, placed directly on concrete or rolled steel joists, have become more popular since the early 1980s, thus challenging the idea that the ideal dance floor must have a sprung or floating wooden floor construction featuring crossbars, padded sleepers, slats, and runners (Figure 95).

A case in point is the Harlequin Corporation's Allegro performance surface. The thick dance surface (0.34 inches) can itself act as a semi-sprung floor. It consists of closed cell foam backing that is nonpermeable to liquids or air, woven mineral fiber reinforcement, a support layer, and a slip-resistant wear coat. It can be overlaid on an uneven concrete floor or a specially designed sprung subfloor, for example, a Harlequin Activity™ Sprung Floor (a permanently installed, fully floating sprung floor system), Liberty™ sprung panels (for either portable or permanent installation), or the Woodspring™ Basketweave, which is perhaps the more typical floor dancers think of using, and includes a triple layer of battens (a

Figure 95 Construction of a Harlequin Activity Sprung Floor System™ at the National Dance Institute of New Mexico in Santa Fe. (Photo by Babak Dowlatshahi, InSight Foto, © 2003)

basketweave pattern of wood), enhanced by shock-absorbent elastomer pads (consisting of various polymers having the elastic properties of natural rubber). Any of these floors can be overlaid with a hardwood surface as well.

The price of various floor systems can vary by a factor of 10. Smaller dance organizations may typically install just a performance surface over an existing floor. Larger organizations using such systems include the Boston Ballet, Aspen Ballet, the Trisha Brown Dance Company, Pacific Northwest Ballet in Seattle, The Joffrey Ballet of Chicago, the Laban Centre in London, professional schools such as the English National Ballet School and the Royal Ballet School, as well as dance programs at Sarah Lawrence College, Bard College, St. Olaf College, California State University, Long Beach, Cornish College for the Arts in Seattle, and Loyola Marymount University in Los Angeles.

Harlequin Corporation CEO and America President Robert Dagger reflects on the evolution of dance flooring and standards for such flooring:

> Sprung dance floors have come a long way since the introduction to North America of the heavy and cumbersome basketweave construction which was probably a Russian development early in the twentieth century. Balanchine subsequently played a leading part in the design of an 8 ft × 4 ft interlocking basketweave panel system which NYCB could tour, but these panels are a brute for anyone without a beefy crew, a semi-trailer, and a deep pocket.
>
> Floors have become lighter, thinner, quieter, and in many cases highly portable. But notably, dancers have become more selective. The days are fast disappearing when they were expected to dance on hard unyielding surfaces. Indeed there is a clear prohibition in the rules of Actors' Equity against dancing on marble or concrete floors for performance or rehearsal. Therefore, the organization stipulated as recently as June 2002 that stage flooring (for dance) should be made of wood and not be laid on nonresilient material. There is a parallel in Europe where the French Ministry of Culture will not authorize subsidy to publicly funded dance schools unless there is a provision for a sprung floor.
>
> Patently, it is of little use installing a resilient floor if the surface is too slippery, or even too blocking (i.e., bringing the dancers to an abrupt stop) for dance. The dance surface must have acceptable friction—or, to use the dancer's term, traction —to promote confidence in the performer. The characteristics of surface friction and resilience are addressed with typical thoroughness in the German standard DIN (Deutsche Industrie Norm) 18032 Part 2. There is, however, the major caveat that the specification applies to sports and athletic activities, not dance. Sportsmen and women wear protective footwear, for example, trainers or sneakers that have protective padding or slip-resistant soles, which require friction and resilience properties different from those of the dancer. Ball bounce may also be a key factor in the drafting of sports floor specifications but inconsequential to dancers.
>
> This anomaly has come to the attention of the Technical Standards Committee of The American Entertainment Services and Technology Association (ESTA), which at the time of writing is drafting a specification for entertainment floors incorporating the interests of Actors' Equity, theatres, performers, and, of course, manufacturers.
>
> Standards notwithstanding, it is almost impossible to control the dance floor environment, especially when a company is touring (unless specified previously in a contract). Many touring companies carry their own portable floor—a suspended dance-floor system, consisting of synthetic material and plywood. It can be laid over any floor that is structurally sound, including a concrete slab.

Thus, given the wide array of dance surfaces and flooring available today, schools and companies should shop around for ease of installation, reconfiguration, maintenance, and durability, as well as selecting a floor with appropriate shock absorption and resilience and excessive springiness for the safe and satisfying execution of the demanding moves dancers are expected to perform.

Sources

Janice Barringer and Sarah Schlesinger, *The Pointe Book: Shoes, Training & Technique* rev. ed. (Hightstown, NJ: Princeton Book Company, Publishers, 1998).

Paul Fiolkowski and Jeff Bauer, "The effects of different dance surfaces on plantar pressures," *Journal of Dance Medicine & Science* 1/2 (1997): 62–66.

Robert Dagger, CEO, Harlequin, personal interview, 2003.

Kenneth Laws, *Physics and the Art of Dance: Understanding Movement* (Oxford: Oxford University Press, 2002), pp. 56–58.

Jay Seals, "Dance surfaces," in Allan J. Ryan and Robert E. Stephens, eds. *Dance Medicine: A Comprehensive Guide* (Chicago: Pluribus Press, Inc./Minneapolis: The Physician and Sportsmedicine, 1987), p. 321.

C

Feet First
Dance Footwear and Footcare

A contributing factor to overuse injury is the lack of protective footwear. Ballet slippers are soft, flexible, and usually made of canvas or leather. Point shoes are more rigid because the toe is "blocked" (i.e., stiffened with glue). Neither shoe offers shock absorption from partnered landings and solo jumps.

Aesthetically, the effect of dancing on point is stunning. It helps to extend the long line of the body and facilitates the execution of multiple pirouettes. But for aerial work the shoe is a liability, providing little shock absorption. Ballerinas complain about the hopping on point required by the Petipa choreography in *Sleeping Beauty*. Depending on the shock absorption properties of the flooring that night, most of the impact is being absorbed by their knees, hips, and spine.

In modern dance, rarely are shoes worn in rehearsal or performance. This is in keeping with the original ideology or cultural traits of modern dance: freedom in movement and expressiveness, without restrictive clothing. For today's modern dancers, it is much safer to wear athletic shoes, as in Elizabeth Streb's work (see Streb profile, Chapter 1). This makes sense for some dancers, and for some choreography. In addition to shock absorption, the athletic shoe provides lateral and hind foot stability. Turns, however, must be carefully negotiated—or avoided—to prevent abrupt, twisting movements that might damage the cartilage in the knee.

For jazz shoes, there are special considerations in selection, if for no other reason than variety. There is an array of shoes to chose from: high- and low-rise slip-ons, split-sole jazz sneakers, shoes with rubber or suede soles, neoprene arch supports, mesh insoles, and even shock absorbers. Some dancers prefer a split-sole design to show off the arch and flexibility of the foot. Other shoes have a rubber split sole, or a suede patch, which allows for faster, smoother turning especially on vinyl or Marley flooring. Some come with half-inch foam heels or contain other lightweight materials (for shock absorption). Others are even reinforced at the toe, which is a common wear point in jazz shoes.

Sources
Janice Barringer and Sarah Schlesinger, *The Pointe Book: Shoes, Training & Technique,* rev. ed. (Hightstown, NJ: Princeton Book Company, Publishers, 1998), pp. 14–15ff.
Linda Sparrowe, "Choose a shoe: a good jazz shoe is a soleful experience," *Dance Magazine* August (2003): 37–39.

D

On Point

Foot problems affect dancers, irrespective of dance style or gender. Yet ballerinas dancing on point have some very predictable, idiom-specific problems. Certainly, ballerinas on point thrill audiences today as much as in 1832 when Marie Taglioni, in a performance of *La Sylphide,* appeared wearing soft satin slippers with darned points and stood on the tips of the shoes. Point shoes today remain both a rite of passage (Figure 96) and a biomechanical challenge for dancers. Weight is transmitted from the toe box through the shank to the ankle bones. The point shoe helps to create a curved line of the foot rather than buckling under the weight of the body (Figure 97).

There is much to consider in choosing, fitting, and wearing point shoes. Dancers must learn, for example, what padding best alleviates pressure. This is especially important for dancers such as Pacific Northwest Ballet's Patricia Barker, who spends up to 8 hours a day in point shoes (Figures 98 through 100).

According to point shoe authority and physician Thomas Novella, more than half the world's ballerinas order shoes from a custom maker. Popular manufacturers include Capezio, popular in the United States and available in a wide variety of sizes and stiffness; Freed, one of the most popular point shoes in Europe and somewhat lighter in weight; Gamba, available in a wide variety of shoes, sizes, and stiffness, useful for dancers with difficult to fit feet; Bloch, lightweight and recommended for the experienced dancer; Chacotte, lightweight, well-made Japanese shoes; and Gaynor-Minden, point shoes made of innovative materials and customized to individual requirements. Dancers are concerned about the fit, comfort, and durability of the shoes, commenting that the "best" shoe is one that "feels right" and permits artistic maneuvers, not necessarily the strongest or most durable.

One risk factor for injury in dancing is wearing "old" point shoes that no longer give adequate support. Point shoes are expensive, and dancers may wear shoes longer than they should. Dancers would welcome innovations that extended the useful life of point shoes. Manufacturers are thus testing new materials and techniques, like reinforcing part of the toe with modern plastics (which also can be somewhat molded to the individual foot shape). Another possibility is covering the outer layer of the upper using fine nylon rather than the traditional satin. Anything to increase the life of the shoe is a boost, since one of the major expenses for students and companies is shoes. Shoes worn only for the last 15

Figure 96 Students (left to right, Nina Deacon, Kelen Laine, Jordan Donahue, Brianne Bell, and Julie McCorkle) at the Nancy Whyte School of Ballet prepare for point class. (Photo by Angela Sterling)

Figure 97 On point. (Sabine Chaland) (Photo by Angela Sterling)

minutes or so of class may last an entire school year. The cost of shoes, padding, and ribbon averages about $75.

Novella gives special considerations in fitting point shoes, including checks for width and length and criteria for size and shank selection (the shank is the interior reinforcement under the long arch of the foot). The evaluation includes looking at bare feet for foot and arch type, taking into account width differences, toe length and shape, and emerging bunions. Shoes need to fit snugly and give support, cradling rather than compressing the

Figure 98 Pacific Northwest Ballet's Patricia Barker takes about 10 minutes to tape her toes in preparing the feet for point work. She positions custom-made rubber padding between her second and third toes using nonslip masking tape (commercially available), wrapping each toe to provide an extra layer for comfort, and with special attention paid to her fourth toe, previously injured from an infected blister. (Photo by Angela Sterling)

Figure 99 Ribbons should be tied carefully to allow the shoe (and foot) proper contact with the floor (demonstrated by Patricia Barker, Pacific Northwest Ballet). (Photo by Angela Sterling)

foot, and allowing for full range of motion of the ankle. (For more, see *The Pointe Book* on how to fit point shoes, prepare them for class use and maintain them, as well as practice exercises for developing strength.)

Improperly fitting point shoes can cause any number of problems, including ingrown toenails (the side edge of the toenail curls and pushes down into the soft skin of the toe, causing irritation or infection) as well as bruised and thickened nails. To avoid the risk of

Figure 100 Pacific Northwest Ballet's Patricia Barker on point. (Photo by Angela Sterling)

infection, dancers should practice good nail hygiene by trimming the nails straight across, with the ideal nail stopping about a millimeter beyond each skin corner, close to the quick at the center. A rough or hooked impacted nail—short of showing signs of infection (red, swollen, warm, and painful)—often can be self-treated. Basically, many nail problems can be avoided, or easily rectified, by following simple procedures such as nail-trimming techniques and paying attention to shoe fit.

Recommendations for good foot hygiene for point dancers and others include:

- *Fungal infections* such as athlete's foot can be avoided by washing feet at least once a day and drying the skin between the toes, as well as wearing sandals or other protective footwear in public showers.
- *Blisters,* caused by continuous friction where the tender skin is rubbed back and forth against the inside of the shoe, can be prevented by taping (see below), and also by lubricating with petroleum jelly or ointment and wrapping the toes in lamb's wool. Using a drying powder can reduce moisture and the chance of getting blisters.
- *Bunions* (a bony knob on the inside of the big toe that forms when the toe angles toward the smaller ones) can be painful. The pain can be reduced by wearing toe spacers made of lamb's wool, moleskin, or foam. Poor technique (i.e., ankle pronation) often is a risk factor.
- *Overly thick calluses* are hard mounds of skin that appear on the bottom or side of the foot and are caused by recurrent pressure from rubbing the skin of the feet against a surface; fungus also may be implicated. Calluses can crack and bleed, causing infections. Soak feet in a bowl of warm water with mild dishwashing soap or cleanser for

10 to15 minutes and then use a pumice stone (carefully) to reduce the callous so that it is level with the skin around it, massaging the area with a formulated skin softener or some emollient such as olive oil. Apply moleskin or other cushioned pads around the callus to help reduce pressure and pain.

- *Corns* result from abnormal pressure from poorly fitting shoes. Dancers can pad spots where corns are forming with moleskin and reconsider the fit of the point shoes. To reduce the size of hard corns, perform foot soaks as described above for 5 to10 minutes; dry and massage the toes with olive oil. Some health professionals recommend rubbing the corn with the coarse side of an emery board, then smoothing with the finer side, and repeating until the corn is even with the skin. Others advise a more conservative treatment of wearing corn pads (moleskin with a hole) or rubberized silicone toe sleeves to prevent pressure against the corn and pain.
- *Soft corns* develop in the moist environment between the toes and usually result from a bone spur of the toe joint, aggravated by point shoes that are too tight across the metatarsal area. To treat, toes should be separated with lamb's wool, cotton, or a commercial toe spacer.

Even with well-fitted point shoes, injuries to the foot and ankle can result. Nevertheless, some helpful pointers can go a long way to preventing injuries:

- Do not wear ribbons too tight—they cut off circulation, mask shoe-fitting problems, and may cause stress to the lower leg.
- Do not allow ribbon knots to apply abnormal pressure to the Achilles tendon.
- If you are knuckling forward on point, look for weaknesses in muscles and problems in alignment.
- Check the heel of point shoes for abnormal wear.
- Do not wear point shoes that are too tight or too large. A point shoe that fits correctly allows full dorsiflexion as well as control of the foot and ankle. A large shoe can increase the propensity to ankle sprains and result in unbalanced muscles. The range of motion needs to be adequate.
- Icing the foot at the end of the day reduces swelling.
- Keep the skin on the feet dry and pliant. It should not dry out so that it cracks or becomes tender. Massaging commercial skin softeners or natural emollients into the skin of the toes (including around the toenails) at night helps; massage each toe and knead the metatarsal arch with the thumbs or some kind of wooden massage roller. Also treat the heels.
- Watch out for fatigue, especially at the end of the day when physical and mental exhaustion is more likely.
- Take the time to properly prepare the feet for point wear, including taping for injury prevention. Dancers use everything from athletic tape to Dr. Scholl's gel and corn pads, toe pads, lamb's wool, gel toe caps, and silicone putty.

Sources

Patricia Barker. On Pointe Shoes: From First Fitting to Curtain Call (video) (Seattle: Pacific Northwest Ballet, 2001).

Janice Barringer and Sarah Schlesinger, *The Pointe Book: Shoes, Training & Techniques,* rev. ed. (Hightstown, NJ: Princeton Book Company, Publishers, 1998).

www.bunheads.com. A source for products that protect the feet in point shoes.

B. W. Cunningham, A. F. DiStefano, N. A. Kirjanov, E. E. Levine, and L. C. Schon, "A comparative mechanical analysis of the point shoe toe box," *American Journal of Sports Medicine 26/4 (1998): 555–561.*

Karen Dacko, "First points: making the coveted shoe work for you," *Dance Magazine* December (2002): 69–73.

Thomas M. Novella, "Management of the dancer's toenails," *Journal of Dance Medicine & Science* 4/4 (2000): 132–136.

Preface

1. See Allan Ryan's excellent review article in the first issue of the *Journal of Dance Medicine & Science* for work in other countries; "Early history of dance medicine," 1/1 (1997): 30–34.

2. According to data compiled by Dance/USA, dancers in the 15 companies in the United States with budgets over $5 million earned $600 to $1,400 per week. While a handful of stars earn more, most other dancers in the 70 to 80 large companies earned $400 to $600 per week. See "Dance in America: Snapfacts 2000," September (2000).

Chapter 1

1. In this book, the term "dancer" refers to one who earns a living (wholly or in part) in an occupation that also is engaged in as an activity by amateurs. Professional dancers perform on a somewhat regular basis in seasonal programs, show runs, or on tour. "Dance student" refers to a dancer who trains to practice the art of movement for recreation, enjoyment, or as a livelihood.

2. Bert Mandelbaum, personal interviews, 1987–1989. Of course, for certain physiological measures such as maximal oxygen intake values, dancers may rank lower than, say, nordic skiers.

3. See Linda H. Hamilton, *Advice for Dancers: Emotional Counsel and Practical Strategies*, rev. ed. (San Francisco: Jossey-Bass Publishers, 1998), p. 55.

4. See Delmas J. Bolin, "Evaluation and management of stress fractures in dancers," *Journal of Dance Medicine & Science* 5/2 (2001): 37–42. *Journal of Dance Medicine & Science* is the official journal of the International Association for Dance Medicine and Science (IADMS).

5. Injury occurs at the site of open epiphyses—areas of new bone cell deposition that allow for growth in bone length.

6. Researchers Shaw Bronner and Lise Worthen, using data from The U.S. Bureau of Labor, the National Dance Education Organization, various listings in *Dance Magazine* and *Dance Teacher Magazine*, and the database of the *Journal of Dance Medicine & Science*, as well as other unpublished sources, estimated the number of children or adults who studied or performed dance in an organized fashion to be 38,000 full- and 38,000 part-time professional dancers and choreographers, with as many as 10,445,000 students, including those in colleges and universities (see Shaw Bronner and Lise Worthen, "The demographics of dance in the United States," *Journal of Dance Medicine & Science* 3/4 (1999): 151–153). Linda Hamilton gives a figure of 20,000 professional dancers in the United States (1998).

7. See L. M. Vincent, *Competing with the Sylph: The Quest for the Perfect Dance Body*, 2nd ed. (Pennington, NJ: Princeton Book Company, Publishers, 1989) and L. M. Vincent, "Disordered eating: confronting the dance aesthetic," *Journal of Dance Medicine & Science* 2/1 (1998): 4–5.

8. There is, however, a movement underway for more widespread screening of dancers to establish norms for body alignment and associated anatomical deviations, and explore what relevance they have for injury, rehabilitation, and performance. See *Journal of Dance Medicine & Science*, 1/3 (1997).

9. Linda H. Hamilton, William G. Hamilton, Michelle P. Warren, Katy Keller, and Marika Molnar, "Factors contributing to the attrition rate in elite ballet students," *Journal of Dance Medicine & Science* 1/4 (1997): 131–138. See also work by Lyle J. Micheli ("Dance injuries: an overview," Paper presented at the Boston Dance Medicine Conference: Update 1998, Boston, October 10) in which he discusses finding only a 5 percent occurrence of the

cavus foot (the unusually high-arched foot, which poorly absorbs shock) suggesting that dancers have been selected out at an early age.

10. See Vincent, *Competing with the Sylph*, p. 162, and Hamilton, *Advice for Dancers*, Chapter 1.
11. Erick Hawkins, personal interviews, 1987–1989.
12. See Gigi Berardi, *Finding Balance*, 1st ed. (Pennington, NJ: Princeton Book Company, Publishers, 1991), p. xviii, for further explanation of the interview process and interviewees.
13. Bill Evans, personal interview, 2003.
14. For more discussion, see the review article by Karim M. Khan, Michelle P. Warren, Amanda Stiehl, Heather A. McKay, and John D. Wark, "Bone mineral density in active and retired ballet dancers," *Journal of Dance Medicine & Science* 3/1 (1999): 15–23.
15. Note that this does not include approaches such as traditional herbal medicine, not because it is unworthy of in-clusion, but more in the interest of speaking of what I know.
16. As well as out of dance completely. See Hamilton, *Advice for Dancers*, Chapter 8.
17. Or calling; Ibid., pp.10ff.
18. This is not unlike other sports, such as rowing and swimming, much less gymnastics and ice skating.
19. This and subsequent quotes are from pages 9 and 158–169 of L. M. Vincent's *Competing with the Sylph*. This book is essential reading for anyone interested in a career in professional ballet and especially for any woman who has struggled to achieve a "perfect body."
20. Ibid.
21. For example, dancers with shallow plié, weak quadriceps, or weak feet are going to have problems rolling through the entire foot when landing in fast-tempo ballets. If the floor is not allowed to absorb the shock from landing—which can be easily triple or quadruple the forces that pass through the foot and ankle—something must, and usually it is the connective tissues of the body, with shock finally transmitted to the bone.
22. Differing characteristics of modern and classical dancers, important for medical care of each, have been noted in the scholarly literature. See David S. Weiss, "Medical care of the professional modern dancer," Paper presented at the tenth Annual Meeting of the International Association for Dance Medicine and Science, Miami, October 27–29, 2000.
23. Oleg Briansky, personal interview, 1989. Eight performances per week in a season would not be uncommon for major professional ballet, modern, and theatrical dance companies. Fewer performances usually means smaller (total) audiences and smaller payrolls, although it is difficult to generalize.
24. It is difficult to compare the wear and tear on different dancers, given the very different variations in length and technical demands of ballets and their choreography. Nevertheless, as a generalization, the more and the longer one dances as part of an ensemble or corps, the more likely the chance of injury. Landing more featured roles might be the best way to prolong a career, but that is not a sure thing, either—soloists and principals may be under more pressure to return too soon from injury.
25. With the claim, "Premiere Modern Dance Company Hits the Road with Renewed Energy."
26. Bill Evans, personal interview, 2001.
27. Daniel Duell, personal interviews, 1987–1989.
28. Portions of this text are from a draft article for publication in *Dance Magazine*.
29. See Gigi Berardi, "The agony of dancing," *Los Angeles Times* May 21 (1989): 61–62.
30. David Howard recalls working on Baryshnikov's foot for 45 minutes before one performance of *Coppélia*. Despite advice to the contrary, the dancer insisted on taping the irritated and inflamed foot and going on with the performance.
31. Danny Grossman, personal interviews, 1987–1989.
32. Anti-inflammatory, over-the-counter drugs enable dancers to keep moving. Ibuprofen, marketed under various trademark names, has probably done as much for dance as sprung wood flooring, making it possible to leap and jump and somersault even when injured. David Howard, international ballet master and coach, recalls dancers at one time commonly taking large doses of the drug, yet caution should be taken given the volume of literature reporting potential harmful effects.
33. Of course, there are many other stressors besides injury in the dancer's life—domestic pressures, the death of colleagues and mentors, and even natural disasters. On October 17, 1989, San Francisco suffered a major earth-quake. The San Francisco Ballet was performing in southern California as scheduled, not knowing if they had homes or family to return to.
34. See Lynda M. Mainwaring, Donna Krasnow, and Gretchen Kerr, "And the dance goes on: psychological impact of injury," *Journal of Dance Medicine & Science* 5/4 (2001): 105–115. The authors note the peculiar stresses of the profession—for where else do people train so hard, for ten years or more, "investing time, money, and energy, with the knowledge that gainful employment is uncertain and that even success may involve living at poverty levels" (p. 106).
35. Ibid., p. 111.

36. Bill Evans, personal interview, 2003. Dancer should be warned that taking ibuprofen, like other nonsteroidal antiinflammatory drugs (NSAIDs), also carries with it the issue that by taking away the pain, which serves as a warning signal, the risk of aggravation or reinjury is increased.

37. Portions of this text are from a draft article for publication.

38. Mainwaring et al., "Psychological impact of injury," p. 112.

39. Throughout their lives, dancers stretch and condition their bodies to achieve a desired line—perfect turnout or beautiful hip hyperextension. While they dance, their muscles are strong to stabilize the hip joint. However, when they stop dancing and become physically inactive, the muscles weaken. Ligament laxity could then be a problem. Thus, continuing to dance and staying active makes sense.

40. K. C. Patrick's editorial introduces the November 2001 (p. 16) issue of *Dance Magazine*, with a special section dedicated to dancers small, large, no longer very young, and with "outrageously difficult challenges."

41. See K. C. Patrick, "Why do we keep doing this?." *Dance Magazine* July (2003): 4.

42. See Merilyn Jackson, "Never stop dancing," *Dance Magazine* November (2001): 50–51.

43. Bill Evans, personal interviews, 2002–2003.

44. K.S. Clippinger and S. Brown, "Editorial," *Journal of Dance Medicine & Science* 1/1 (1997): 5.

45. Researchers Ruth and John Solomon, Lyle Micheli, and E. McGray have pioneered research on the epidemiological, medical, and financial aspects of injuries to dancers of the Boston Ballet company over a 5-year period (1993–1998). Their work explains how company choices regarding a variety of health care providers and when to claim major expenses have resulted in savings to the company in excess of $1.2 million. See R. Solomon et al., "The 'cost' of injuries in a professional ballet company: a five-year study," *Medical Problems of Performing Artists* 14/4 (1999): 164–169.

46. Murray Louis, personal interviews, 1987–1989.

47. Merrill Ashley, *Dancing for Balanchine* (New York: E. P. Dutton, Inc., 1984) pp. 217–218.

48. Keith Sabado, Risa Steinberg, personal interviews, 1987–1989.

49. From Mabel E. Todd's classic title, *The Thinking Body: a Study of the Balancing Forces of Dynamic Man* (Brooklyn: Dance Horizons, Inc., 1937).

50. K.C. Patrick, "Why do we keep doing this?"

51. Wendy Perron, personal interviews, 1987–1989.

52. Patricia McBride, Jerel Hilding, personal interviews, 1987–1989. Patricia McBride is now associate artistic director and teacher at North Carolina Dance Theater. Jerel Hilding is associate professor of music and dance at the University of Kansas.

53. See Hamilton, *Advice for Dancers*, Chapters 1 and 7.

54. As discussed in the *Seattle University News* (Nick Gallo, "Turning point," Winter (2003): 12–15), "the university education does something more than give them a credential, in what could be an entreé, a chance at a future, it oh so humanizes what, in general, is life in a most dehumanizing world—of ballet. When so much of ballet asks the dancers to be anything but . . . in the university classroom, anything goes . . ." In the article by Gallo, he comments on this ". . . In a short span of time, the heady conversation includes references to cloning, comas, slavery, St. Augustine, Plato's polis, Ayn Rand's Objectivism, and *The Elephant Man* . . . .[the instructor] drives home a key point: Throughout history people have used their own definitions of 'human' to scratch off those who are different." Such discussion serves to humanize the dancer's world, coming to class straight from a 9-hour stint of rehearsals.

55. *Takaderme* was choreographed by a former company member, Robert Battle, and is often performed by Parsons dancer Katarzyna Skarpetowska. Skarpetowska also choreographed *Stand Back*, created originally for the Chicago-based Hubbard Street 2. Parsons often produces the work of his dancers, even to the point of looking for such talent in the dancers he auditions.

56. Steinberg, a former José Limón company member, master teacher, and solo performer, was profiled in the first edition of *Finding Balance* and appears on the cover of the book.

Chapter 2

1. See Stephen F. Conti and Yue Shuen Wong, "Foot and ankle injuries in the dancer," *Journal of Dance Medicine & Science* 5/2 (2001): 43–50.

2. See Boni Rietveld, "Dance injuries in the older dancer: comparison with younger dancers," *Journal of Dance Medicine & Science* 4/1 (2000): 16–19.

3. See the thoughtful review by Gretchen Kerr, Donna Krasnow, and Lynda Mainwaring in "The nature of dance injuries," *Medical Problems of Performing Artists* 7/1 (1992): 25–29.

4. See Marijeanne Liederbach, "General considerations for guiding dance injury rehabilitation," *Journal of Dance Medicine & Science* 4/2 (2000): 54–65. These figures can vary: see James G. Garrick, "Early identification of musculoskeletal complaints and injuries among female ballet students," *Journal of Dance Medicine & Science* 3/2 (1999): 80–83.

5. However, as researchers Eva Ramel and Ulrich Moritz note, an acute injury such as an ankle sprain may be the result of a tired artist in an overload work situation. See "Work conditions and musculoskeletal disorders in ballet dancers at three theaters in Sweden," in Fadi Bejjani, ed., *Current Research in Arts Medicine: A Compendium of the MedArt International 1992 World Congress on Arts and Medicine* (Pennington, NJ: a cappella books, 1993), Chapter 57.

6. Liederbach, "General considerations," p. 54.

7. Others offer a definition as simply "time lost from performing," which borrows from sports medicine classifications, "time lost from play." See S. Bronner and B. Brownstein, "Profile of dance injuries in a Broadway show: a discussion of issues in dance medicine epidemiology," *Journal of Orthopaedic and Sports Physical Therapy* 26/2(1997): 87–94.

8. Garrick offers, "a musculoskeletal problem, arising from professional dance activities that resulted in the generation of medical costs and the filing of an insurance claim." See "Early identification of musculoskeletal complaints and injuries," p. 82.

9. Ibid.

10. Ibid, p. 80.

11. Robert E. Stephens, "The etiology of injuries in ballet," in Allan J. Ryan and Robert E. Stephens, eds., *Dance Medicine: A Comprehensive Guide* (Chicago: Pluribus Press/Minneapolis: The Physician and Sportsmedicine, 1987), p. l6.

12. See Michelina C. Cassella, Christine Ploski, Elizabeth Sullivan, and Lyle Micheli, "Transition dance class: rehabilitation through dance," *Journal of Dance Medicine & Science* 3/4 (1999): 139–143.

13. See Delmas J. Bolin, "Evaluation and management of stress fractures in dancers," *Journal of Dance Medicine & Science* 5/2 (2001): 37–42.

14. Statistics vary, with men showing more lower-spine, shoulder, and neck injuries, and modern dancers, in general, presenting with more knee and back disorders. General statements such as this necessarily exclude particular populations; see Lynda Mainwaring, Donna Krasnow, and Lauren Young, "A teacher's guide to helping young dancers cope with psychological aspects of hip injuries," *Journal of Dance Education* 3/2 (2003): 57–64. Some studies show the greatest proportion of ballet injuries found in 13- to 18-year-olds; see Lynda M. Mainwaring, Donna Krasnow, and Gretchen Kerr, "And the dance goes on: psychological impact of injury," *Journal of Dance Medicine & Science* 5/4 (2001): 105–115. See also Freddie H. Fu and James J. Irrgang, Introduction to special issue on lower extremity musculoskeletal disorders in dancers—Part 1, *Journal of Dance Medicine & Science* 5/1 (2001): 5; J. Christopher Potts and James J. Irrgang, "Principles of rehabilitation of lower extremity injuries in dancers," *Journal of Dance Medicine & Science* 5/2 (2001): 51–61; C. Nilsson, J. Leanderson, A. Wykman, and L. E. Strender, "The injury panorama in a Swedish professional ballet company," *Knee Surgery, Sports Traumatology, Arthroscopy* 9/4 (2001): 242–246; Liederbach, "General considerations."

15. For an excellent discussion of upper-body disorders and rehabilitation, see *Medicine and Science in Sports and Exercise: Special Symposium Issue* 21/5 (1989): S119-S157.

16. David M. Jenkinson and Delmas J. Bolin, "Knee overuse injuries in dance," *Journal of Dance Medicine & Science* 5/1 (2001): 16.

17. For a note on technique, see Gigi Berardi, "Scottish country dancing has a young soul," *Dance Magazine* November (2000): 64–65.

18. Donna Krasnow and Motaz Kabbani, "Dance science research and the modern dancer," *Medical Problems of Performing Artists* 14/1 (1999): 16–20.

19. Gigi Berardi, research conducted April 2001 and 2002.

20. Paul Bowler, personal interviews, 2001. Also see Paul Bowler profile, Chapter 6.

21. See Juan Bosco Calvo and Luis Gomez-Pellico, "Flamenco dance injures: the Spanish experience," paper presented at the tenth annual meeting of the International Association for Dance Medicine & Science, Miami, FL, October 27–29, 2000.

22. M. Elizabeth Pedersen and Virginia Wilmerding, "Injury profiles of student and professional dancers," *Journal of Dance Medicine & Science* 2/3 (1998): 108–114.

23. M. Elizabeth Pedersen, M. Virginia Wilmerding, J. Milani, and J. Mancha, "Measures of plantar flexion and dorsiflexion strength in Flamenco dancers," *Medical Problems of Performing Artists* 14/3 (1999): 107–112.

24. See Sachi Shimosaka and Harumi Morishita, "Injuries and physical fitness of Japanese traditional dancers," paper presented at the ninth annual meeting of the International Association for Dance Medicine & Science, Tring, England, October 24–26, 1999.

25. Bronner and Brownstein, "Profile of dance injuries."

26. See Aileen Young and Lorna Paul, "Incidence of Achilles tendon injuries in competitive Highland dancers," *Journal of Dance Medicine & Science* 6/2 (2002): 46–49.

27. See Liederbach, "General considerations."

28. See L. Henry, "Leg length discrepancy in the professional dancer," *Journal of Back and Musculoskeletal Rehabilitation* 5/3 (1995): 209–217.

29. Material in this section draws from Liederbach, "General considerations," as well as material in Lyle J. Micheli, "Dance injuries: an overview," paper presented at the Dance Medicine Conference: Update 1998, Boston, October 10, 1998, in Proceedings, *Journal of Dance Medicine & Science* 3/1 (1999): 28–32.

30. Certainly, other schema for classifications of risks exist, including that given in Gigi Berardi, "Dancing over thirty and far beyond: case studies of older-aged dancers and the factors that contribute to the longevity of their performing careers," M.S. thesis, UCLA, 1988. A schema by Yiannis Koutedakis and Craig Sharp includes *direct effects*—having to do with biomechanics, heredity, medical history, psychology (stress control, motivation, goal setting); technology and material science (shoes, dance surfaces), and physiology (physical fitness variables such as aerobic and anaerobic capabilities, muscular strength and power, joint mobility, muscle flexibility, and body composition)—and *indirect effects* such as artistic choreography, costumes, environmental factors, individual (financial state), managerial (administration), and so on. See Yiannis Koutedakis and N. C. Craig Sharp, *The Fit and Healthy Dancer* (New York: John Wiley & Sons, 1999), p. 54.

31. See the excellent review article by Donna Krasnow, Rita Monasterio, and Steven J. Chatfield, "Emerging concepts of posture and alignment," *Medical Problems of Performing Artists* 16/1 (2001): 8–16.

32. Potts and Irrgang, "Principles of rehabilitation," p. 59.

33. See Anne Millington, "The physiological and psychological effects of summer school dance training," paper presented at the ninth annual meeting of the International Association for Dance Medicine & Science, Tring, England, October 24–26, 1999. Also, Micheli, "Dance injuries: an overview," discusses training oversights.

34. See Garrick, "Early identification of musculoskeletal complaints and injuries," p. 83.

35. Liederbach, "General considerations," p. 58.

36. Janice Barringer and Sarah Schlesinger, *The Pointe Book: Shoes, Training & Technique*, rev. ed. (Hightstown, NJ: Princeton Book Company, Publishers, 1998).

37. See Marijeanne Liederbach, "The role of fatigue in dance injuries," paper presented at the tenth annual meeting of the International Association for Dance Medicine & Science, Miami, FL, October 27–29, 2000, and Linda Hamilton, "Advice for dancers," *Dance Magazine* June (2003): 13. Also see Marijeanne Liederbach and Julietta M. Compagno, "Psychological aspects of fatigue-related injuries in dancers," *Journal of Dance Medicine & Science* 5/4 (2001): 116–120.

38. For more on finding balance in the dancer's routine workday and how to work hard without overload, see the first chapter of Daniel Nagrin's, *How to Dance Forever: Surviving Against the Odds* (New York: William Morrow and Co., Inc., 1988).

39. See Richard T. Braver's "Prerequisites for going on point" (Englewood, NJ: Active Foot and Ankle Care Center, 2003.) Or see capeziodance.com.

40. See Pierre d'Hemecourt, "Ballet injuries of the lumbar spine," paper presented at the Dance Medicine Conference: Update 1998, Boston, October 10, 1998. In Proceedings, *Journal of Dance Medicine & Science* 3/1 (1999): 30. Also see Anthony Luke and Lyle J. Micheli, "Management of injuries in the young dancer," *Journal of Dance Medicine & Science* 4/1 (2000): 6, and Micheli, "Dance injuries: an overview."

41. Linda H. Hamilton, William G. Hamilton, Michelle P. Warren, Katy Keller, and Marika Molnar, "Factors contributing to the attrition rate in elite ballet students," *Journal of Dance Medicine & Science* 1/4 (1997): 131–138.

42. See Micheli, "Dance injuries: an overview." See also discussion by David Stone, "Hip problems in dancers," *Journal of Dance Medicine & Science* 5/1 (2001): 8–9, on how 16- to 18-year-old ballet students were able to increase external hip rotation (although the 4 degree difference was thought to have questionable clinical significance).

43. See Mainwaring et al., "A teacher's guide;" William G. Hamilton, Michelle P. Warren, and Linda Hamilton, "Physical and psychological aspects of dance medicine," in Bejjani, ed. *Current Research in Arts Medicine*, Chapter 51 (this review covers all common orthopedic problems for classical ballet dancers). Also see Fadi Bejjani, "Occupational disorders of dancers," in Bejjani, ed. *Current Research in Arts Medicine*, Chapter 65.

44. See Katie Lundon, Lindsay Melcher, and Krista Bray, "Stress fractures in ballet: a twenty-five year review," *Journal of Dance Medicine & Science* 3/3 (1999): 101.

45. Ibid.

46. For a good discussion of risk factors for stress fractures, see M. L. Omey, L. J. Micheli, and P. G. Gerbino II, "Idiopathic scoliosis and spondylolysis in the female athlete," *Clinical Orthopaedics and Related Research* 372 (2000): 74–84.

47. See Stone, "Hip problems of dancers." See also the work of Ruth Solomon in clinical settings: "Techniques for addressing tendinitis of the hip: stop the snap, crackle and pop!" paper presented at the tenth annual meeting of the International Association for Dance Medicine & Science, Miami, Florida, October 27–29, 2000.

48. Carol C. Teitz, "Hip and knee injuries in dancers," *Journal of Dance Medicine & Science* 4/1 (2000): 23–29.

49. Jenkinson and Bolin, "Knee overuse injuries," pp. 16–17.

50. Note that this is not necessarily the same thing as the knee being "over the foot" in a lunge, especially if the dancer has femoral anteversion and tibial torsion.

51. Where excessive pronation or supination is indicated, orthotics may help. See Richard T. Braver, "Insights on orthotic treatment of ballet injuries," *Podiatry Today* 17/6 (2004): 21–26. Also see Suzanne Martin, "Health and fitness for life," *Dance Magazine* June (2003): 40.

52. See Donna Krasnow, Lynda Mainwaring, and Gretchen Kerr, "Injury, stress, and perfectionism in young dancers and gymnasts," *Journal of Dance Medicine & Science 3/2 (1999): 51–58.*

53. See Luke and Micheli, "Management of injuries," p. 6.

54. See The Education Committee of the International Association for Dance Medicine & Science, "The challenge of the adolescent dancer," *Journal of Dance Medicine & Science* 5/3 (2001): 94–95. For pre-professional female ballet dancers, puberty may be delayed. See the work of Hamilton, et al., "Attrition rate in elite ballet students."

55. Ibid.

56. Lyle J. Micheli, "Dance injuries: an overview."

57. Luana Poggini, Stefania Losasso, and Stefania Iannone, "Injuries during the dancer's growth spurt: etiology, prevention, and treatment," *Journal of Dance Medicine & Science* 3/2 (1999): 73–79.

58. Such adolescent growth characteristics may put the dancer at risk for many possible injuries: mechanical back pain, spondylolysis or spondylolisthesis (spinal vertebrae disorders), iliopsoas (hip flexor) tendinitis, patellofemoral pain, stress fractures of the tibia and fibula (lower leg), Achilles tendinitis, and ankle sprain, among others. See R. Solomon, T. Brown, P. G. Gerbino, and L. J. Micheli, "The young dancer," *Clinics in Sports Medicine* 19/4 (2000): 717–739.

59. Children with hyperlaxity may sustain dislocations and ligament sprains and need strengthening exercises to control joint motion and improve alignment; children with poor flexibility are more susceptible to muscle strains and tendinitis and should stretch more, including use of proprioceptive neuromuscular facilitation (stretching) methods. See Luke and Micheli, "Management of injuries," p. 7.

60. Mainwaring et al., "A teachers guide," p. 61. Also see Solomon et al., "The young dancer."

61. Rita Smilkstein, "How the brain learns: research, theory, and classroom application," paper presented at the "Transforming Campuses Through Learning Communities" conference of the Washington Center for the Improvement of Undergraduate Education, Seattle, WA, February, 2000.

62. Ibid.

63. Linda H. Hamilton, *Advice for Dancers: Emotional Counsel and Practical Strategies*, rev. ed. (San Francisco: Jossey-Bass Publishers, 1998), p. 55. Also see Linda H. Hamilton, "A psychological profile of the adolescent dancer," *Journal of Dance Medicine & Science* 3/2 (1999): 50; Linda H. Hamilton and W. G. Hamilton, "Occupational stress in classical ballet: the impact in different cultures," *Medical Problems of Performing Artists* 9/2 (1994): 35–38; and, M. Horosko and J. R. F. Kupersmith, *The Dancer's Survival Manual* (New York: Harper & Row, 1987).

64. Susan A. Lee, "Adolescent issues in a psychological approach to dancers," *Journal of Dance Medicine & Science* 5/4 (2001): 121, 123; Krasnow and Kabbani, "Dance science research," pp. 16–20; and, J. M. Schnitt, D. Schnitt, and S. Lee, "Psychological issues in the clinical approach to dancers," in R. T. Sataloff, A. G. Brandfonbrener, R. J. Lederman, eds. *Performing Arts Medicine*, 2nd ed. (San Diego: Singular Publishing Co., 1998), p. 359.

65. Luke and Micheli, "Management of injuries," p. 14.

66. Ibid. Also see N. Vaisman, H. Voet, A. Akivis, and I. Sieve-Ner, "Weight perception of adolescent dancing school students," *Archives of Pediatrics and Adolescent Medicine* 150/2 (1996): 187–190, and "Special issue: eating behavior, reproductive health, and osteoporosis," *Journal of Dance Medicine & Science* 2/1 (1998).

67. See Bolin, "Evaluation and management of stress fractures."

68. Ibid. Note that intense training greater than 5 hours per day can impart a six-fold increase in stress fractures; the odds are greatly increased if the dancer has amenorrhea. See N. Kadel, C. Teitz, and R. Kronmal, "Stress fractures in ballet dancers," *American Journal of Sports Medicine* 20/4 (1992): 445–449. Also see Jordan D. Metzl, "The developing dancer," paper presented at the tenth annual meeting of the International Association for Dance Medicine & Science, Miami, FL, October 27–29, 2000.

69. See S. Abraham, "Eating and weight controlling behaviors of young ballet dancers," *Psychopathology* 29/4 (1996): 218–222, and N. Bettle, O. Bettle, U. Neumarker, and K. J. Neumarker, "Adolescent ballet school students: their quest for body weight change," *Psychopathology* 31/3 (1998): 153–159.

70. See Jennifer M. Stacey, "The physiological development of the adolescent dancer," *Journal of Dance Medicine & Science* 3/2 (1999): 62, and Hamilton et al., "Attrition rate in elite ballet students."

71. See U. Kujala, A. Oksanen, S. Taimela, and J. J. Salminen, "Training does not increase maximal lumbar extension in healthy adolescents," *Clinical Biomechanics* 12/3 (1997): 181–184.

72. See Craig Philips, "Strength training of dancers during the adolescent growth spurt," *Journal of Dance Medicine & Science* 3/2 (1999): 66–72.

73. Poggini et al., "Injuries during the dancer's growth spurt," p. 75.

74. See Solomon, "Techniques for addressing tendinitis." Also see Teitz, "Hip and knee injuries," pp. 23–24, for a good discussion of involvement of the iliotibial or iliopsoas tendons, related inflammation, and options for healing the irritated and painful tendon. Also see D. L. Janzen, E. Partridge, M. Logan, D. G. Connell, and C. P. Duncan, "The snapping hip: clinical and imaging findings in transient subluxation of the iliopsoas tendon," *Journal de l'Association Canadienne des Radiologistes* 47/3 (1996): 202–208.

75. Ibid.

76. Ibid.

77. D.J. Popalisky and M. G. Herbert, "Defining the performing artist: how a health psychology course integrates into university performing arts training," *Medical Problems of Performing Artists* 15/4 (2000): 148–154.

78. See "Special issue: dance screening," *Journal of Dance Medicine & Science* 1/3 (1997). Note commentary by Karen Clippinger and Janice Plastino and articles by Ruth Solomon and lead authors Itzhak Siev-Ner, Marijeanne Liederbach, and Marika Molnar.

79. Dancers may not recognize an injury perhaps to avoid the "disruption of self" emanating from it. See Mainwaring et al., "And the dance goes on," p. 105, and Kerr et al., "The nature of dance injuries," p. 25.

80. Liederbach, "General considerations," p. 54.

81. Potts and Irrgang, "Principles of rehabilitation," pp. 51–52.

82. For example, in Pacific Northwest Ballet's Sleeping Beauty in 2003, a principal dancer with a minor ankle injury danced the role of Lilac Fairy instead of the more demanding Aurora.

83. See Potts and Irrgang, "Principles of rehabilitation," p. 53.

84. Ibid., p. 52.

85. William Weintraub, *Tendon and Ligament Healing: A New Approach Through Manual Therapy* (Berkeley, CA: North Atlantic Books, 1999), p. 27.

86. For information on manipulation and adjustments, especially in the later stages of healing, see the discussion in Karel Lewit, *Manipulative Therapy in Rehabilitation of the Locomotor System*, 2nd ed. (Boston: Butterworth-Heinemann, 1991), and William H. Kirkaldy-Willis, ed., *Managing Low Back Pain* (New York: Churchill Livingstone, 1983).

87. Potts and Irrgang, "Principles of rehabilitation," pp. 53ff.

88. Ibid. Note that the fully maturing scar tissue may take months to form (assuming collagen tissue has a turnover rate of about 9 months).

89. See Solomon et al., "Techniques for addressing tendinitis."

90. See Daniel Nagrin's *How to Dance Forever*, pp. 119–166, for an excellent description of some healers and their methods of treatment.

91. Although Brown clearly states his concerns that treatment plans should be the result of a careful risk-benefit analysis of all available treatment options and, preferably, with well-designed intervention studies as well as case reports, he acknowledges that, to date, CAM data generally do not provide the evidence typically used in producing standards-of-care guidelines. This is in line with the conclusions of a NIH-appointed panel. The panel noted that research into the efficacy of CAM is needed and, at the very least, that there should be a listing of resources within the NIH for medical and lay communities, including bibliographies, expert directories, an online CAM database, and a clearinghouse for public education resources. It is interesting to note that accrediting bodies were first established for chiropractic, acupuncture, and naturopathy, yet only for chiropractic is licensure required in all states. See Scott E. Brown, "The efficacy of complementary and alternative medicine," *Journal of Dance Medicine & Science* 2/3 (1998): 117–119.

92. Ibid., p. 117.

93. Admittedly, it is odd to define something by what it is not. By comparison, would it make sense to characterize organic food as that which is not sold in all large supermarkets? (see Gigi Berardi, "The Lenses of Culture," unpublished paper, available from the author, Western Washington University, Bellingham, WA). Furthermore, the finding that CAM are not taught more widely at American medical schools or are not generally available at American hospitals does not mean that they are not being taught. Schools of such healing practices exist—Bastyr in Seattle, Washington, and Axelsson's Institute in Stockholm are but two examples.

94. See Nagrin, *How to Dance Forever*, p. 175.

95. See Nancy Gamboian, Steven J. Chatfield, and Marjorie H. Woollacott, "Further effects of somatic training on pelvic tilt and lumbar lordosis alignment during quiet stance and dynamic dance movement," *Journal of Dance Medicine & Science* 4/3 (2000): 90–98. Also see Carol M. Davis, ed. *Complementary Therapies in Rehabilitation: Holistic Approaches for Prevention and Wellness* (Thorofare, NJ: Slack, Inc.,1996), an impressive volume of complementary body/mind therapies of myofascial release, Rolfing, biofeedback, yoga, T'ai Chi, Alexander, Feldenkrais, Trager, several forms of traditional Chinese medicine, and homeopathy, all of which are disciplines unto themselves, yet also exist as part of holistic treatments.

96. See *Dance Medicine Resource Guide*, originated by Jan Dunn and edited by Marshall Hagins (Andover, NJ: J. Michael Ryan Publishing, Inc., 2003).

97. Brown, "The efficacy of complementary and alternative medicine," p. 117.

98. See T. Nickenig, "Grace under pressure," *Advances for Directors in Rehabilitation* 10/5 (2001): 55–58, for a discussion of the directed education required on both sides of the clinician-patient relationship. Also see Eric Franklin's *Dynamic Alignment Through Imagery* (Champaign, IL: Human Kinetics, 1996) for the history and leading figures of somatic therapies and a review of the various disciplines.

99. See Brown, "The efficacy of complementary and alternative medicine," p. 118. Also see "Guiding principles for research in complementary and alternative medicine," *Journal of Dance Medicine & Science* 2/3 (1998): 115–116.

100. Liederbach, "General considerations," p. 54.

101. Allan J. Ryan and Robert E. Stephens, *The Dancer's Complete Guide to Healthcare and a Long Career* (Chicago: Bonus Books, 1988), pp. 162–163.

102. Liederbach, "General considerations," p. 54.

103. Ibid. See Table 4 on p. 62 for a listing in the Liederbach article for such functional tests for dance.

104. See Potts and Irrgang, "Principles of rehabilitation."

105. Linda Hamilton, "Advice for dancers," *Dance Magazine* January (1995): 94–95.

106. See Gigi Berardi, "Proprioceptive training following acute Achilles injury in dance," *Impulse* 3/13 (1995): 200–213.

107. See Gigi Berardi, "Early mobilization after Achilles tendon repair," *Your Patient and Fitness* 10/2 (1996): 23–30.

108. See Bill Russell, "Proprioceptive rehabilitation in dancers' injuries," *Kinesiology and Medicine for Dance* 14/2: (1992): 27–38; Christopher M. Norris, *Back Stability* (Champaign, IL: Human Kinetics, 2000), pp. 79ff and 197ff; and C. Buz Swanik, Scott M. Lephart, Frank P. Giannantonio, and Freddie H. Fu, "Reestablishing proprioception and neuromuscular control in the ACL-injured athlete," *Journal of Sport Rehabilitation* 6/2 (1997): 182–206.

109. Liederbach, "General considerations."

110. Thomas W. Myers, *Anatomy Trains: Myofascial Meridians for Manual and Movement Therapists* (Edinburgh: Churchill Livingstone, 2001).

111. Myofascial meridian refers to an interlinked series of connected tracts of sinews and muscles that are lines of pull based on standard western anatomy. These are lines that transmit strain and movement through the body's myofascia around the skeleton. They girdle the body, as with the meridians of longitude and latitude, defining geography and geometry within the body's fascia.

112. See a "Brief Overview of Neural Reflexes" and "Neural Mechanisms and Flexibility" by Donna Krasow, unpublished papers available from the author at Dept. of Dance, Faculty of Fine Arts, York University, 4700 Keele St., Toronto Ontario M3J1P3, Canada. Also see Robert E. Stephens, "The neuroanatomical and biomechanical basis of flexibility exercises in dance," in R. Solomon, S. Minton, and J. Solomon, eds. *Preventing dance injuries: An interdisciplinary perspective*, (Reston, VA: American Alliance for Health, Physical Education, Recreation and Dance, 1990), Chapter 13.

113. Weintraub, *Tendon and Ligament Healing*.

114. Ibid., pp. 3–13, contains a good discussion of the standard medical view for unresponsive chronic injuries, and alternatives.

115. For advice on the importance of questioning a medical diagnosis, especially when the physical therapy assessment and treatment response do not support it, see N.F. Quarrier and A. B. Wightman, "A ballet dancer with chronic hip pain due to a lesser trochanter bony avulsion: the challenge of a different diagnosis," *Journal of Orthopaedic and Sports Physical Therapy* 28/3 (1998): 168–173.

116. See Krasnow's work such as, "C-I training: the merger of conditioning and imagery as an alternative training methodology for dance," *Medical Problems of Performing Artists* March 12/1: 3–8.

117. See Glenna Batson's work, such as: "Traditional and nontraditional approaches to performing arts physical therapy: the dance medicine perspective," *Orthopaedic Physical Therapy Clinics of North America* 6/2 (1997): 207–230; "Stretching technique: a somatic learning model. Part II Training purposivity through Sweigard ideokinesis," *Impulse* 2 (1994): 39–58; and "Conscious use of the human body in movement: the peripheral neuroanatomic basis of the Alexander technique," *Medical Problems of Performing Artists* 11/1 (1996): 3–11.

118. See Franklin's work, such as, *Conditioning for Dance: Training for Peak Performance in All Dance Forms* (Champaign, IL: Human Kinetics, 2004).

119. See, for example, Minton's work, *Dance: Mind & Body* (Champaign, IL: Human Kinetics, 2003).

120. See Solomon's work cited throughout this chapter as well as the video, *Anatomy as a Master Image in Training Dancers* (Santa Cruz, CA: Ruth Solomon, 1988).

121. Potts and Irrgang, "Principles of rehabilitation," p. 56, and Noa Spector-Flock, *Get Stronger by Stretching with Thera-Band®*, 2nd ed. (Hightstown, NJ: Princeton Book Company, Publishers, 2002). Also see Franklin, *Conditioning for Dance*, pp. 213–233.

122. The following are source materials for the discussion of Pilates: Brent D. Anderson and Aaron Spector, "Introduction to Pilates-based rehabilitation," *Orthopaedic Physical Therapy Clinics of North America* (Complementary Medicine), 9/3 (2000): 395–410; Jan Dunn, "Pilates—an exercise and rehabilitation system for the '90s," appearing as "Il metodo Pilates negli Stati Uniti: Origine, evoluzione ed applicazioni pratiche,"

Choregraphie: Studi e ricerche sulla danza 6/11 (1998): 81–91; P. Hodges and C. Richardson, "Inefficient muscular stabilization of the lumbar spine associated with low back pain: a motor control evaluation of transversus abdominis," *Spine* 21/2 (1996): 2640–2650; Michele Meyer, "Fitness," *Lear's* January (1994): 38–39; Potts and Irrgang, "Principles of rehabilitation," p. 58; C. Richardson, G. Jull, P. Hodges, and J. Hides, *Therapeutic Exercise for Spinal Segmental Stabilization in Low Back Pain* (Edinburgh: Churchill Livingstone, 1999); Karen Springen, "Concentrating on the body's 'core,'" *Newsweek* January 20 (2003); and, Nora St. John, "The changing face of Pilates," *Body-Mind-Spirit* (2002): 6–8.

123. Pilates' childhood frailty was a strong motivator in his commitment to becoming stronger. He studied yoga, martial arts, Zen meditation, and Greek and Roman training exercises. He worked with medical professionals, including his wife, Clara, a nurse.

124. The foot board lessens the amount of hip flexion seen with the bar and facilitates full foot proprioception—essential not only in rehabilitation but also in correcting poor foot/leg mechanics.

125. Adapted from Weintraub, *Tendon and Ligament Healing*, pp. 83–95.

126. Richard Braver, D.P.M., has developed an orthotic for dancers that slips onto the bottom of the dancer's foot, which is appropriate for class and rehearsal; some dancers also use it in performance. It should not be regarded as a substitute for the strengthening and flexibility work that is needed to correct alignment and muscle use. A variation on the orthotic, the Braver Ballet Device, made by the Allied Orthotics Lab in Indianapolis, Indiana, can be worn with point shoes. It slips onto the bottom of the foot and limits excessive ankle rolling in and rolling out and is designed to benefit the dancer in relevé. It differs from a traditional orthotic in that it gives the most support under the ball of the foot rather than the arch. As with many of the examples given in this chapter, dancers should seek medical and health professionals knowledgeable about dancers and dance injuries for their own treatment and rehabilitation. See Braver, "Insights on orthotic treatment." Also see Barringer and Schlesinger, *The Pointe Book*.

127. See Weintraub, *Tendon and Ligament Healing*, pp. 96ff.

128. Physician Boni Rietveld advises a "JOJO schedule" for strength training following surgical repair. After mobility of the foot is restored, Phase 1 includes working through the foot, from demi-plié to relevé and back on two legs, with two hands on the barre, progressing to one hand on the barre, balancing on the injured leg. Phase 2 allows for jumping, initially using both legs, with two hands on the barre. See "follow-up care" by Boni Rietveld, unpublished paper.

129. Admittedly, the truncated presentation here does not provide extensive evidence-based data and narrative. For more, see Weintraub, *Tendon and Ligament Healing*, pp. 96–106, for a full discussion.

130. Glenna Batson, "Stretching technique: a somatic learning model. Part I: Training sensory responsivity," *Impulse* 1/2 (1993): 127.

131. Sandra Minton, "Exploring the mind/body connection with imagery," *Kinesiology and Medicine for Dance* 14/1 (1991/2): 29–32. Also see Minton, *Dance: Mind & Body*.

132. Irene Dowd, *Taking Root to Fly* (Hadley, MA: Commonwealth Printing, 1981), p. 2

133. Franklin, *Conditioning for Dance*, pp. 18–19.

134. Stuart McGill makes a strong case for fast walking as an important component of a fitness program, particularly when one of the goals is core stability. See *Low Back Disorders: Evidence-Based Prevention and Rehabilitation* (Champaign, IL: Human Kinetics, 2002), p. 218.

135. For example, see L. Mouchnino, R. Aurenty, J. Massion, and A. Pedotti, "Coordination between equilibrium and head-spine orientation during leg movement: a new strategy built up by training," *Journal of Neurophysiology* 67/6 (1992): 1587–1598, and F. Horak, L. Nasher, and H. Diener, "Postural strategies associated with somatosensory and vestibular loss," *Experimental Brain Research* 82/1 (1990): 167–177.

136. Systems that promote proprioceptive capacity and balance include those that are being applied to elementary education, such as work in the Structure-of-Intellect Learning Styles and Sensory Motor Integration, based on the learning theories of J. P. Guilford of the University of Southern California.

137. For any of these approaches, functional tests may be used. See Liederbach, "General considerations," pp. 61–62.

138. A common source of pain in the lower back is a weak and tight psoas muscle. The psoas attaches to the lower thoracic and all of the lumbar vertebrae and inserts on the inside of the femur. The pull on the lower spine is tremendous when the muscle is tight. This is especially true since many of us spend much of our waking moments in hip flexion (for example, any movement requiring the dancer to raise the leg to the front), either sitting or dancing. Although, in recent times, there has been a concern that deeper abdominal muscles, the internal and external obliques, and the transversus abdominis be strengthened in any abdominal conditioning program (see Judy Gantz, "The relationship between intra-abdominal pressure and dance training," *Kinesiology for Dance* 9/4 [1987]: 15–18), Stuart McGill raises questions about the action of the psoas as a hip flexor and spine stabilizer, as well as the role of intra-abdominal pressure in reducing spinal compression. See McGill, *Low Back Disorders*, p. 112.

139. Y. Koutedakis, P.J. Pacy, R.J. Carson, and F. Dick, "Health and fitness in professional dancers," *Medical Problems of Performing Artists* 12/1 (1997): 23–27.

140. See also exercises developed in the Group Back Education Program at New York City Ballet by physical thera-pist Elizabeth Henry, performed in three sets of 10 repetitions and including lumbar bracing and stabilization. See Donald R. Murphy with Craig Liebenson and Gary F. Ierna, *Lumbar Spinal Stabilization: Floor Exercises* (RISES, Inc./P.O. Box 657, Mt. Sinai, NY 11766) for good explanations of standard bracing exercises (pelvic tilt in supine and quadruped positions), abdominal bracing (supine, kneeling, standing), and various supine arm and leg raises.

141. See Cassella et al., "Transition dance class."

142. Ibid., p. 143.

143. See Emmett W. Hines, *Fitness Swimming* (Champaign, IL: Human Kinetics, 1999).

144. See Thomas M. Novella, "Shim set therapy for the dancer's foot," *Journal of Dance Medicine & Science* 5/3 (2001): 87–93.

145. See Batson, "Traditional and nontraditional approaches"; Franklin, *Conditioning for Dance*; Krasnow, "C-I Training"; Minton, *Dance: Mind & Body*; and Solomon, *Anatomy as a Master Image.*

146. Batson, "Traditional and nontraditional approaches."

147. For more on the psychological and psychosocial impact of injury on the dancer, including disruption to the ath-lete/dancer's sense of identity and coping strategies as a function of individual differences in dancer personality, available social support, and levels of knowledge and available information about injury and recovery, see Mainwaring et al, "And the dance goes on." Also, see the *Journal of Dance Medicine & Science* special issues (in their entirety) on "Psychological issues in dance medicine"—Part one (5/4 [2001]) and Part two (6/1 [2002]), as well as earlier articles: Donna Krasnow, Gretchen Kerr, and Lynda Mainwaring, "Psychology of dealing with the injured dancer," *Medical Problems of Performing Artists* March (1994): 7–9, and Lynda Mainwaring, Gretchen Kerr, and Donna Krasnow, "Psychological correlates of dance injuries," *Medical Problems of Performing Artists* 8/1 (1993): 3–6.

148. Mainwaring et al., "And the dance goes on," and Hamilton, *Advice for Dancers: Emotional Counsel and Practical Strategies.*

149. See Batson, "Traditional and nontraditional approaches."

150. See Ruth Solomon, "The 'cost' of injuries in a professional ballet company: a five-year study," paper presented at the ninth annual meeting of the International Association for Dance Medicine & Science, Tring, England, October 24–26, 1999; and see R. Solomon, J. Solomon, L. J. Micheli, and E. McGray Jr., "The 'cost' of injuries in a professional ballet company: a five-year study," *Medical Problems of Performing Artists* 14/4 (1999): 164–169.

151. Ramel and Moritz, "Work conditions and musculoskeletal disorders," p. 22.

152. Ibid., pp. 219, 222.

153. As also given in Eva Ramel and Ulrich Moritz, "Psychosocial factors at work and their association with profes-sional ballet dancers' musculoskeletal disorders," *Medical Problems of Performing Artists* 13/2 (1998): 66–74, dis-satisfaction with work and muscle tension were the two biggest factors in injuries.

154. See Gigi Berardi, "Circus + dance = Cirque du Soleil," *Dance Magazine* September (2002): 30–33.

155. Mainwaring et al., "A teacher's guide," p. 63.

156. Hamilton et al., "Attrition rate in elite ballet students," pp. 135–137, and Jessica Shenton and Rachel Seghers, "An example of dance health education in practice," paper presented at the ninth annual meeting of the International Association for Dance Medicine & Science, Tring, England, October 24–26, 1999.

157. This, from *Dance Insider Online*, " . . . Catherine Cabeen enters upstage in the same walk and balances for what seems like forever, before creeping back off stage, only to repeat the same sequence again. Of course Jones picked the perfect dancer for this role. With her long pliable legs and exquisitely arched feet that, when raised to relevé, resemble the strokes of calligraphy, Cabeen is a pleasure to watch."—Vanessa Manko Flash review 3, 2–5: Jones Redux "D-Man in The Waters" performance at Lincoln Center, spring 2002.

158. George Balanchine and Francis Mason, *Balanchine's Festival of Ballet: Scene-by-Scene Stories of 404 Classical and Contemporary Ballets* (London: W.H. Allen, 1978), p. 632.

159. As discussed in this chapter and elsewhere, strengthening the core is a critical first step in the rehabilitation of any injury, as well as being a critical component of general conditioning (see Chapter 4). Nadeau's exercises con-sisted of rotational work, eventually with weights, and also work on proprioception, using balance boards at var-ious slants, to develop balance and coordination. Some of the nonprop work included side-walking, with her legs tied together—also to develop alignment when various senses are challenged in space.

160. Gigi Berardi, "Seattle," *Dance International* Winter (2003): 46–47.

Chapter 3

1. See Robert E. Stephens, "The etiology of injuries in ballet," in Allan J. Ryan and Robert E. Stephens, eds. *Dance Medicine: A Comprehensive Guide* (Chicago: Pluribus Press, Inc./Minneapolis: The Physician and Sportsmedicine, 1987), p. 20.
2. Risa Steinberg and Erick Hawkins, personal interviews, 1987–1989.
3. See M. A. Barnes, D. Krasnow, S. J. Tupling, and M. Thomas, "Knee rotation in classical dancers during the grand-plié," *Medical Problems of Performing Artists* 15/4 (2000): 140–147, and E. Trepman, R. E. Gellman, L. J. Micheli, and C. J. De Luca, "Electromyographic analysis of grand-plié in ballet and modern dancers," *Medicine and Science in Sports and Exercise* 30/12 (1998): 1708–1720.
4. Stuart Wright, *Dancer's Guide to Injuries of the Lower Extremity* (New York: Cornwall Books, 1985), p. 14.
5. See J. Christopher Potts and James J. Irrgang, "Principles of rehabilitation of lower extremity injuries," *Journal of Dance Medicine & Science* 5/2 (2001): 51–61.
6. Boni Rietveld, "Compensatory mechanisms for insufficient turn-out of the hips and their adverse effects in dance: anatomy of muscles (that should be) used in turn-out and turn-out movement," paper presented at the eleventh annual meeting of the International Association for Dance Medicine & Science, Alcala de Henares, Spain, November 1–3, 2001.
7. Luana Poggini, Anna Paola Pace, and Donatella Di Mastromatteo, "Relationship between technical faults and dance injuries: correction and prevention," in Fadi J. Bejjani, ed. *Current Research in Arts Medicine: A Compendium of the Med Art International 1992 World Congress on Arts and Medicine* (Pennington, NJ: a cappella books, 1993), Chapter 49.
8. Julie Kent, besides starring in *Dancers*, also is the 2000 recipient of the Prix Benois de la Danse, as reported in *Dance International* 31/3 (2003): 5–8.
9. In the words of educator Mabel E. Todd, author of *The Thinking Body: A Study of the Balancing Forces of Dynamic Man* (Brooklyn: Dance Horizons, Inc., 1937).
10. Bill Evans, personal interview, 2003.
11. M. Virginia Wilmerding, Vivian H. Heyward, Molly King, Kurt J. Fiedler, Christine A. Stidley, Stuart B. Pett, and Bill Evans, "Electromyographic comparison of the développé devant at barre and centre," *Journal of Dance Medicine & Science* 5/3 (2001): 69–74. Also see Donna Krasnow, Rita Monasterio, and Steven J. Chatfield, "Emerging concepts of posture and alignment," *Problems of Performing Artists* 16/1 (2001): 8–16.
12. Marshall Hagins, letter to the editor, *Journal of Dance Medicine & Science* 6/2 (2002): 68.
13. See Stuart McGill, *Low Back Disorders: Evidence-Based Prevention and Rehabilitation.* (Champaign, IL: Human Kinetics, 2002), Chapters 2–4.
14. Ibid.
15. New research-based ideas are found in journals such as *Medical Problems of Performing Artists* and *Journal of Dance Medicine & Science*, as well as in sports and medical literature.
16. Kenneth Laws, *The Physics of Dance* (New York: Schirmer Books, 1984), p. 9.
17. Kenneth Laws, *Physics and the Art of Dance: Understanding Movement* (Oxford: Oxford University Press, 2002), p. vi.
18. Ibid.
19. See Thomas M. Welsh and Steven J. Chatfield, "Within-subject research designs for dance medicine and science," *Journal of Dance Medicine & Science* 1/1 (1997): 16–21, for a good discussion of group comparison research designs as well as within-subject research designs as a useful alternative for answering questions important to dance medicine. See also Steven J. Chatfield and M. H. Woollacott, "Electromyographic and kinematic analysis of movement repatterning in dance," *Impulse* 4/3 (1996): 220–234.
20. Karen S. Clippinger and Scott E. Brown, "New millennium technology and dance medicine and science," *Journal of Dance Medicine & Science* 4/3 (2000): 84–85.
21. See Yiannis Koutedakis and N. C. Craig Sharp, *The Fit and Healthy Dancer* (New York: John Wiley & Sons, 1999).
22. For an excellent discussion of biomechanics applied to dance, see Priscilla M. Clarkson and Margaret Skrinar, eds. *Science of Dance Training* (Champaign, IL: Human Kinetics, 1988), Chapter 8. For further discussion of dance kinesiology, see the following articles in *Kinesiology for Dance*: Kenneth Laws, "Dance kinesiology—difficulties and directions," 7/1 (1984): 6–7; Sue Stigleman, "Dance kinesiology: The field and its literature" (No. 15 (June 1981): 5–9); and Sally Fitt, "The importance of kinesiology for dancers" (No. 1 [May 1977]: 6–7). *Kinesiology for Dance* was a journal devoted entirely to the study of dance science in human movement. Starting in 1977, it published articles ranging from the art of centering to the effect of plyometric training on dancers' vertical jump height to medical treatment for common skin lesions of the feet. Twelve years after its inception, the publication was expanded as a refereed journal with the title *Kinesiology and Medicine for Dance*, cofounded and edited by this author and published by Princeton Periodicals, Inc., in Pennington, New Jersey.
23. Luana Poggini, Stefania Losasso, Manuela Cerreto, and Lucia Cesari, "Jump ability in novice ballet dancers before and after training," *Journal of Dance Medicine & Science* 1/2 (1997): 46–50.

24. Michele R. Scharff-Olson, Henry N. Williford, and Jennifer A. Brown, "Injuries associated with current dance-exercise practices," *Journal of Dance Medicine & Science* 3/4 (1999): 144–150.

25. See John M. Wilson, "Evolution as the master model for understanding biomechanics," paper presented at the ninth annual meeting of the International Association for Dance Medicine & Science, Tring, England, October 24–26, 1999.

26. Adapted from Laws, *Physics and the Art of Dance*, Chapters 5 and 9. Laws' book is fascinating to read and one of the finest examples of the marriage of science and art in the literature today.

27. Shaw Bronner and colleagues discuss the three-dimensional kinematic study of the arabesque using three different levels of training: professionals with a minimum of 10 years of dance training, advanced students, and beginner-intermediate students. The study provided insight into the underlying control of movement dynamics and the effectiveness of training techniques. Success depended on the mastery of postural control and segmental velocities. See Shaw Bronner, Bruce Brownstein, Lise Worthen, and Sarah Ames, "Skill acquisition and mastery in performance of a complex dance movement," paper presented at the tenth annual meeting of the International Association for Dance Medicine & Science, Miami, FL, October 27–29, 2000.

28. Laws, *Physics and the Art of Dance*, pp. 21–22.

29. Ibid., pp. 19–33.

30. Dancers often speak of "torques" on the body. Daniel Nagrin gives a good definition of torque as it is sometimes used in dance in *How to Dance Forever: Surviving Against the Odds* (New York: William Morrow and Company, Inc., 1988), p. 96. He describes a torque at the knee—a twisting force on one part of the body from another—which could possibly injure the knee.

31. Another illustration of the grand jeté floating illusion shows Carrie Imler (profiled in Chapter 1, who now is a principal at Pacific Northwest Ballet but was a student at Central Pennsylvania Youth Ballet when these images were taken) in a remarkable split, high in the air; the sequence shows her center of gravity and head height frame by frame. (Available through the Department of Physics, Dickinson College, Carlisle, PA.)

32. For further discussion, see Lei Li, with Kenneth Laws, "The physical analysis of Da She Van Tiao," *Kinesiology for Dance* 11/4 (1989): 9–11; Kenneth Laws and Kyong Lee, "The grand jeté: a physical analysis," *Kinesiology for Dance* 11/4 (1989) pp. 12–13.

33. Kenneth Laws, "Physics and the potential for dance injury," *Medical Problems of Performing Artists* 1/3 (1986): 88.

34. See the excellent discussion by Kenneth Laws regarding the timing of the extension of the arms and legs. Laws explains how, when the arms are almost straight, a greater vertical force may be exerted (Laws, *Physics and the Art of Dance*, p. 146).

35. For an excellent discussion of the knee, see Ronald Quirk, "The dancer's knee," in Ryan and Stephens, eds. *Dance Medicine: A Comprehensive Guide,* Chapter 11; for femoral angle and torsion, tibial torsion, and limited plantar flexion due to different anatomical variations, see Robert E. Stephens, "The etiology of injuries in ballet," in Ryan and Stephens, *Dance Medicine: A Comprehensive Guide*, Chapter 2.

36. Karen Clippinger-Robertson, "Flexibility in dance," *Kinesiology and Medicine for Dance* 12/2 (1990): 1–16, and *Flexibility for Aerobics and Fitness* (Seattle, WA: Seattle Sports Medicine, 1987).

37. Clippinger-Robertson, ibid.

38. Some of which are included under the term "complementary therapies," used in Chapter 2. "Complementary therapies," however, has little meaning in the context of this chapter—they are not "in addition to" any standard training, but rather, stand alone.

39. Eric Franklin, *Dynamic Alignment Through Imagery* (Champaign, IL: Human Kinetics, 1996), p. 3 and Jeanne Achterberg, *Imagery in Healing* (Boston: Shambhala Publications, 1985).

40. Franklin, ibid., p. 4.

41. Thomas Hanna, *Somatics: Reawakening the Mind's Control of Movement, Flexibility, and Health* (Menlo Park, CA: Addison-Wesley Publishing Company, 1988).

42. See Nancy Gamboian, Steven J. Chatfield, and Marjorie H. Woollacott, "Further effects of somatic training on pelvic tilt and lumbar lordosis alignment during quiet stance and dynamic dance movement," *Journal of Dance Medicine & Science* 4/3 (2000): 90–98.

43. See Rachel Kaplan, ed. *Moving Toward Life: Five Decades of Transformational Dance* (Hanover, NH: Wesleyan University Press, 1995).

44. See Eric Franklin, *Dynamic Alignment* and *Dance Imagery for Technique and Performance* (Champaign, IL: Human Kinetics, 1996).

45. See Nancy Gamboian, Steven J. Chatfield, Marjorie H. Woollacott, Sherrie Barr, and Gary A. King, "Effect of dance technique training and somatic training on pelvic tilt and lumbar lordosis alignment during quiet stance and dynamic dance movement," *Journal of Dance Medicine & Science* 3/1 (1999): 5–14, for a review of the literature on conditioning with imagery and other applications, with cautions about the need for a reliable protocol that can quantify changes resulting from somatic training.

46. Krasnow et al., "Emerging concepts of posture and alignment," p. 13. The authors also raise questions about how dancers transfer what is learned at an unconscious level during static alignment to dynamic situations.

47. Measures that have been used in studies looking at alignment are reported in journals such as *Physical Therapy* (see review in Gamboian et al., "Effect of dance technique training").

48. Ibid. and Gamboian et al., "Further effects of somatic training."

49. In reporting their findings, they build on the pioneering studies of Donna Krasnow and colleagues in the field of C-I training and in the study of dynamic alignment.

50. Martha Myers, "Body therapies and the modern dancer," *Dance Magazine* supplement. (New York: Dance Magazine, Inc., 1983).

51. See Glenna Batson, "Stretching technique: a somatic learning model. Part I: training sensory responsivity," *Impulse* 1/2 (1993): 127.

52. Practitioner certification programs are available. Contact the School for Body-Mind Centering in Amherst, MA, as well as other institutions such as the Center for the Alexander Technique in Menlo Park, California.

53. See discussion of Cohen's work in William Weintraub, *Tendon and Ligament Healing: A New Approach Through Manual Therapy* (Berkeley, CA: North Atlantic Books, 1999), pp. 10, 40–41, 53–55. Cohen's work is often applied to respiratory, digestive, circulatory, and hormonal systems as well, with an emphasis on child development as it relates to the evolutionary stages of other animals. See Cohen's *Sensing, Feeling, and Action: The Experiential Anatomy of Body-Mind Centering* (Northampton, MA: Contact Editions, 1993), based on previously unpublished articles in *Contact Quarterly*.

54. Lulu E. Sweigard, *Human Movement Potential: Its Ideokinetic Facilitation* (New York: Harper & Row, Publishers, 1974).

55. For more, see Franklin, *Dynamic Alignment*, pp. 3–12; Sweigard, *Human Movement Potential*; and, Irene Dowd, *Taking Root to Fly* (Northampton, MA: Contact Editions, 1990). Dowd was a student of Sweigard's and her assistant at the Juilliard School in New York in the early 1970s.

56. Constructive rest position: with the arms folded across the chest, knees bent so that the feet are resting parallel on the floor, and the teacher/facilitator giving verbal cues, imagine moving from one body part to the next, using different though related imagery.

57. See diagram, Franklin, *Dynamic Alignment*, p. xii.

58. Sweigard, *Human Movement Potential*, p. 233.

59. See Franklin, *Dynamic Alignment*, for more on the origins and uses of imagery, the biomechanical and anatomical foundation for understanding complex imagery, and hundreds of anatomical imagery exercises to increase body awareness, and exercises to promote healthy posture and alignment. *Dance Imagery for Technique and Performance* also contains imaging exercises, such as "Imagine you're lying on soft clay or a sandy beach" (p. 11), "Imagine that you can take in oxygen through every part of your body" (p. 18), and "Imagine you are a soap bubble wobbling as it floats" (p. 43), as well as exercises using imagery for the ballet barre. For example, for battement, tendu, and jeté, imagine "your back remains wide, even billowing like a sail when you tendu and dégagé" (p. 101). As noted in a review that I wrote in *Journal of Dance Medicine & Science* (1/2 [1997]: 78), his work could have even other applications, to dance writing perhaps: "With Franklin's creative suggestions and guidance, maybe we will sculpt our written dance texts as well as the moving ones."

60. Eric Franklin, *Pelvic Power: Mind/Body Exercises for Strength, Flexibility, Posture, and Balance for Men and Women* (Hightstown, NJ: Elysian Editions, Princeton Book Company, Publishers, 2002). See also the work of Kathe Wallace (www.kathewallace.com), focusing on lumbopelvic girdle and pelvic floor strengthening and stabilizing.

61. It is interesting to note that Alexander's observations and experiments on vocal problems have been applauded by noted scientists such as ethnologist Nikolaas Tinbergen.

62. F. Matthias Alexander, *The Universal Constant in Living* (New York: Dutton, 1941), p. 10.

63. For more on inhibition, primary control, and freeing the neck, see Jerry Sontag, ed. *Curiosity Recaptured: Exploring Ways We Think and Move* (San Francisco: Mornum Time Press, 1996).

64. Mornum Time Press in San Francisco specializes in books on education, including on the Alexander Technique. See *The Act of Living: Talks on the Alexander Technique* (1999) and also *An Examined Life: Marjory Barlow and the Alexander Technique: in Conversation with Trevor Allan Davies* (2002). Barlow began studies with her uncle, F. M. Alexander, at the age of 17. The conversations provide insights into the history and development of the technique, and the effects of applying this technique over a lifetime.

65. Jerry Sontag, ed. *Thinking Aloud: Talks on Teaching the Alexander Technique* (San Francisco: Mornum Time Press, 1994).

66. (San Fransico: Mornum Time Press, 1995).

67. Accredited training programs are approved by organizations such as the North American Society of Teachers of the Alexander Technique, the American Center for the Alexander Technique (ACAT), and the Society of Teachers of the Alexander Technique (STAT) in London.

68. Martha Myers, "Body therapies and the modern dancer: the Alexander Technique," *Dance Magazine* April (1980): 92.
69. Sontag, *Curiosity Recaptured.*
70. Ibid., p. 70.
71. Laws, *Physics and the Art of Dance*, p. 85.
72. Traditionally, correction (and assessment) of technique remained the domain of dance teachers who were not always educated in anatomy and movement mechanics, and who perhaps could not advise on injury prevention and treatment. But educator Judy Gantz notes, "Today, this process is more frequently carried out by dance specialists who have both a dance-science and dance-training background, such as dance kinesiologists, physical therapists, and dance-medicine professionals." Judy Gantz, "Evaluation of faulty dance technique patterns: a working model," *Kinesiology and Medicine for Dance* 12/1 (1989): 1–11. Gantz goes on to discuss how to define and identify faulty dance coordination patterns and develop a working framework of analysis to assess faulty technique.
73. See Kitty Daniels, "Teaching anatomically-sound dance technique: the ballet barre," paper presented at the ninth annual meeting of the International Association for Dance Medicine & Science, Tring, England, October 24–26, 1999. Also see Donna Krasnow and Steven J. Chatfield, "Dance science and the dance technique class," *Impulse* 4/2 (1996): 162–172.
74. Daniels, ibid.
75. Risa Steinberg and Erick Hawkins, personal interviews, 1987–1989.
76. McGill, *Low Back Disorders.*
77. Ibid.
78. Erick Hawkins, personal interviews, 1987–1989.
79. Jan Hyatt, personal interviews, 1987–1989 and 2001.
80. Pam Paulson, personal communication, 2002.

Chapter 4

1. "Strength" in this chapter refers to muscular strength, and, to a lesser extent, muscular endurance.
2. Unless otherwise stated, "endurance" refers to cardiorespiratory endurance.
3. See J. Christopher Potts and James J. Irrgang, "Principles of rehabilitation of lower extremity injuries," *Journal of Dance Medicine & Science* 5/2 (2001): 51–61; quote p. 58. Potts and Irrgang note that it is not uncommon for dancers to lack strength and endurance in the quadriceps, abdominal muscles and core stabilizers, dorsiflexors, and the intrinsic muscles of the foot. Dancers also have calf tightness (from training in relevé) and hip flexor tightness (from overuse, e.g., making compensations for poor turnout and extension).
4. Y. Koutedakis, P. J. Pacy, R. J. Carson, and F. Dick, "Health and fitness in professional dancers," *Medical Problems of Performing Artists* 12/1 (1997): 23–27.
5. See Marijeanne Liederbach, "General considerations for guiding dance injury rehabilitation," *Journal of Dance Medicine & Science* 4/2 (2000): 54–65.
6. Karen Clippinger-Robertson, "Principles of dance training," in Priscilla M. Clarkson and Margaret Skrinar, eds. *Science of Dance Training* (Champaign, IL: Human Kinetics Publishers, Inc., 1988), p. 45.
7. See a "Brief Overview of Neural Reflexes" and "Neural Mechanisms and Flexibility" by Donna Krasnow, unpublished papers available from the author at the Dept. of Dance, Faculty of Fine Arts, York University, 4700 Keele St., Toronto, Ontario M3J1P3, Canada. Also see Robert E Stephens, "The neuroanatomical and biomechanical basis of flexibility exercises in dance," in R. Solomon, S. Minton, and J. Solomon, eds. *Preventing dance injuries: An interdisciplinary perspective* (Reston, VA: American Alliance for Health, Physical Education, Recreation and Dance, 1990), Chapter 13.
8. Cynthia Harvey, quoted in Kenneth Laws, *Physics and the Art of Dance: Understanding Movement* (Oxford: Oxford University Press, 2002), pp. xix–xx.
9. See Gayenne Grossman and M. Virginia Wilmerding, "The effect of conditioning on the height of dancer's extension in à la seconde," *Journal of Dance Medicine & Science* 4/4 (2000): 117–121 for more details. The therapeutic intervention consisted of a modified leg raise (with one set of 10 lifts then three sets of 10 lifts over a 6-week period), using only the weight of the leg as resistance, with the thigh externally rotated, the knee slightly flexed, and the quadriceps relaxed, simulating an attitude position.
10. In the words of Koutedakis and Sharp, " . . . many dancers seem not wholly to treat their body as the main instrument for their art." Yiannis Koutedakis and N. C. Sharp, *The Fit and Healthy Dancer* (New York: John Wiley & Sons, 1999), p. xxii.
11. See Yiannis Koutedakis, "The effects of physical fitness on dance ability," paper presented at the ninth annual meeting of the International Association for Dance Medicine & Science, Tring, England, October 24–26, 1999.
12. Koutedakis and Sharp, *The Fit and Healthy Dancer.*
13. Ibid, p. xxii.

14. Yiannis Koutedakis, "'Burnout' in dance: the physiological viewpoint," *Journal of Dance Medicine & Science* 4/4 (2000): 125.

15. Koutedakis and Sharp, *The Fit and Healthy Dancer*.

16. Ibid., pp. 91–92.

17. Ibid., p. xxiii.

18. Craig Phillips defines strength as the peak force or torque developed during a maximal voluntary effort. See Craig Phillips, "Strength training of dancers during the adolescent growth spurt," *Journal of Dance Medicine & Science* 3/2 (1999): 69.

19. Ibid., p. 70.

20. Researcher Craig Phillips reviews the literature and provides some general guidelines: Warm up appropriately, without excessive stretching; begin with an exercise that uses low resistance and body weight and focuses on core stabilization; train all major muscle groups, ensuring that movement in all directions is balanced and there is no overemphasis on flexion; work the muscles through their entire range of motion; emphasize endurance training in that the number of repetitions should remain high; avoid maximum loading; cool down with moderate stretching. See: C. J. R. Blimkie and O. Bar-Or, "Trainability of muscle strength, power, and endurance during childhood," in O. Bar-Or, ed. *Child and Adolescent Athlete* (London: Blackwell Science, 1996); Steven J. Fleck and William J. Kraemer, *Designing Resistance Training Programs*, 2nd ed. (Champaign, IL: Human Kinetics Publishers, Inc., 1997). See also Douglas Brooks, *Effective Strength Training: Analysis and Technique for Upper-Body, Lower-Body, and Trunk Exercies* (Champaign, IL: Human Kinetics Publishers, Inc., 2001,) pp. 199–216; Phillips, "Strength training of dancers during the adolescent growth spurt," and a position paper and literature review from the National Strength and Conditioning Association (NCSA), "Youth resistance training," *Journal of Dance Medicine & Science* 2/2 (1998): 73.

21. See Gayanne Grossman and Mary Virginia Wilmerding, "The relationship between iliopsoas conditioning and hip extension in dancers," paper presented at the eighth annual meeting of the International Association for Dance Medicine & Science, Hartford, CT, October 30-November 1, 1998.

22. Phillips, "Strength training of dancers during the adolescent growth spurt." p. 69.

23. Grossman and Wilmerding, "Iliopsoas conditioning and hip extension," p. 120.

24. Daniel Duell, personal interviews, 1987–1989.

25. Adapted from Brooks, *Effective Strength Training*, pp. 57, 256–257.

26. For reference and further discussion of the information in this list, see Christopher M. Norris, *Back Stability* (Champaign, IL: Human Kinetics Publishers, Inc., 2000), pp. 7–8.

27. Brooks, *Effective Strength Training*, p. 89.

28. See also Katherine C. Buroker and James A. Schwane, "Does postexercise static stretching alleviate delayed muscle soreness?" *The Physician and Sportsmedicine* 17/6 (1989): 65–83.

29. Koutedakis and Sharp, p. 162.

30. Erick Hawkins, personal interviews, 1987–1999.

31. D. H. Krasnow, "C-I training: the merger of conditioning and imagery as an alternative training methodology for dance," *Medical Problems of Performing Artists* 12/1 (1997): 3–8.

32. For example, see Maxine Tobias and John Patrick Sullivan, *Complete Stretching: A New Exercise Program for Health and Vitality* (New York: Alfred A. Knopf, 1998), which recommends instruction by teachers trained in the system of B. K. S. Iyengar, familiar with the use of props such as belts, blankets, and blocks to ease stretch and strengthening work of various positions.

33. To these we also could add Craniosacral Therapy, Integrated Movement Exercise, Kinetic Awareness, Klein Technique, Body Mind Centering, Feldenkrais Method, Skinner Releasing Technique, The Zena Rommett Floor-barre Technique, and the Trager Approach. See Wendy Perron, "Guide: bodywork approaches," *Dance Magazine* November (2000): 74.

34. Quotes in this section are from Kathryn Karipides, personal interviews, 1987–1989 and 2003.

35. See Niels Bukh, Emily R. Andrews, and Karen Vesterdal, *Fundamental Gymnastics: The Basis of Rational Physical Development* (New York: E.P. Dutton & Co., 1928), pp. ix-x, 2.

36. Ibid., pp. 2, 15.

37. Stuart McGill, *Low Back Disorders: Evidence-Based Prevention and Rehabilitation* (Champaign, IL: Human Kinetics Publishers, Inc., 2002).

38. McGill notes that power athletes in such situations tend to "sip" the air at the upper end of the tidal volume. Allowing more air out of the lungs causes spine stability to drop dramatically. Dancers, when lifting partners, experience much the same. Pers. comm., October 2003.

39. See McGill, *Low Back Disorders*, p. 247.

40. Ibid., and Dixie Stanforth, Philip R. Stanforth, Stephanie R. Hahn, and Allison Phillips, "A 10-week training study comparing resistaball and traditional trunk training," *Journal of Dance Medicine & Science* 2/4 (1998): 134–140.

41. See P. Hodges and C. Richardson, "Inefficient muscular stabilisation of the lumbar spine associated with low back pain: a motor control evaluation of transversus abdominis," *Spine* 21/2 (1996): 2640–2650; C. Richardson, G. Jull, P. Hodges, and J. Hides, *Therapeutic Exercise for Spinal Segmental Stabilization in Low Back Pain* (Edinburgh: Churchill Livingstone, 1999); and Norris, *Back Stability*.

42. See A. Nitz and D. Peck, "Comparison of muscle spindle concentrations in large and small human epaxial muscles acting in parallel combinations." *American Surgeon* 52/5 (1986): 273–277. See also Alec Kay's "An Extensive literature review of the lumbar multifidus: biomechanics," *The Journal of Manual & Manipulative Therapy* 9/1 (2001): 17–39 and "An extensive literature review of lumbar multifidus: anatomy," *The Journal of Manual & Manipulative Therapy* 8/3 (2000): 102–114. as well as Kay's "The role of the lumbar multifidus in manual therapy in patients with chronic low back pain and lumbar segmental instability: an extensive literature review." Doctoral dissertation, Ola Grimsby Institute, 2001.

43. See J. H. Wilke, S. Wolf, L. Claes, M. Arand, and A. Wiesand, "Stability increase of the lumbar spine with different muscle groups: A biomechanical in vitro study," *Spine* 20/2 (1995): 192–198.

44. See Michael J. Alter, *Science of Flexibility, 3rd ed.* (Champaign, IL: Human Kinetics Publishers, Inc., 2004). See also the classic work of B. K. S. Iyengar, *Light on Yoga* (New York: Schocken Books, 1979), for discussion of the derivation of the word, "yoga," from "yuj," meaning to bind, attach, and yoke. It implies, "to direct and concentrate one's attention; to use and apply" (p. 19). In the ancient writing of the *Yoga sutras*, there are several categories of physiological practices and spiritual exercises, called *angas* or "limbs."

45. See S.C. Vasu, *The Gheranda Samhita: A treatise on Hatha Yoga* (Adyar, Madras, India: Theosophical, 1933), p. 25, as quoted in Alter, *Science of Flexibility*, p. 4.

46. Alter, ibid.

47. Lori Brungard, "Dancers discover yoga benefits," *Dance Magazine* November (2000): 75.

48. For more (much more), see Tobias and Sullivan, *Complete Stretching*.

49. In Pilates conditioning sessions, Pilates Method floor work usually follows Pilates machine-assisted conditioning, i.e., it is suggested that people try the floor work once they have reached a certain level of conditioning.

50. Ann McMillan, Luc Proteau, and Rose-Marie Lebe, "The effect of Pilates-based training on dancers' dynamic posture," *Journal of Dance Medicine & Science* 2/3 (1998): 101–107.

51. Juliu Horvath is the creator of GYROTONIC EXPANSION SYSTEM®, GYROTONIC®, and GYROKINESIS®, which are registered trademarks of Gyrotonic Sales, Inc. and are used with permission. For more, see www.gyrotonic.com.

52. See Potts and Irrgang, "Principles of rehabilitation;" J. M. Gamboa and S. P. Galagher, "Developing a comprehensive warmup and conditioning program for performing artists," *Orthopaedic Physical Therapy Clinics of North America* 5/4 (1996): 515–546; and B. F. French and G. Giammanco, "Developing a work hardening program for the performing artists," *Orthopaedic Physical Therapy Clinics of North America* 6/2 (1997): 231–243.

53. See Brooks, *Effective Strength Training*, for a good discussion of interchangeable terms used for strength training (resistance training, weight training, and so on).

54. For a history of GAS dating back to 1936, see Hans Selye, *Stress Without Distress* (New York: J.P. Lippincott, 1974).

55. L. L. Ploutz, P. A. Tesch, R. L. Biro, and G. Dudley, " Effect of resistance training on muscle use during exercise," *Journal of Applied Physiology* 76/4 (1994): 1675–1681.

56. W.J. Kraemer, S.J. Fleck, and W.J. Evans, "Strength and power training: physiological mechanisms of adaptation," *Exercise Sport Sciences Reviews* 24 (1996): 363–397.

57. See Chris Hughes and Phillip Page, "Scientific basis of elastic resistance," and Phillip Page, "Dosing of elastic resistance exercise" in Phillip Page and Todd S. Ellenbecker, eds. *The Scientific and Clinical Application of Elastic Resistance* (Champaign, IL: Human Kinetics Publishers, Inc., 2003), pp. 3–4 and 21–27. See also Alter, *Science of Flexibility*, pp. 170–171. Exhaustion and injury may result if a program is not carefully constructed.

58. Clippinger-Robertson, "Principles of dance training," p. 50.

59. For further discussion, see ibid., pp. 51, 64; and John Garhammer, *Sports Illustrated Strength Training* (New York: Harper & Row, Publishers, 1986), pp. 29–32. See also Steven J. Fleck and William J. Kraemer, *Designing Resistance Training Programs*, 2nd ed. (Champaign, IL: Human Kinetics Publishers, Inc., 1997); and Brooks, *Effective Strength Training*, p. 236–237.

60. See Koutedakis and Sharp, *The Fit and Healthy Dancer*, pp. 156–159.

61. Note that there are many factors to be taken into consideration when designing a program—individual needs and goals, time available, muscle fiber type to be worked. See Everett Aaberg, *Resistance Training Instruction: Advanced Principles and Techniques for Fitness Professionals* (Champaign, IL: Human Kinetics Publishers, Inc., 1999), pp. 49–60.

62. A repetition is a complete movement of a particular exercise and typically consists of a concentric or lifting muscle action, and an eccentric, or lowering of the resistance. A set is a group of repetitions performed continuously. See Fleck and Kraemer, *Designing Resistance Training Programs*, p. 5.

63. At least one set per exercise should be worked until "fatigue," from a fitness perspective, in order to make strength gains (Brooks, *Effective Strength Training*, pp. 238ff). Brooks also recommends training with high reps (15 to 20), low weights, and working up to 8 to 12 or 6 to 10 reps with higher weights. Those who are already fit but want to realize further strength gains will need to condition at least three times a week.

64. Norris, *Back Stability*.

65. See Fleck and Kraemer, *Designing Resistance Training Programs*, pp. 92–93, for a good discussion of exercise order.

66. For more information, see Garhammer, *Strength Training*, pp. 189–199; Donald Chu, "Planned progression," *Idea Today* 7/8 (1989): 30–35; Aaberg, *Resistance Training Instruction*, pp. 57–59; and Brooks, *Effective Strength Training*. As Brooks notes (pp. 230–231), periodization can involve training with a variety of activity, with varied and progressive intensities, and in 4- to 6- week training plans (referred to as a mesocycle, compared to a 7-day, short-term plan, a microcycle, or a yearly organizational plan, a macrocycle). Progressive load should not be increased for more than 4- to 6- continuous weeks. Between mesocycles, periods of recovery are needed. In a sense, dancers are used to such cycles of intense work (with fatigue) followed by recovery. See also Koutedakis and Sharp, The F*it and Healthy Dancer*, p. 159.

67. See Fleck and Kraemer, *Designing Resistance Training Programs*, pp. 38–43.

68. Noa Spector-Flock, *Get Stronger by Stretching with Thera-Band* (Hightstown, NJ: Princeton Book Company, Publishers). See also Aaberg, *Resistance Training Instruction*.

69. Page and Ellenbecker, *Elastic Resistance*.

70. Ibid., for more information on scientific evidence surrounding the use and effectiveness of the bands.

71. Spector-Flock, *Get Stronger by Stretching with Thera-Band*, pp. 11–12.

72. See Page, "Dosing of elastic resistance exercise."

73. For additional information and guidelines when using the bands, see Patricia A. VanGalen, *Exercising with DYNA-BAND Total Body Toner: Basic Guidelines for the Instructor* (Akron, OH: The Hygienic Corporation, 1987) and Page and Ellenbecker, *Elastic Resistance*. Note that all exercises should be performed only after a suitable warmup.

74. Spector-Flock, *Get Stronger by Stretching with Thera-Band*, pp. 13–14.

75. Ibid., pp. 154–156.

76. Phillip Page, "Integrated uses of elastic resistance," in Page and Ellenbecker, eds. *Elastic Resistance* , pp. 181–188.

77. For further discussion, see Garhammer, *Strength Training*, pp. 53ff.

78. See M. H. Stone and H. Bryant, *Weight Training: A Scientific Approach* (Minneapolis: Burgess International Group, Inc., 1987).

79. This lift is usually performed with a barbell. For further instructions and for cautionary notes, see Garhammer, *Strength Training*, pp. 127–129.

80. Kent Stowell, telephone interview, 2003.

81. For an excellent discussion, see Maria Junco, "Pilates technique," *Dance Teacher Now* 10/9 (1988): 27–30. Also see McMillan et al., "Pilates-based training." See also S. S. Fitt, J. Sturman, and S. McClain-Smith, "Effects of Pilates-based conditioning on strength, alignment, and range of motion in university ballet and modern dance majors," *Kinesiology and Medicine for Dance* 16/1 (1994): 36–51.

82. Koutedakis and Sharp, *The Fit and Healthy Dancer*, p. 91.

83. In one study, the morphology of the heart—the left ventricle's muscular wall—was similar to that seen in athletes trained for strength. See J. L. Cohen, P. K. Gupta, E. Lichistein, and K. D. Chadda, "The heart of a dancer: noninvasive cardiac evaluation of professional ballet dancers," *American Journal of Cardiology* 45/5 (1980): 959–965.

84. Matthew Wyon, Andrew Head, Craig Sharp, and Emma Redding, "The cardiorespiratory responses to modern dance classes: differences between university, graduate, and professional classes," *Journal of Dance Medicine & Science* 6/2 (2002): 41–45.

85. Emma Redding and Matthew Wyon, "Strengths and weaknesses of current methods for evaluating the aerobic power of dancers," *Journal of Dance Medicine & Science* 7/1 (2003): 10–16.

86. Ibid., p. 12.

87. To obtain an estimate of maximal heart rate (also called "maximum exercise heart rate"), subtract the person's age from 220 (e.g., the maximal attainable heart rate of a 20-year-old is 220 – 20 or about 200 bpm, or beats per minute). For a more accurate estimate of calculating maximal and training heart rates, see Sally Fitt, *Dance Kinesiology* (New York: Schirmer Books, 1988), Chapters 14, 19, and Fleck and Kraemer, *Designing Resistance Training Programs*. Exercise at 70 percent is often referred to as "conversational exercise" (i.e., it is possible to hold a conversation while exercising without being exhausted). In the case of the 20-year old dancer, 70 percent × 200 = 140. To realize fitness gains, a typical training zone is working at 70 to 90 percent of the maximal heart rate, in this case, between 140 and 180 bpm.

88. J. L. Cohen, K. R. Segal, I. Witriol, and W. D. McArdle, "Cardiorespiratory responses to ballet exercise and the VO_2max of elite ballet dancers," *Medicine and Science in Sports and Exercise* 14/3 (1982): 212–217.

89. However, interesting work shows that both energy systems are vital. Except for high-intensity exercise lasting less than 30 seconds, most exercise uses both energy systems in varying amounts. Even at 2 minutes of exercise, the ratio between aerobic and anaerobic energy production is 50:50, and even after 70 seconds of intensive exercise, the aerobic system contributes 47 percent of the energy.

90. See Koutedakis and Sharp, *The Fit and Healthy Dancer*, pp. 72ff, for a discussion of the development of energy systems at the muscle fiber level.

91. J. R. Sutton, "Limitations to maximal oxygen uptake," *Sports Medicine* 13/2 (1992): 127–133.

92. This point is disputed among dance scientists. Some argue that one hour of intense interval-burst anaerobic activity will, over a 24-hour life period, "burn" more fat than one hour of aerobic endurance training over the same 24-hour life period. The former exercise simply mobilizes more fat after the workout (this can be hours later), the latter during the workout. Few people, however, can sustain an intense interval-burst anaerobic activity for even one hour.

93. See Steven Chatfield and William C. Byrnes, "Cardiovascular aspects of dance," in Clarkson and Skrinar, eds. *Science of Dance Training*, Chapter 6. VO_2max is the maximum amount of oxygen that an individual can utilize to produce energy required for work expressed in units of milliliters of oxygen per kilogram of body weight per minute. It is considered an acceptable measure of the ability of the cardiorespiratory system to deliver oxygen to the working muscle.

94. Wyon et al., "Cardiorespiratory responses," p. 41. (See also the first edition of *Finding Balance*, pp. 137–138.)

95. J. H. Rimmer, D. Jay, and S. A. Plowman, "Physiological characteristics of trained dancers and intensity level of ballet class and rehearsal," *Impulse* 2/2 (1994): 97–105.

96. Wyon et al., "Cardiorespiratory responses"; See also J. A. DeGuzman, "Dance as a contributor to cardiovascular fitness and alteration of body composition," *Journal of Physical Education and Recreation* 50/4 (1979): 88–91; J. L. Cohen, K. R. Segal, I. Witriol, and W. D. McArdle, "Cardiorespiratory responses to ballet exercise and the VO_2max of elite ballet dancers," *Medicine and Science in Sports and Exercise* 14/3 (1982): 212–217; and P. G. Schantz and P. O. Astrand, "Physiological characteristics of classical ballet," *Medicine and Science in Sports and Exercise* 16/5 (1984): 472–476. See also commentary by Karen Clippinger on measuring and evaluating aerobic capacity in dancers in "Fitness, dance, and health," *Journal of Dance Medicine & Science* 1/1 (1997): 27–29. See Redding and Wyon, "Evaluating the aerobic power of dancers," for a good discussion of the limitations of apparatus in such research, including past studies conducted with Douglas bags as the main method of gas analysis and heart rate monitors. Also Thomas M. Welsh, "A primer on measuring dancer capacities," *Journal of Dance Medicine & Science* 7/1 (2003): 5–9, and Thomas M. Welsh, "Ethical standards for experimental research with dancers," *Dance Research Journal* 31/1 (1999): 86–99, for a discussion of technical and ethical standards for research with dancers.

97. Chatfield and Byrnes, "Cardiovascular aspects of dance," pp. 103–104.

98. See Fleck and Kraemer, *Designing Resistance Training Programs*, pp. 7–8; and Debbie C. Lieber, Richard L. Lieber, and William C. Adams, "Effects of run-training and swim-training at similar absolute intensities on treadmill VO_2max," *Medicine and Science in Sports and Exercise* 21/6 (1989): 655–661. Whether or not there is "transfer" in aerobic capacity from cycling to running to swim training is debated.

99. Dennis M. Davidson, "Dance and cardiorespiratory fitness," in Caroline G. Shell, ed. *The Dancer as Athlete: The 1984 Olympic Scientific Congress Proceedings* (Champaign, IL: Human Kinetics Publishers, Inc., 1986), p. 137. Swimming is excellent exercise, although to avoid shoulder and back problems, dancers should be certain that their upper body is properly conditioned before embarking on a swimming regimen.

100. American College of Sports Medicine, "Position Stand: the recommended quantity and quality of exercise for developing and maintaining cardiorespiratory and muscular fitness in healthy adults," *Medicine and Science in Sports and Exercise* 22/2 (1990): 265–274.

101. Clippinger, "Fitness, dance, and health," p. 28. See also Koutedakis and Sharp, *The Fit and Healthy Dancer*, pp. 104–105.

102. Redding and Wyon, "Evaluating the aerobic power of dancers," p. 12.

103. Koutedakis and Sharp, *The Fit and Healthy Dancer*, p. 104.

104. This increase was approximately 8 percent. These data were for a nondance population. See the short review article by Bryant Stamford, "How much should I exercise?" *The Physician and Sportsmedicine* 17/7 (1989): 150. See also Clippinger, "Fitness, dance, and health," p. 28.

105. Clippinger, ibid.

106. The results are conflicting as to whether or not intermittent versus continuous exercise results in greater caloric expenditure over a 24-hour life period. The reason the intermittent may be more effective is that the participant gets tired and works less hard as with continuous and heavy exercise.

107. Also see Koutedakis and Sharp, *The Fit and Healthy Dancer*, pp. 104–105, and Fleck and Kraemer, *Designing Resistant Training Programs*, pp. 66–69.

108. Steven N. Blair, Harold W. Kohl III, Ralph S. Paffenbarger, Debra G. Clark, Kenneth H. Cooper, and Larry W. Gibbons, "Physical fitness and all-cause mortality: a prospective study of healthy men and women," *Journal of the American Medical Association* 262/17 (1989): 2395–2401.

109. See commentary in Claudia Kallo, "Health for life," *Newsweek* January 20 (2003): 60–64.

110. Weak inward rotators may be secondary to structural problems in causing injury, for example, retroversion of the neck of the femur, resulting in the "toed-out" running.

111. Emmett Hines, *Fitness Swimming* (Champaign, IL: Human Kinetics Publishers, Inc., 1999). It is interesting to note that the core stability so important in dance also is essential to acquiring aquatic posture, line, and balance (to reduce resistance and increase stroke length in the water). Thus, swimming is very effective cross training. Jim Williams, personal communication, 2004.

112. See Clippinger's discussion of moderate exercise, "Fitness, dance, and health," p. 28.

113. For further information, see Debbie Rosas and Carlos Rosas, with Katherine Martin, *Nonimpact Aerobics* (New York: Avon Books, 1988).

114. For more information, see Robin Chmelar and Sally Fitt, *Diet for Dancers* (Pennington, NJ: Princeton Book Co., Publishers, 1990).

115. See Stefanos Volianitis, Yiannis Koutedakis, and Ray J. Carson, "Warm-up: a brief review," *Journal of Dance Medicine & Science* 5/3 (2001): 77–78.

116. Koutedakis and Sharp, *The Fit and Healthy Dancer*, p. 128.

117. Ibid., pp. 128–129. Any number of factors can affect muscle flexibility and joint mobility. These include structure of bony surfaces, structure of articular cartilage, joint-capsule laxity, ligaments, synovial fluid, muscle/tendon length, fibrous or elastic connective tissue, muscle fat content, stretch/relaxation techniques, age, gender, body type, fitness levels, environmental factors such as room temperature, and psychological stress.

118. Alter categorizes flexibility with three types: *static flexibility* refers to the range of motion about a joint irrespective of speed; *ballistic flexibility* is associated with bouncing or rhythmic motion; *dynamic flexibility* refers to the ability to use a range of joint movement when moving at a normal or fast speed. See Alter, *Science of Flexibility*, p. 3.

119. See Clippinger-Robertson, "Principles of dance training," p. 60.

120. Robert E. Stephens, "The neuroanatomical and biomechanical basis of flexibility exercises in dance," in R. Solomon, S. Minton, and J. Solomon, eds. *Preventing Dance Injuries: An Interdisciplinary Perspective,* (Reston, VA: American Alliance for Health, Physical Education, Recreation and Dance, 1990), see Chapter 13.

121. See also Volianitis et al., "Warm-Up," p. 78.

122. Alter, *Science of Flexibility*, p. 9.

123. L. M. Gannon and H. A. Bird, "The quantification of joint laxity in dancers and gymnasts," *Journal of Sports Sciences* 17/9 (1999): 743–750.

124. See Karen Clippinger-Robertson, "Flexibility in dance," *Kinesiology and Medicine for Dance* 12/2 (1990): 1.

125. Koutedakis and Sharp, *The Fit and Healthy Dancer*, p. 134.

126. Alter, *Science of Flexibility*, p. 2.

127. Ibid.

128. P. Beighton, R. Grahame, and H. Bird, "Hypermobility in the performing arts and sport," in Beighton, P. R. Grahame, and H. Bird, eds. *Hypermobility of Joints*, 3rd ed. (London: Springer-Verlag London Ltd., 1999), pp. 125–145.

129. Lyle J. Micheli, "Dance injuries: an overview," paper presented at the Dance Medicine Conference: Update 1998, Boston, October 10, 1998. In Proceedings, *Journal of Dance Medicine & Science* 3/1 (1999): 28–32.

130. Craig Phillips, "Is there a limit to stretching?" paper presented at the ninth annual meeting of the International Association for Dance Medicine & Science, Tring, England, October 24–26, 1999.

131. See T. Hortobagyi, J. Faludi, J. Tohanyi, and B. Merkeley, "Effects of intense 'stretching'-flexibility training on the mechanical profile of the knee extensors and on the range of motion of the hip joint," *International Journal of Sports Medicine* 6 (1985): 317–321.

132. For a very interesting discussion of the neurophysiology of flexibility, see Alter, *Science of Flexibility*, pp. 85–104 and Stephens, "The neuroanatomical and biomechanical basis of flexibility," pp. 271–292.

133. H. A. de Vries, "Evaluation of static stretching procedures for improvement of flexibility," *Research Quarterly* 33/2 (1962): 222–229.

134. See Robert Stephens's excellent discussion of the difference between elastic deformation of tissue, occurring within the muscle cell, and the longer-lasting plastic deformation, occurring in the connective tissue in "The neuroanatomical and biomechanical basis of flexibility," pp. 284–285.

135. See G. H. Van Gyn, "Contemporary stretching techniques: theory and application," in Shell, ed. *The Dancer as Athlete,* Chapter 10.

136. See Stephens, "The neuroanatomical and biomechanical basis of flexibility." p. 274, for the benefits of relaxation (deep breathing, positive visualization) in reducing muscle tone (tightness).

137. Alter, *Science of Flexibility*, p. 3.

138. See Alter, ibid., p. 176, for a critique of static stretching, some of it having to do with the typical exclusion of additional useful forms of stretch.

139. See N. Wolkodoff, "Physiology and application of flexibility programs," paper presented at the IDEA One-to-One Fitness Conference, Los Angeles, California, April 14–16, 1989.

140. Alter, *Science of Flexibility*, p. 173.

141. Koutedakis and Sharp, *The Fit and Healthy Dancer*, p. 139. Other potential problems with ballistic stretching have to do with inadequate tissue adaptation and inadequate neurological adaptation. Incorporating ballistic stretching as part of a progressive velocity flexibility program seems to overcome some of these disadvantages. See Alter, *Science of Flexibility*, p. 174 and pp. 127–136 for a discussion of muscle soreness and preventive measures.

142. H. Kabat, together with physical therapists Margaret Knott and Dorothy Voss, first developed the methods in his clinical work; L. E. Holt and colleagues applied them to general conditioning regimens. See H. Kabat, M. McLeod, and C. Holt, "The practical application of proprioceptive neuromuscular facilitation," *Physiotherapy* 45/4 (1959); H. Kabat, "Proprioceptive facilitation in therapeutic exercise," in S. Licht, ed. *Therapeutic Exercise* (New Haven, CT: Williams and Wilkins, 1965), pp. 87–92; L. E. Holt and R. K. Smith, "The effects of selected stretching programs on active and passive flexibility," in J. Terauds, ed. *Biomechanics in Sport* (Del Mar, CA: Research Center for Sports, 1983), pp. 54–67; and L. E. Holt, T. M. Travis, and T. Okita, "Comparative study of three stretching techniques," *Perceptual and Motor Skills* 31/2 (1970): 611–616.

143. Robert E. McAtee and Jeff Charland, *Facilitated Stretching: Assisted and Unassisted PNF Stretching Made Easy*, 2nd ed. (Champaign, IL: Human Kinetics Publishers, Inc., 1999), p. 14.

144. There is some debate as to exactly how long this stretch should be held—perhaps not more than 5 seconds—to reduce the risk of delayed muscle soreness.

145. For further discussion, see Van Gyn, "Contemporary stretching techniques." See Alter, *Science of Flexibility*, pp. 185–188, for discussion of the many different types of PNF techniques available.

146. See Alter, ibid., pp. 180–189, for a more complete discussion of the pros and cons of passive and active stretching. McAtee and Charland effectively address many of these concerns in *Facilitated Stretching*.

147. Alter, *Science of Flexibility*, p. 158.

148. See Beighton et al., "Hypermobility in the performing arts and sport."

149. Alter, in *Science of Flexibility*, gives a guideline of stretching once a day to maintain flexibility.

150. Ibid., pp. 170–171. Alter includes a good discussion of specific adaptation to imposed demand (SAID) overload principle, and overstretching principle.

151. Ibid., p. 170. Alter includes a good overview of the recommendations for holding each stretch; 15 to 30 seconds seems reasonable.

152. Judy Alter, *Stretch and Strengthen* (Boston: Houghton Mifflin, 1986) and *Surviving Exercise: Judy Alter's Safe and Sane Exercise Program* (Boston: Houghton Mifflin, 1983). See also Alter, *Science of Flexibility*, pp. 209–228 for a discussion of controversial stretches. Much of his discussion refers to Judy Alter's work.

153. Adapted from Ruth Lindsey and Charles Corbin, "Questionable exercises—some safer alternatives," *Journal of Physical Education, Recreation and Dance* 60/8 (1989): 26–32.

154. Adapted from Alter's *Surviving Exercise*. See also Karen Clippinger-Robertson, "Components of an aerobic dance-exercise class," in *Aerobic Dance-Exercise Instructor Manual* (San Diego: IDEA Foundation, 1987), Chapter 5; Elizabeth Stevenson, "Hyperflexion of the knee," *CAPHERD Journal Times* 52/2 (1989): 21–22. Lindsey and Corbin, ibid., also offer an excellent discussion of other exercises to avoid, such as double leg lifts, donkey kicks, and deep squatting exercises.

155. A very interesting dialogue regarding "potentially dangerous" exercises has been conducted by Karen Clippinger-Robertson, one of dance science's foremost proponents, and physician-editor James Garrick, among others. An important point emerges from this debate: if work with professional athletes and dancers is one-on-one in a clinical setting, some potentially dangerous exercises are not that "dangerous."

156. See Alter, *Science of Flexibility*, pp. 211–228, for a thoughtful discussion of "X-rated exercises," analysis of risk factors, and risk reduction. The same also could be said for the concerns about sit-ups raised by Stuart McGill, *Low Back Disorders*, earlier in this chapter.

157. See Alter, pp. 214–215, for a discussion of further modifications of the hurdler's stretch (e.g., using blankets, bolsters, mats, or props).

158. Clippinger, "Fitness, dance, and health," p. 29.

159. Koutedakis, "'Burnout' in dance."

160. Karen S. Clippinger, "Complementary use of open and closed kinetic chain exercises," *Journal of Dance Medicine & Science* 6/3 (2002): 77–78.

161. See D. H. Krasnow, S. J. Chatfield, S. Barr, J. L. Jensen, and J. S. Dufek, "Imagery and conditioning practices for dancers," *Dance Research Journal* 29/1 (1997): 43–64, and Krasnow, "C-I training." Also see Ruth Solomon, *Anatomy as a Master Image in Training Dancers* (Santa Cruz, CA: Ruth Solomon, 1988).

162. Eileen M. Wanke, "The cinder track in the ballet studio: an integrated endurance training to prevent injuries," paper presented at the ninth annual meeting of the International Association for Dance Medicine & Science, Tring, England, October 24–26, 1999.

163. Eric Franklin, *Conditioning for Dance: Training for Peak Performance in All Dance Forms* (Champaign, IL: Human Kinetics Publishers, Inc., 2004). See also his *Pelvic Power: Mind/Body Exercises for Strength, Flexibility, Posture, and Balance for Men and Women.* (Hightstown, NJ: Elysian Editions, Princeton Book Company Publishers, 2002).

164. Krasnow, "C-I training," p. 5.

165. For more on this, see Donna Krasnow's video sequence on *C-I Training*, available from Krasnow at Dept. of Dance, Faculty of Fine Arts, York University, 4700 Keele St., Toronto, Ontario M3J1P3, Canada. Also see Solomon, *Anatomy as a Master Image.*

166. Mark Buckingham and Rachel-Ann Rist, "The challenges of implementing fitness training sessions for professional dance students," paper presented at the eighth annual meeting of the International Association for Dance Medicine & Science, Hartford, Connecticut, October 30-November 1, 1998.

167. Murray Louis, *On Dance* (Pennington, NJ: a capella books, 1992) p. 1.

168. Ibid., p.18.

169. Ibid., p. 21.

170. "The Nikolais Legacy," *Dance Magazine* September (2003): 32.

171. Louis, *On Dance*, p. 16.

OTHER SOURCES

Warming Up

Jay Blahnik, *Full-Body Flexibility* (Champaign, IL: Human Kinetics Publishers, Inc., 2003).

Daniel L. Kohut, *Musical Performance: Learning Theory and Pedagogy* (Englewood Cliffs, NJ: Prentice-Hall, 1985).

Yiannis Koutedakis and N. C. Sharp, *The Fit and Healthy Dancer* (New York: John Wiley & Sons, 1999), pp. 152, 166, 167, 171.

Eric W. Krenz, *Gaining Control: Turning Stress into an Asset with Modified Autogenic Training* (Salt Lake City, UT: L.L.P. Associates, 1983).

Stefanos Volianitis, Yiannis Koutedakis, and Ray J. Carson, "Warm-up: a brief review," *Journal of Dance Medicine & Science* 5/3 (2001): 77–78.

Pilates Method

Scott Brown, "Pilates: man or method," *Journal of Dance Medicine & Science* 3/4 (1999): 137–138.

Scott Brown, "Pilates: where are we now?" *Journal of Dance Medicine & Science* 6/4 (2002): 108–109.

Ann McMillan, Luc Proteau, and Rose-Marie Lebe, "The effect of Pilates-based training on dancers' dynamic posture," *Journal of Dance Medicine & Science* 2/3 (1998): 101–107.

Michele Meyer, "Fitness," *Lear's* January (1994): 38–39.

Noa Spector-Flock, *Get Stronger by Stretching with Thera-Band*, 2nd ed. (Hightstown, NJ: Princeton Book Company, Publishers, 2002), pp. 9–10.

Nora St. John, "The changing face of Pilates," *Body-Mind-Spirit* (2002): 6–8.

For information, see material available from the Pilates Method Alliance (www.pilatesmethodalliance.org), which recommends a certification program of 375 hours for an entry-level teacher on the mat and apparatus, and a minimum of 100 hours for the mat. See also Polestar Education (www.polestareducation.com) as well as www.pilates-studio.com, www.the-method.com, www.balancedbody.com, and www.stottpilates.com.

Chapter 5

1. Much has been written on this in connection to stress fractures; see references in Chapter 2.

2. Mary Yannakoulia and Antonia-Leda Matalas, "Nutrition intervention for dancers," *Journal of Dance Medicine & Science* 4/3 (2000): 103.

3. Carbohydrates are needed for normal metabolism, maintenance of body homeostasis, as well as the energy needed to perform; poor nutrient intake in general can compromise oxygen consumption and aerobic capacity. See Wanda Koszewski, Joanne S. Chopak, and Barton P. Buxton, "Risk factors for disordered eating in athletes," *Athletic Therapy Today* 2/2 (1997): 7. Some researchers estimate the percentage of calories from fat in dancers' diets to be as high as two thirds; the average for the United States population is closer to 40 percent. See Jane M. Bonbright, "The nutritional status of female ballet dancers 15 to 18 years of age," *Dance Research Journal* 21/2 (1989): 9–14. At the very least, disordered eating leads to sleep disturbance, difficulty in concentrating, mood swings, irritability, and anxiety. See Laura S. Hurley and Alfred Roncarati, "A profile of the Female Athlete Triad," *Athletic Therapy Today* 2/2 (1997): 14–19. In some cases, not enough fats rich in desirable nutrients (omega-3

fatty acids) are being consumed. See Yiannis Koutedakis and N. C. Craig Sharp, *The Fit and Healthy Dancer* (New York: John Wiley & Sons, 1999), p. 240.

4. See the review in Yannakoulia and Matalas, "Nutrition intervention for dancers," p. 104.

5. S. C. Sandri, "On dancers and diet," *International Journal of Sport Nutrition* 3/3: 334–342.

6. Calcium is problematic since it is needed in large amounts and dancers often reject one good source, dairy products. In one study, Clarkson reports that dancers with stress fractures tended to avoid dairy products. See Priscilla M. Clarkson, "An overview of nutrition for female dancers," *Journal of Dance Medicine & Science* 2/1 (1998): 32–34. Other good sources of calcium are sardines, or other fish with bones, legumes, certain green vegetables and seeds. See Robin D. Chmelar and Sally S. Fitt, *Diet for Dancers: A Complete Guide to Nutrition and Weight Control* (Pennington, NJ: Princeton Book Co., Publishers, 1990), pp. 52–54. Iron, too, is a concern, although with adequate caloric intake, it should not be a problem. Although heme iron (such as that found in red meat) is more absorbable than nonheme (plant sources), dancers can increase the available amount by consuming adequate amounts of calories, emphasizing whole grains, legumes, dried fruit, and dark, leafy vegetables in their diet, and, to increase the availability, taking vitamin C (for example, in a fortified drink) with food.

7. Bonbright, "The nutritional status of female ballet dancers," pp. 12–13. Also see Chmelar and Fitt, *Diet for Dancers*, pp. 55–56, and Lynne Myszkewycz and Yiannis Koutedakis, "Injuries, amenorrhea and osteoporosis in active females: an overview," *Journal of Dance Medicine & Science* 2/3 (1998): 88–95.

8. See Linda H. Hamilton, *Advice for Dancers: Emotional Counsel and Practical Strategies*, rev. ed. (San Francisco: Jossey-Bass Publishers, 1998), pp. 62–67; Nancy I. Williams, "Reproductive function and low energy availability in exercising females: a review of clinical and hormonal effects," *Journal of Dance Medicine & Science* 2/1 (1998): 19–31; L. M. Vincent, "Dancers and the war with water and salt," *Kinesiology and Medicine for Dance* 12/2 (1990): 40–49, and *Competing with the Sylph*, 2nd ed. (Princeton, NJ: Princeton Book Company, Publishers, 1989). See also Sharon A. Armann, Christine L. Wells, Susanne S. Cheung, Stuart L. Posner, Ronald J. Fischer, Judith A. Pachtman, and Russell P. Chick, "Bone mass, menstrual abnormalities, dietary intake, and body composition in classical ballerinas," *Kinesiology and Medicine for Dance* 13/1 (1990): 1–15.

9. See, for example, M. N. Hassapidou and A. Manstrantoni, "Dietary intakes of elite female athletes in Greece," *Journal of Human Nutrition and Dietetics* 14/5 (2001): 391–396.

10. Refer to Table 4 for sources and citations. Note that such studies are subject to measurement errors, as discussed by the researchers, and underreporting is a problem.

11. Even the 1,923 value that Clarkson gives for a 90-lb 12-year-old girl, with moderate exercise is well above the figures for females given in Table 4. See Clarkson, "An overview of nutrition," p. 37. In a study of 21 female university dance majors, not one dancer was found to fall within the compliance range of good to excellent nutrition. See also Catherine Culnane and Donna Deutsch, "Dancer disordered eating: comparison of disordered eating behavior and nutritional status among female dancers," *Journal of Dance Medicine & Science* 2/3 (1998): 95–100.

12. Food and Nutrition Board, 2002. Dietary Reference Intakes for Energy, Carbohydrate, Fiber, Fat, Fatty Acids, Cholesterol, Protein, and Amino Acids. (Washington, DC: Institute of Medicine, National Academies.)

13. Bonbright, "The nutritional status of female ballet dancers," pp. 12–13.

14. Clarkson, "An overview of nutrition," p. 33.

15. K.A. Beals and M.M. Manore, "The prevalence and consequences of subclinical eating disorders in female athletes," *International Journal of Sport Nutrition* 4/2 (1994): 175–195.

16. Balanced does not necessarily mean equal.

17. This includes primary amenorrhea (absence of menstruation), irregular menstrual cycles, and lack of three consecutive menstrual cycles. See Culnane and Deutsch, "Dancer disordered eating."

18. Potential medical complications include gastric and esophageal irritation and bleeding, gastric dilation, large-bowel abnormalities, anemia, impaired renal function, and cardiovascular problems. See Hurley and Roncarati, "A profile of the Female Athlete Triad."

19. See Culnane and Deutsch, "Dancer disordered eating," p. 96. Also see Hurley and Roncarati, ibid., p. 14.

20. Ibid.

21. For example, there are dancers with disordered eating who do not meet the strict criteria for eating disorders defined by the American Psychiatric Association, *Diagnostic and Statistical Manual of Mental Disorders*, 4th ed. (Washington, DC: American Psychiatric Association, 1994). See also Culnane and Deutsch, "Dancer disordered eating."

22. Ibid. Two standard diagnostic criteria for anorexia, for example, are a body weight 16 percent below normal and scores on a standard eating attitudes assessment in the symptomatic range.

23. Source material for this section includes the following references: Steven J. Chatfield, "The health of our dancers: what is and what is to be?" *Journal of Dance Medicine & Science* 2/1 (1998): 3; Culnane and Deutsch, "Dancer disordered eating"; Linda H. Hamilton, "A psychological profile of the adolescent dancer," *Journal of Dance Medicine & Science* 3/2 (1999): 48–58; Linda H. Hamilton, William G. Hamilton, Michelle P. Warren, Katy Keller, and Marika Molnar, "Factors contributing to the attrition rate in elite ballet students," *Journal of Dance Medicine*

& *Science* 1/4 (1997): 131–138; B. A. Kaufman, M. P. Warren, and L. Hamilton, "Intervention in an elite ballet school: an attempt at decreasing eating disorders and injury," *Women's Studies International Forum* 19/5 (1996): 545–549; Karim M. Khan, Michelle P. Warren, Amanda Stiehl, Heather A. McKay, and John D. Wark, "Bone mineral density in active and retired ballet dancers," *Journal of Dance Medicine & Science* 3/1 (1999): 15–23; Donna Krasnow, Lynda Mainwaring, and Gretchen Kerr, "Injury, stress, and perfectionism in young dancers and gymnasts," *Journal of Dance Medicine & Science* 3/2 (1999): 51–58; Katie Lundon, Lindsay Melcher, and Krista Bray, "Stress fractures in ballet: a twenty-five year review," *Journal of Dance Medicine & Science* 3/3 (1999): 101–107; Dave P. Nelson and Steven J. Chatfield, "What do we really know from the literature about the prevalence of anorexia nervosa in female ballet dancers?" *Journal of Dance Medicine & Science* 2/1 (1998): 6–13; Luana Poggini, Stefania Losasso, and Stefania Iannone, "Injuries during the dancer's growth spurt: etiology, prevention, and treatment," *Journal of Dance Medicine & Science* 3/2 (1999): 73–79; Bonnie E. Robson, "Disordered eating in high school dance students: some practical considerations," *Journal of Dance Medicine & Science* 6/1 (2002): 7–13; Judy Sonnenberg, "Etiology, diagnosis, and early intervention for eating disorders," *Journal of Dance Medicine & Science* 2/1 (1998): 14–18; L. M. Vincent, "Disordered eating: confronting the dance aesthetic," *Journal of Dance Medicine & Science* 2/1 (1998): 4–5; Williams, "Reproductive function and low energy availability;" Yannakoulia and Matalas, "Nutrition intervention for dancers."

24. Sonnenberg, "Etiology, diagnosis, and early intervention."
25. Ibid.
26. Khan et al., "Bone mineral density in active and retired ballet dancers."
27. For a good discussion on this compulsive behavior, see "Overcoming the ten-pound obsession," *Tufts University Diet and Nutrition Letter* 6/11 (1989): 3–6.
28. Hamilton, "A psychological profile of the adolescent dancer," p. 49.
29. Elizabeth L. Snell, "Some nutritional strategies for healthy weight management in adolescent ballet dancers," *Medical Problems of Performing Artists* 13/3 (1998): 117–119.
30. Koszewski et al., "Risk factors for disordered eating," p. 7.
31. They are categorized as monosaccharides, a six-carbon sugar group such as glucose, fructose, and galactose; disaccharides, consisting of two sugar molecules, such as glucose and fructose to form sucrose; and polysaccharides, consisting of three or more sugar molecules, most commonly, cellulose, starch, and glycogen.
32. For an excellent discussion of energy nutrients and energy/exercise metabolism, see Koutedakis and Sharp, *The Fit and Healthy Dancer,* pp. 3–50; Bruce Abernethy, Vaughan Kippers, Laurel Traeger Mackinnon, Robert J. Neal, and Stephanie Hanrahan, *The Biophysical Foundations of Human Movement* (Champaign, IL: Human Kinetics, 1997), Chapters 12 and 13; and, Frank I. Katch and William D. McArdle, *Nutrition, Weight Control, and Exercise* (Philadelphia: Lea & Febiger, 1988), Chapters 1 and 4. See also William D. McArdle, Frank I. Katch, and Victor L. Katch, *Exercise Physiology, Energy, Nutrition and Human Performance,* (Philadelphia: Lippincott, Williams & Williams, 2001).
33. Koutedakis and Sharp, *The Fit and Healthy Dancer,* p. 26. Also see www.joslin.harvard.edu/education/library/carbohydrates.shtml for information related to Glycemic Index, especially for people with diabetes. The "*glycemic index*" emerged as a concept from work at the University of Toronto. The "*glycemic load*" as a concept was developed by researchers from the Harvard School of Public Health.
34. Also, elevated insulin encourages the conversion of carbohydrate to fat. See Abernethy et al., *The Biophysical Foundations,* pp. 206–207.
35. AHA (American Heart Association), *Heart Cuisine* (Los Angeles: AHA, undated).
36. See Koutedakis and Sharp, *The Fit and Healthy Dancer,* p. 31. Other groups of fat include: phospholipids, important in blood clotting; cholesterol, present in all animal cells and important in the production of bile and reproductive hormones; and lipoproteins, responsible for transporting fat in the blood. Examples of lipoproteins are the high-density lipoproteins (HDL), which contain a relatively larger amount of protein and less cholesterol than their lower-density or LDL counterparts, and are responsible for returning cholesterol to the liver for disposal.
37. All foods contain protein because it is an important constituent of animal and plant cells, either structurally—to hold the cell together—or as enzymes that increase the rate of chemical reaction in the cell. Foods that contain relatively large amounts of water, such as vegetables and fruits, have small amounts of protein compared with grains, nuts, dried beans, and animal products.
38. See Brian B. Cook and Gordon W. Stewart, *Strength Basics: Your Guide to Resistance Training for Health and Optimal Performance* (Champaign, IL: Human Kinetics, 1996), p. 17.
39. Abernethy et al., *The Biophysical Foundations,* pp. 207–208.
40. AHA, *Heart Cuisine,* pp. 121–122.
41. National Research Council, *Recommended Dietary Allowances,* (Washington, DC: National Academies, 1980) pp. 166, 168. See also the general discussion in the tenth edition of the Council's *Recommended Dietary Allowances* and in *Diet and Health,* both published in 1989 by the National Academy of Sciences (National Academy Press). See also Abernethy et al., *The Biophysical Foundations,* pp. 208–209.

42. Recommendations for hydration and rehydration vary slightly. See Clarkson, "An overview of nutrition," p. 38.

43. Because it is not possible for humans to adapt to inadequate water intake or excessive daily losses through urine, feces, sweating, vomiting, dieting, diffusion through the skin, and exhalation of water vapor, dehydration inevitably results. Dehydration compromises the body's ability to function in many ways: by reducing muscular strength, lowering plasma and blood volumes, depleting liver glycogen stores, and more. Basically, as a person sweats, body fluids are lost, which results in a lowered available volume of blood to provide oxygen and nutrients to working muscles and to deliver heat to the skin for body thermoregulation. As dehydration increases, the heart rate increases, the blood flow to the skin decreases, body temperature increases, performance declines, and movement becomes labored. Even before pronounced thirst is experienced, the person may suffer fatigue, loss of coordination, irritability, and, in the susceptible, cramps.

44. See L. M. Vincent, "Dancers and the war with water and salt." Also see Abernethy et al., *The Biophysical Foundations*, pp. 208–209.

45. Elizabeth L. Snell, "Keep your dancers dancing with liquid assets and iron," paper presented at the tenth annual meeting of the International Association for Dance Medicine & Science, Miami, Florida, October 27–29, 2000.

46. Suzanne Martin, "Health and fitness for life," *Dance Magazine* April (2003): 51.

47. BMR is defined as the minimum level of energy needed to sustain the body's vital functions in the waking state. Technically, the BMR is usually determined by measuring oxygen consumption in a thermoneutral environment under very strict protocols. When the effects of temperature are not controlled in calorimetry studies (for example, the subject is exercising at whatever the ambient room temperature is for that particular day), it is the RMR that is measured.

48. See Abernethy et al., *The Biophysical Foundations*, p. 165.

49. For a detailed review of the evidence supporting a significant genetic component affecting RMR (after accounting for the effects of age, sex, and body composition), see Eric T. Poehlman, "A review: exercise and its influence on resting energy metabolism in man," *Medicine and Science in Sports and Exercise* 21/5 (1989): 515–525.

50. For a discussion of other biological factors related to size that predict an animal's RMR, see Abernethy et al., *The Biophysical Foundations*, p. 165. The text also includes the now famous mouse-to-elephant curve discussed by K. Schmidt-Nielson, *Scaling: Why Is Animal Size So Important?* (Cambridge: Cambridge University Press, 1991), p. 57. Also see Koutedakis and Yiannis, *Fit and Healthy Dancer*, p. 9.

51. I use "sex" rather than "gender" here to denote influences due primarily to biology rather than culture.

52. See Katch and McArdle, *Nutrition, Weight Control, and Exercise*, pp. 102–103.

53. RDAs are defined as "The levels of intake of essential nutrients considered, in the judgment of the Committee on Dietary Allowances of the Food and Nutrition Board on the basis of available scientific knowledge, to be adequate to meet the known nutritional needs of practically all healthy persons." These were meant to be guidelines for healthy, sedentary populations. The estimates were based on a number of techniques, including collection of data on nutrient intake from the food supply of healthy people, review of epidemiological studies when clinical consequences of nutrient deficiencies were found to be correctable by dietary improvement, biochemical measures that assessed the degree of tissue saturation or adequacy of molecular function in relation to nutrient intake, as well as various nutrient balance studies. Once the data from the estimates are compiled and the recommended level of nutrient intake is indicated, the requirement is increased by an amount sufficient to meet the needs of all members of the population and to take into account inefficient utilization by the body of the nutrient (e.g., iron). The RDA, by necessity, then represents rather generous recommendations because estimated average requirements are increased to take into account individual biological variability. See National Research Council (NRC), *Recommended Dietary Allowances*, p. 1.

54. Food and Nutrition Board, Institute of Medicine. *Dietary Reference Intakes: Vitamins.*

55. Clarkson, "An overview of nutrition," p. 33.

56. E. R. Pariser and M. Wallerstein, "Fish protein concentrate: lessons for future food supplementation" (1980), in Gigi M. Berardi, ed. *World Food, Population and Development.* (Totowa, NJ: Rowman and Allanheld, 1985), p. 243.

57. Food and Nutrition Board, *Dietary Reference Intakes* (Washington, DC: Institute of Medicine, National Academies, 2002).

58. Ibid.

59. Ibid.

60. Ibid.

61. Abernethy et al., *The Biophysical Foundations*, pp. 204–209.

62. See Chmelar and Fitt, *Diet for Dancers*. Their recommendations suggest a food pyramid, with carbohydrates at the base. Note, however, that many female dancers have difficulty trying to lose weight with protein intakes below 15 percent of calories, and when the total caloric intake is less than 1,200 kcal.

63. Chmelar and Fitt, *Diet for Dancers*, p. 50.

64. Ibid., p. 91.

65. Ibid.

66. Bonbright, "The nutritional status of female ballet dancers," p. 12.

67. Clarkson, "An overview of nutrition," p. 34.

68. Ibid, p. 35.

69. See Paul A. Mole, Judith S. Stern, Cynthia L. Schultz, Edmund M. Bernauer, and Bryan J. Holcomb, "Exercise reverses depressed metabolic rate produced by severe caloric restriction," *Medicine and Science in Sports and Exercise* 2/1 (1989): 29–33.

70. Bonbright, "The nutritional status of female ballet dancers," p. 11.

71. For a good discussion of body fat and dance, including genetic influences on body composition, see Chmelar and Fitt, *Diet for Dancers*, pp. 10–11, 27–41, and Koutedakis and Sharp, *Fit and Healthy Dancer*, pp. 232–236; also, the introduction to M. Virginia Wilmerding, Ann L. Gibson, Christine M. Mermier, and Kathryn Allison Bivens, "Body composition analysis in dancers: methods and recommendations," *Journal of Dance Medicine & Science* 7/1 (2003): 24–25.

72. Ibid.

73. For a comprehensive discussion of fuel homeostasis, see Abernethy et al., *The Biophysical Foundations*, Chapter 12, and Harriet Wallberg-Henriksson, "Acute exercise: fuel homeostasis and glucose transport in insulin-dependent diabetes mellitus," *Medicine and Science in Sports and Exercise* 21/4 (1989): 356–361.

74. For a review of the literature on the extent to which purposeful physical exercise (by trained and untrained individuals) can increase basal or resting energy expenditure, see Poehlman, "Exercise and its influence on resting energy metabolism," and Wallberg-Henriksson, "Acute exercise."

75. Katch and McArdle, *Nutrition, Weight Control, and Exercise*, p. 94; Chmelar and Fitt, *Diet for Dancers*.

76. Geoffrey Cowley, "A better way to eat," *Newsweek* January 20 (2003): 47.

77. See Jean Carper, "Myths make me nuts," *USA Weekend* September 26–28 (2003): 4, with comments from Harvard's Walter Willett.

78. Ibid., pp. 47–48.

79. Diana Schwarzbein and Nancy Deville, *The Schwarzbein Principle* (Deerfield Beach, FL: Health Communications, Inc., 1999), p. 119. Also see the more recent (and moderate) *The South Beach Diet* by Arthur Agatston (NY: Random House, 2003).

80. The Glycemic Index is a measure of how fast insulin rises in response to the amount of sugar entering the portal vein at any given moment, ibid., p. 123. It also is discussed earlier in this chapter.

81. Ibid., pp. 124–125. The idea here is that carbohydrates—*all* carbohydrates—are sugar (recall that complex carbohydrates are three or more connected sugar molecules). It is easy to consume several plates of pasta or a box of cereal before feeling satiated, because carbohydrates have to go through an entire digestive and absorption process before the brain stops indicating hunger. See also Chmelar and Fitt, *Diet for Dancers*. However, note that the Glycemic Index for foods varies from individual to individual. Also see caveats given earlier in the chapter.

82. Avoid "damaged fats:" trans-fatty acids, hydrogenated fat—bottled salad dressings, cream substitutes, deep-fat fried foods, high-fat meats cooked at high temperatures, hydrogenated oil, imitation mayonnaise, sour cream, margarine, processed foods and fast foods using hydrogenated oils, and sandwich spreads.

83. Abernethy et al., *The Biophysical Foundations*, p. 204–209. Dancers who suffer from irregular eating habits and/or physical cravings (e.g., for sugar) should consult a physician, dietician, or healthcare expert. Special diets can then be recommended.

84. Allegra Kent, with James and Constance Camner, *The Dancers' Body Book* (New York: William Morrow and Company, Inc., 1984), p. 59.

85. See Chmelar and Fitt, *Diet for Dancers*.

86. Koutedakis and Clark, *Fit and Healthy Dancer*, Chapter 9. Most carbohydrates are absorbed relatively quickly, producing a sudden increase in blood glucose. When this happens, glucose is readily diffused into cells. As insulin is released, the liver and other cells are stimulated to convert glucose to glycogen and fat, and the breakdown of fats and proteins is temporarily inhibited.

87. This makes sense, since the fastest rate of glycogen resynthesis occurs in the 2 hours following strenuous exercise.

88. Ibid., and Clarkson, "An overview of nutrition," p. 35.

89. Nerve cells in the brain (hypothalamus) detect this condition of deprivation and generate nerve impulses that signal hunger to the conscious part of the brain, the cortex.

90. Dancers should try to avoid "carbohydrate backlash," i.e., attempts to demonize or sanctify (see "Pasta fights back amid low-carb trend" by the Associated Press, filed February 18, 2004 and available at NYTimes.com)—but rather try to access information, even in the popular literature, that attempts to present many sides of the issue. See "Going beyond Atkins" by Walter C. Willet, M.D. (one of the pioneers in carbohydrate study) and Patrick J. Skerrett in *Newsweek* January 19 (2004): 45–48.

Chapter 6

1. See F. C. Bakker, "Personality differences between young dancers and non-dancers," *Personality and Individual Differences* 12/7 (1991): 671–681.

2. See work coauthored with developmental psychologist Susan Lee, J. M. Schnitt, D. Schnitt, and S. Lee, "Psychological issues in the clinical approach to dancers," in R. T. Sataloff, A. Brandfonbrener, R. J. Lederman, eds. *Performing Arts Medicine*, 2nd ed. (San Diego: Singular Publishing Co., 1998), p. 359.

3. Ruth Solomon, John Solomon, Lyle J. Micheli, John J. Saunders, and David Zurakowski, "Using the Test of Attentional and Interpersonal Style (TAIS) for profiling and counseling dancers," *Journal of Dance Medicine & Science* 6/4 (2002): 126.

4. Linda Hamilton, "Dancers' Health Survey, Part II: from injury to peak performance," *Dance Magazine* February (1997): 60–65.

5. Stanley E. Greben, "Career transitions in professional dancers," *Journal of Dance Medicine & Science* 6/1 (2002): 15.

6. Solomon et al., "Using the Test of Attentional and Interpersonal Style," p. 124.

7. Gigi Berardi, "Bill Evans: changing the body and geography of modern dance," *Dance Magazine* October (2003): 38–43.

8. Linda Hamilton, *Advice for Dancers: Emotional Counsel and Practical Strategies* (San Francisco: Jossey-Bass Publishers, 1998), pp. 14–15.

9. Some of this resembles what psychologist Albert Ellis calls Rational-Emotive Therapy. See any of his works (some of which are co-authored), titles such as *Growth Through Reason, A New Guide to Rational Living, A Guide to Personal Happiness, Rational-Emotive Therapy and Cognitive Behavior Therapy*, and *How to Stubbornly Refuse to Make Yourself Miserable About Anything—Yes, Anything.*" The last book is available through Lyle Stuart, Inc. in Secaucus, New Jersey.

10. Hamilton, *Advice for Dancers*, p. 14.

11. Ibid., pp. 141–142.

12. New York: Luminous Press, 2001.

13. See Rita Smilkstein, "Acquiring knowledge and keeping it," *Gamut: A Forum for Teachers and Learners* (Seattle: Seattle Community College District), p. 43.

14. Focusing on what "should" happen feeds into irrational beliefs. See note 8.

15. See James G. Garrick, "Early identification of musculoskeletal complaints and injuries among female ballet students," *Journal of Dance Medicine & Science* 3/2 (1999): 80–83.

16. Italics are my emphasis. Susan Bordo, "The empire of images in our world of bodies," *The Chronicle of Higher Education* December 19 (2003): B7.

17. Ibid. Bordo is the author of U*nbearable Weight: Feminism, Western Culture, and the Body* (Berkeley: University of California Press, 2004).

18. In social sciences, we might call such an idea triangulation—using numerous sources to validate information.

19. Greben, "Career transitions," p. 16.

20. See www.nytimes.com/2003/09 /07/movies/moviesspecial

21. "National Public Radio, August 13, 2003.

22. Thomas M. Smith, *Raising the Barre: The Geographic, Financial and Economic Trends of Nonprofit Dance Companies*. Research Division Report 44, National Endowment for the Arts. (Washington, DC: National Endowment for the Arts, Research Division. August 2003).

23. Ibid., pp. 5–6.

24. Nevertheless, smaller nonprofit companies may have taken quite a hit; it is difficult to know from the report, since data are not separated by size of budgets. It is clear that ballet has typically dominated in terms of grants received. For example, in 1988–1990, the average ballet company grant (a little over $100,000) was almost two and a half times larger than the average modern company grant, and at least five times larger than the average ethnic company grant. By 1995, the gap was narrowing, but still there. Ibid., p. 34.

25. Murray Louis, *Murray Louis: On Dance* (Pennington, NJ: a cappella books, 1992), pp. 18–19.

26. Susie Dinan, "Life after a professional career," Chapter 13 in Koutedakis and Sharp, *The Fit and Healthy Dancer*.

27. Greben, "Career transitions."

28. Alexander Dubé, personal interview, 2003.

29. Indeed, Angela Sterling, the photographer for this edition of *Finding Balance*, transitioned successfully from a ballet career (soloist, Pacific Northwest Ballet) to dance and fashion photographer.

30. Stanley E. Greben, "Career transitions."

31. Lauren Gordon, personal interview, 2003.

32. Linda H. Hamilton, Edward Bristow, and Michael J. Byars, "College programs for professional ballet dancers: the impact on career transition," *Journal of Dance Medicine & Science* 6/1 (2002): 20–23.

33. Kathryn Karipides, personal interview, 1987–1989 and 2003.

34. Risa Steinberg, personal interview, 1987–1989.

Appendix A

1. Pers. comm., Boni Rietveld.

Glossaries

DANCE

à la seconde   A position or movement in which one leg is extended directly to the side of the body, either with the toe touching the floor or with the leg lifted to various heights.

adagio   A slow, sustained tempo in a particular movement; section of a ballet class; pas de deux. Adagio movements are characterized by continuity, fluidity, and apparent ease of execution.

allegro   A fast, lively tempo or movement characterized by a quality of lightness, quickness, and buoyancy. Allegro also refers to a section of a ballet class.

arabesque   A pose or movement in which one leg is raised directly behind the body. The supporting leg may be fully extended, flexed, or on point, but the raised leg must be fully extended. If the raised leg is bent, the position or movement is called attitude derrière.

attitude turns   Turns on one leg in which the other leg is lifted either to the front, to the side, or to the back. The knee of the lifted leg is bent, usually at a 90-degree angle. As in arabesque, the supporting leg may be fully extended, flexed, or on demi- or full-point.

barre   The railing used to provide support for dancers during specific exercises in a dance class; a specific section of a dance class. The barre section of a dance class features exercises that build strength and agility of particular muscle groups. In a center barre, such exercises are performed away from and without the support of the barre; in a floor barre, they are performed while lying on the floor.

batterie   Steps in which the legs beat together in a scissorlike motion. Petite batterie are small-beat steps, such as brisé and entrechat, that demand precision and quickness. Grande batterie are large-beat steps, such as cabrioles and grands jetés en tournant battus, that require elevation and strength.

brisé   A small beating step that travels. Brisé begins by brushing the working leg away from the supporting leg, beating the legs together in the air, and landing on either one or both legs.

cabriole   An elevation step in which the stretched legs beat in the air.

classical ballet   Ballet based on the danse d'école or codified theatrical dance principles.

corps, corps de ballet   Group or ensemble members of a dance or ballet company.

courtier   A member of the royal court.

danseur noble   A leading male dancer who embodies classical ballet style.

demi-plié   See **plié**.

demi-pointe   ("half-pointe," "half-toe") Balancing or moving on the balls of the feet.

développé   A folding, then unfolding or extension, of one leg in any direction.

en croix   ("in the shape of a cross") A pattern of repetition in which an action is performed to the front, to the side, and then to the back in sequence.

en l'air ("in the air") Any action or movement in which either one or both legs leave the ground, as in tour en l'air or rond de jambe en l'air (see **rond de jambe**).

entrechat A beating step in which the legs cross and uncross a certain number of times.

ethnic (or world) dance Dance of a specific region or culture.

fifth position A closed position of the feet in which the legs are turned out from the hip and the heel of the front foot is placed close to the big toe joint of the foot behind.

first position A closed position of the feet in which the legs are turned out from the hip with both heels close together and the toes pointing away from the midline of the body.

fondu A flexion or bending of the supporting leg.

Graham contraction A stylized abdominal contraction with the head falling backward in hyperextension and the arms reaching forward with wrists hyperextended; basic to the technique developed by Martha Graham.

grand allegro A section of a ballet or class that combines large jumps, batterie, and turns. It is usually one of the final combinations of a ballet class.

grand battement ("large beat") A large kick in which the working leg is forcefully raised, then lowered with control, in any direction.

grand jeté ("large leap") A leap or jeté is an active transfer of weight from one foot to the other in which both feet leave the floor. A grand jeté is a forceful spring from one foot to the other in which the gesturing or unsupported leg is thrust into the direction of the leap.

grand plié See **plié**.

grande batterie See **batterie**.

modern dance A term used to indicate dance or styles of dance arising in the twentieth century and not as codified as classical ballet technique.

pas A simple step or movement that involves a transfer of weight.

pas de deux A dance or series of steps performed by two people; a duet.

pathogenic choreography Movements or sequences that are potentially hazardous owing to extreme physical stresses or demands placed on the body.

petite batterie ("small beats") See **batterie**.

pirouette A turn of the body on one leg.

plié A flexion or bending of one or both legs: demi-, partial; grand, full.

point, pointe, sur les pointes Balancing or moving on the tips of the toes, usually with the support of a blocked shoe.

premier danseur A leading male ballet dancer.

relevé Raising the body through plantar flexion ("extending" the foot while maintaining contact with the floor) of either one or both ankles.

rond de jambe A circling action of the whole leg, executed with the foot leading either away from the body (en dehors) or toward the body (en dedans). Rond de jambe may be performed with the toe maintaining contact with the floor (à terre) or with the toe off the floor (en l'air).

show dance Theatrical dance styles used in musicals, revues, and music videos. Show dance often combines characteristics of jazz, tap, and ballet.

soloist A solo dancer.

tendu Pointing the foot and stretching the leg continuously in a particular direction (e.g., behind the body—tendu derrière), with the toe maintaining contact with the floor.

tour en l'air A turn in the air that usually starts in fifth position demi-plié and returns to fifth or an open position. During the turn, the body is held vertically and the legs are held tightly together.

tour jeté, grand jeté en tournant entrelacé, grand jeté dessus en tournant A large turning leap in which the legs pass closely together as the body changes direction in the air to finally land in an arabesque.

turnout External rotation of the entire leg, most of which occurs at the hip.

unitard   A type of dance apparel that combines the traditional tights and leotard of ballet into a sleek, one-piece garment.

MEDICAL AND TECHNICAL

abduction   Movement of an extremity or limb segment away from the midline of the body.

abductors   Muscles that move the extremities or limb segments away from the midline of the body.

acetabulum   The cup-shaped depression of the pelvis that constitutes the socket for the head of the femur. The acetabulum is also commonly called the "hip socket."

Achilles tendon   The tendon that connects the calcaneous (the heel bone) to the muscles of the calf (gastrocnemius, soleus, and plantaris).

acromion process   The outside edge of the spine of the scapula; it articulates with the clavicle (collarbone).

acupuncturist   A healer trained in strategic placing of thin needles in the muscles of the body to relieve pain and effect cure.

adduction   Movement of an extremity or limb segment toward or beyond the midline of the body.

adductors   Muscles that move the extremities or limb segments toward the midline of the body.

aerobic activity   Continuous and relatively moderate exercise that is at least 12 to 15 minutes in duration.

amenorrhea   Absence of menstruation.

anaerobic   ("without oxygen") Refers to energy systems in which heat energy is ultimately generated in the absence of oxygen, usually through relatively short workouts.

angle of femoral anteversion   The angle created by the neck of the femur and the shaft of the femur in the transverse plane, which is affected by the amount of torsion or rotation intrinsic to the femur or hip. With a high angle of anteversion (greater than 12 degrees), the femur is rotated to the front, making turnout of the leg difficult. With a low angle (less than 12 degrees, called retroversion), the femur has a more posterior rotation, making turnout of the leg easier.

anorexia nervosa   An eating disorder characterized by severe emaciation resulting from self-imposed weight loss.

anterior   Refers to the front side of the body.

anterior cruciate ligament (ACL)   Stabilizing ligament crossing through the knee. In combination with the posterior cruciate ligament, stabilizes anterior/posterior motion between femur and tibia.

anterior deltoid   A cap-shaped muscular formation covering the anterior portion of the shoulder joint.

anterior hip capsule   The front portion of the hip capsule.

anterior pelvic tilt   A forward tilt of the pelvis that increases the curve of the lumbar spine (hyperextension).

arthritis   Inflammation of a joint.

arthroscope   An instrument that is equipped with a light and camera for viewing inside a joint during surgery.

arthroscopy   Surgery on the interior of a joint using an arthroscope. May also be used for diagnosis of disorders.

ballistic stretch   A stretch that involves rapid bouncing, lunging, or bobbing.

biceps brachii   A two-headed muscle of the anterior portion of the upper arm.

biomechanics   The study of the principles and laws of mechanics applied to the function of human movement, usually using quantitative data.

body therapist or somatic educator   A practitioner trained in a somatics discipline (e.g., Bartenieff Fundamentals, Feldenkrais, Ideokinesis) for movement rehabilitation.

bulimia   An eating disorder characterized by compulsive eating, usually followed by self-induced vomiting.

bunion   A deformity of the first metatarsal phalangeal joint, characterized by an enlarged bump at the inside of the big-toe joint.

bursa   A fluid-filled sac.

bursitis   Inflammation of a bursa.

carpals   Bones of the wrist.

cartilage   The nonvascular connective tissue that interfaces between the bones of the joint.

cathartics   Medications that increase the rate of bowel evacuation.

chiropractor   A licensed, certified practitioner who manipulates neuromuscular structures of the body to restore and maintain their proper functioning.

chondromalacia   Degeneration or inflammation of the cartilage under the patella.

cinematography, cinematographic analysis   The use of film to analyze movement.

clavicle   The collarbone. This bone articulates with the sternum (the breastbone) and the acromion process of the scapula.

coccyx   The tailbone, or last three to five vertebrae of the spine.

collagen   The major protein of connective tissue, cartilage, and bone.

compression fracture   A break—usually in bone or cartilage—caused by increased pressure from external forces.

concentric contraction   A contraction of the muscle fibers that causes the muscle to shorten.

coracobrachialis   A muscle that originates in the coracoid process of the scapula and inserts in the medial border of the humerus.

cortisone   A steroidal medication used to decrease inflammation.

CPR   Cardiopulmonary resuscitation.

crepitus   Noise within a joint.

deltoid muscle   A triangular-shaped muscle of the shoulder that connects the clavicle and scapula to the humerus.

diaphragm muscle   A muscular membrane that separates the abdominal cavity from the thoracic cavity.

dietician   A practitioner who examines the relationship of diet to health for the maintenance of health and prevention of disease.

distal   An extremity or limb segment situated away from the center of the body.

diuretics   Substances that promote urination, thus decreasing fluid retention.

dorsiflexion or ankle flexion   Bending action of the ankle or foot joints that causes the top of the foot or toes to come closer to the shin.

eccentric contraction   A contraction of the muscle that causes the muscle to lengthen against resistance.

electromyography   A method of testing muscle action: electrodes are inserted into specific muscles and the electrical action potentials of the muscles are recorded and analyzed.

emetics   Agents that promote vomiting.

epiphysis   The area of a bone where growth occurs during physical maturation.

erector spinae   Muscles of the back that hold the spine erect.

eversion   Raising the lateral border of the foot so that the foot rests mostly on its inner edge. Also a component of rolling in and winging the foot.

extension   Extending a limb or body part; increasing the angle at a joint, such as straightening a knee.

external, outward, or lateral rotation   Turning or movement of a joint in the transverse plane, away from the midline of the body.

fascial sheath   A covering of connective tissue that envelops a muscle.

femur   The thigh bone.

flexion   Decreasing the angle at a joint, such as bending an elbow.

frontal plane The plane that runs through the body from side to side and separates the front of the body from the back. Actions such as abduction and adduction occur in the frontal plane.

functional flexibility The range of motion actually used during dance movements.

gastrocnemius The large calf muscle that assists in plantar flexion—pointing the toe, relevé, or pushing off the ground (jumping).

general practitioner A physician trained to take care of a broad range of medical conditions such as common illnesses, minor injuries, and trauma; a family physician.

glenohumeral adductors Adductors of the glenohumeral (shoulder) joint, including pectoralis major, latissimus dorsi, teres major, and coracobrachialis.

gluteus maximus The largest of the three gluteal muscles located in the buttocks. Gluteus maximus acts as a hip extensor in forceful movements.

goniometer A device that measures the angle between different body segments.

groin The junction of the thigh and the trunk.

gynecology Branch of medicine dealing with women's health.

hamstrings A group of muscles in the back of the thigh that cross both the hip and the knee.

healer A person who claims to heal by a specific method, system, or philosophy, such as Christian Science, "new thought," and laying on of hands. More generally, the term refers to an individual who has been trained in one of a number of culturally conventional and nonconventional healing practices.

heel lifts Noncompressible pads placed inside one or both shoes.

herniated disc A condition that occurs when the integrity of the outer fibrous covering of the disc—the anulus fibrosus—becomes weakened and the internal gelatinous body of the disc—the nucleus pulposus—projects through the covering. This causes compression on adjacent structures, nerves, and connective tissue.

high instep A high-arched foot; a bony-appearing area just in front of the ankle, mostly common in highly arched feet.

homeopath A practitioner of the system of therapy developed by Samuel Hahnemann, which treats disorders using minute doses of medication that, in healthy persons, would produce symptoms of the disorder.

humerus The long bone of the upper arm.

hyperextension Extreme extension; an increase of the angle between two joints to greater than 180 degrees.

ibuprofen A nonsteroidal anti-inflammatory medication used in the management of pain and inflammation. Previously available only by prescription, it is now an over-the-counter medication.

ideokinesis The art and science of the visualization of movement patterns.

iliofemoral ligament ("Y ligament") A triangular ligament that connects the anterior inferior spine of the ilium, the rim of the acetabulum, and the femur. It inhibits hyperextension of the hip joint.

iliopsoas Major hip flexors. Iliacus and psoas major muscles. Psoas major originates on the vertebral bodies of the twelfth thoracic to the fifth lumbar vertebrae. Iliacus originates on the iliac crest and fossa. Both join and attach at the lesser trochanter of the femur.

internal, or medial or inward, rotation Turning or movement of a joint in the transverse plane toward the midline of the body.

internist A physician who specializes in the diagnosis and treatment of nonsurgical diseases, especially in adults.

intra-abdominal pressure Pressure within the abdominal cavity created by the tonus of abdominal muscles. Muscles of the pelvic floor and diaphragm assist in influencing intra-abdominal pressure. This pressure helps to support internal organs and structures.

inversion   Raising the medial or inside border of the foot so that the foot rests mostly on its outer edge. Also a component of rolling out and sickling.

inward rotators   Muscles that effect movement toward the midline of the body in the transverse plane.

ischial tuberosities   The "sit bones"; the lowest bony protrusions of the ischium.

ischium   One of the three bones that comprise the os coxa. The ischium is the lowest part of the pelvis.

isometric contraction   A muscular contraction in which there is no change in muscle length.

ketosis   Metabolic adaptation in which the body converts fatty acids and amino acids into ketone bodies (metabolized as carbohydrate substitutes). This allows the body to survive for extended periods of time without external sources of glucose.

kilocalorie   ("Calorie") The amount of heat required to raise the temperature of one kilogram of water by 1°C.

kinesiologist   A practitioner trained in the science and study of movement and the structures of the body involved in movement.

kinesiology   The qualitative and quantitative analysis of human movement as it relates to the neuromuscular system.

kinesthetic; kinesthesia   The sensation of body movement, position, and tension perceived by the nerves, muscles, tendons, and joints.

lactic acid   A metabolic by-product of strenuous muscular exertion.

lateral   Away from the midline of the body, for example, the outer side of the arms and legs.

latissimus dorsi   Broad muscle of the back and upper arm that originates on the spinous processes of the lower thoracic and lumbar vertebrae, the sacrum, the iliac crest, and the lower three or four ribs.

laxative   Substance that promotes bowel movement.

lever   A rigid body or object, such as a bone, that rotates around a fulcrum or axis. Levers operate on the principle that a force applied to one end of the lever will cause the other end to move in a direction opposite to the force applied.

ligaments   Sheets or bands of tissue that connect bones and limit the end-range of motion.

longitudinal arch   The arch on the underside of the foot that runs from the heel to the base of the toes.

lumbar compression   Compression of the lumbar region of the spine, most stressful when landing from a jump or lifting a heavy object.

lumbar intervertebral discs   The discs located between the lumbar vertebrae.

MRI   (Magnetic resonance imaging) A method to view a cross section of body tissue.

massage therapist   A practitioner who uses massage for the treatment or amelioration of specific neuromuscular or soft tissue problems.

medial   Toward or near the midline of the body, for example, the inner edge of the knee or ankle.

menisci, lateral and medial (sing., meniscus)   Crescent-shaped cartilaginous structures located in the knee joint.

metacarpals   The five bones of the hand located just proximal to each finger.

metatarsals   The five bones of the foot located just proximal to each toe.

moment arm   The perpendicular distance between the line of force application and the axis of a lever.

multifidus   One of the extensor muscles of the spine; critical in creating stability.

muscular imbalance   Altered (less than ideal) relationship between muscle groups. May be due to deficits in strength, flexibility, proprioception, or activation.

neurologist   A physician who specializes in the treatment of neurological disorders.

neuromuscular patterning   The patterning of motor innervation of skeletal muscles.

neurovascular   Refers to arteries, veins, and nerves.

nutritionist   A practitioner trained in the study of food and drink needs of human beings for health or prevention of illness.

obliques, internal and external   Lateral abdominal muscles that contribute to intra-abdominal pressure.

orthopedist   A physician trained in the medical, surgical, and physical methods required for the diagnosis and treatment of skeletal system disorders.

orthotic   A device to create support; most commonly used to support the foot.

os trigonum   A small triangular bone, sometimes present as part of the ankle (talus) bone.

osteopath   A practitioner trained in specific manipulative measures in addition to the normative diagnostic and therapeutic measures of medicine.

osteoporosis   Premature bone loss.

outward rotators   Muscles that effect movement away from the midline of the body in the transverse plane.

paravertebral   Alongside the vertebrae or the spine.

patella   The knee cap.

patella chondromalacia   Softening (wear or tear) of the cartilage on the underside of the knee cap.

pectoralis major   A muscle of the chest that originates at the clavicle, the manubrium, the body of the sternum, and the first through sixth ribs and attaches at the humerus.

peroneal tendinitis   Inflammation of the tendons on the outside of the leg.

peroneus longus and brevis   Two muscles of the lower leg: **peroneus brevis** originates on the fibula and attaches at the fifth metatarsal; **peroneus longus** originates on the upper and outer surfaces of the fibula and tibia and inserts behind the lateral malleolus and continues under the foot and attaches to the medial cuneiform and first metatarsal.

phalanges   Bones of the toes or fingers.

physiatrist   Medical specialty for rehabilitative medicine.

physical therapist   A licensed professional trained in the evaluation and treatment of biomechanical movement disorders of the musculoskeletal system.

plantar fascia   The sheet of fibrous tissue that supports muscles of the sole of the foot.

plantar fasciitis   Ligament inflammation that causes pain in the sole or heel of the foot.

plantar flexion   Moving the plantar (sole) surface of the foot downward. Commonly called "pointing the toe" in dance.

plyometrics   Exercise where the muscle is stretched in a loaded pattern, then immediately contracted (e.g., jumping down off a box and then immediately springing up).

podiatrist   A practitioner concerned with the diagnosis, treatment, and rehabilitation of injuries and diseases of the human foot and ankle and those structures above that are affected by their actions.

posterior   Refers to the back surface or rear portion of the body.

posterior pelvic tilt   A tilt of the pelvis that reduces the curve of the lower lumbar spine ("tucking").

pronation   Of the foot: lifting the outside edge of the foot (also called "rolling in"). Of the forearm: inward rotation of the lower arm that turns the palm toward the body.

prone   Lying face down.

Proprioceptive neuromuscular facilitation (PNF)   A stretching technique in which isometric contraction against resistance is followed by muscle relaxation and then static stretching to achieve increased range of motion.

proprioceptivity   Sensitivity to stimuli arising from muscles, tendons, and other tissues; sense of feeling, of balance.

proximal   An extremity or limb segment situated toward the center of the body.

posas   A muscle that flexes the hip and connects the lumbar spine to the femur.

psychiatrist   A physician who specializes in the diagnosis and treatment of mental diseases and disorders.

psychologist   A licensed practitioner concerned with human mental and behavioral processes.

psychotherapist   A psychiatrist or psychologist trained in the treatment of emotional, behavioral, personality, or psychiatric disorders. Verbal or nonverbal processes of communication, rather than chemical measures, may be used in treating clients.

quadriceps   A group of four muscles of the upper thigh that extend the knee: rectus femoris, vastus lateralis, vastus intermedius, and vastus medialis.

renal toxicity   Toxicity that affects normal kidney function.

retroversion   A femoral angle of torsion less than 12 degrees. This condition facilitates external rotation of the lower extremity, especially during movement.

Rolfing practitioner   One trained in the theories of Ida Rolf, which emphasize deep tissue manipulation.

rolling in   Pronation or eversion of the foot; lifting the outside border of the foot off the ground.

rolling out   Supination or inversion, of the foot; lifting the inside border of the foot off the ground.

ROM   Range of motion.

rotator cuff   A group of four muscles (subscapularis, supraspinatus, infraspinatus, and teres minor) that help to maintain contact between the head of the humerus and the scapula.

rubber bands   Elastic materials, for example, tension bands and surgical tubing, used to provide a source of external resistance for stretching and strengthening muscles.

sagittal plane   The plane that runs from the front to the back of the body. Actions such as flexion, extension, and hyperextension occur in the sagittal plane.

scapular downward rotation   Rotation of the scapula so that the lower point of the scapula moves toward the spine or midline of the body.

Shiatsu practitioner   One who uses the method of Shiatsu, or pressure points, in a therapeutic setting.

shinsplints   A stress condition of the lower leg that results in pain, swelling, and soreness of the muscles.

sickling   Pointing the foot—or plantar flexion—without equal tension on both sides of the ankle; the foot appears to be inverted (i.e., as if more weight is placed on its outer edge).

somatic   Pertaining to the body.

spasm   An involuntary muscular contraction; it may have various causes.

spinal discs   Cartilaginous discs that lie between the vertebrae to provide cushioning and shock absorption.

sprain   Injury to soft and connective tissues surrounding a joint, resulting in stretching or tearing of the ligaments with ensuing pain, swelling, and sometimes bruising.

static flexibility   The passive range of motion possible at a joint or series of joints.

strain   Injury to muscle resulting in pain, swelling, and bruising.

strapping, taping   Using tape or other materials to provide external support during the healing process.

stress fracture   Fracture (break) of a bone caused by repeated stress or overuse. Stress fractures are accompanied by pain and inflammation of the surrounding tissue, and may be difficult to diagnose.

supination   Of the foot: lifting the inside edge of the foot; also called rolling out or sickling. Of the forearm: outward rotation of the lower arm that turns the palm away from the body.

supine   Lying face up.

surgical tubing   Elastic tubing used to provide resistance for strengthening.

talocalcaneal or subtalar joint   The joint between the talus (the ankle bone) and the calcaneus (the heel).

talocrural joint   The ankle joint, formed by the tibia, fibula, and dome of the talus.

talus   The ankle bone. The talus articulates with the tibia and fibula to create the ankle joint.

taping   See **strapping**.

tendinitis   Inflammation of the tendon, resulting in pain, restricted motion, and crepitus within the tendon sheath.

teres major   A thick muscle that originates on the lower portion of the scapula, runs under the armpit, and attaches to the front of the humerus.

torque (moment of force)   In common usage, torque refers to a rotary or twisting force. Technically, a torque (of a lever) is the product of the force and the moment arm.

torsion   The amount of twist inherent in a structure, such as a bone or a joint. Femoral torsion, the amount of twist inherent in the thigh bone, affects the amount of natural rotation (internal and external) of the leg. Less than 12 degrees of femoral torsion is called retroversion; greater than 12 degrees of torsion is called anteversion (see **angle of femoral anteversion**). Tibial torsion is the amount of external twist intrinsic to the tibia. Excessive tibial torsion can create knee problems. Tibial torsion less than 12 degrees contributes to pigeon-toed gait and pronation.

traction   A pulling force.

transverse or horizontal plane   The plane that runs parallel to the ground. Actions such as internal and external rotation occur in the transverse plane.

transverse abdominis   Part of the abdominal musculature; may be referred to as the TA. It is critical in supporting torso and spinal stability.

ultrasound   A therapeutic method that employs high-frequency sound waves.

valgus (common usage)   In the knees: knees are pointed inward, giving a knock-kneed appearance. In the foot: foot has a rolled-in appearance.

varus (common usage)   In the knees: knees are apart, giving a bowlegged appearance. In the foot: foot looks as if it has a high arch.

winging   Eversion of the foot, accompanied by plantar flexion. Commonly employed to give the desired line to the leg in arabesque.

Y ligament   Iliofemoral ligament.

Index

Boldface items indicate illustrations

About the Author

(Photo by Angela Sterling)

Gigi Berardi has studied and written about dance for more than 20 years. She holds an MA in dance from UCLA and has trained in dance in the United States, England, Italy, and Kenya. Her academic background and performing experience allow her to combine her interests in the natural and social sciences with her passion for dance, as both critic and writer. Over 150 articles and reviews by Ms. Berardi have appeared in *Dance Magazine*, *Dance International*, the *Los Angeles Times*, the *Anchorage Daily News*, *The Olympian*, *The Bellingham Herald*, and scientific journals such as *BioScience*, *Human Organization*, and *Ethics, Place, and Environment*. Her public radio features (for KSKA, Anchorage) have been recognized by the Society of Professional Journalists. She has served on the Board of Directors of the Dance Critics Association, is a member of the American Society of Journalists and Authors, and currently is book review editor for the *Journal of Dance Medicine & Science*. A professor at Western Washington University, she received the university's Diversity Achievement Award in 2004. *Finding Balance* is her fifth book.